SO-EKL-973

THIS EDITED BOOK IS AN EMINENTLY readable and understandable work on two very important subjects of national and international concern featuring solid contributions from productive practitioners. While we all may think we are knowledgeable about the necessity for corruption to be absent from private and institutional governance, this book explores the subject in such breadth and depth as to enlarge any future consideration. The oft-unrecognized and little-discussed interrelationship between intelligence (charmingly described in the book as "foresight") and governance is outlined so well that intelligence, security and governance must henceforth be considered together as a seamless triangle. This is an excellent book which I highly recommend for university and advanced high school students.

— Alex Morrison, CD MSc MA
  Founding President, Pearson Peacekeeping Centre
  Former Director, School of Peace and Conflict Studies,
  Royal Roads University

THIS EDITED BOOK IS A NOVEL approach to examining the many dependencies and inter-dependencies of governance and security in a global context. The thesis introduces the need for a new approach and a new understanding that decision making on major issues relating not just to physical security but human, environmental, economic, resource and cultural security all need to find solutions within an agreed or common understanding of these interdependencies.

The groundwork for understanding the thesis is based on Royal Roads University – Roger Girouard's Featured Essay based in part on his experiences as Commander of the Joint Canadian Contingent on the UN Integrated Mission in East Timor. He is followed by nineteen academics and practitioners, from around the world who write on widely diverse topics such as State-Caused Ethnic Conflict; Gender, State and Security; Adaptive Water Governance; Policing and Governance; Harmony and Order and Good Governance for a More Secure World. No matter what the topic, they all relate their articles back to Girouard's introductory essay calling for a better understanding of Governance and Security.

This is an important new work for use by graduate and undergraduate students as well as national decision-makers alike.

— Vice Admiral (ret'd) Gary L. Garnett, CMM CD
  Former Vice Chief of the Canadian Defence Staff

THIS BOOK IS INDEED TIMELY AND interesting from both an academic and practitioner's view point.

I regret that I could not contribute as one of the authors.

— Adeolu Ade Adewumi
Principal Consultant, 4Solutions Multi-Consult (4SM)
Conflict and Security Management, Nigeria

ANYONE INTERESTED IN GOVERNANCE AND SECURITY issues will gain new insights when reading this edited volume. Scholars from a number of different contexts share their reflections and experiences of promoting and practicing governance. Scholars and practitioners of environmental security, gender security, food security and peacebuilding will read and re-read this book.

— Rebecca Spence, PhD
Faculty, University of New England, Armidale, NSW, Australia
Peaceworks Pty Ltd

THIS FASCINATING COLLECTION OF ARTICLES EXPLORES the transformative changes that would be needed if governance and security were to be defined in terms of the communities they affect rather than by Hobbesian rulers. It is an enlightening, thought-provoking set of papers, raising challenging questions.

— Hugh Miall, PhD
Professor of International Relations at the University of Kent
Previously, Director of the Richardson Institute for Peace Studies at Lancaster University
Established author in Peace and Conflict Studies; his latest book is *Contemporary Conflict Resolution*, with Oliver Ramsbottom and Ton Woodhouse.

THE CONTRIBUTORS TO *GOVERNANCE AND SECURITY AS A UNITARY CONCEPT*, and orchestra conductors Rippon and Kemp, have provided a compelling and interesting analysis of Girouard's "complex and murky" subject – governance and security as a unitary concept. As a senior police officer who has served in United Nations missions and as a current international private security practitioner, this work aided me to reconcile long-rooted ideas acquired through my own international service in public and private security. This book provides important information which causes one to reflect on the ethics associated with the current state of security in the world today. Hats off to the professionals who have contributed to this anthology; it makes a solid contribution to academia – future practitioners – and to those of us who are currently practicing in the field.

— Superintendent Len Babin, Royal Canadian Mounted Police (Ret'd)
Canadian Government Envoy to the Presidential Police Reform Commission of Guatemala 2011–12
President, Primoris Associates Inc., a foremost international corporate security consultancy

# GOVERNANCE AND SECURITY
## as a Unitary Concept

**Dedicated to** those who have served and do serve
the cause of peace, good governance, and global security

# GOVERNANCE AND SECURITY
## as a Unitary Concept

TOM RIPPON AND GRAHAM KEMP, editors

---

WRITTEN BY...
Eric Abitbol
Quassy Adjapawn
Laura Balbuena González
Alan Breakspear
Rosemary Cairns
Michael Canares
Les Chipperfield
Dale Christenson
Roy Cullen
Douglas Fry
Roger Girouard
Peter Gizewski
Graham Kemp
Barbara Mann
Moses Muthoki
Mary-Anne Neal
Tom Rippon
Susanne Thiessen
Serge Vidalis
María Eugenia Villarreal

FOREWORD BY... Terrance Power

**PUBLISHING HOUSE**

151 Howe Street, Victoria BC Canada V8V 4K5
*in collaboration with*

## *Avalon Institute Inc.*

© 2012, Tom Rippon and Graham Kemp.
All rights reserved.
Without limiting the rights under copyright reserved above, no part
of this publication may be reproduced, stored in or introduced into
a retrieval system, or transmitted, in any form or by any means
(electronic, mechanical, photocopying, recording or otherwise),
without the prior written permission of both the copyright owner
and the publisher of this book.

Sally Jennings of *pto-editing.com* provided editorial assistance.

*For rights information and bulk orders,
please contact the publishers through*
www.agiopublishing.com

**_Governance and Security
as a Unitary Concept_**
ISBN 978-1-897435-83-0 (trade paperback)
ISBN 978-1-897435-84-7 (ebook)
ISBN 978-1-897435-85-4 (casebound)

Cataloguing information available from
Library and Archives Canada.
Printed on acid-free paper.
Agio Publishing House is a socially responsible company,
measuring success on a triple-bottom-line basis.
10  9  8  7  6  5  4  3  2  1c

# TABLE OF CONTENTS

| | | |
|---|---|---|
| *Foreword* | Terrance Power | i |
| *Introduction* | Tom Rippon | iii |
| *Contributing Authors* | | xi |
| *Featured Essay*<br>On Governance and Security | Roger Girouard | 1 |

**SECTION I:**
**ESTABLISHING STRUCTURES**

| | | |
|---|---|---|
| State-Caused Ethnic Conflicts: The Need to Reverse and Re-Structure the Educational Policies in the Northern Region of Ghana | Quassy Adjapawn | 23 |
| A Perspective on Governance for Human Security | Rosemary Cairns | 51 |
| Growing Up Kikuyu | Mary-Anne Neal and Moses Muthoki | 77 |

**SECTION II:**
**DIMENSIONS OF SECURITY**

| | | |
|---|---|---|
| Gender, State and Security: Examining the Issue of Vulnerability From a Gender Perspective | Laura Balbuena González | 91 |
| Trafficking of Boys and Young Men in Guatemala | María Eugenia Villarreal | 101 |
| Governance for Security and Security for Governance in Outlaw Motorcycle Gangs | Tom Rippon | 113 |

**SECTION III:**
**PERSPECTIVES ON RESOURCE SECURITY**

| | | |
|---|---|---|
| On Adaptive Water Governance: Producing an Equitable and Reflexive Hydro-politics of Security and Peace | Eric Abitbol | 131 |

| | | |
|---|---|---|
| Intelligence: The Unseen Instrument of Governance | Alan Breakspear | 145 |
| Policing and Governance | Les Chipperfield | 157 |
| Private Security and Military Companies: Securing the Peace? | Serge Vidalis | 185 |

SECTION IV:
STATES WITHIN STATES AND STATES OF CO-OPERATION

| | | |
|---|---|---|
| Leadership Development for First Nations Governance in British Columbia | Susanne Thiessen | 199 |
| Governance and the Creation of Peace Systems | Douglas Fry | 231 |

SECTION V:
RULES TO ENSURE GOOD GOVERNANCE AND SECURITY

| | | |
|---|---|---|
| Good Governance and a More Secure World – Natural Bedfellows | Roy Cullen | 261 |
| From Security Strategy to Project Governance | Dale Christenson | 275 |

SECTION VI:
CHALLENGES TO ASSURING SECURITY

| | | |
|---|---|---|
| Governance for Peace and Development | Michael Canares | 287 |

SECTION VII:
NON-EUROPEAN GOVERNANCE

| | | |
|---|---|---|
| Harmony and Order: Governance and Security the Aztec Way | Graham Kemp | 317 |
| Governance, Turtle-Island Style | Barbara Mann | 331 |

SECTION VIII:
A COMPREHENSIVE APPROACH

| | | |
|---|---|---|
| The Comprehensive Approach: An Idea Whose Time Has Arrived | Peter Gizewski | 355 |

SUMMARY OF OUR ASPIRATIONS

| | | |
|---|---|---|
| *Conclusion* Governance and Security – A Unitary Concept | Graham Kemp | 377 |

# FOREWORD

## TERRANCE POWER, PhD

---

We live in dangerous times, times that require the adoption of new mental models for state governance and security.

Rippon and Kemp have produced and edited a remarkable collection of short readings spanning a wide range of geopolitical, economic, societal and historic reflections on state governance and security. The challenges examined include *inter alia* those faced by failing states; the need for resource security; a determination of the appropriate level of cooperation between states, and states within states, to include a brief look at British Columbia's First Nations' governance; identifying the benchmarks and the provision of a litmus test for good governance; examining concepts and notions relating to nation states in constant flux; a brief glance at two non-European perceptions of governance and security; and finally, an examination of state governance and security at the micro and macro levels in McLuhan's Global Village.

The authors frequently offer a way forward, grounded in lessons learned from history. Collectively, the readings provide interdisciplinary,

---

multi-dimensional solutions. The beauty of their solutions is that, for the most part, governance and security are frequently treated as a merged and interrelated entity that demonstrates these subject areas' complementary dynamic interaction. In Section VIII, Gizewski calls for a comprehensive approach to the challenges, and provides the reader with a stimulating framework for consideration. One would hope that Canada's and other nations' decision makers will in due course gain awareness of Gizewski's findings.

There are eight sections from which the reader might choose to start. Whichever reading is selected, the reader will be correct. The reader will find a number of core ideas threaded throughout the topic's eight sections which, taken as a whole, reveal the governance and security mosaic.

This timely and comprehensive primer provides governance and security practitioners and students an excellent entrée to the field. The authors, each standing on a different terrain, provide wide-ranging, insightful, and richly diverse perspectives. This work should be on the library shelves of every undergraduate and graduate student and national decision maker who is deeply concerned about state governance and security. The reader will find the book's contents timely, relevant and profound.

*Professor Terrance Power, PhD*
*Wharton Fellow, Royal Roads University, Victoria, Canada*

# INTRODUCTION

## On Governance and Security as a Unitary Concept

TOM RIPPON, PhD

---

Growing global insecurity and failing governance have prompted debates that continue to influence policy decisions including, more recently, positions on global warming at the Copenhagen Climate Summit. The proceedings of this gathering of representatives of nation-states reflect the insecurities and limited ability of leaders to establish a common forum for governance and security not just of their respective territories but also their interests in the context of the global community. The dialogue from this meeting exposed a diversity of views on governance and their relationship to a perceived sense of security, fortified by a collective awareness of resource scarcity.

The inability of the leaders to arrive at a consensus (other than to meet again at an unspecified time) brought to the forefront the reality that human security and civil society require an all-embracing framework for governance and security. One is reminded of the previous failures in international co-operation to establish the security of the human future, such as the Hague Peace Conventions of 1899 and 1907, the Treaty of Versailles of 1919, and the World Disarmament Conferences of 1932 and 1933, with such disastrous results.

The issues influencing governance and security in the global village are as diverse as the multi-national cultures; hence, any solutions require an inter-disciplinary, multi-dimensional approach. A sustainable solution to governance and security challenges cannot reflect an insular, silo approach akin to Versailles. Instead, it must come from an examination of governance and security as a unitary concept. The concept should reflect the inter- and intra-relationships, an innovative approach not previously examined. The relationships should accommodate the existing political diversity of actors and the social, economic, resource and environmental dimensions intricately woven into the fabric of the phenomenon. For this to happen, there is an urgent need to establish a discourse on that framework and an equally urgent need to draw from a diversity of experiences and ideas. The strength of this innovative approach, as reflected in this book, is achieved by cross-referencing the overlapping of theories presented by the international array of authors.

In support of this approach, Kooiman asserts, "If governance is going to make an impression as a societal practice and a scholarly activity, it has to be multi-faceted. Scholarly discussion, supporting or criticising governance of whatever kind has to be multi- or interdisciplinary in nature."[1] The scholarly collection of essays in this edited book has been collated to examine these multi-faceted issues and begin dialogue that goes beyond the Eurocentric perspective which has dominated much of the literature to date. The book is a single source that presents diverse issues affecting the inter-relationship of governance and security, and how these issues influence decision-making in a global context.

Governance and security have been examined previously as separate entities, yet through complementary dynamic interaction, one influences and is influenced by the other. Governance may create security but security feeds back into governance, which establishes the nature of good governance, re-enforcing and supporting its structure. By security, one does not mean just physical security, but also human, environmental, economic, resource and cultural security.

Having taught in disciplines of human security, business management, strategic studies and political science, the editors and authors have been challenged to create a single compilation of contemporary commentaries that would meet the learning outcomes. The book is designed to be a reference for undergraduate and graduate programs that examine comparative analysis as an andragogical learning methodology. Professors can use particular chapters and assign them for their lectures for the standard twelve- to fourteen-week term. Instructors may select a series of chapters to lead discussions in comparative analysis seeking prognoses and positions through critical thinking and in-depth analysis, either face-to-face or in an online symmetrical or asymmetrical discourse forum.

The themed sections offer an overlap of ideas between the different chapters; this is the potency of its design. Chapters examine strengths and weaknesses of nation-states in their governance and security, reflecting on nation-states and institutions labelled as failed states and those regarded as sustainable.

The book begins with **Roger Girouard**'s article, whose call for a better understanding of both governance and security was premised upon experience with United Nations peacekeeping missions, such as the UN Integrated Mission in Timor-Leste and the subsequent UN Transitional Administration in Timor-Leste, *inter alia*. These and other multi-national interventions with failed and failing states spurred the inspiration for the book. Other contributors subsequently segue their discussions to Girouard's arguments.

The chapters present articles from authors embedded in and analysing states, with firsthand experience of the state's successes and failings. Each author proposes some theory with an in-depth analysis, theories for reflection in new contexts, and the interplay of theory and concepts. Thus, the book provides both emic and etic perspectives for comparative analysis in academic disciplines, and for reflection by those motivated by the challenges in grappling with issues of failed and failing states, and the interrelationship with governance and security.

In Section I, **Quassy Adjapawn**, from Ghana, discusses the need to restrict and re-structure educational policies for the North Region of Ghana, to establish better ethnic security. In the failing of Somalia as a nation-state and Serbia as a state resulting from internal strife and civil war, **Rosemary Cairns** discusses the means to re-establish governance and security in such situations. She asserts that one must look for solutions in that society's political and cultural traditions rather than imposing solutions from without. **Mary-Anne Neal** and **Moses Muthoki** provide a view of failing governance and security not from the perspective of the observer but from the person facing the experience, a youth from Kenya.

It is a reminder, if needed, that failing governance leads to cycles of inept security and concomitant corruption, and has a human price. The Honourable **Roy Cullen** discusses the latter in Section V.

In Section II, authors examine a breadth of issues reflecting multi-faceted dimensions of security that leaders in nation-states often fail to perceive as a high priority. This failure restricts their forms of governance and thus limits their ability to deliver real security. Gender security is one such dimension overlooked almost worldwide. **Laura Balbuena González** from Peru raises this issue. Its lack of recognition has consequences that go beyond just female rights, as **María Eugenia Villarreal** reveals in her chapter on child sex-trafficking in Guatemala. In the same vein, **Tom Rippon** examines governance and security in a group within the state, outlawed motorcycle gangs. The governance and security of these outlier organizations reveal that there are always human issues (whether established formally or informally) and awareness that the state is not the sole source of governance and security for its citizens. Counter-cultures with their own forms of governance and security exist in society.

Section III presents perspectives on resource security. **Eric Abitbol** examines the issues of water security, a growing international problem affecting governance and security. It is necessary to be aware of the dynamic interaction between governance and security to ensure resource security. **Alan Breakspear** presents an innovative argument for open intelligence as a necessary resource for good governance and security. In the wake of WikiLeaks, intelligence security has become as important a resource issue as water security. **Les Chipperfield** and **Serge Vidalis** examine the role of police, military and private security agencies and their impact on the governance and security of resources in and outside the borders of nation-states.

Section IV reviews states within states and states of cooperation. Girouard focuses on nation states, but the world is more complex. Inter- and intra-national issues of governance and security occur. Several societies are colonized; the ruling elite is a different culture from its peoples. In this regard, issues of cultural or ethnic security arise. **Susanne Thiessen** examines the development of interaction between leaders of First Nations and the Nation-State of Canada, and with the Province of British

Columbia. She contemplates how governance can come into being to keep cultural security between these societies. From an international perspective, we have **Douglas Fry**'s chapter on the European experience of state co-operation in the European Union, an overarching structure with state-like jurisdictions. Today, the financial structure has come under forced review as states and financial institutions default on their fiscal responsibilities.

Section V looks at rules created to assure good governance and security and what happens when corruption overshadows such rules. In his chapter, the Honourable **Roy Cullen** asserts that sustainable governance and security can be achieved only when those who govern are not influenced by corruption. He argues that an accurate barometer of good governance in any society is the degree of corruption that permeates the security of that society, like a sickness causing havoc in its wake. **Dale Christenson** looks at good governance and security from the perspective of project governance. He concurs with Girouard's observation that governance is the complex and often murky construct of people, organizations and rules that exist to run the nation-state. This definition is relevant and consistent, and can be unilaterally applied to the definition of project governance. The successful governance of a nation is no less important than the success of a project. The implications of failed projects in a state's critical infrastructure are reflected in the story of the Kenyan youth growing up, written by Mary-Anne Neal and Moses Muthoki (in Section I).

Section VI examines the challenges faced by those mandated to assure security as defined by good governance in nation-states having to respond to constant flux. **Michael Canares** presents the Philippines as an example of a nation-state in constant flux between good and bad governance as mirrored in periods of peace or violence. National security problems in the country are met with the conventional solution of deploying the military to restore and maintain peace and order, rather than civil police. Militarization, he argues, is necessary but not sufficient for sustainable peace, a manifestation of good governance. Canares' thesis converges with that proposed by Chipperfield on policing and governance, and Vidalis on private security and military companies employed to secure peace. Canares' theories overlap with concepts proposed by Rippon, who suggests that governance and security are issues of groups in society. The group issues demonstrate that as we attempt to form international constructs from diverse states, we realize that societies are themselves constructs of diverse smaller societies with their own governance and security issues. When the defence of core values of a nation-state is sub-contracted to external gladiators, security is compromised by corruption, as noted by the Honourable Roy Cullen.

Section VII presents two non-European traditions of governance and security, of the Aztecs and Native Americans of what is today the Eastern United States, as presented by **Graham Kemp** and **Barbara Mann**. These authors supply not only a new source of cultural ideas for good governance and security but they challenge our concepts of good and bad practices. Their respective theses call into question the prevailing Eurocentric viewpoints and examine, more objectively, their own cultural worldviews. Barbara Mann's discussion of Turtle Island First Nations complements positions presented by Susanne Thiessen in her discussion of First Nations leadership development in British Columbia.

The book finishes in Section VIII with **Peter Gizewski**'s call for a Comprehensive Approach (CA) to governance and security, whose time has come. Gizewski emphasizes that our future depends on the establishment of the unitary concept for good and successful governance and security. CA is a framework that is needed to recognize the mechanics of the interaction and the forces affecting it. Above all, CA allows a set of dynamics to emerge with an awareness of the forces that will develop. As Girouard suggests, a simple set of static rules or laws will not create good governance or a more secure future for humanity. It is, as he notes, a murky and complex affair. To create clarity, we need to begin a thorough and extensive discourse.

**Graham Kemp** closes the book with a summary of our aspirations and the melding of positions postulated by all the contributing authors. We see this edited book as the beginning of a discourse on governance and security as a unitary concept rather than two complementary but separate entities. One hopes that it will promote consensus at the next Copenhagen Climate Summit, and influence discussions and decisions regarding failed and failing states, societies, institutions and organizations in the inter- and intra-related matrix of the global village. The construct of the book is an innovative way of approaching the multidimensional attributes of governance and security. The strength and virtue of the book is the diversity and the overlapping perspectives of the authors, looking in, from within.

ENDNOTES

1    J. Kooiman. *Governing as Governance* (London, UK: Sage, 2003), 6.

# CONTRIBUTING AUTHORS

**Eric Abitbol,** PhD (Cand.), is a Chevening Scholar, completing his doctorate (ABD) at the University of Bradford's Department of Peace Studies (UK). His FQRSC-funded research deconstructs discourses of water development in the Israel-Palestinian conflict, assessing hydropolitical practices and opportunities for building peace in the Middle East. A theorist-practitioner, Abitbol recently conducted a Conflict and Peace Effects Study for the Red Sea Dead Sea Conveyance (RSDSC) project led by the World Bank. He was the co-coordinator of the AVOW research project (Adaptive Visions of Water in the Middle East) housed at York University. He was the founding coordinator of the University of the Streets Café public conversation initiative (Institute in Community Development, Concordia University), and for many years published and edited *Cantilevers* peace and conflict resolution magazine. Abithol is currently an international editorial advisor with the *Journal of Peacebuilding and Development* based at the American University in Washington, DC. He has worked for International Alert (UK), the Minority Rights Group (UK), WaterAid (UK) and other INGOs. A researcher-practitioner, Abitbol maintains a peace research, publishing and consulting practice, Peacemedia-paixmédia. He teaches political science at Concordia University (Montreal) and publishes his work as an Associate Fellow of York University's Institute for Research and Innovation in Sustainability (IRIS).

**Quassy Adjapawn,** PhD, is a human security expert. He is the director of Peaceworks Foundation, West Africa. He has a blend of academic interests ranging from professional experiences in organizational management and development to strategic planning and marketing in peace and conflict studies. In line with his academic pursuits, his interests include peace and conflict, especially the ethnic conflicts in sub-Saharan Africa. He is an adjunct lecturer at Ghana Institute of Management and Public Administration (GIMPA). His articles have appeared in such learned journals as *Global Development Studies*, the *Australasian Review of African Studies*, the *Guild of Independent Scholars*, the *Journal of Alternate Perspectives in Social Science*.

**Laura Balbuena González**, PhD (Cand.), is completing doctoral studies in political science from the New School for Social Research of New York. She holds an MA in political science from the same university and a BA in philosophy from the Pontificia Universidad Católica del Perú (PUCP). Balbuena González is a researcher and consultant on gender issues, having published articles and given keynote addresses on the subject in different countries. She is currently a professor at the Political Science Department at PUCP and director of Peru Programs at the Institute for Study Abroad, Butler University. Balbuena González has taught at the sociological department of Ramapo College and has been a minority scholar in residence at the political science department of the Illinois State University at Normal. She is secretary general of the Latin American Peace Research Association (CLAIP) and a member of the board of the International Peace Research Association Foundation (IPRAF) and of the executive council of the Peru Section of the Latin American Studies Association (LASA).

**Alan Breakspear,** BA, ndc, is a graduate of the University of Western Ontario, in English and French, and an alumnus of Canada's National Defence College. During his 30-year career in Canada's federal Public Service, he served as analyst and manager (to assistant deputy minister level) in intelligence, and in policy, program and resource management functions, in the Communications Security Establishment, Privy Council Office, Treasury Board Secretariat, Canadian Security Intelligence Service and the Solicitor General Secretariat. After leaving government,

Breakspear ran a consulting practice from 1994 providing professional services in competitive intelligence, knowledge management, strategic early warning and enterprise risk management to a range of client organizations. Since moving to Victoria in 2007, he has taught a course in intelligence and public policy at the University of British Columbia and the University of Victoria. He has taught competitive intelligence in many settings, including the University of Ottawa's EMBA program and the training programs of several federal departments and corporate clients. He served as chair of the Science, Technology & Environment Program Advisory Board of Royal Roads University (Victoria, BC) from 2001 to 2006, and assisted Royal Roads in developing its graduate programs in knowledge management. Breakspear has been a member of several professional societies. He is active in the Canadian Association for Security & Intelligence Studies (CASIS) and the International Association for Intelligence Education (IAFIE). He is past president of the Victoria Branch of the Canadian International Council (CIC), a national association devoted to improving the public debate on Canada's foreign policy.

**Rosemary Cairns,** MA, has been involved in community development work in northern Canada and Serbia, and election observation with the UN and OSCE in South Africa, Bosnia, Ukraine, Serbia and Georgia. She has a particular interest in locally driven peacebuilding and development in conflicted and "underdeveloped" parts of the world. She has researched how people built peace for themselves in Somaliland and the Brčko District in Bosnia. Cairns currently works with local peacebuilders in Sri Lanka, Zimbabwe, DRC and southern Sudan to develop local indicators for measuring their achievements, through UK-based Peace Direct. A former journalist, she maintains Hopebuilding wiki to distribute stories of local achievement from around the world. In 2009, she published *Islands of Achievement: How People are Rebuilding After War Ends* (Leipzig, GR: VDM-Vertag).

**Michael Canares,** MSc, is currently the monitoring and evaluation officer of the Provincial Road Management Facility Project, a project funded by the Australian Agency for International Development in the

Philippines. He previously taught for ten years at Holy Name University (Philippines) and served as research associate at the Centre for Research and Local Governance. He has an MSc in development studies from the London School of Economics and Political Science, with previous degrees in accountancy, business education, and law from Philippine universities. Canares's research interests are poverty, local governance, local development, peace and non-violence. He was trained in the evaluation of peace-building programs at the International Conflict Research Institute (UK), development and inequality at Brown University (US), and evaluation of sustainable development at the Research Institute for Managing Sustainability (Austria). His work has recently been published in the *Journal for Small Business and Entrepreneurship* and in an edited volume on urbanization and development by the Oxford University Press.

**Les Chipperfield,** BBA, joined the Royal Canadian Mounted Police in 1966. He spent the next 20 years in New Brunswick, five years in Manitoba and five years in Regina, retiring in 1996 with the rank of superintendent. He then became the deputy chief of police in Fredericton, NB for seven years followed by four years as executive director of the Atlantic Police Academy in Summerside, PEI. Over his 41 years in policing, he has been involved in a broad spectrum of operational and administrative duties with a concentration on adult education in a justice environment in later years. Chipperfield holds a BBA from UNB, graduating as the Outstanding Business Student, and is the recipient of various awards and decorations. He retired in 2007.

**Dale Christenson,** PhD, is the founder and president of the Project Management Centre of Excellence Inc. He is a certified management consultant and project management professional and specializes in project management consulting and training. Christenson is the former executive director of the Province of British Columbia's Project Management Centre of Excellence. He had been the acting assistant deputy minister of the Business Transformation and Learning Services Division as well as the Leadership Centre of BC. Prior to assuming this position, he worked as the director of project management for the Ministry of

Human Resources. He held a number of management positions in the Criminal Justice Branch and after 12 years left to pursue responsibilities in the Chief Information Office, where he also assumed the roles of project director, e-BC Strategy and director of the newly formed Results Management Office. Christenson completed a doctorate in project management from the Royal Melbourne Institute of Technology University in Australia. He holds undergraduate and graduate degrees, diplomas and certificates in criminology, counselling psychology and project management. He has 10 peer-reviewed journal articles to his credit and is a frequent speaker at conferences. He is the winner of the Project Management Institute (PMI) Project of the Year (2007).

**The Honourable Roy Cullen**, PC, BA, MPA, qualified as a Canadian chartered accountant. He was initially elected to the House of Commons in Ottawa in a by-election in 1996 and was re-elected in 1997, 2000, 2004, and in the 2006 general elections. He retired from the Canadian House of Commons in 2008. Cullen served as chair of the House of Commons Standing Committee on Finance; as parliamentary secretary to the minister of finance; as parliamentary secretary to the deputy prime minister and the minister for public safety and emergency preparedness; and as chair of the Ontario Liberal caucus. He was sworn in as a member of the Queen's Privy Council for Canada in 2006. He also served as official opposition critic for natural resources. During his career, Cullen served as an assistant deputy minister in the British Columbia Ministry of Forests and as a vice-president in the Noranda Forest Group (now Norbord). During his tenure as parliamentary secretary to the minister of finance, Cullen was involved in designing and implementing Canada's anti-money-laundering regime. He has been active in the Global Organization of Parliamentarians against Corruption (GOPAC) in the international fight against corruption and money laundering. He has spoken out about these scourges and has played a leadership role at several anti-corruption and anti-money-laundering workshops and conferences. Cullen currently serves as a director of GOPAC, and as team leader of the GOPAC Anti-Money Laundering Global Task Force. In 2008 he completed a book, *The Poverty of Corrupt Nations,* in which he examines the relationship between corrupt leaders and poverty; as a result of the misappropriation of public assets by elected and senior officials, millions of citizens around the world are being deprived of the basic human right of the chance to move out of the ranks of the poor. He offers a Twenty-Point Plan as a way of attacking these vexing problems.

**Douglas Fry,** PhD, received his doctorate in anthropology from Indiana University in 1986 based on a combined ethological and ethnological field study of aggression among the Zapotec people of Oaxaca, Mexico. Fry is currently professor and docent in the Developmental Psychology Program at Åbo Akademi University in Vasa, Finland; concurrently, he is an adjunct research scientist in the Bureau of Applied Research in Anthropology at the University of Arizona. Fry has written on aggression, conflict, and conflict resolution from various theoretical perspectives. His articles have been published in journals such as the *American Anthropologist, Aggressive Behaviour, Child Development, Human Organization*, the *Journal of Aggression, Conflict Resolution and Peace Research*, and *Sex Roles*. Fry is the author of *The Human Potential for Peace* (Oxford University Press, 2006) and *Beyond War* (Oxford University Press, 2007). He is co-editor with Kaj Björkqvist of *Cultural Variation in Conflict Resolution: Alternatives to Violence* (Erlbaum, 1997) and with Graham Kemp of *Keeping the Peace: Conflict Resolution and Peaceful Societies around the World* (Routledge, 2004). He is an Associate Editor of the *Encyclopedia of Violence, Peace, and Conflict, Volumes 1-3, second edition* (Elsevier/Academic Press, 2008). In 2005, Fry was awarded Åbo Akademi University's Harry Elvings Teaching Excellence Award.

**Roger Girouard,** MA, Rear Admiral (ret'd), served in the Canadian Navy for 34 years, following the command route to lead two Canadian missions overseas and head Canada's west coast navy. Experienced in offshore operations, joint and interagency missions, disaster management as well as the realm of HR management, he retired from the Canadian Forces in September 2007. Roger Girouard recently completed the Canadian Coast Guard Inquiry into the tragic sinking of the *l'Acadien*

*II*, a sealing vessel home ported in the Magdelene Islands. He is an associate professor at Royal Roads University.

**Peter Gizewski,** PhD, is a senior defence scientist with the Centre for Operational Research and Analysis (DRDC-CORA), Department of National Defence, and currently serves as the strategic analyst to the Land Capabilities and Designs Operational Research Team (LCDORT) in Kingston, Ontario. He was educated at the University of Toronto (Trinity College) and Columbia University, where he was a Canadian Department of National Defence Fellow in Military and Strategic Studies and a MacArthur Fellow in Conflict, Peace and Security. Gizewski worked for over nine years as a foreign and defence policy analyst at the Canadian Institute of International Peace and Security (CIIPS), and the Canadian Centre for Global Security (CCGS) in Ottawa. He was also senior associate at the Peace and Conflict Studies Program, University of Toronto, and postdoctoral associate in Non-Proliferation Arms Control and Disarmament (NACD) at the York Centre for International and Security Studies, York University.

**Graham Kemp,** PhD, is a peace researcher and Director of Lentz Foundation for Peace Education and Research, Leeds Metropolitan University, UK. He was co-editor with Douglas Fry, *Keeping the Peace: Conflict Resolution and Peaceful Societies Around the World.* He is a regular contributor to the work of the International Peace Research Association (Nonviolent Study group) and the International Society for Research on Aggression.

**Barbara Mann,** PhD, is an Ohio Bear Clan Seneca, scholar and assistant professor at the University of Toledo, Ohio, USA. She has authored eleven books, the latest of which is *The Tainted Gift* (2009), on the deliberate spread of disease to Natives by settlers as a land-clearing tactic. Her internationally famous *Iroquoian Women: The Gantowisas* (2001, 2004, 2007) is in its third printing. She has written three other internationally known books, *George Washington's War on Native America* (2005, 2007), *Daughters of Mother Earth* (2006)—released in paperback as *Make a Beautiful Way* (2008)—and *Native Americans, Archaeologists and the Mounds* (2003, 2006). In addition, Mann has recently published articles on the little-known connection between James Fenimore Cooper and Jane Austen; her book on the topic, *The Cooper Connection*, is due out from AMS Press in 2012. Mann is also the author of dozens of chapters and articles, especially including *"A Sign in the Sky: Dating the League of the Haudenosaunee"* (1997), today considered seminal. Her *"'Where Are Your Women?' Missing in Action"* (2006) has been anthologized, while her *"Greenville Treaty of 1795: Pen-and-Ink Witchcraft in the Struggle for the Old Northwest"* (2004) is highly referenced.

**Moses Muthoki,** BEd, a husband and father of two is a licensed teacher, a youth leader and a public servant. His concern with governance and ethnicity in Kenya motivated him to write a novel on tribalism. He is committed to building capacity in Kenyan youth and achieving peace among Kenyan communities. Muthoki is a facilitator and coordinator of youth activities in his home community.

**Mary-Anne Neal,** MEd, is a mother of four, teacher, writer, public servant, coach, consultant and community contributor. She recently returned from Kenya where she worked with a team of colleagues in Teachers Without Borders. She has earned awards for such varied accomplishments as: *Most Enthusiastic Teacher, Excellence in Written Communication, Public Speaking,* and *Outstanding Achievement.* Neal has facilitated workshops and delivered keynote addresses and presentations to more than 3,000 people in British Columbia. She is a passionate college instructor of leadership and communication skills.

**Tom Rippon,** PhD, completed his doctoral studies at the University of New England, Armidale, NSW, Australia. He publishes and presents papers nationally and internationally, and peer reviews manuscripts for publication in journals. Rippon's research interests include culture of peace, cultures of war and violence, governance and security, ethics, and the efficacy of United Nations missions. Rippon has a professional affiliation with the International Peace Research Association, Canadian Pugwash Group,

International Society for Research on Aggression, American Psychological Associations, Academy of Management, Canadian International Congress, and Society for the Study of Peace, Conflict and Violence.

**Susanne Thiessen,** PhD (Cand.), is of Haida and Scottish ancestry and grew up on the west coast of British Columbia. She has combined a fine arts background with an MBA from the University of Victoria and is currently working on a doctorate in business with a specialization in leadership at Northcentral University. She has been involved in leading and managing Indigenous businesses and organizations in BC for 17 years. Thiessen is a faculty member in the School of Business at Camosun College and leads the Indigenous Business Leadership program. Her cultural background, experiences in developing, managing and delivering programs to Indigenous learners, and her approach to teaching have helped her to create learning environments for Indigenous learners where their perspectives are valued and applied. Through her research, Thiessen is interested in balancing Indigenous perspectives and ways of knowing with non-Indigenous approaches in order to reclaim and revalidate Indigenous approaches to leadership.

**Serge E. Vidalis**, PhD (Cand.), is a retired Canadian naval officer who served in Naval Special Operations and possesses expertise in maritime counter-terrorism, mine warfare and explosive ordnance disposal. His career included a five-year departure from the navy when he served as a police officer in British Columbia, Canada. Vidalis returned to active duty within weeks of September 11, 2001, and was deployed in March 2003 to the Arabian Sea in support of Operation Apollo and Operation Enduring Freedom where he led a special protection team. Vidalis holds a master of arts degree in conflict analysis and management with specialization in political, ethnic and security issues. He is currently a doctoral candidate at the University of British Columbia researching the impact of culture on western security strategies and terrorism. He is also the president of Blue Force Global, Special Services Group Ltd., a firm specializing in strategic security and emergency management services.

**María Eugenia Villarreal**, PhD, completed her doctoral studies at the Universidad Nacional Autónoma de México, México City. For 15 years, she has been working in Mexico and Central America researching child protection, the exploitation of children for sexual purposes, the trafficking of children, child pornography and sexual exploitation in tourism. Eugenia Villarreal has been a council member for the International Peace Research Association, convener of the International Commission of Human Rights (IPRA), and council member of the Global Alliance Against Traffic in Women. She has published and presented papers, and contributed to edited books, nationally and internationally.

*FEATURED ESSAY*

# ON GOVERNANCE AND SECURITY

ROGER GIROUARD, MA

---

## INTRODUCTION AND CONCEPT

The great amorphous gyre of contemporary human interaction has been evolving since mankind emerged as the prime social beast to walk the Earth. Calculating, adaptive and communal, humans sought governance as a controlling and enabling model long before a national government or a United Nations was conceived. A social tenet inherited somehow from the great apes, humankind has made use of governance, structure and hierarchy, of custom and regulation, for a very long time.

Like the concept of family, the theme of governance is familiar to all cultures and regions. It surfaces in our youth through the games we play and pervades our social conduct as habit through to our burial rites. It may well be inevitable in modern life in one form or another. Even anarchists have a pecking order, revolutionaries and terrorists an alternative regime. *"The man"* is at once benevolent and oppressive. Most of all, he is necessary.

To consider governance is to ponder how humanity makes things work. It is the investigation of humankind's successes and failures in simply being, as much as in progressing. It is the assessment of a culture's societal mechanisms and ruling structure, and of the interfaces with the cultures that abut its sphere of influence. It is the study of the imperfect works and processes upon which the very survival of a society, a nation or of humankind may depend. If, in the persistent global economic turmoil of 2012, economics is deservedly known as the dismal science, then governance, in this same complex and risky worldwide milieu, must be seen as the indispensable science. Governance in modern human affairs determines action or gridlock, wealth or penury, peace or conflict, health or illness, progress or arrested development.

At a fundamental human level, governance is how parents manage a home. Governance, traditional and familiar, is how a village elder oversees his or her small dominion. Governance, complex and imperfect as it is, is how the multi-faceted elements of modern society, including nation states, consider and choose. Like parenthood, it needs a standard of expertise and wisdom, which often falls far short of the needs. We make do, to be sure, but run our families, villages and nations better when governance is delivered by the experienced and the studious or at least the well read rather than the naïve, ambitious and the expeditious.

## DEFINITIONS

Governance, of course, comes in varying forms. Corporations and non-governmental organizations have governance elements, as do First Nations in Canada. The United Nations is an amalgam of governance institutions, primarily in the form represented by its member states but symbolized as much by its constituent segments, from the Security Council to UNICEF. Nation-states themselves, rooted in the Treaty of Westphalia (1648), have governmental entities as varied as human culture, which serve to encompass, manage and exert the responsibilities and requirements of the state.

For the purpose of this discussion, governance is the complex and often murky construct of people, organizations and rules that exist to run the nation-state. Whether considering topics on the financial turmoil of the moment, defence and security issues or property and water rights, a recurring theme in each is that of *governance*. Concerns over Haiti, Afghanistan, North Korea, Iran and a host of other states remind us that security issues are embedded in any governance model. The subject matter can be bureaucratic and is often decidedly unglamorous, yet governance is the crucible for choices for good or ill that touch virtually every part of our daily lives. It determines the success or failure of fragile and emerging states. It sets the conditions for deciding the quality of life of a nation and whether or not a population's human capital will achieve its potential or be left to wallow unfulfilled.

Governance is the means by which state will and power is exercised. It is the process by which every social action is effected, whether by code or word of mouth. It is the apparatus by which the disastrous tipping point is avoided and the positive change calculated and implemented. While most people perceive the threats to humanity posed by nuclear proliferation, climate change or the next pandemic, it is, in fact, the dearth of trusted and effective governance that permits these concerns to menace us at all. It is fair to argue that a governance gap can be apparent at many levels and in many jurisdictions. The challenges of failed and fragile states, of emerging nations dealing with a new spurt of commerce or industrialization of the consequences of newfound wealth and the distribution of this largesse, represent an unmet opportunity for understanding and mitigation. The consequences of these changes in parallel with their effect on the physical and social environment are profoundly in need of study, analysis and recommendations. In our own neighbourhood, British Columbia, Canada and Cascadia, we bear witness to challenges to society that derive from inadequate governance models, evident in near-field threat issues, whether they are related to homelessness, environmental degradation, economics or health-care. Good governance is the hope of every citizen, a result of both wisdom and service. Governance is the human interface between a nation's laws and its citizens. Applied with fairness, compassion and pragmatism, governance is limited only by the energy, knowledge and imagination of its practitioners. Greed, paranoia and intolerance deliver the opposite end of the spectrum.

It is commonly said that the prime function of the state and its apparatus is the protection of the borders and of the people. While acknowledging that in some regimes the emphasis is on the former rather than the latter, the predominant approach of the modern state emphasizes the security of the people in a fairly broad context. Indeed, the discussion of what comprises *human security* in this age of rights, sustainability and transparency is, in itself, a complex theme.

Equally complex is the concept that the government *is* the citizenry. Even the Bolsheviks used this theme, so it is not an exclusively democratic concept. It refers to a system where the machinery of government and the body politic become co-influencers, where a moral contract emerges among the politician, the bureaucrat and the citizen. The totalitarian state takes a "trust me to do the thinking" approach and uses ideology and the security apparatchik to mitigate the next revolution. In the summer of 2009, it was impossible to reflect on the post-election turmoil in Iran when considering this approach to governance. The Führer and the Party have been replaced in the hierarchy by the Ayatollah in a theocracy, but the dictatorship remains. Democracies tend to be more engaging, at least in theory, seeking the electorate's approval at each election cycle, giving the masses the option to "throw the bums out" should conditions require. Both democracies and totalitarian regimes at least touch on the aspect of civic engagement and the duties, if not rights, of citizenship. Both lament the efficacy of the two-way conversation, which the term "engagement" denotes. In a democracy, this lament can be expressed publicly.

What makes a state? What elements, physical or ethereal, combine to form an entity recognizable as a member of the international order we call nations? In *First Democracy*, Woodruff describes seven non-negotiable elements or "ideas" required of the democratic state:

1.  Harmony;
2.  Rule of law;
3.  Freedom;
4.  Natural equality;
5.  Citizen wisdom;
6.  Reasoning without knowledge; and
7.  General education.

Most factors clearly place the emphasis on an enlightened and engaged populace rather than on the engine of government. This appears to be in contrast to the current experience in many modern democracies as exemplified by the voting trends of the last 50 years. This trend refers all the more to the importance of the governance model, its capacity for satisfying citizen engagement, and the morals and values set in place for those charged with the role of governing.

In examining the responsibilities of the sovereign national body, Ghani, Lockhart and Carnahan discuss the ten functions of the state:

1. Legitimate monopoly on the means of violence;
2. Administrative control;
3. Management of public finances;
4. Investment in human capital;
5. Delineation of citizenship rights and duties;
6. Provision of infrastructure services;
7. Formation of the market;
8. Management of the state's assets (including the environment, natural resources and cultural assets);
9. International relations (including entering into international contracts and public borrowing); and
10. Rule of law.[1]

Overlaps with Woodruff are apparent, as is a divide regarding the prerogative of the sovereign entity and that of the citizenry. Well executed, we might conceive of separate, intertwined and complementary energies. Where benevolence is in lesser supply, the executions take a different form such as the Gulag, the torture chamber or the propensity for "disappearing." Democratic or dictatorial, the functions are deployed and governance exists.

## POLITICAL IMPACT ON GOVERNANCE

Political expediency is a reality and it is worth exploring the idea of political impact on governance before looking at the structural elements of the governance machine. While governance is not politics, *per se*, it is clearly an enterprise often enmeshed in the political realities of the society in which it seeks to engage. It is subject to the scrutiny of politicians (elected or not) and exposed to the withering glare of the body politic, public opinion and an often indelicate, polarized and even raucous public debate. Ideology, the rights agenda, political correctness, special interests, preventative theory and faith have all been ingredients in the public discourse of nations and in the crafting of the resultant legislation.

## THE ANASTAZI THEORY

In the American southwest were a people called the Anastazi. They were the precursors of the Pueblo society, a culture largely lost to the sands of time. Although traces of their presence exist in the archaeological record, the direct line to the Pueblo is lost. It is known that the Anastazi migrated from their established homeland in the 12th and 13th centuries but their reasons and their subsequent path are unknown. Many ascribe their disappearance to climate change, disease or an unrecorded cultural competitor. I have another theory.

The Anastazi were a developed and successful civilization. They succeeded in agriculture, architecture, engineering and law. In fact, they became the world's first aggressively litigious society, flirting with and flitting amongst a spectrum of legal styles. They established scripts that served as precedents and regulated family hierarchies and constructs (the Napoleonic Code). They developed conventions and tablets outlawing certain actions (English Common Law) and then expanded their regulatory regime to codify what was permitted, outlawing everything else (German Rule of Law). They experimented, combined and integrated the most complex legal framework known in pre-history while their society became so pre-occupied with legal frameworks and outcomes that daily living took on an increasingly inferior place in the people's energies and attentions.

So complex, so tightly constrained and so restrictive were the laws, oversight and enforcement by which the society was literally bound, that less and less commerce, agriculture or daily living took place. The people became so litigious and legalistic in their dealings between parties that less was being done, which had a profound and inexorable impact on the quality of life.

Indeed, people were starving because no one had time to tend the gardens or work the fields. Irrigation stopped for want of decisions on the appeals in court and treaty pronouncements describing sharing regimes. Doctors had abandoned their practice for fear of lawsuits, which resulted in an increasing mortality rate. The civic discourse had disappeared completely because of incessant libel actions. Lifesaving products could not reach the market because of impossible standards for proving them safe. Government collapsed as every vote was mired in the courts, including that of electing the judges.

The rules that the Anastazi had once been so proud of, and the legal framework, once a symbol of their advanced status, had outsmarted them. Initiated to make the system work more efficiently, the litigious culture had become mired in regulatory and governance molasses. The Anastazi were dying of rules and knowing they were breaking the law, those who could went away and started again somewhere else.

It is evident that governance is not in and of itself *rules*. As illustrated in the Anastazi Theory above, rules are the enabler by which governance enacts and functions. Badly applied, like any tool poorly used, unintended and counter-productive consequences are spawned.

Returning to the meaning of governance, perhaps it is best to leave the definition loose. One-size-fits-all has not been a successful human approach historically. A more flexible perspective is that governance is what is required to implement the will and needs of the people. Analogies are often instructive, so think of the horseman and rider as an example of national aims embodied. Neither horse nor rider is governance; saddle, stirrups and bridle are useless alone but are powerful enablers, fitted on a strong and smart horse mounted by a skilful rider. And there it is. Effective governance is more about an amalgamated whole, just as the horse and rider are not individuals. They become a powerful team, each independent but co-dependent for success. Governance needs a seasoned rider who can give a horse its head but pull the reins in when needed and yet share in the results, happiness and satisfaction they build together. In this sense, governance verging on statesmanship seems a worthy aspiration.

## AN EXPLORATION OF
## THE ELEMENTS OF GOVERNANCE

Ancient Rome, the Ottoman Empire and the colonial expanse of the British Empire each functioned through bureaucracy and rules, the core elements of the engine we call governance. Whatever the age, the ideology or the result, it is fair to say that most of modern humanity hopes their governance model delivers security, stability and service. Still in use today in the signature of government correspondence, *Your Obedient Servant* describes, at least in mythology, the competent, fair and efficient civil servant upon which nations and their politicians so often depend.

If the first role of government is the security of the state, the prime role of the civil service is supporting government, traditionally through anonymous results. What should we make of the larger construct, cultural elements and systemic realities? Given a wealth of models and approaches, it is difficult to determine the boundaries of the engine of governance. Roots and tendrils reach into unintended and sometimes illegal segments of society and the state. However far they reach, the intent of governance is one of management and direction rather than of power and control. Even in the non-democratic context of the dictatorship, governance is a requirement. In the ideological model, history and culture appear to be the determining factors in forming the state's approach to governance; thus, North Korea, Indonesia, Chile and Iceland have each arrived at a different place in the early 21st century. The past notwithstanding, the morals and values of the day drive the conduct of politics and governance, presuming one accepts delineation between the two as related to the different roles of the politician and the unelected official.

Indeed, at the heart of the assessment of governance lie the bureaucrat, the functionary and the civil servant. A noble calling in pharaonic Egypt, ancient China, the Ottoman Empire and Victorian England, the modern stereotype is less kind. The reality is that good souls still hope to serve even in modern bureaucracy. A notion familiar to many Canadians is that of "peace, order and good government" as the prime deliverable of any elected body and of the politicians we put into office. Although an imperfect theme, it remains an important and noble goal in the affairs of contemporary society. Security, stability and ethical leadership are key parts of the concept. The notion of peace, order and good governance, as rendered in the affairs of state, requires that security, stability and ethical service exist in that state. It is delivered by those who would rule in spite of the form of government and the model in place. Security, stability and ethical service require balance, a fact which demands judgment amongst those charged with meeting the expectations raised by the tenets of peace, order and good government.

Peace has historically been derived from security, a term once reserved largely for the military practitioner. With the escalating effects of globalization, the term now includes everything from the security of the state to the well-being of the people and their quality of life. It includes health, employment and access to resources, education and opportunity. The existence of a secure society is the foundation of effective governance and the two are required for the sustained improvement of the body politic and the quality of life. Governance and security are inextricably linked.

Order results from a mature society with a sense of public responsibility and openness to dialogue and discourse. Civics is related to the art and the act of citizenship, the domain of rights and responsibilities afforded an individual as a member of the state. It comprises issues of relationship, voice, access and obligation. It is a topic deeply and indelibly linked to culture and tradition, as much as statute and code. Embedded in the concept of order, the elements of a nation's security include the constabulary, guided and constrained by pertinent policies and laws, at least in theory. Again, the theme of balance and judgement arise.

Good government is a more nebulous concept. It sometimes concerns pomp and ceremony, often concerns the civil service and is invariably an unexciting image. This is where the heart of governance lies. It includes laws, policies, functionaries, statecraft and, of course, messaging or the art of effective communication. Each aspect is vital in building success for the nation. Whether considering a council of the elders or Westminster, the apparatus for pondering, deliberating, deciding and executing those decisions is a human endeavour to be appreciated. The structure of government, the traditions and laws, and the mechanism for permitting the public voice on topics of concern are all essential elements of the effective governance model.

The tale of the Anastazi Theory should not be considered too jaundiced a view of the laws, the courts or the constabulary's value to the citizenry or to governance. The tale is allegorical, a cautionary tale, and is not intended to recommend that we eschew all for nothing. It refers rather to the need for balance, the very symbol that Lady Justice holds forth for us all to contemplate. Rule-sets and tradition provide structure and predictability for the social construct. One can argue its place on the political spectrum from libertarianism to socialism and back to the law-and-order agenda but few people want anarchy. While lawyers may poll only a slightly higher worth than a bank CEO in this post-fiscal-meltdown season, the need for a legal construct and the judiciary to interpret it are in the end unarguable.

Stepping back to consider how the ingredients form the whole, the themes of complexity, balance, layering and inter-connectedness become apparent. A systemic perspective is required to see the mass of activity contributing to the governance engine. In the same way, an eye for detail and the common touch are invaluable in reaching down into the trenches and gleaning the information necessary and sufficient to make it all work. Differentiation, the great art that entwines both leadership and management, is the means by which those who govern well, succeed.

As in horsemanship, the constituent parts of governance are complex, with many skill elements lingering unseen or indeed forgotten until circumstances demand. What is even more complex is the spectacular array of interrelationships upon which successful governance is dependant, through the dominant political model. Much of this relationship dynamic falls under the rubric of civil society and is vital to the health and effectiveness of the ship of state. Figure 1 illustrates a simplified representation of this intra-state network of communities, which is in fact the state, and with which its governance mechanisms must work.

Figure 1. Intra-state Governance

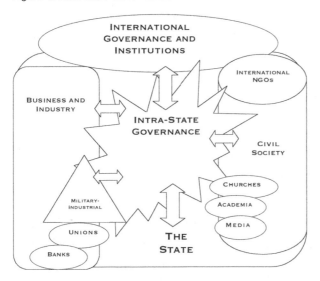

## CONTEXT OF THE FUNCTIONING OF GOVERNANCE

While much of our discussion about governance has been rooted in the perspective of democratic states, one must accept that even dictatorships have governance. Stalin, Hitler and Pol Pot had very effective systems that endured for a time at least. Many features of their regimes perfectly parallel elements found in democracies, reminding us that the tool of governance is, in fact, a politically creed-neutral entity, subject to the ideologies of the leadership and the state, and of the powerful bureaucracies that emerge to become decision-brokers in their own right. We must differentiate between the aim, the implement and the result. In the real world, all three are intertwined to be sure, guided and constrained by the checks and balances that are themselves a vital facet of the reality of governance.

Mao pondered the issue at length, motivated as he was by amalgamating the massive and complex crucible of China under his rule. He considered six key criteria to guide decisions and actions:

1. Words and actions should help unite and not divide the people of our various nationalities;

2. They should be beneficial and not harmful to socialist transformation and socialist construction;

3. They should help to consolidate and not undermine or weaken the people's democratic dictatorship;

4. They should help to consolidate and not undermine or weaken democratic centralism;

5. They should help to strengthen and not discard or weaken the leadership of the Communist Party; and

6. They should be beneficial and not harmful to international socialist unity and the unity of the peace-loving people of the world.

The use of the term "people's democratic dictatorship" illustrates that blatant ideological or even politically correct terminology will often conspire to deliver Kafkaesque results in the discussion of rule and governance. Is this a political-science equivalent of *and then a miracle happens*? *Oz*, the *Mad Hatter, 1984* and the movie *Brazil*, perhaps one of the most haunting tales on film, all refer to the potential madness of power and control through politics and government. Of course, governance is not necessarily democracy. The caveman had governance, gleaned from the clan's culture, size and strength. Governance by club, both the weapon and the social connotation, is a concept that is still familiar, sometimes even in democracies.

If governance does not deliver by default a freedom, service or democratic orientation, the history of the 20th century seems to suggest it should. In the modern context of human affairs and in the hopeful longing of those who want more, we seem forced to distinguish governance as deserving of a higher order of leadership and of effect. Whatever our position on the political spectrum, we seek less selfishness, fewer Swiss bank accounts and more tolerance, sustainability and a better, more broadly shared, quality of life. Most of all, we seek stewardship and servant leadership over self-interest and power for its own sake. It is perhaps more of an ideal than an ideology but one that can be found in the hearts and minds of the conservative, the libertarian and the socialist alike. Values and ethics not only matter but they ought to be at the core of the national personality, even in states of an eclectic cultural mosaic. Where once Divine Right emanated from lineage and physical power, the modern legitimacy of the 21st-century state and its leaders is becoming increasingly rooted in the prospect of leadership as vocation for (and with) the people for the good of the nation, integrated with the neighbourhood of nations. Governance for good. Now there's a concept worth working towards.

Still today, many states fail the litmus test of good government. The North Korean police state, Iranian rigged elections, and the xenophobia of Myanmar all reflect regimes intent on survival where the people, through ideology or religious zeal, are seen as chattels. Even Mao's successors remain preoccupied with the survival of the Party as the embodiment of the state. Although their pragmatism has delivered considerable progress in terms of quality of life and even freedom, this often appears as a concern for legitimacy and a mechanism for fending off the counter-revolution, should the populace become too dissatisfied with Communist rule. It is better that the people be just slightly dissatisfied, it seems.

Rest assured that Western democracies too have their imperfections, with or without a relativistic perspective to tint the assessment. Dark days with minorities, freedom of speech, constraints on liberties and electoral impropriety fill the annals of living history, if only to confirm the fact that governance is hard and complex. It demands a principled approach as much as a deft hand, no matter what the "-ism" or "-ocracy" at play.

Failed, fragile and emergent states face the greatest challenge (from a historical, cultural and economic perspective) in arriving at an effective and survivable governance construct. Nevertheless, sizeable odds have not stopped the steady increase in the number of entities generally recognized as "countries," reaching some 195 national bodies. Nationhood remains a dream that captures the human imagination, even while the spread of religious ideology represents a unity of a different and sometimes competitive sort. These simultaneous themes refer in part to the internal tensions of scenarios such those in Haiti, Somalia, the Balkans or even Pakistan. Amplifying this domestic challenge is the dog-eat-dog reality of a crowded international community. The community is at best subject to *realpolitik* and economic self-interest, and at worst is the field of play of malicious and deadly manipulation rooted in any of a thousand motivations and aspirations. Whether entrenched in nationalism or nihilism, we have only to ponder Chechnya, the Gaza Strip or Rwanda to acknowledge the quagmire that concurrent intra- and extra-territorial strife can create. No wonder the countries fashioned since the United Nations was formed have had such a hard go of it.

Post-colonial Africa remains, perhaps, the most tragic example of three generations of a depressing and incessant game of international snakes and ladders. The annals of the blame dialogue related to the continent could fill volumes. Billions of dollars, thousands of soldiers in combat, peacekeeping and peace-making missions, plus an infinity of international engagements have done too little for too few. The untapped human potential there waits in desperation and, frequently, violent despair. For those who subscribe to the theory that insanity means doing the same thing over and over while expecting different results, what happens in Africa seems to fit the formula.

Perhaps more than any human lesson, the living laboratory that is Africa cries out for governance models that integrate the need for security, embed the best of the anthropological and cultural foundations of the societies and, most importantly, popularize service to the whole over self-interest. As complex as the struggles of Africa are, they are not only about money, not all the result of badly drawn maps, not exclusively about resources and riches, not only about tensions between clans, and never about the weakness of the black races. Whatever the ills, they have all been exacerbated in Africa by a weakness in governance.

Whether property rights, micro-credit, resource sharing, combating corruption or managing tax revenues (every single one a governance issue) the recurring theme of the potential for beneficial change suggests that grass-roots and intra-state governance is first and foremost the leverage point for stepping away from the insanity of repeating the same thing over and over. Reflecting on the current insanity, and on the billions invested to date, some propose giving up on Africa, as if abandoning the population to the radicals, drug lords and pirates will somehow be cheaper in the long run. Until now, the governance effort has yet to be tried; the possibility of breaking the repeated behaviour exists. Despite the seemingly intractable tribulation we see in Africa, an effective governance agenda represents real hope for the next right step. Perhaps the solution for Africa does not lie in the UN, the AU or the IMF and the top-down solutions of a hundred other acronyms. Perhaps for Africa, the solutions lie in the villages and the family groups. We return again to the power of governance. For Africa, the first step may lie in not giving up before the work begins or perceiving only a dark end that gives us the excuse to walk away.

## TO PONDER, TO MUSE, TO REFLECT

In 1965, Barry McGuire hit the radio waves with the powerful and enduring political lament and protest song called *Eve of Destruction*. As a rallying cry for action, it was superb. As a predictor of imminent conflagration, it was completely wrong. What we can dispassionately glean from this song is that Malthusian chants sell or that predicting doom helps mobilize change. But what happens when the dark clouds seem so dire and the end so imminent that the populace checks out? Fifty years on, we can see profound change for the good in America and across this planet, assuming we are willing to see it. It did not happen by accident but by an amalgam of work by governments, activists, power brokers, citizens and organizations. It wasn't easy or often elegant but much good has been done.

To state that governance is profoundly difficult is to offer a simplification that is elegant in the extreme. It is easier to kibitz, cajole or complain than to do. It *is*, in fact, easier to destroy ourselves than to heal the ugliness around us or fight the evil in the dark spaces where so many of us fear to tread. Apologists, cynics and anarchists would have us do just that but, despite the naysayers, mankind is not easily given to surrender. Certainly, good leadership entails tenacity as much as vision.

In simplistic terms, there are three types of people in the world: wolves, sheep and sheepdogs. The good men and women who fall into the latter category don't give up in their good works. Sadly, neither do the wolves with their agenda of self-interest and harm. Retrenchment or isolationism is not what humanity or the planet on which we live are in need of today. The economic, societal and ecological complexities of the moment require engagement, engagement and engagement. To do less is to abdicate our responsibilities to ourselves, each other and our inheritors.

Determining to do something right is the first step. The second, deciding how, is the tougher challenge. The good intentions that pave the road to hell speak volumes and are more than anything the cause of hesitation, lest gold, blood, reputation or moral standing be the cost. Patton's statement "take no counsel of your fears" helps to reinforce the spine, especially in apparent no-win situations where only least-worst options remain. "It's the craftsman, not the tools" approach may be useful in harnessing energy, budgets and attention, as long as one can also accept that scenarios are affected as much by uncontrollable realities as by human foibles, which may in fact be mitigated some of the time.

The more fundamental question being considered is simply: Are we our brother's keeper? The self-interested corollary, which also begs an answer, especially in our connected global village is: Do we have the right to prevent the turmoil there from coming here? An absolute yes or no for either question is difficult to arrive at but with even a graduated "it depends," the implications are significant. It has traditionally been democracies that ponder the question of just or humanitarian intervention the most.

For those who rail about a 20th century of rampant Westernism and blame the ills and evils of the world on the USA or their Allies, there are three names: Hitler, Stalin, Mao. They are guilty of over a billion dead among them, and more hate and lasting resentment than all the sponsored-in-the-USA errors or alleged and assumed conspiracies the nations of the West, combined, have ever amassed. These three were totalitarians and totalitarianism, whether Fascism, Nazism, Communism or Radical Islamism, remains the gravest threat to both have and have-not populations. Notwithstanding what some may offer as rays of light inside these three evil regimes, their ills always outweigh their benevolent rhetoric. The Commonwealth, the Allies, NATO, the European Union, and la Francophonie may be imperfect but they have left more on the positive side of the ledger over the last 100 years than the opposite style of regimes ever will. This is not an apologist's tale but a fair accounting of history.

Democracy has long admitted its foibles and imperfections. This admission is, in part, so that it may guard against losing its humility and, in turn, seek to take more than it gives to its community. In the larger context, democracies too must aim to survive through what is described as a clash of civilizations. Harshly put, we are perhaps facing the barbarians of the 21st century – people who have no love of life and luxuriate in the deaths of their own children, let alone the deaths of their enemy's child. This sad truth is what separates us and not finance, means or the rich-poor divide. Poverty has survived many centuries without this level of hate, driven by ideological absolutism or religious zeal entwined with a bloodlust for power and control. The world's Al Qaedas have no desire to improve the lot of the masses. The Taliban never worked to heal root causes but strove to dominate and subjugate, to dim their world into another Dark Age. Welcome to the 21st century, where things are hard again and *heavy lifting* is the only way. It is said that there are no atheists in a foxhole and it could fairly be said that there are no pacifists in a knife-fight. Taken further, in the new world order, there are no innocents in a suicide bombing – they are all combatants. Welcome to the new *total* war never envisaged by Bismarck.

The real issue we must come to grips with is whether intervention causes radicalism or self-isolation enables it? Neither political analysis nor social sciences have determined the answer and we may never know. Perhaps, instead of focusing on the 2% of humanity that is propounding the violent cancer of murderous radicalism, we should examine the more general malaise of the disenfranchised and the vulnerable. Even those who disavow the theory of "root cause" can at least support an examination of the quality of life on the bottom tier of humanity on humanitarian grounds. The business case is even stronger if one accepts that stability is good for business. Values, compassion, systemic thinking and inclusiveness, along with humility, openness and sensitivity all bear fruit. So too does decisive action, sometimes uncomfortable, but required and effective in a balanced approach. The theme of reward and consequence, the carrot and the stick, is simplistic but human.

Perhaps the point is not about the delivery of democracy and the torpedoes be damned. As well intentioned as the Bush administration may have been, the "you're with us or against us" message was counter-productive. So was the theme of injecting democracy to make the world better. The mad rush to that end has sometimes delivered sad unintended consequences. With patience as a premise and a prospect for the least wrong done over the longer term, the point is to deliver the fundamentals first. The herder, peasant, peon, serf in Somalia, Kurdistan, Guatemala or Myanmar has no interest in the Chablis diplomacy of Geneva or the technicolour dreams of the human rights agenda. She would be satisfied to eat a little more, to die a little less. You may recall Mackenzie King's mid-World War II election platform vacillation of "conscription if necessary but not necessarily conscription." We may now consider "perhaps democracy, but better democracy when ready."

So what do we focus upon? The need for governance calls for integrated research, analysis and coherent effort. The following serves to temper the perspective taken on embarking on such a quest:

1.  Address broad and integrated themes supportive to the intra-state governance domain, whatever the political construct in place;
2.  Maximize quality of life initiatives and structures;
3.  Integrate security, stability and economic concepts;
4.  Differentiate the consequences of sharing and redistribution, of aid and dependence, of self-worth and self-determination; and
5.  No matter the desire to assist, eschew ideological imperialism and the "we know better" conundrum.

In considering this list, a crucial perspective for assistance and intervention is that described by the term *anthropologically correct*. The term expresses the extreme opposite of political correctness, that notorious term describing a world of apolitical androgyny, where an artificial sameness aims to expunge, insult or offend. This is a domain where tolerance is a violent act.

The anthropologically correct viewer readily admits, celebrates and takes into account historical and cultural differences. With sincere curiosity, he or she seeks out the styles and strengths and aims to embed such elements into systems, even while existing in the complex modern world. Rather than denying cultural roots or eradicating perceived colonial mechanisms, the approach seeks to integrate, maximize and deploy the best of what works, while adapting and improving along the way. More than anything, it is a process that seeks the roots of servant leadership in every culture it perceives, with the goal of making service a sign of strength rather than weakness.

Depending on your place in the world order, hope can be a luxury, vision, mirage or a singular thread by which one clings to survival. It is not unfair to state that the only souls with a right to hope are those who depend upon it the most. For the rest of us, our relationship with hope is that of delivering it, not of holding onto it. Governance and security, as a unitary concept, is about those who have the will and the power and the vision to deliver on the hope of those around us who are in need. The string of activity that emerges follows the look, see, hear, scrutinize, plan and do sequencing. It is an iterative cycle with the aim of constant improvement. It is absolutely unoriginal in the realm of change management. It is worth starting now with a governance lens.

## REFERENCES

Ackerman, P., and J. Duvall. A *Force More Powerful – A Century of Non-violent Conflict*. New York, NY: Palgrave, 2000.

Amstutz, M. R. *International Conflict and Cooperation: An Introduction to World Politics*. Bel Air, CA: William C. Brown, 1995.

Bessler, M., and K. Seki. "Civil-Military Relations in Armed Conflicts: A Humanitarian Perspective." An excerpt from *Liaison, A Journal of Civil-Military Humanitarian Relief Collaborations* III, no. 3 (2006).

Cairns, R. *Islands of Achievement: How People are Rebuilding After War Ends: Locally-driven Strategies Offer New Models for International Peacebuilding in Conflict-torn Societies*. Berlin, Ger: VDM Verlag, 2009.

Chomsky, N. *Failed States – The Abuse of Power and the Assault on Democracy*. New York, NY: Owl Books, 2006.

Eberly, D. *The Rise of Global Civil Society Building Community and Nations from the Bottom Up.* New York, NY: Encounter Books, 2008.

Fettweiss, C. J. "Freedom Fighters and Zealots: Al Qaeda in Historical Perspective." *Political Science Quarterly* 124, no. 2 (Summer 2009).

Friedman, T. L. "A New Hope for Peace." *New York Times* (August 4, 2009).

Ghani, A., C. Lockhart, and M. Carnahan. *Closing the Sovereignty Gap: An Approach to State-Building.* Working Paper 253, Overseas Development Institute, London, 2005.

Hubert, D. "Humanitarian Advocacy Campaigns: Lessons on Government Civil-Society Collaboration." Chapter 7 in *Joint Action for Prevention – Civil Society and Government Cooperation on Conflict Prevention and Peacebuilding*, Issue Paper, 4 December 2007. In Paul van Tongeren and Christine van Empel (Eds.). *European Centre for Conflict Prevention/Global Secretariat of the Global Partnership for the Prevention of Armed Conflict.* The Netherlands. <http://www.gppac.net/uploads/File/Programmes/Interaction%20and %20 Advocacy/Issue%20Paper%204%20December%202007%20Gov-CSO%20 cooperation.pdf> (15 September, 2009).

Huntington, S. P. "How Countries Democratize." *Political Science Quarterly* 124, no. 1 (Spring 2009/1991).

Lanoszka, A. *The World Trade Organization: Changing Dynamics in the Global Political Economy.* London, UK: Lynne Rienner Publishers, 2009.

Lewis, S. *Race Against Time.* 2005 Massey Lecture Series. Toronto, ON: House of Anansi Press, 2005.

McGuire, B. "*Eve of Destruction.*" 1965 <http://artists.letssingit.com/barry-mc-guire-lyrics-eve-of-destruction-s1m88lj> (15 September 2009).

Molden, D. ed. *Water for Food Water for Life: A Comprehensive Assessment of Water Management in Agriculture.* International Water Management Institute Standalone Summary, 14 February 2007.

Mueller, J. "War Has Almost Ceased to Exist: An Assessment." *Political Science Quarterly* 124, no. 2 (Summer, 2009).

Tse-Tung, M. *On the Correct Handling of Contradictions Among the People.* Peking, CH: Foreign Languages Press, 1966/1957.

Woodruff, P. *First Democracy.* New York, NY: Oxford University Press, 2005.

## ENDNOTES

[1] A. Ghani, C. Lockhart and M. Carnahan. *Closing the Sovereignty Gap: An Approach to State-Building.* Working Paper 253, Overseas Development Institute, London, 2005.

SECTION I

---

# ESTABLISHING STRUCTURES

---

# STATE-CAUSED ETHNIC CONFLICTS: THE NEED TO REVERSE AND RE-STRUCTURE THE EDUCATIONAL POLICIES IN THE NORTHERN REGION OF GHANA

**QUASSY ADJAPAWN, PhD**

## INTRODUCTION

The study in *Two Faces of Education in Ethnic Conflict* by Bush and Saltarelli contests the popular notion that education is inexorably a force for good.[1] It reveals that education can be manipulated to drive a wedge between people, rather than drawing them closer together. The study reveals that denial of education can be used as a weapon of war and the cultivation of inclusive citizenship as a benefit. It emphasises the need for peace-building education to deal with principles and goals, including the demilitarisation of the mind, the introduction of alternatives to suspicion, hatred and violence, and the value of memory.[2] Girouard proposes a similar dualistic perspective of "action or gridlock, wealth or penury, peace or conflict, health or illness, progress or arrested development." Governance must be delivered and administered by those who are both experienced and educated.

It may not be unusual to suggest that in sub-Saharan Africa (SSA), the lack of education contributes to lawlessness, societal breakdown and conflict. Works by peace and conflict researchers support this notion as applicable to the Northern Region of Ghana.[3,4] Similarly, in Sierra Leone and Liberia, the lack of opportunity for education or any kind of planned future created squads of disaffected youth ripe for recruitment.[5,6] Amid the complexities and chaos in education and conflict lies the fact that education in general, and peace education in particular, are vital in the management of conflict.

In terms of *Complexity Theories and Conflict*, the issue with educational theory is that there has not been enough research into the contribution of schooling and violence. The emphasis has been on the contribution to inequality, looking at reproduction of social class or gender relations, while the reproduction of conflict has received far less attention.[7] Drawing on research in 52 countries affected by conflict, Buckland[8] examines the role that education could play, both in terms of conflict prevention and in the reconstruction of post-conflict societies. According to Easterly:

> Africa's poor growth and resulting low income is associated with low schooling, political instability, underdeveloped financial systems, distorted foreign exchange markets, high government deficits, and insufficient infrastructure. High ethnic diversity is closely associated with low schooling, underdeveloped financial systems, distorted foreign exchange markets, and insufficient infrastructure. While motivated by Africa, these results are not particular to Africa.[9]

Education provides an environment of relative stability and normalcy for children even amid the instability and unpredictability of war. It provides them with an opportunity to learn so that they can have a chance to gain at least some of the most basic skills that will allow them to contribute to society and, in time, to support their family. As stated by the former UNICEF boss, Carol Bellamy, it was a tragedy that much was not done to educate those living for many years in refugee camps.[10]

In April 2009, the World Bank's Director for Education, Beth King, announced that the World Bank had doubled its education financing in low- and middle-income countries to $4.09 billion to help poor countries battle threats to their educational systems during the global economic crisis.[11] That is a welcome announcement but it seems that these monies are not well channelled to the areas where they are most needed. In Sierra Leone, for example, the education sector is in crisis as thousands of teachers go unpaid (Fofana, 2009).[12] The ruling government has refused to pay the salaries of almost 3,000 teachers, while looking to recruit thousands more. The New Security Foundation chairman, Dr. Harold Elletson, rightly said that education is the forgotten aspect of post-conflict humanitarian aid and aid for refugees. It is no wonder that, a decade since MDG's universal primary education for every child by 2015 was adopted, 100 million children are still not attending primary school.[13] And of these, 50% are in countries that are either suffering from conflict or recovering from it.[14]

## RELATIONSHIPS AMONGST ETHNIC GROUPS

In trying to understand the background of the situation, it is important to realize that the antipathy that has dogged the relationship between ethnic groups in the Northern Region of Ghana is a product of the political configuration that the British colonialists imposed on them.[15] The main feature of this configuration was Indirect Rule, which the British developed for the ethnic groups and chieftaincies. As part of Indirect Rule, the British colonialists forced the historically non-centralized ethnic groups and their allies under the political jurisdiction of the Dagombas and their allies, and the acephalous Kusasis were said to have been forced under the cephalous Mamprusis. Social amenities and other benefits were reserved mainly for the chiefly centralized groups while the non-centralized groups went without. As noted by Staniland quoting Sir Gordon Guggisberg on British policy of rule:

> Our policy must be to maintain any Paramount Chiefs that exist and gradually absorb under these any small communities scattered about. What we should aim at is that someday the Dagombas, Gonjas and Mamprusis should become strong native states. Each will have its own little Public Works Department and carry on its own business with the Political Officer as a Resident and Adviser. Each state will be more or less self-contained.[16]

This political inequality resulted in tensions between the ethnic groups that persisted until the conditions came to be viewed as bitterly

Table 1. Inter-ethnic Conflicts Fought Between 1980 and 2002

| Date | | Ethnic Groups | Concerns Raised | Cost of War |
|---|---|---|---|---|
| 1 | 1980 | Gonjas-Vaglas | Chieftaincy and land | Unknown |
| 2 | 1981 | Konkombas-Nanumbas | Chieftaincy and land | 118 dead, and houses burnt |
| 3 | 1982 | Mamprusi – Kusasi | Chieftaincy and land | Unknown |
| 4 | 1984 | Konkombas-Bimobas | Chieftaincy and land | 60 dead and many displaced |
| 5 | 1984 | Mamprusi – Kusasi | Chieftaincy | 150 killed |
| 6 | 1985 | Mamprusi – Kusasi | Chieftaincy | Unknown |
| 7 | 1985-86 | Konkombas-Bimobas | Chieftaincy and land | 78 dead, several displaced |
| 8 | 1986-87 | Kombas-Bimobas | Chieftaincy and land | 26 dead, assets destroyed |
| 9 | 1989 | Konkombas-Bimobas | Chieftaincy and land | 20 dead |
| 10 | 1990 | Konkombas-Nawuris | Chieftaincy and land | Unknown |
| 11 | 1991 | Nawuris-Gonjas | Chieftaincy and land | 78 Dead |
| 12 | 1992 | Gonjas-Nawuris | Chieftaincy and land | Unknown |
| 13 | 1992 | Konkombas (and allies)-Gonjas | Chieftaincy and land | High death toll 19 |
| 14 | 1993 | Konkombas-Mossis20 | Chieftaincy | Unknown |
| 15 | 1994-95 | Konkombas-Dagombas and allies | Chieftaincy and land | 15,000 dead, 200,000 displaced, 442 villages burnt. |
| 16 | 1997 | Mos-Gonjas | Chieftaincy | 800 people displaced. |
| 17 | 2000 | Mamprusi – Kusasi | Chieftaincy | No account of lives lost. Assets burnt |
| 18 | 2000 | Mamprusi – Kusasi | Chieftaincy | 40 dead, property destroyed |
| 19 | 2001 | Mamprusi – Kusasi | Chieftaincy | 50 dead, 150 injured, 5,000 displaced, property burnt. |

Source: Adjapawn (2010)

unfair by the oppressed. Rebellion resulted and the oppressors resisted attempts to alter the *status quo* to shift the balance of power, resulting in twists and turns. As noted by Staniland:

> Despite this assertion of suzerainty, the Dagomba kingdom seems never to have exercised close control over the Konkomba: administration took the form of slave raiding and punitive expeditions. The Konkombas were by no means assimilated. Relations between them and the Dagomba were distant and hostile: there was little, if any, mixing by marriage.[17]

Since 1957 when Ghana gained independence from the British, the successive postcolonial governments have done little to reverse the scene set by London. Subsequent policies on land, chieftaincy, and allocation of resources have rather served to endanger the already fragile relationships in the Northern Region of Ghana. The most prominent 23 of over 30 conflicts fought are tabled below (see Tables 1 and 2). It is important to note that the tables document only the conflicts with higher tolls. Events that resulted in lower counts such as the Konkomba – Bimoba conflict in 2007 (three dead and three houses in the Jimbali area burnt)[18] are not documented here.

Table 2. Intra-ethnic Conflicts Fought Between 1980 and 2002

| Date | | Ethnic groups | Concerns raised | Cost of war |
|---|---|---|---|---|
| 1 | 1986-87 | Dagombas' chieftaincy crisis | Chieftaincy | Unknown |
| 2 | 2000 | Bimobas' war | Land | Unknown |
| 3 | 2002 | Dagombas' chieftaincy crisis | Chieftaincy | 49 dead, 1000s displaced |
| 4 | 2002 | Bimobas' war | Land | 2 dead, 1,200 displaced, assets destroyed. |

Source: Adjapawn (2010)

The Mamprusis fought six times over the same period, not with any other ethnic group in the Northern Region but against the Kusasis in the Upper East Region. Tables 1 and 2 show inter and intra-ethnic conflicts between 1980 and 2002.[19, 20]

The Northern Region of Ghana, with Tamale as its capital, is the largest region and covers 70,383 square kilometres, about 30% of the total area of the country. It has a population of 1,805,428[21] with only 25.7 persons per square kilometre as against the national average of 78.9.[22] To understand the discussions in the following sections on the groups' interactions and subsequent conflicts, it is necessary to be familiar with the ethnographical map (Figure 1) and a summary of the region and its inhabitants (Table 3).

Figure 1. Ethnography of the Northern Region of Ghana

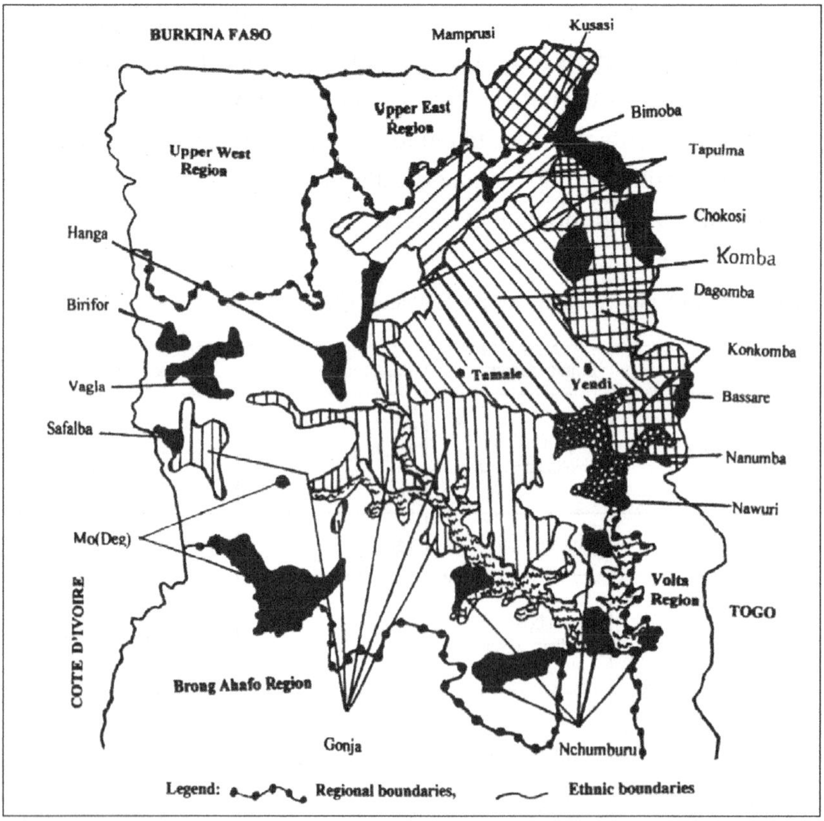

Source: Adjapawn (2010)

Note that some of the ethnic groups appear more than once in their groupings and some are known by more than one name. As seen in Table 3, the groups have interesting demographic representations, from the Dagombas, who have the greatest numerical strength, to the Tapulmas, whose representation the recent National Population and Housing Census (2000) found to be infinitesimally small. The two neighbouring regions in the North, the Upper West and Upper East, have 31.2 and

Table 3. Ethnic Groups in Northern Region – Ghana

| | Ethnic Groups | Population Distribution of Ethnic Groups in the Northern Region, Ghana | | | | |
|---|---|---|---|---|---|---|
| | | Total National Population | Total Regional Population | Ethnic size as % of National Population | Ethnic size as % of Regional Population | % of Ethnics in the Region |
| 1 | Dagomba | 747,924 | 594,865 | 4.3 | 32.90 | 79.50 |
| 2 | Konkomba | 474,293 | 305,575 | 2.7 | 16.90 | 64.40 |
| 3 | Gonja | 211,703 | 131,814 | 1.2 | 7.30 | 62.30 |
| 4 | Mamprusi | 200,393 | 132,494 | 1.1 | 7.30 | 66.10 |
| 5 | Bimoba | 113,130 | 49,013 | 0.6 | 2.70 | 43.30 |
| 6 | Nanumba | 78,812 | 45,414 | 0.5 | 2.50 | 57.60 |
| 7 | Chokosi | 63,910 | 35,898 | 0.4 | 2.00 | 56.30 |
| 8 | Bassare | 51,299 | 20,331 | 0.3 | 1.10 | 39.60 |
| 9 | Nchumburu | 113,334 | 13,624 | 0.6 | 0.80 | 12.00 |
| 10 | Vagla | 41,684 | 5,205 | 0.2 | 0.30 | 12.50 |
| 11 | Mo (Deg) | 55,174 | 5,178 | 0.3 | 0.30 | 9.40 |
| 12 | Safalba | 7,827 | 2,159 | - | 0.10 | 27.60 |
| 13 | Birifor | n/a | n/a | n/a | n/a | n/a |
| 14 | Hanga | n/a | n/a | n/a | n/a | n/a |
| 15 | Komba | n/a | n/a | n/a | n/a | n/a |
| 16 | Nawuri | n/a | n/a | n/a | n/a | n/a |
| 17 | Tapulma | n/a | n/a | n/a | n/a | n/a |

Source: Population Figures from Government of Ghana, 2000
Population and Housing Census, 2000.

104 people per square kilometre respectively, making the region the least populated.[23] The Northern Region has 20 administrative districts and is shared between 17 main linguistically distinct ethnic groups.

## ETHNIC CONFLICT AS AN AGENT OF DESTRUCTION

Human losses and destruction of property are hard to record in such a preponderantly illiterate society.[24] Though the focus of the study is the Northern Region of Ghana, the conflicts sometimes spill over to other parts of the country where feuding groups clash, resulting in death and the destruction of property. As recently as 25 August 2008, an ethnic clash occurred between the feuding groups, but this time at Konkomba Market at Agbgbloshie in Accra, the capital city. Three people were butchered to death with machetes.[25] Due to its erratic nature and the subsequent spillover, recording the dead and destruction of property has always become problematic.

In the Northern Region, the majority[26] of the inhabitants are Muslims whose teachings dictate immediate burial of the dead. Also, to win a psychological victory, in the case of the Konkombas, their women, who in times of war serve as the rearguard, are responsible for immediately burying their dead men and supplying the warriors with food and water.[27,28] The problem with counting the dead results in conflicting recorded figures. For example, Ada van der Linde and Naylor claim that the Guinea Fowl war in 1994-1995 claimed 15,000[29] lives, whereas Pul records that at least 2,000 died. However, they all agree that over 200,000[30] people were displaced and 442 villages and settlements were burnt down. Also destroyed were vehicles and private and public properties including schools, churches and clinics.[31]

## EDUCATIONAL NEGLECT: COLONIAL GOVERNMENTS

The days of colonialism saw an established and sustained system of inequality whereby education was offered to the princes, especially the sons of senior chiefs in the north. It was not until the 1950s, with the arrival in the north of missionaries along with their clinics and schools, that such facilities became available to all commoners including the non-chiefly ethnic groups. Through Indirect Rule, during the major part of colonisation, the British kept a tight control on education and missionary policies in order to maintain the traditional institutions that were facilitating their smooth administration.[32] These policies had seemingly left the protectorate of the Northern Territories to suffer and they are still suffering from serious educational disadvantages compared to the Ashanti and the Gold Coast colonies in the south. This was evident in 1957 at the time of independence; the Northern Region had only one university graduate.[33]

During the colonial period, education received little attention in the Northern Region of Ghana. It was not perceived as a life-saving initiative like health and nutritional rehabilitation. From the experiences that the colonialists had in the Ashanti Kingdom and the Gold Coast Colony, they deliberately wanted to slow down the educational process in the Northern Region, if not neglect the inhabitants completely. The British colonial administration ensured the late introduction of education in the Northern Territories and in some areas there were restrictions. Education started in 1908 with four boys, who were sent to Cape Coast in the Gold Coast colony and, in 1909, when Tamale School was established, the boys were transferred to Tamale in the Northern Territories. By 1925, it was clear that areas like Yendi, Bawku and Bole needed schools but not at the expense of Achimota College that was opened in Accra in the south. The British administration responded that:

> Owing to the necessity of rigid economy and to the fact that considerable expenditure will be incurred in the near future in the building of Achimota College, His Excellency has decided that no additional day Primary School will be opened in the Northern Territories during the next three or four years.[34]

Three phases were established in educational policies in the Northern Territories. During the first phase, the colonizers raised no concern about integrating educational and administrative issues. The foreign missionaries were allowed to operate but with the caveat that their operations were not to interfere with areas where Islam was strong. The second phase was marked by the announcement by F. G. Guggisberg in 1919 that education was to be established in the protectorate but it should be encouraged not to break down the traditional institutions, as was the case of the Ashanti and the Gold Coast colonies. In effect, Standard III (Elementary Primary 6) education was to be limited as the maximum that the system could bear. Their only option was to migrate to the south as unskilled labourers in the mines and the plantations. During the third phase, in line with Native Administration, the traditional authorities were urged to send their children to school, but the provision of labour was seen as a higher priority than education. The chief commissioner in the Protectorate pointed out the need to establish special schools to train a new generation of chiefs, but English language should be enforced as the lasting benefit rather than forcing the commissioners and their administrators to learn one of the many languages of the ethnic groups.

In the Northern Territories, the intake at the Tamale school in 1913 was as following: 43 Dagombas, 5 Gonjas, and 10 were identified as children of southerners employed by the government. There was no enrolment for anyone from the acephalous ethnic groups. A step supposed to improve education was introduced in 1915, where pupils completing Standard VII (Elementary Middle Form 4) were recruited as teachers on the basis that employment of the local natives would encourage the parents to send their children to school. There were better-qualified teachers in Ashanti and the Gold Coast colonies but in the Northern Territories, the British administration continued to recruit Standard VII leavers as teachers. By 1935, schools in the north had a serious shortage of qualified teachers, but the provincial inspector of schools could not be convinced to bring in qualified teachers from the south, who by then had better education than their compatriots in the north. The British were aware that the standard of education in the south was better than in the north, yet their attempt to improve the educational system in the north settled on recruiting local Standard VII (Elementary Middle Form 4) as teachers, instead of bringing better qualified teachers from the south. The provincial inspector for education notes:

> The teachers from outside the Northern Territories (from the south) although they were competent and efficient as such, did

not exercise a beneficial influence on the boys in the direction of instilling in them a sense of their civic responsibilities.[35]

Bening (1977) notes that the denial of the qualified teachers from the south was to shield the northerners from the movements that were protesting against the colonial rule in the south.[36] A few attempts by the missionaries to be involved in schools met resistance from the British administration because they were deemed to be subversive and thus not allowed to operate freely. Despite the weaknesses in education, the provincial commissioner found it unnecessary to revamp the educational system in the north. Bening states:

> To give these primitive children more advanced education would be a doubtful blessing at present. It might tend to make them discontented with their lot. Is our population so large at present that we can afford to educate natives for work on the coast? On the other hand if they, on leaving school, return to their families with advanced education, will this make for peace in the household? Will these educated youth go back to work on the farms?[37]

In the Ashanti kingdom and the Gold Coast colony, education was steadily improving with better-qualified teachers. Meanwhile in the north, presumably due to limited development or isolation, Governor Guggisberg decided to integrate traditional values slowly into the educational system. The seemingly deliberate attempt to delay the northerners' education as compared to the southerners was noted in 1919 (see Table 4). At that time there were only four government schools in the Northern Territories with a population of 694,000, while Ashanti, with a population of 448,000 had four government schools and nineteen government-assisted schools. In a sense, the colonial administration seemed to be guarding against the mistakes they made in the south. Governor Guggisberg noted:

> It is obvious that to do anything at the present moment that would extend the education system in the Northern Territories would be extremely inadvisable. In the Northern Territories we

have a virgin ground on which to work, as far as education is concerned, guided by the lessons brought to us by the failures in the colony and Ashanti.[38]

Table 4. Gold Coast Educational System in 1919[39]

| Gold Coast Colony Area | Number of Gov Schools | Government-assisted Mission Schools | Pupils Enrolled | |
|---|---|---|---|---|
| | | | Boys | Girls |
| Eastern Province | 5 | 114 | 12,130 | 2,877 |
| Central Province | 3 | 42 | 5,723 | 1,107 |
| Western Province | 3 | 19 | 2,370 | 321 |
| Ashanti Colony | 4 | 19 | 2,292 | 287 |
| Northern Territory | 4 | - | 203 | 8 |

Source: The author and compilation from sessional paper
No. XVII, 1918 –1919, CO 98/31

Whether intentionally or by oversight, the two committees that were set in 1918 and 1920 by Clifford and Guggisberg, respectively, to investigate and report on the progress of education in the three colonies did not make mention of the Northern Territories. By 1939, the Northern Territory continued to lag behind the other colonies in education. In 1931, the total number of children in the north was estimated at 184,000 boys and 168,480 girls, but out of these only 600 boys and 65 girls were enrolled in schools. Meanwhile in that year, the total enrolments in the southern colonies including Togoland mandate were 43,825 boys and 14,534 girls.

The research conducted for this chapter unearthed no document to support the idea that the British colonialists favoured Islamization in Ghana. However, a political conference held in 1933 in the Northern Territories endorsed the Education Department's concerns about the way in which the Catholic Mission schools seemed to be springing up in an uncontrolled manner. This is an indication of the concerns of the then government.[40] Duncan-Johnstone,[41] then chief commissioner of the Northern Territories (CCNT) feared that the Catholic Mission schools would have a disintegrating effect on the social system that he was trying to build.[42]

Whilst Hodgkin, Ferguson and Seidu have recorded a positive and steady process of Islamization during the colonial days in the Northern Territories, Goody, Hodgkin, Ferguson, Seidu, Sundkler and Steed note that the steady process of Islamization resulted from the undisclosed support for Islam and concern about Christianity by the British government. On the other hand, other researchers note the British colonial authorities did not perceive Islam as a threat to their administration and therefore Muslims received little attention or were left alone.

As mentioned earlier, education was deliberately introduced at a later stage and with tight control – the level of attainment was restricted in order to facilitate smooth administration in the north. When the Christian missionaries wanted to help, they were cautioned. Border policies that united the western part of Togoland with the Gold Coast have resulted in opponents and proponents of the ethnic conflicts re-writing history to the disadvantage of others who are denied land and political representation. The acute economic destitution and lack of development being witnessed today in the Northern Region of Ghana have their origins in historical underpinnings based on poor governance. Such politico-economic development recipes, according to Collier's groundbreaking work, create an environment where ethnic conflicts thrive.

It sounds reasonable that the denial of qualified teachers from the south was to shield the Northern Territories from awareness movements that were protesting against the British in the south (Field note 2005/37). The British knew that the Northern Territories was at the time lagging behind in education, they further restricted the missions in their activities to guard their interest. In his groundbreaking work to establish the link between Conflict and Development (or the lack of it), Collier asserts:

Civil war is now an important issue for development. War retards development but conversely development retards war. This double causation gives rise to virtuous and vicious circles. Where development succeeds, countries become progressively safer from violent conflicts, making subsequent development easier. Where development fails, countries are at higher risk of becoming conflict trapped, in which war wrecks the economy and increases the risk of further war.[43]

## EDUCATIONAL NEGLECT: POSTCOLONIAL GOVERNMENTS

It was revealed that though the 1992 Ghana Constitution provides for Free Compulsory and Universal Basic Education (FCUBE) and enjoins the state to make higher education progressively accessible to all, allocations of public subsidies to support educational institutions are skewed against the north and favour the south. State subsidies per schoolchild by region favour the prosperous regions in the south. For primary schools, the south receives fewer subsidies mainly due to good private institutions that cater for foreign diplomats and the well-to-do families. With the poorest regions benefiting least from public spending, this presents a great challenge in the fight against poverty.

The national averages for the pupil-teacher ratios in primary and junior secondary schools (JSS) are 43 and 32 respectively. However, shortages of teachers in the Northern Region result in high teacher-pupil ratios and over-crowded classrooms. It is thus plausible that the appalling pattern of schooling in the region as compared to the south could be the result of this disparity. The literacy rate among adults in

Figure 2. State Subsidies for Schools

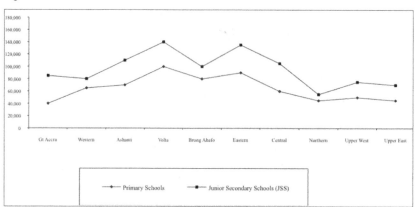

Source: Adapted but modified from S. Canagarajah and X. Ye, 2001.

the area is lower than 5%, and about 40% of school-age children are out of school.[44]

Despite under-staffing and lack of adequate resources, primary school education is readily available in the north. However, out of 260 communities surveyed in the Northern Region, 13 have no primary schools and children living at Namango in the Mamprusi East district wishing to attend primary school have to journey 28 kilometres. In a survey of Junior Secondary Schools (JSS),[45] the people of Buipe-Yipala in the Gonja West district have to travel 50 kilometres to attend JSS. It might sound unbelievable that pupils at Banda-Nkwanta in the Bole district in Northern Region have to travel 90 kilometres to the nearest Senior Secondary Schools (SSS), but this is the reality.

Given the lack of schools in the Northern Region, it is not surprising to note that they are behind in education.[46] These precarious educational systems in the three Northern Regions explain the relatively poor educational standards in the north. The national average for those who have attended preschool or no school stands at 47.7%. In the Greater Accra Region, the figure is 28.8%, but in the Northern Region the figure stands at 78.6%. Nationally, those who have attained tertiary education

Table 5. Northern Region's Educational Characteristics Compared with Greater Accra Region and National

| | Northern Region | Greater Accra | National | Percentage (%) |
|---|---|---|---|---|
| Education Characteristics | 1,639,327 | 2,714,517 | 17,282,545 | 100 |
| None or pre-school | 1,288,064 | 782,337 | 8,240,625 | 47.7 |
| Primary | 174,727 | 470,715 | 3,210,917 | 18.6 |
| Middle/JSS | 73,721 | 763,607 | 3,642,567 | 21.1 |
| Secondary/SSS | 52,078 | 336,050 | 1,045,140 | 6.0 |
| Vocational/Technical | 14,919 | 142,695 | 386,559 | 2.2 |
| Post Sec. (Agric/Nurse) | 17,374 | 58,488 | 266,323 | 1.5 |
| Tertiary | 18,444 | 160,625 | 490,414 | 2.8 |

Source: Population and Housing Census, 2000, Ghana Statistical Services.

account for 2.8%; in the Greater Accra Region this reaches 5.9%, while in the Northern Region it is a mere 1.1%.[47]

Detailed analysis reveals a substantial difference between girls and boys when it comes to school attendance, especially in the rural areas and in the Northern Region. For those who do attend school, there is a higher girls' dropout rate. There are also disturbing signs of declining access to tertiary education. Only about 10% of basic schools, mainly based in the south, produce nearly 70% of students admitted to Ghana's tertiary institutions.[48] The continuing brain drain out of the Northern Region and inability to retain trained manpower shows the sustainability problems.

The selective development pattern, which was initially started by the colonialists, still prevails against the north, but in favour of the south.

> The whole of the Northern Region has only one university, but various campuses. In the south, there are over 15 universities, both private and government. Pupils who are brilliant enough to further their education are deterred by accommodation and distance problems. (Executive, Student Representative Council 079)

Had the British education policies been applied evenly across the three colonies at the time, the underdevelopment, unemployment and recurring ethnic conflicts would have been minimised.

> Places like Bole, Yendi, Damongo, Gushiegu and Savelugu needed schools but the British spent in excess to build huge schools like Achimota College in Accra in the south. That amount could have built four moderate schools in these areas but they did not. Due to the considerable expenditure incurred in the building of Achimota College, not even an additional primary school was opened in the Northern Territories at the time Achimota College was being built. (Retired teacher 101)

A National Reserve Ranger at Bole National Park stressed:

> With such restrictions on education, it was another way of the British making sure that pupils upon completion of Standard III would not be fit for any job but still migrate to the south

to work on the plantations and the mines. (National Reserve Ranger 102)

## SADA: A SHOW OF CAPACITY AND WILLINGNESS OR FACE-SAVING?

The call to bridge the north-south gap has prompted the formation of the Savannah Accelerated Development Authority (SADA), which is an independent agency for organising a far-reaching development agenda for the Northern Savannah Ecological Zone in Ghana. The agency's main thrust is to promote sustainable development and the strategy will provide opportunities for poor peasants, especially women, to own economic assets, sustain their food crop production and protect the fragile eco-system of the northern savannah by managing the flood-prone riverbeds better. In August 2010, parliament passed the SADA bill into law after which it received presidential approval in September 2010. This was an initiative to bridge the socio-economic gap between the savannah regions of Northern Ghana and the rest of the country. The imbalance in the industrial distribution resulted in a massive exodus of people from the Northern Region to the south. To survive, the females become *kayayo* (porters) and the males do other odd jobs such as pushing carts. Posterity will judge SADA as a face-saving exercise or as an agency that reversed and revamped the destitution of the Northern Region of Ghana.

## CONCLUSION

It is apparent that, whether by design or oversight, the Northern Region of Ghana has been denied sufficient education. Education is a human right and offers a way to break the cycle of poverty. During the launching of the 2008 Global Action Week of the Ghana National Education Campaign Coalition, there was a call to make quality education a reality for all children, particularly in the Northern Region. Nevertheless, this was said about the current situation:

> The enrolment and retention of girls in schools in the Northern Region has not improved much. The gender parity index

decreased from 0.88% during the 2006/2007 academic year to 0.83% in 2007/2008. At the Basic Education Certificate Examination (BECE), the region recorded a 53.6% pass in 2004, which reduced to 46.1% in 2005 and appreciated marginally to 47.6% in 2006. In 2008, out of the 21,594 candidates who registered and participated in the BECE, 13,550 were boys and 8,044 were girls, respectively. The primary school enrolment is currently 377,328 as against the estimated population of 442,927 children between six and eleven years, with about 65,599 (14.8%) of children in that age group out of school.[49]

With about 80% of the inhabitants in the region declared poor, poverty, unemployment and other economic issues are pervasive. It is apparent that if youth are faced with the option of poverty, unemployment and destitution, they might be more inclined to join a rebellion where they might have better opportunities. In the case of the Northern Region, it is obvious that people in higher places, such as politicians, have been influencing the poor and destitute youth to take up arms. Although it has been said that education in general can be manipulated as both positive and negative forces of conflict[50] peace education in particular (which deals with the principles and goals of demilitarisation, conflict management, peacemaking, conflict resolution and non-violence) should be considered the best option for the situation in the Northern Region of Ghana.[51]

Education for peace is one of the eight pillars of UNESCO's Culture of Peace initiative, developed by Dr. David Adams during the 1990s. With education, comes hope. As described by Girouard, hope "can be luxury, vision, mirage or a singular threat by which one clings to survival." State-caused ethnic conflict diminishes hope but hope can be revived through education. In the case of the Northern Region of Ghana, there is a need to reverse and re-structure the education policies that have left a legacy of discrimination as a result of biased, prejudiced governance. Good governance and security, as a unitary concept, is the key to hope.

## REFLECTIONS

1. The epitaph to colonialism notes that the colonial government adopted the strategy of indirect rule with good intentions. However, the strategy altered the traditional chieftaincy system and land issues, thus affecting the indigenous settings they met. Although developing the Northern Region was not the government's priority, neglect of educational services in the area, coupled with endemic poverty and destitution, have set the scene for conflict. According to Roger Girouard, effective governance is more about an amalgamated whole – bringing on board all available resources for maximum and effective output. In this part of the world, where politics is based on "winner takes all," the best resource persons in opposition or the minority are hardly considered for a position. Unfortunately, the post-colonial governments have barely changed most of the governance and security apparatus the colonial government left behind.

2. In West Africa, where authoritarianism and poor governance are rife, some political commentaries paint democracy as a fraud or at least short of the so-called good governance advocated by the West. Democracy per se should be admirable but, in context, the terminology can be elusive and conflicting. A simple observation supports the notion that good governance requires a degree of economic prosperity.

   Developed countries like Canada vote on the premise of "peace, order and good government" to elect politicians into office. Elsewhere, depending on the nation, the willingness and capacity of politicians, the expectations of the people, the history and drive, and the definition of governance varies. In Ghana where a recent survey put the police service at the top of corruption ladder, the bureaucratic function of the state is questionable. Peace has historically been derived from security but would that require peace education of the citizenry? In a situation where selective development has been the agenda since the colonial era and indeed continues, conflict-prone areas will continue to suffer recurrences of conflict and the people will remain trapped in the vicious cycle of poverty. After all, it is argued that good governance requires a degree of economic prosperity. Governance and security as understood and practised in the West will require commitment, economic prosperity, capacity and willingness. The roadmap should be designed and owned by the indigenes who will be affected and their beneficiaries.

## REVIEW QUESTIONS

1. Most ethnic conflicts are sited in countries that were formally colonised. Do you support or refute the notion that colonialism is in part responsible for the numerous ethnic conflicts around the globe. State your reasons?

2. Would you consider that most the emerging conflicts such as oil-and-gas-related conflicts in countries that have just started drilling might have some links to the century-old ethnic conflicts?

3. Technology abounds! Sure. How can modern technology be used to curtail or bring about sustainable peace?

4. Most of the published literature on governance and security is dominated by foreign scholars who employ Western uni-linear paradigms encapsulated in neo-modernisation frameworks. What would you suggest as practical and effective approaches to governance and security in Africa as a whole and Ghana in particular?

REFERENCES

Abdul-Majeeb, Y. *Guns Inside Coffins.* <http://www.modernghana.com/Ghana-Home/NewsArchive/news_details.asp?id=VFZSSmVFNVVXWGs9&related=coffins&menu_id=1&sub_menu_id=313&menu_id2=0> (13 January 2007).

Addae-Mensah, I. *Education in Ghana: A Tool for Social Mobility or Social Stratification?* Accra, Ghana: Academy of Arts and Sciences, 2000.

Adedze, V. *Three Killed in Konkomba, Bimoba Conflict.* 2007. <http://www.ghanaculture.gov.gh/index1.php?linkid=65&archiveid=770&page=1&adate=18/09/2007> (23 August 2009).

Adjapawn Q. "Why Does Northern Ghana Stay Poor: Lack of Governmental Will or a Lack of Capacity." *The Australasia Review of African Studies* XXVII, no. 2 (2006): 31-48.

Adjapawn Q. and Jonathan Makuwira. "Sub-Sahara Africa and the Millennium Development Goals: Issues, Perspectives, Tensions and Contradictions." *Global Development Studies* 4 (2006): 229-247.

Adjapawn Q. *Ambiguous Peace: Unmasking the Hidden Truth about the Protracted Ethnic Conflicts in the Northern Region of Ghana.* Accra, Ghana: DELCAM Press, 2010.

Amidu (Honourable), Martin, A. B. K. *The History and Rationale for the National Architecture for Peace in Ghana and a National Peace Council Bill.* Paper delivered at the United Nations, New York, 17 December 2010.

Azam J-P. "The Redistributive State and Conflicts in Africa." *Journal of Peace Research* 38, no. 4 (July 2001): 429-444.

Bacho F. Z. I., E. K. Musah and A. Mahama. Report on the Assessment of Rehabilitation Needs of Victims in the Conflict Area of the Northern Region, *Inter-NGO Consortium*, Tamale, 1996.

Bellamy, C. *International Conference on War-Affected Children.* Speech Delivered on 13 September 2000 at Winnipeg. <http://www.unicef.org/media/media_11863.html> (23 August 2000).

Bening, R. B. "Colonial Development Policy in Northern Ghana, 1898-1950." *Bulletin of the Ghana Geographical Association* 17 (1975): 65-79.

Bening, B. R. *A History of Education in Northern Ghana: 1907-1976.* Accra, Ghana: Ghana Universities Press, 1990.

Brass, P. *Ethnic Groups and the State.* London, UK: Croom Helm, 1985.

Brass. P. *Riots and Pogroms.* London, UK: Macmillan, 1996.

Brass, P. *Theft of an Idol: Text and Context in the Representation of Collective Violence.* Princeton, NJ: Princeton University Press, 1997.

Buckland, P. *Reshaping the Future: Education and Post-Conflict Reconstruction.* Washington, DC: World Bank Publications, 2004.

Bush K. D. and D. Saltarelli. *The Two Faces of Education in Ethnic Conflict: Towards a Peacebuilding Education for Children.* Florence, Italy: United Nations Children's Fund, Innocenti Research Centre, 2000.

Canagarajah, S. and X. Ye. *Public Health and Education Spending in Ghana in 1992-98: Issues of Equity and Efficiency, Poverty Reduction and Economic Management (PREM).* Washington DC: World Bank Policy Research Working Paper no. 2579, April 2001. <http://papers.ssrn.com/sol3/papers.cfm?abstract_id=632648> (12 March 2006).

Collier P., and A. Hoeffler. "On the Incidence of Civil War in Africa," *Journal of Conflict Resolution* 46, no. 1 (2002): 13-28.

Collier, P. *Breaking the Conflict Trap, Civil War and Development Policy.* A World Bank Policy Research Book. Washington DC: The World Bank, 2003.

Daabu, M. A. *Agbogbloshie Deaths Rise to Three*. 2009. <http://www.moderng-hana.com/news/234834/1/agbogbloshie-deaths-rise-to-three.html> (26 August 2009).

DFID. *The Causes of Conflict in Africa*, Consultation Document by the Cabinet Sub-Committee on Conflict Prevention in Africa. London, UK: DFID, 2001.

Easterly, W. *Can Institutions Resolve Ethnic Conflict?* Policy Research Working Paper no. 2482, Washington DC: The World Bank Development Research Group, Macroeconomics and Growth, 2000.

Easterly W. and R. Levine. *Africa Growth Tragedy: Policies and Ethnic Divisions*. 1997. <http://www.mitpressjournals.org.ezproxy.une.edu.au/doi/abs/10.1162/003355300555466> (23 August 2011).

Ferguson, P. *Islamization in Dagbon: A Study of the Alfanema of Yendi.* Unpublished Ph.D. Thesis, University of Cambridge, UK, 1972.

Ferguson P., and I. Wilks. "Chiefs, Constitutions and the British in Northern Ghana." In *West African Chiefs,* edited by M. Crowder and O. Ikime. New York, NY: Ile Ife Publisher, 1970.

Fofana, L., *Education-Sierra Leone: Schools in Crisis as Thousands of Teachers go Unpaid*, Inter Press Service, IPS Freetown. <http://www.ipsnews.net/africa/nota.asp?idnews=48218> (26 August 2009).

Fuller, A. A. "Toward an Emancipatory Methodology for Peace Research," *A Journal of Peace Research: Peace and Change*. 5 March 2009. <http://www3.interscience.wiley.com/journal/122207391/issue> (23 August 2009).

Ghana Population and Housing Census, 2000.

Goodhand, J. *Violent Conflict, Poverty and Chronic Poverty*. Chronic Poverty Research Centre (CPRC) Working Paper no. 6, 2001.

Goody J. "A Note on the Penetration of Islam into the West of the Northern Territories of the Gold Coast." *Transactions of the Cold Coast and Togoland Historical Society* 1, no. II (1953): 45-46.

Goody, J. *The Ethnography of the Northern Territories of the Gold Coast, West of the White Volta*. London, UK: The Colonial Office, 1954.

Goody, J. "The Over-Kingdom of Gonja." In *West African Kingdoms in the Nineteenth Century,* edited by D. Forde and P. M. Kaberry. London, UK: Oxford University Press, 1967.

Herbert, S. "From Spy to Okay Guy: Trust and Validity in Fieldwork with the Police." *Geographical Review* 91, no.1-2 (2001): 304-310.

Hodgkin, T. "The Islamic Literacy Tradition in Ghana." In *Islam in Tropical Africa,* edited by I. M. Lewis. London, UK: Oxford University Press, 1966.

Ignatieff, M. *The Warrior's Honour: Ethnic War and the Modern Conscience*. New York, NY: Henry Holt and Company, 1995.

Kasfir, N. "Explaining Ethnic Political Participation." *World Politics* 31, no. 3 (1979): 365-388.

Kleinman, S. "Field-Workers' Feelings: What We Feel, Who We Are, How We Analyse." In *Experiencing Fieldwork: An Inside View of Qualitative Research*, edited by William Shaffir and Robert Stebbins. Newbury Park, London and New Delhi: Sage, 1991.

Mahama, I., *Ethnic Conflicts In Northern Ghana*. Cyber Systems, Tamale, 2003.

Mekenkamp M., van Tongeren, P., and van de Veen, H. *Searching For Peace in Africa: An Overview of Conflict Prevention and Management Activities*. Utrecht, the Netherlands: European Platform for Conflict Prevention and Transformation, 1999.

Minichiello, V. *In-Depth Interviewing: Principles, Techniques, Analysis* (2nd ed.). Melbourne, Australia: Longman, 1995.

O'Brien, D. "A Lost Generation? Youth Identity and State Decay in West Africa." In *Postcolonial Identities in West Africa*, edited by R. Werbner and T. Ranger. London, UK: Zed Books, 1996.

Population and Housing Census. Ghana Statistical Services, 2000.

Pul, H. A. S. *Exclusion, Association and Violence: Trends and Triggers of Ethnic Conflicts in Northern Ghana*. Unpublished Master's Degree Thesis presented to the McAnutly College and Graduate School of Arts, Duquesne, 2002.

Richards, P. "Rebellion in Liberia and Sierra Leone: A Crisis of Youth?" In *Conflict in Africa,* edited by O. Furley. London, UK: Tauris, 1995.

Seidu, S. A. *The Influence of Islam on the Dagbamba in the Twentieth Century*. Unpublished M. Phil Thesis, University of Ghana, Legon, 1989.

Soyinka-Airewele, P. "Subjectivities of Violence and the Dilemmas of Transitional Governance." *West Africa Review* no. 6 (2004).

Staniland, M. *The Lions of Dagbon: Political Change in Northern Ghana*. Cambridge, UK: Cambridge University Press, 1975.

Sundkler, B., and C. Steed. *A History of the Church in Africa*. Cambridge, UK: Cambridge University Press, 2000.

Talentino, A. "Rethinking Conflict Resolution: Matching Problems and Solutions." *Peace and Conflict Studies* 10, no. 1 (Spring 2003).

Thomas, R. G. "Forced Labour in British West Africa: The Case of Northern Territories of Gold Coast, 1906-1927." *The Journal of African History* 14, no. 1 (1973): 79-103.

Thomas, R. G. "Education in Northern Ghana 1906-1940: A Study in Colonial Paradox." *The International Journal of African Historical Studies* 7, no. 3 (1974): 427-467.

UNESCO EFA Monitoring Report, 2009.

Vail, L. *The Creation of Tribalism in Southern Africa.* Berkeley, CA: University of California Press, 1989.

Van der Linde, Ada, and Rachel Naylor. *Building Sustainable Peace: Conflict, Conciliation and Civil Society in Northern Ghana.* An Oxfam Working Paper, 2002.

Wheeler, H. C. *NEP Annual Report*, NAGA, ADM 56/1/33 (1912).

## ENDNOTES

1.    K. D. Bush and D. Saltarelli. *The Two Faces of Education in Ethnic Conflict: Towards a Peacebuilding Education for Children.* (Florence, Italy: United Nations Children's Fund, Innocenti Research Centre, 2000).

2.    K. D. Bush and D. Saltarelli. *The Two Faces of Education in Ethnic Conflict: Towards a Peacebuilding Education for Children.* (Florence, Italy: United Nations Children's Fund, Innocenti Research Centre, 2000).

3.    H. A. S. Pul. *Exclusion, Association and Violence: Trends and Triggers of Ethnic Conflicts in Northern Ghana.* Unpublished Master's Degree Thesis presented to the McAnutly College and Graduate School of Arts, Duquesne, 2002.

4.    Q. Adjapawn. *Ambiguous Peace: Unmasking the Hidden Truth about the Protracted Ethnic Conflicts in the Northern Region of Ghana.* (Accra: DELCAM Press, 2010).

5.    P. Richards. "Rebellion in Liberia and Sierra Leone: A Crisis of Youth?" In *Conflict in Africa,* ed. O. Furley. (London, UK: Tauris, 1995).

6.    D. O'Brien. "A Lost Generation? Youth Identity and State Decay in West Africa." In *Postcolonial Identities in West Africa*, ed. R. Werbner and T. Ranger. (London, UK: Zed Books, 1996).

7.    P. Buckland. *Reshaping the Future: Education and Post-Conflict Reconstruction.* (Washington DC: World Bank Publications, 2004).

8.    Buckland, P. *Reshaping the Future: Education and Post-Conflict Reconstruction.* Washington DC: World Bank Publications, 2004.

9.    W. Easterly. *Can Institutions Resolve Ethnic Conflict?* Policy Research Working Paper no. 2482. (Washington DC: The World Bank Development Research Group, Macroeconomics and Growth, 2000).

10.    C. Bellamy. *International Conference on War-affected Children.* Speech Delivered on 13 September 2000 at Winnipeg. <http://www.unicef.org/media/media_11863.html> (23 August 2000).

11.    See http://www.afrol.com/articles/33112

12.    Read about the crisis in schools in Sierra Leone by Lansana Fofana: *Education-Sierra Leone: Schools in Crisis as Thousands of Teachers go Unpaid,* at Inter Press Service, IPS Freetown, from: http://www.ipsnews.net/africa/nota.asp?idnews=48218

13    Q. Adjapawn and Jonathan Makuwira. "Sub-Sahara Africa and the Millennium
      Development Goals: Issues, Perspectives, Tensions and Contradictions." *Global
      Development Studies* 4 (2006), 229-247.

14    *Education 'Forgotten' in Post-Conflict Aid*: http://www.elearning-africa.com/newsportal/
      english/news199.php

15    Martin, A. B. K Amidu. *The History and Rationale for the National Architecture
      for Peace in Ghana and a National Peace Council Bill*. Paper delivered at the United
      Nations, New York, 17 December 2010.

16    M. Staniland. *The Lions of Dagbon: Political Change in Northern Ghana*. (Cambridge,
      UK: Cambridge University Press, 1975), 4.

17    M. Staniland. *The Lions of Dagbon: Political Change in Northern Ghana*. (Cambridge,
      UK: Cambridge University Press, 1975), 4.

18    V. Adedze. *Three Killed in Konkomba, Bimoba Conflict*. 2007. <http://www.ghanaculture.
      gov.gh/index1.php?linkid=65&archiveid=770&page=1&adate=18/09/2007> (23 August
      2009).

19    It is very hard to put a figure on the death toll since each side tried to hide their casual-
      ties to win a psychological victory over the other.

20    Ethnologically the Mossis are related to the Dagombas, but they do have their own
      language and religion, with most members being Muslim. They share common trad-
      itions with the Dagomba, Mamprusi and other northern Ghanaian groups. Even
      though they originated from Burkina Faso and have been in the Northern Region for
      hundreds of years, they are the most isolated and form a fairly cohesive group. Often,
      they migrate to live in the Ashanti and Brong-Ahafo regions where they worked on
      farms belonging to natives of these regions. http://www.cidcm.umd.edu/mar/assessment.
      asp?groupId=45203

21    According to the figures of the 2000 Government of Ghana Population and Housing
      Census.

22    Ghana Population and Housing Census 2000.

23    Source: Population figures from Government of Ghana, 2000 Population and Housing
      Census.

24    See Population and Housing Census, 2000, Ghana Statistical Services, Government of
      Ghana.

25    Read from Ghanaweb Friday, 28 August 2009 - Konkombas: We have nothing to do
      with clashes, from: http://www.ghanaweb.com/GhanaHomePage/NewsArchive/artikel.
      php?ID=167736

26    Out of 1,815,408 population of Northern Region, 1,022,331 are Muslims
      (56%), see Population and Housing Census, 2000, Ghana Statistical Services,
      Government of Ghana, Summary Report on Final Results, p. 26.

27   H. A. S.Pul. *Exclusion, Association and Violence: Trends and Triggers of Ethnic conflicts in Northern Ghana*. Unpublished Master's Degree Thesis presented to the McAnutly College and Graduate School of Arts, Duquesne (2002).

28   Mahama, I. *Ethnic Conflicts In Northern Ghana*, Cyber Systems, Tamale, 2003.

29   See Ada van der Linde and Rachel Naylor, 2002, Building Sustainable Peace: Conflict, Conciliation and Civil Society in Northern Ghana, An Oxfam Working Paper.

30   200,000 figure has been recorded by Ada van der Linde and Rachel Naylor (2002): 28, Pul (2002) and by Bacho, Musah and Mahama (1996), 1.

31   See Pul (2002), Ministry of Food and Agriculture - MoFA (1994) and Ada van der Linde and Rachel Naylor (2002).

32   R. G. Thomas. "Education in Northern Ghana, 1906-1940: A Study in Colonial Paradox", *The International Journal of African Historical Studies* 7, no. 3 (1974), 427-467.

33   See Roger, 1974.

34   Cited in B. R. Bening. *A History of Education in Northern Ghana: 1907-1976*. (Accra: Ghana Universities Press, 1990).

35   Cited in B. R. Bening (1975), 65-79.

36   Bening, B. R. (1975)

37   See NEP Annual Report, 1912 by Captain Wheeler, NAGA (now called PRAAD), ADM 56/1/33.

38   Ghana National Archives (now called PRAAD), File Number ADM/56/1/88, letter Number 30/M.P.2189/24 dated 6th January 1925, cited in R. B. Bening (1976), 25.

39   From sessional paper 17, 1918 –1919, CO 98/31.

40   M. Staniland. *The Lions of Dagbon: Political Change in Northern Ghana* (Cambridge, UK: Cambridge University Press, 1975).

41   He had been in Gold Coast since 1913 but serving mainly in the Colony, later, was transferred to the Northern Territories and in 1933 became Commonwealth Commissioner of Northern Territories (CCNT). He was charged with upholding and furtherance of Indirect Rule after previous successors like Walker-Leigh and Major F. W. F. Jackson. See M. Staniland, *The Lions of Dagbon: Political Change in Northern Ghana*. (Cambridge University Press, London, 1975), 100.

42   M. Staniland (1975), 100.

43   P. Collier. *Breaking the Conflict Trap, Civil War and Development Policy*. A World Bank Policy Research Book (Washington DC: The World Bank, 2003).

44   Ghana Education Service Internal Budget Book, 2002.

45 Equivalent of Middle School

46 Q. Adjapawn. "Why Does Northern Ghana Stay Poor: Lack of Governmental Will or a Lack of Capacity." *The Australasia Review of African Studies* 27, no. 2 (2006), 31-48.

47 Figures are derived from Ghana Population and Housing Census, 2000, Ghana Statistical Services.

48 I. Addae-Mensah. *Education in Ghana: A Tool for Social Mobility or Social Stratification?* (Accra: Ghana Academy of Arts and Sciences, 2000).

49 John Kwesi Hobenu, Northern Regional Director of Education, made the observation at the Northern Regional Education Sector Annual Review meeting in Tamale. The three-day meeting served as a participatory forum for stakeholders to assess the overall educational status in terms of achievements, challenges and strategize for improved educational performance. See Northern Region records low enrolment, retention of girls in schools at: <http://www.ghanaweb.com/GhanaHomePage/NewsArchive/artikel.php?ID=143530>

50 K. D. Bush and D. Saltarelli. *The Two Faces of Education in Ethnic Conflict: Towards a Peacebuilding Education for Children.* (Florence, Italy: United Nations Children's Fund, Innocenti Research Centre, 2000).

51 Q. Adjapawn. *Elusive peace: Interrogating the inter-ethnic conflicts in the Northern Region of Ghana (Konkombas and Dagombas), Unpublished PhD* thesis, University of New England, Armidale, Australia, 2008.

# A PERSPECTIVE ON
# GOVERNANCE FOR HUMAN SECURITY

## ROSEMARY CAIRNS, MA

## INTRODUCTION

Ever since I discovered the concept of "human security" and the associated activity of "peace-building," I have been far more interested in what works than in what doesn't work. It thrills me that more people are using this approach. When I began studying human security, most of the stories I read seemed more a litany of failure than an exemplar of achievement.

Perhaps this is because I am an academic only by accident, much more comfortable in the field than in the classroom. My work has been in community development, election administration and observation, and women's organizations; thus, my focus has been on the practical. When I first began doing this work, I looked to facilitation, mediation and adult education to learn the skills and terminology I needed.

As I sat in a hotel room in Belgrade on September 11th, 2001, about to help a team of people decide which 60 communities we should work with in Western Serbia and which 60 projects they could start on, the world changed. Suddenly, the terminology of scholars and policy makers began to have a real and practical effect on the kind of work I was doing in the field although I didn't realize it at the time. It was not just about governance or security but about governance and security as a singular concept.

Equally important was the notion of governance and security from the perspective of the people involved in the process of governance and security. In his opening chapter, Girouard suggests, "Like the concept of family, governance as a theme is familiar to all cultures and regions" but governance by whose standards? Governance alone is a complex concept; governance without a security apparatus is a recipe for a failed state. Girouard rightly asserts, "The discussion of what comprises human security in this age of rights, sustainability and transparency is, in itself, a complex theme."

An academic discourse arose on the notion of "failed states" and the danger they posed to the world outside their borders. The answers that began to be batted around in academic circles seemed to focus on how "They" could become more like "Us," the developed states that were successful. New approaches were prescribed by those outside the state or in the state but did not include the people.

Perhaps I am a natural contrarian but I began to wonder about the notion of success. Slowly, I realized that this definition of success came from our historical experience in Western Europe and North America. Like the aboriginal tribes whose land our ancestors occupied when they came to North America, we tended to think of ourselves as "the people," and our experience as the only experience.

## DEFINING SUCCESS

I began to wonder about the people who lived in those failed states. Did they think of themselves as residents of a failed state? What did success look like from their perspective? (And as a corollary – did we, as residents of developed states, feel we were able to influence our governments in the ways we expected residents of the so-called failed states to do?) Were there examples of how they had built peace, security and good governance after conflict? Could we learn from how they had done it?

That led me to research in Somaliland, the northwestern part of Somalia, and the District of Brčko, in Northern Bosnia. Both Somalia and Bosnia had experienced dreadful wars in which thousands had been killed or had disappeared. Cities had been as devastated as any in Europe during the Second World War, when the international community had intervened with resources, technology and a conviction that "we" could fix things.

Somalia, in fact, was the original failed state that led academics to coin the term and to wonder about whether a new notion of international trusteeship was needed when states could not look after their own affairs or care for their own people. Subsequently, this discussion led to the notion of the "responsibility to protect" (R2P), which was the idea that the international community had an obligation to intervene when states were not protecting their own people.

But what did we do when we got there? That did not seem nearly as clear and, despite their prescriptive role, most academics did not have the field experience on which they could draw to provide answers. The people working in the field were far too busy to write about what they were doing and learning.

## ASKING THOSE WHO DID IT

It seemed to me that the most practical way to find out what worked was to ask people who had managed to build peace for themselves. So that was what I did, in the summer and fall of 2009, with support from Canada's Social Sciences and Humanities Research Council and Royal Roads University. I asked people in Somaliland and the Brčko District how they built peace and how they rebuilt governance and security as a singular construct to maintain peace. Subsequently, through my work as an external evaluator for the UK-based charity, Peace Direct, I have been able to ask that question of people in other countries that have experienced conflict. How do they build peace and what does it look like from their point of view? And so I have come to a few conclusions.

The first conclusion is that no one from outside a country can rebuild peace or good governance for people in that country. We can serve as peacekeepers, of course, and keep the warring parties apart. But when it comes to rebuilding peace in a sustainable way or for development activities, the job must be done by the people of that country for themselves.

"But, but, but…" I can hear you saying. "But they haven't done it and they can't do it without our help." On that point, I agree. They need our help but it must be offered in a spirit of partnership and sharing, not with the attitude that we know better than they do. I like the way the Community Development Resource Association in Cape Town explains the difference. They call it "horizontal" learning when neighbours learn from neighbours and "vertical" learning when experts teach students. So what can we share as neighbours?

## TWO NARRATIVES

Living in Western Serbia between 2001 and 2003 and travelling extensively around the countryside showed me two things. The first was the physical impact of the international bombing campaign in 1999 that had been intended to stop Serbian president Slobodan Milošević from carrying out ethnic cleansing in the Serbian province of Kosovo. For two years, I lived just up the street from the hole in the ground that had once been the Užice post office building, now called in jest the "Užice swimming pool" because it was filled with stagnant water. Near Čačak, we drove across a bridge that had been so destabilized by the bombing of a nearby factory that cars had to crawl across at 10 mph. Every time I went to Belgrade, I could see the downtown buildings that had been hit by cruise missiles. I heard stories from the people I got to know about what it had been like to know that bombers were flying overhead and might drop their bombs on you. Even when I went walking in the countryside around Užice, I could see abandoned factories by the side of the path; it was apparent that the infrastructure of the economy in rural areas had just collapsed.

The second thing I realized was that it was actually the people of Serbia who had been responsible for removing Milošević from office. It was the result of many years of patient, brave, persistent and creative protest. This homegrown campaign would ultimately contribute to the Orange revolution in Ukraine, the Rose revolution in Georgia, and so many other similar changes that Serbian activists were banned from travelling to several Eastern European countries. Yet the people I talked to in Canada often thought it was the bombing campaign and not the homegrown protest that had been responsible for forcing Milošević out and for installing a democratic government under Zoran Djindjic.

As I learned more about Serbia, I realized that the bombing campaign was a devastating blow to an infrastructure that was already fragile and failing, the legacy of years of underinvestment and authoritarian and politicized state management. In Western Serbia, just across the Drina from Bosnia, the impact was even greater. Most municipalities, having opposed Milošević's policies for some years, had been starved of infrastructure resources by his government precisely because of that opposition, even as they were coping with the conflict in Bosnia.

Their roads were rutted; many of their public buildings had been turned into centres to house refugees; their water and power systems were near collapse. Trains were old and often in poor shape. Buses were privately run. The former Yugoslav health care system, once a model of preventive health care, had virtually collapsed, so that people had to go to private clinics and pharmacies for care, if they could afford it. The public system had virtually no medicine and no equipment, even if it still had dedicated doctors who continued to care for people. But the people in small communities were still doing their best to help out their displaced neighbours by building homes for them and caring for those who were vulnerable.

Our mandate was to encourage small community-run projects to rebuild infrastructure, social services, and economic development. It had been modelled on a US pilot project in Lebanon and it was intended to support democratization by encouraging local community ownership of projects. It did much good but I slowly came to realize that in many ways, we were sewing patches on to a garment that was disintegrating and already so heavily patched that it was virtually made up of patches.

People needed to make a new garment rather than put more patches on the old one. But it needed to be a garment of their own design, made in a way that suited them and their society, not a North American garment. It was hard for them to muster the knowledge, resources and energy to design a new garment when everything around them seemed to be collapsing. There were so many needs and so few resources, and a few people seemed to own the bulk of the country's resources.

## STARTING ANEW

It could be a very discouraging picture and for many Serbs, it is. Many felt they had risked their own lives to bring change and they felt cheated. The changes they wanted to see had not come to pass. Many believed that they had not finished the job they started on October 5th, 2000 and when Djindjic was assassinated in 2003, they talked about what they should have done on October 6th, which was to deal with organized crime.

In talking with many people, I realized that they did not know how to make the changes they wanted. Their system and their education had not prepared them for that. They had learned a particular way to deal with the system and that system had changed much faster than their ways of creating change. The average person could not keep up.

So in some ways, the total collapse that happened in Somalia and Bosnia made it easier to start over again, although I do not mean to diminish the terrible suffering that happened in both places. This time, people wanted to do things differently. A number of scholars have noted that total state collapse offers a chance to do things differently rather than rebuilding what didn't work in the first place. Sadly, their insights have been little heeded in the international attempts to rebuild Somalia as a state.

In the northwestern corner of the former state of Somalia, people were quite clear. They wanted a decentralized system, one that did not allow power to be aggregated in the hands of just a few. They wanted, as much as possible, to translate the checks and balances in their traditional clan-based system into a system of government.

Even their liberation struggle was democratic, and deliberately so. The men who risked their lives to fight Said-Barre's government were determined that their liberation movement was not going to become a one-man band, and so they created a system of collective leadership and accountability that functioned, even in the hardest times of their struggle. The fighters elected their delegates to sit on the central committee that led the struggle and those leaders were accountable to them. Unlike any other liberation movement in Africa, the SNM turned over power peacefully to a civilian-led government after a two-year transition.

## A UNIQUE BLEND OF TRADITION AND MODERNITY

Part of the SNM's process was to incorporate the elder-led guurti system of traditional leadership and conflict resolution in its struggle. The communities themselves supported the fighters; the elders, or guurti, resolved any disputes that arose between them. So it was natural for the SNM to turn to the guurti when they faced the challenge of creating a community-led peace process once Said-Barre's forces had been driven out of Somaliland.

This process eventually led to the creation of a blend of traditional and modern governance with an elected president and vice-president and parliament balanced by a House of Guurti or elders' senate, which held many of the responsibilities for protecting peace and culture. Even the positions of president and vice-president, despite being an artifact of another political culture, reflected local cultures, as the incumbents were deliberately chosen from two clans as a way of balancing power.

The process of peace and rebuilding governance followed the traditional Somali ways of doing things. As they had done for centuries, the men of the community met under the tree and discussed issues, while everyone else who wanted to could watch. The public observation meant various conclusions and arguments were tested in the community, ensuring that what was said at larger meetings really reflected a community consensus. It was truly a bottom-up process. Even though it was led by the men, as is Somali custom, the women were watching carefully and did not hesitate to bar the door, pushing men back into the room if they felt the men were leaving before a consensus had been reached. A similar process happens in aboriginal politics in Northern Canada but because the women's input, for so many years, happened in private, observers sometimes felt the women were not participating. Visiting homes and seeing the active discussion would soon change that viewpoint!

It is hard to overstate how big an accomplishment this was, in a region and a city, Hargeisa, which had been razed in the late 1980s by Said-Barre's forces. The only building left undamaged was the colonial-era Governor's Palace, from which Said-Barre's son-in-law, General Morgan, led the bombardment of Hargeisa from the air and from the ground. He apparently made a videotape of this process and I am told you can hear him telling his men that a house or building here or there had been missed. Hargeisa was reduced to rubble; everything was destroyed. Thousands of people had been killed or injured. It was a society that had been devastated in all but spirit.

## CHOOSING RECONCILIATION

In this setting, people chose reconciliation over revenge, as they knew there would be no future in an endless round of settling old scores. The main clans in Somaliland had been on different sides, with some supporting the SNM and some the government. Even the rebuilding process was disrupted several times by fighting between militias affiliated with different clans, made up primarily of young men who had learned that guns brought them power and the ability to accumulate resources. It was clear to all that continuing to fight, at any level, would just devastate their cities all over again.

This choice of reconciliation, even in the face of the dreadful things that people had suffered, is one that is made by other people in equally difficult situations. One of the key lessons we learned, when peace-builders from 12 countries came together in Peace Direct's first Peace Exchange in Nairobi in February 2010, was the importance of an inclusive, reconciliatory process. People with real experience in dealing with militias talked of the importance of befriending the leaders; others talked of the importance of involving tribal leadership in peace-building and rebuilding; all were clear on the importance of not leaving anyone out.

When I asked them how they knew their communities were becoming more peaceful, they came up with a long list of indicators in the areas of establishing personal security and in enhancing social relationships. These were far more important, in terms of building peace after conflict, than creating institutions or building an economy. They were, clearly, the basic building blocks on which everything else rested.

The Community Development Resource Association in Cape Town, which has done a great deal of work with community-based organizations in Southern Africa, says that there are three kinds of social change:

emergent, transformative, and projectable. I see it as being like an iceberg, with emergent and transformative change being the largest chunk of the iceberg under the waterline while projectable change is the small part of the berg that you can see above the water.

## EMERGENT AND TRANSFORMATIVE CHANGE

Emergent change is what happens when conflict has just finished. People are traumatized and don't trust each other or even themselves. Relationships have been damaged or destroyed and people no longer know how to work together on anything. Learning how to trust and rebuild relationships is a delicate process that takes time. People have to learn how to live together again. CDRA calls the role of outsiders in this process "accompaniment." This means being there with people as they make their path by walking it and providing whatever help they need as they ask for it, not pushing them faster than they can go. This is a process they must do for themselves. In *Towards Restoring Life in Cambodian Villages*, Meas Nee puts it beautifully:

> The village is like a basket that has been broken and the pieces scattered. The pieces are still there but not everyone can see them. What has been broken can be rewoven slowly and gradually but only by those who will take the time to stay close to the village people and build trust with them.

> I know for certain that this can be achieved, even though it must be done slowly and carefully. Eventually the village people become the weavers and they carry the task forward. The basket will be better than before, but first it must be something like the same.

War makes people feel hopeless and paralyses the mind so one cannot think about the future, Meas Nee says. It seems impossible to think of new ideas or start projects. His advice to people who want to work in this situation is to go very slowly indeed:

> In the beginning simply try to make the people feel at home

with you. Join in with them. Don't be stressed with projects. Slowly ... sit under the shadow of the trees with the families and listen to them. Sit in the cool of the night. Don't feel ashamed that you waste time. You are gradually learning to understand people's strengths, people's problems, people's feelings. Spend time to talk with them. It is a matter of rebuilding spirit, life and relationships. Where community development has worked well the thing that has happened is not the projects. It is the people of the community moving together to support each other.

## BUILDING RELATIONSHIPS

The point Meas Nee makes about the time involved in this process is reflected in Henri Bura Ladyi's work with militias in Eastern Congo. He explains that you cannot just call up a militia leader and say, "Let's talk about getting your men back from the bush." What this means in practical terms is that he must first build a relationship with the leader. He does this by finding out who the leader's trusted associates are. He uses all his own sources to try and make a link with those people. He explains who he is and what he does. It takes a lot of airtime on a mobile phone and a lot of patience, as it takes place on their schedule, not his.

Gradually, if those associates begin to trust him, he may be able to speak to that militia leader. One day, perhaps, the leader will come in a taxi to visit Henri and will expect Henri to pay the taxi fare, as the militia leader has no money. It will be necessary to have a meal or coffee together to get to know one another. The leader may invite Henri to come and visit him in the bush. Only then, once there is a relationship, will it be possible for Henri to talk about bringing those militia soldiers back from the bush.

If they get to that point, the leader will probably want to have a feast in the bush and Henri may need to contribute to that. Then, finally, there may come the time when the militia comes back from the bush and only at that point can Henri begin to work with them and the community in what we might call a project. That project rests on the whole body of work he has done in emergent and transformative change, in creating trust and building relationships. This change is largely unseen by the outside world.

In Brčko, local people rebuilt their relationships but the international community facilitated that process by creating safe places where people could meet. Initially, carefully selected people (the moderately inclined) were invited to attend meetings and a military escort from the IFOR base came to bring the guests to the base for the meeting. Eventually, as trust built, the meetings were held in the Brčko supervisor's office. Gradually, people were able to work together in their own District Assembly, which now is a model for Bosnia as a whole.

Carefully nurtured and supported, this process eventually created a situation where the moderate community grew and the extremists became a small group. This was made possible, in large part, because the supervisor modelled an attitude of listening respectfully and of building relationships that made a huge impact on the people he worked with, although he himself did not realize it at the time. It just seemed to him to be the normal courtesy one extends to others, learned in small town US Midwest.

## HUMANIZING THE EX-MILITIAS

In Somaliland, the relationship building happened in the hundreds of small community meetings that fed into other larger meetings. Trust was nurtured through disarmament and reintegration camps, created by the government at the urging of the elders and funded by local businesses, which humanized young ex-militia men by reintroducing them to the values and beliefs of their own society and of Islam. This was necessary, the elders realized, because Said-Barre had deliberately militarized the entire society in order to control it.

The humanizing was a process that CDRA would call "transformative" change, which can be a difficult but an energetic stage. People learn behaviours from the society around them. In the case of a society that has experienced great conflict, they need to unlearn behaviours as well. The Somaliland process recognized the importance of giving these young men something to do and some way to make a living, so they did not use their guns to make a living.

In Southern Sudan, where the introduction of guns turned the role of young men upside down from protectors of their community to, often, predators on their community, some people saw the same need. They knew that in the turmoil of war, guns gave young men power, prestige and a way to make a living. Peace often leaves them with no power, no prestige and no way to earn money. Disarming them without creating an alternative for them to make a living was not sustainable.

In Somaliland, the two processes were combined. Militias were demobilized into camps where they learned or relearned their cultural values and how to be humans once again, and then they were enrolled in the peacetime army and police. This army was much larger than Somaliland actually needed but it appears to have been the easiest way to keep the young men active and employed so they did not disrupt the rebuilding process. Local businessmen funded the disarmament camps because the international community did not help.

There are some brilliant examples of how to combine these two things in Southern Sudan, unfortunately not nearly as well known as they should be. In one case, SWIDAP worked with the leader of one of the white army militias (so called because the young men in dry-season cattle camps, where they care for the community's cattle, cover themselves with ashes to protect them from flies and insects) to help him buy two trucks and create a trucking company. Before that, the young men were raiding cattle, often destroying homes, killing people and raping women. The two trucks, used in transporting goods for others along roads they controlled, gave them a practical alternative that earned them money.

Other community-based organizations were created to give the young men training in making blocks for building and in drilling boreholes for water. These activities brilliantly addressed the problem of insecurity by keeping the young men busy in activities that supported the community-rebuilding process so that they were not tempted to continue raiding and destroying. Thus, they no longer needed their guns and were willing to hand them over to their tribal chiefs. Of course, security increased dramatically in the communities in which the young men had formerly created chaos.

## THE IMPORTANCE OF LOCAL KNOWLEDGE

These activities work because they come from local knowledge of the causes of conflict, from local contacts and relationships, and from a locally driven peace process. Internationally driven DDR processes, in contrast, often deal with only a part of this process and often at a much higher cost. Such processes tend to deal with the technical aspects, ignoring the trust and relationship-building steps and the need to set both problem and solution in a local context. Often our international intervention is "stovepiped," because there are so many specialized agencies with specific mandates that we can't see the connections between problems and activities that are so clear to local people.

In Southern Sudan, the first attempt to disarm militias ended in disaster because traditional community leadership had been disrupted by the way guns had turned the social order upside down. Another reason was because the young men's pleas for alternatives to cattle raiding and compensation for their guns were not heeded. A second attempt, in which the community peace-building capacity had first been reinforced by a series of trust-building meetings and in which alternative activities were found for the young men, ended peacefully and largely satisfactorily.

In Sri Lanka, a popular approach to the long-running conflict was to hold multi-religious dialogues involving religious leaders. It took local people who were Buddhist to see that a lack of preparatory work with Buddhist clergy meant that these dialogues often turned into monologues driven by those clergy, while other religious leaders sat in silence. They were able to speak with the Buddhist clergy and learned that their educational process meant they had been isolated from modern learning and often felt insecure in these dialogues when faced with religious leaders who *did* know about modern learning and the outside world. The Buddhist clergy wanted to learn but no one had approached them to talk about how they could do that.

Based on their knowledge and social position, the local people were able to work with the Buddhist clergy to show them that there was no conflict between Buddhist beliefs and conflict transformation theory. In fact, they concluded, Buddhist belief had actually discovered the key aspects of this theory long before the term "conflict transformation" had ever been coined. This powerful work in building trust and relationships with the Buddhist clergy led to transformative change, dramatic changes in the relationships among all clergies and created true multi-religious dialogues that are helping to build peace in communities that have been divided by bitter conflict for decades. Because Buddhist Sinhalese are the majority of the population and thus will decide on political solutions that can create sustainable peace, such dialogues have an impact far beyond religious ceremonies.

In Brčko, the collaborative working relationship between international staff and local people, and the approach taken by the supervisor, meant that institution-building took into account things that were vitally important locally. They included changing street names, using symbols, and respecting each other's religious and community celebrations. Thus institution building contributed to, and grew out of, relationship building and was highly sensitive to symbolic issues that made sense locally.

## A SHARED AGENDA

In the case of Brčko, it helped greatly that the arbitration panel, which had studied Brčko for several years, issued a clear "to do" list when it made its final decision. Everyone knew the contents of the list; it formed a shared agenda and timetable. It meant the supervisor could go ahead with his work, citing the list, and it gave a clear framework for local people to move ahead as well.

Local politicians used the supervisor's powers to legislate change that was needed but for various reasons they were unable to agree to among themselves. They knew that pushing further to reach an agreement would disturb or destroy the relationships needed to work on other areas. They would ask the supervisor to issue an order requiring that a specific thing be done so they could all move on to other things.

One clear example was the supervisory order legislating multi-ethnic education in Brčko schools. In other areas of Bosnia, students still go to schools based on their ethnic background. In Brčko, however, students all go to mixed schools. It was very controversial even though many people wanted it done. The politicians asked the supervisor to order it because they could not reach agreement among themselves.

This decision has contributed greatly to improving the climate in Brčko. Students meet students from other cultures at school, rather than just hearing about other cultures or religions from their parents or religious leaders. They can reach their own conclusions about each other. This was an important lesson, learned some years earlier in Northern Ireland, about the power of building relationships among young people to counteract the pictures of the "other" drawn by their parents.

One US project designed to foster improved understanding between Israeli and Palestinian youth takes them to the Balkans to see what happens in war and how people are rebuilding even after divisive conflict. It is, by their reports, both a sobering and a joyful experience, as young Israelis and Palestinians realize that in many ways, their country's conflict is not an exceptional one.

## THE ROLE OF BUSINESS

In Somaliland, business people played a key role in the rebuilding process. They were invited to take part in the community discussions, not just to contribute money for rebuilding. Their work created both infrastructure and jobs, of course, but they were seen as an essential part of the peace-building process as well, and saw themselves as having a role and taking an opportunity.

The first hotel in Hargeisa, for example, was built by a man who was working in the Saudi oilfields. He had heard a BBC broadcast that said people from Djibouti were flying in to the city only for day-long meetings because there was nowhere to stay. He bought a piece of land, provided money to start building, arranged for the building supplies to be sent in because there was nowhere to buy them locally and hired people to start building. When the money ran out, he sent money regularly from his salary to finish the building. It was not just a business but a community service and is still regarded in that light by people in Hargeisa.

The first new university created in Somaliland was funded by people working in the oil fields who knew the importance of education for youth, and who contributed from their salaries to allow the community to create it. These days, there are a number of universities and it is a powerful experience to see hundreds of students graduate, ready to serve their communities in teaching, law, medicine and business.

A second major hotel in Hargeisa was built by an expatriate businessman in the poorer, south side of the city, to the surprise of many, and has contributed greatly to building peace among clans. So, too, did the hospital built by Edna Adan Ismail, who was once married to Somaliland's first prime minister and served as Somaliland's foreign minister. She built her hospital on the land on which, during Said-Barre's time, many Somalilanders had been executed, and which had subsequently been piled high with garbage by local people. Local women made bricks; she sold her jewellery to buy the toilets and washbasins. Somalis from the diaspora helped by sending money.

In Brčko, people who had been isolated from each other by the war were able to meet in the Arizona market that sprang up on the edge of the city, as everyone needed to buy and sell goods. The connections were rebuilt through the market at a time when the district was divided between two entities and there was so much distrust that they could not visit one another freely. The market contributed greatly to building peace in the district.

Provision of regulated services such as telecommunications had been used by Said-Barre to handicap communication and community services in Somaliland. The mobile phone revolution, taken up avidly by local businessmen after 1991, meant that everyone could have access to telecommunications, not just those in the few areas where telephone poles had been installed. In Somaliland, too, one far-seeing man created a remittance company with such worldwide scope that you can pay in money in Canada and have it arrive in Hargeisa electronically minutes later or send money from Hargeisa to London and have the transfer completed by the time you have finished signing the paperwork.

## SEEING FROM INSIDE THE COMMUNITY

This link works so well because people see how things are linked together. They see that if they do this, they can affect that. People who work in international development often don't see these connections because the design of much international peace-building and development tends to be a more technical process involving beneficiaries, indicators and spending money. So much time has to be spent in making the process work that there is no time to get to know the community well enough to see how things fit together.

As North America has become a more sophisticated society and moved away from its roots in family and community, we have lost sight of the fact that most of Eastern Europe and Africa sees family and community in quite a different way. Just as with aboriginal people in Northern Canada, people in Africa and Eastern Europe begin to get to know others by finding out where they are from and who they are connected to. Family and place defines who you are as a person; it gives you your history. The place where your ancestors are buried is sacred ground.

So, for example, when the man who served as Brčko District's first speaker, who came from another part of Bosnia, chose to bury his son in Brčko after his tragic death in a car accident, he was saying something important to the people of Brčko. He was committing himself to the community's destiny, just as he was when he made sure he attended the community and village celebrations held by different groups, not just the ones held by his own people.

In his brilliant book, *Africa: The Politics of Suffering and Smiling*, the Africanist scholar Patrick Chabal makes the same point. Africans are connected to their village, their tribe, their age group and their land in ways that are profoundly different from current North American culture. This connection to community puts a premium on generosity because it is in sharing with one's own people that one becomes human, Chabal suggests. Colonial politics in Africa often defined people purely in terms of ethnicity, missing the importance of the places of birth and burial as a marker of community, he says. Without understanding this deep connection between one's land, ancestors, and belief system, outsiders cannot possibly see the connections and linkages that local people do.

## REBUILDING GOVERNANCE AND SECURITY

Without the work in emergent and transformative change done by local peace-builders in communities around the world, rebuilding or changing governance can become a divisive process. When there is distrust, people hold on to the institutions that seem to represent their interests, even if those institutions do not work well. Changing the institutions requires trust and understanding.

The people of Somaliland decided to take back their independence after some of the liberation groups in the south broke an agreement that all of the groups would gather after the war and decide on a future federal structure for Somalia. People were acutely aware that the future of an independent government would depend on people outside so they made their choice from systems that had been introduced from outside, that outsiders would understand: a presidential system, a prime ministerial system or a rotating presidency. From their viewpoint, they were concerned about the need for strong leadership, knowing the challenges that lay ahead, and so they reached out to the most experienced of their political leadership, balancing that with a man who had considerable experience in the SNM struggle.

In hindsight, it seems that one of the problems they faced was that there were so few systems to choose from. Somalia had had a prime ministerial system and it collapsed because the clans fought so hard for resources, as they had always done in the past. Somalia had an autocratic presidential system and it turned into a militarized state that went against all the values of pastoral democracy. Yugoslavia had had a rotating presidency and it collapsed as the leaders fought for power. We don't seem to have a truly decentralized system that gives power to people while still having a government that serves their needs.

Even in the United States, which sees itself as the pre-eminent democracy, one can see the debate about the nature of government continuing today. So it is not an easy question to resolve. In many ways, the most successful examples of how to do it come from the developing world rather than the developed world.

Developing a decentralized government system, although a key concern for people in Somaliland, seemed to be something that they could leave for a later time once they had rebuilt. They used their own clan- or beel-based system to choose the members of parliament, the president and vice-president for more than a decade and this appears to have worked fairly well.

## THE NEED FOR INFRASTRUCTURE

Somaliland moved away from that system to a multi-party system in large part because they wanted recognition from the outside world and the resources it would bring to rebuild the infrastructure. They did their best to make it a balanced system, choosing to limit the number of parties to three to avoid the clan-based proliferation of parties that had doomed Somalia. They had the parties chosen based on the outcome of the first local elections, held in 2002.

They have encountered a number of problems recently, not all of their own making. After their first highly successful and self-organized 2003 election, for example, international donors decided to support a sophisticated voter registration system, one that I don't think is used anywhere in the world. One can debate, of course, whether it would have been more productive for donors to contribute that money towards building roads, water sources, or sustainable development. They don't do this because the world does not recognize Somaliland's independence. The point is that the registration exercise produced a flawed list, despite the huge donor investment, which in turn complicated Somaliland's internal politics.

Behind the scenes of the subsequent crisis, elders continued to use the traditional Somali systems of dispute resolution and community reconciliation to bring the parties together. As an outside observer, I cannot help but think that all this energy and resources would have been much better invested in exploring the challenging question of how to bring together traditional and modern systems of governance in a way that respects both.

This process is slowly happening in Somaliland and I hold out hope that, just as they led the way in Africa in rebuilding peace and governance after terrible conflict in a community-driven inclusive process, they can find ways to solve this dilemma. The dilemma is causing havoc as the outside world intervenes in traditional societies like Afghanistan and Iraq and tries to modernize them without understanding what it is doing.

In Brčko, international expertise in municipal administration and law reform meant that local people were able to choose from the best examples in the world, taken from Eastern Europe, North America and Western Europe. The experts shared their knowledge so people could make the best choices for new systems. Sadly, elsewhere in Bosnia, internationals did not choose to learn from these innovations. Systems were reshaped in an integrated way and with full local participation so that people could see the linkages between laws, policies and systems. As a consequence, Brčko has systems for public review of the budget and regularly produces a balanced budget, which cannot be found anywhere else in BiH.

Similarly, even as Somalilanders were gathering themselves to rebuild, the UN agency Habitat worked with them to rebuild municipal structures and systems so that they could begin, once again, to raise funds locally to provide services and administer systems from scratch. Said a local mayor, "What we needed was expertise, not money." Too often in Somalia's past, money has been a force that divides rather than unites, he noted, especially when it came from outside and was seen as a resource to be fought over rather than shared widely.

## CONCLUDING THOUGHTS

### OUR ROLE

Assuming you have followed me thus far, you may be wondering "Well, what is our role, then, if I accept all this?" I would like to offer a few thoughts from what I have learned and from what others have shared with me. Their own ideas, of course, may be different. My first thoughts are in terms of those who go elsewhere to build peace or development as some of you reading this book may be considering. I concur with Girouard when he says, "Governance and security, as a unitary concept, is about those who have the will and the power and the vision delivering on the hope of those around us who are in need." Based on this idea, I offer my observations.

Firstly, I believe that anyone who wants to take part in peace-building or international development should spend time trying to create social change in his or her home community. Learning the challenges involved in doing this, in a setting where you understand the culture and the language, gives you the requisite sense of humility when you try and do this somewhere else, in someone else's culture and language.

The second thing I have learned is the importance of being a human being. This means, in practical terms, not losing sight of our common shared humanity as we try to manage a development project or a peace-building process. I have seen people doing their best but losing their way in trying to meet the technical demands of designing and delivering programs and "burning money" fast enough to satisfy donors. To use a common human development cliché, they become a "human doing" rather than a "human being."

I gave this advice to a friend who went to Africa as a member of a UN peacekeeping force. I was a bit hesitant, thinking it might sound like the impractical, lovey-dovey stuff that many soldiers think is how peace-builders approach their task. But it summed up all I had learned, in the most succinct way possible: "Be human."

He carried out the peacekeeping tasks assigned to him. In his spare time, he got a bicycle and rode out in the countryside on his bike rather than in a fancy four-wheel drive and so of course he got to know people in a different way. He took time to talk with the children who always clustered, in the morning, around the compound fence. If someone had sent pencils or toys from Canada, he shared them. He collected plastic bottles from inside the compound and gave them to the children, who sold them in the village market to merchants who needed containers for oil. If he had nothing else, he smiled and asked how they were.

He came back to Canada, as so many of us do, struggling with how to absorb what he had learned there and often feeling frustrated with the international systems he saw close up. He wondered if his work had meant anything. And then, in a moment of grace, a friend told me a story written by someone who had subsequently gone to the same place. It was a powerful demonstration of how much his decision to be human had had on the community and on other peacekeepers. He learned, in a way few of us are privileged to do, that he had made a huge difference not just by being a peacekeeper but by being a human being who shared with other human beings.

## TAKE YOUR TIME

My second thoughts relate to what we should do when we get there. Firstly, take the time to get to know the community. If the community is just recovering from conflict, take heed of Meas Nee's sage advice. Go slowly. Get to know people. Let them set the pace. Help them when they ask for help. Do not tell them how to do things. Model peace-building in your own life.

Be aware of the importance of the emergent and transformative stages of creating social change. Know that people must rebuild their relationships and trust in one another. Know you can help by listening, asking questions, identifying the moderately inclined and giving them a safe place to meet, and by helping them identify small and concrete projects that will help improve their community as they slowly learn how to work together again.

Do not reinforce extremism by responding only to extremist views. A long time ago, when my younger daughter was in elementary school, the principal decided that the way to encourage good behaviour was to reward good behaviour. So they began, during assemblies, to honour students who had done good things and, of course, bad behaviour began to decrease because it was not reinforced. This is not just a lesson for elementary school students.

Model respect, model the ability to listen, and keep your temper. Don't jump to conclusions about how the situation arose or which are the good guys or the bad guys. Everyone needs to be involved in rebuilding and your attitude can help model an inclusive approach. Learn people's names. Learn the names of their children. Ask how they are doing, each time you see them. Truly listen when they tell you. Don't feel that your work is more important than sitting over tea with people. This *is* your work, just as it is their work. If it is not done, nothing much else that is sustainable will happen.

## A SHARED AGENDA

Know and respect the power you hold and know, too, that you may be able to see things more clearly than the people in the community whose experiences have been so scarred by the war. Tell stories from your own experience when the time seems right but avoid telling people what they should do, even if it might seem so obvious to you. If you have lived a full life, they will respect the stories you tell, just as you respect the stories they tell of how they survived. Just like people everywhere, they will learn far more from the stories you tell than from any lectures you might be tempted to deliver.

Live in the community where you are working. Even if you do not live in the same conditions as local people, they will regard you differently than if you live somewhere else and just drive in for a few days now and then. Among other things, it gives people time to invite you for tea on the weekends. As Greg Mortenson discovered when he was building schools in Afghanistan, the power of sharing three cups of tea cannot be over-estimated.

Help to set a shared agenda for the community that everyone can work towards, but do it only after you have listened long and often, and tested your conclusions as widely as you can in that setting. Such a framework helps people organize their work and achieve productive results in a situation that otherwise seems chaotic and uncertain. It also helps ensure that donor resources are focused on meeting real community needs.

Make sure you work from the agenda. Take responsibility for carrying out the tasks assigned to you. Model effective working styles as you do so, knowing that people are watching what you do and that this is much more powerful than what you say.

Don't overload people with tasks. Accompany them as they learn to rebuild their communities, their governance and their economy. See where small amounts of resources will help and give those without strings attached, once you have agreed what they will be used for. Celebrate achievement, praise people for their accomplishments, and honour their efforts. Enjoy the people you work with.

Model effective working styles and inclusive team leadership. Be willing to make decisions and take responsibility for them, if you are in charge. Don't blame others if things don't work – just learn and share the lessons you have learned from seeing what didn't work. Model effective ways of evaluating and learning from experience.

Find good people to work with and trust their capacity. Given that they have emerged from war, they don't have a resumé for you to assess. In Brčko, the youngest person ever hired to work with the supervisor ended up managing a portfolio worth millions of dollars and did it brilliantly, at age 22. She has managed economic development, helped write laws, helped carry out one of the most successful rebuilding projects in modern history, and now she can't find appropriate work because outsiders don't believe a 30-something has actually done all that.

HONOUR CAPACITY

If the community has rebuilt trust and relationships and the capacity to work together again, honour and celebrate that capacity. Ask people what they need help with. What do they need to do next? If they need help in learning how to work together at more sophisticated levels of change, find resources that help them learn how to do this in a participatory and effective way.

If you have the authority, organize the donors' work, based on what you know about the community's situation and needs. Bring them together and focus their work on the key priorities identified by the community. Do your best to make sure they do this work in a way that will benefit the community most. Connect them with the people they need to know in the community.

A community may need roads to be built or rebuilt. This can be done very quickly with heavy equipment but where there are few jobs and a fragile economy, it may be more important to do this in the most labour-intensive way possible. Keep the bigger picture in mind.

Encourage and support local economic development, even if it emerges first in unregulated ways. The Arizona market in Brčko, for example, built peace as effectively as any official effort by creating a place where people could meet together again after the war and talk to each other, as well as buying and selling goods. The supervisor found a way to shape that emergent market into a more official structure, avoiding the temptation to shut it down precisely because it was unregulated.

Advocate for the community. Outsiders have contacts and the ability to shape how the outside world sees a community that they know only from headlines. Tell the community's story. Celebrate its achievements. Honour its people and give them credit for what they have accomplished. This does not diminish you or your accomplishments.

Finally, make sure their accomplishments show up in the academic journals and the academic discourse, which influences the policies made by the international community. Share the story of how they built peace, how they rebuilt trust and relationships, and how they rebuilt their society and governance.

Share their challenges as well as their accomplishments. These challenges are important learning opportunities for all societies. Treat them with the respect they deserve. If the challenges were easily resolved, the people would already have resolved them. If we all work together horizontally, as neighbours, to understand these challenges and see if we can find ways to resolve them, we will all be better served.

"There are respected and good-hearted informal leaders in every village I have seen," Meas Nee says of Cambodia but it is true of everywhere. Nee states:

> They have hopes for peace and for restoring the life of their village. If they recognise the same qualities in the community development workers who befriend the village, they will enlist

our help. They will begin to show us that there is a way forward despite the problems. If we win their respect we will be invited into their company.

## REVIEW QUESTIONS

1.  This chapter argues that rebuilding trust and relationships is a key aspect of recreating governance after conflict and that the international community can aid that process by helping to create safe places for moderately inclined people to meet. How might you use these insights in developing an intervention plan for a post-conflict situation?

2.  "Projects," in post-conflict settings, rest on a great deal of work in trust-building and repairing of relationships that has been done by local people. Sometimes international projects effectively disrupt these achievements, unintentionally, because this work is largely invisible. How might you factor this kind of "emergent" and "transformative" change into your post-conflict intervention planning?

3.  One of the challenges for communities and regions emerging from conflict is to design a new system of governance that is both effective and inclusive. What lessons can you draw from the experiences of Somaliland and Brčko in terms of how they re-designed their systems of governance?

4.  Schooling is often a casualty of conflict, leaving a generation of young men who only know how to earn a living through using a gun. Young men with guns who don't see a future for themselves can destabilize any society. What lessons do you draw from the experiences of Somaliland and Southern Sudan in finding constructive ways to engage such young men? How do these experiences contrast with the conventional international approach to demobilization, disarmament and reintegration?

# GROWING UP KIKUYU

## MARY-ANNE NEAL, MEd AND MOSES MUTHOKI, BEd

"The condition of Africa is bound to that of the
world. We all share one planet and are one humanity."
~ Wangari Maathai, *The Challenge for Africa*

This chapter describes the life of a Kikuyu boy growing up in Kenya
over the past thirty years during an era when the governance structure
changed rapidly. Lacking the primary elements that form the foundation of governance and security (peace, order and good government),
the resulting chaos and violence in Kenya are obvious even to a child.
"The theme is familiar to all cultures and regions," as Girouard suggests
in his introductory chapter. "It is the study of the imperfect works and
the processes upon which the very survival of a society, of a nation, of
mankind, may well and truly depend."

Raised in the town of Molo, which was a hotbed of racial tension,
Moses Muthoki quickly learned that ethnic rivalries run deep. His personal story takes place in the context of this political climate.

## CONTEXT

We believe that Africa, the cradle of humanity and the source of the
world's earliest technologies, was originally populated by many small
communities of people with distinct languages, cultures and traditions.
During the late 1800s, the continent on which human life began was
carved into countries by European colonists. Through written records,
widespread racism, violence and power struggles have become apparent

in communities throughout Africa. Kenya, a country of 41 million people, located on the east coast of Africa squarely over the equator, has not emerged unscathed.

Kenya is an amalgam of people, wildlife and geographically special ecosystems. Forty-two tribes live in Kenya. Most tribes are Christian, with pockets of Muslims and people who follow indigenous beliefs. Kenya shares borders with five countries: Sudan, Ethiopia, Somalia, Tanzania, and Uganda. Many inhabitants of these countries are ethnically related to Kenya's peoples. Uganda and Tanzania share with Kenya a history of British colonial rule.[1]

## INTRODUCTION

The topography of the country varies greatly and includes mountains, lakes, forests and valleys, plains, deserts, bush and coast. The major cities (Nairobi, Mombasa, Nakuru, Kisumu and Eldoret) are separated by large expanses of fields cultivated for tea, coffee and other cash crops.

Kenya's standard of living, once relatively high compared to much of sub-Saharan Africa, considered East and Central Africa's biggest economy, growing at 7% in 2007, has declined in recent years due to political turmoil. About 75% of the workforce is engaged in agriculture, mainly as subsistence farmers living close to the land, raising goats and chickens and living in small villages. Much of the natural vegetation was stripped in the 1940s, when an invasion of settlers led to forest destruction and timber poaching in order to grow cash crops and raise domesticated animals. Efforts to reclaim land and grow trees have been outpaced by logging and charcoal making. Despite legislation passed in 2002 declaring all forests free from human activity, the level of deforestation in the country has increased.

The concept of governance as a "complex and often murky construct of people, organizations and rules" (Girouard) is the basis of the process through which the people of Kenya are restructuring their society. According to the introductory chapter, peace, order and good government are the prime deliverables of any elected body. This chapter explores these underpinnings of governance in the Kenyan context.

**Peace** includes everything from security to the well-being of the people and their quality of life including health, employment, education and access to resources. Peace is the goal of many Kenyan people, regardless of tribal affiliation.

**Order** is required for stability. It is linked to culture, tradition, statutes, codes, balance and judgment. In Kenya, tribal suspicions have been fuelled by recent governments, which have emphasized their differences and inequities, especially with regard to land. Over the past fifty years, these perceived inequities have contributed to a lack of order.

**Good government** means ethical leadership, including laws, policies, functionaries, statecraft and communication. An effective bureaucracy is the foundation of a smoothly functioning society. All aspects of good government have been lacking in Kenya.

## A BRIEF HISTORY

Kenya's political history is of the greatest relevance to the topic of governance. Over the ages Bantu have migrated to Kenya. Arab traders settled on the coast, establishing Mombasa, Malindi and Zanzibar, and trading with the Arab world and India for ivory and slaves. The Persian Kilwa Sultanate ruled the Swahili Coast from the 10th century. In 1414 relations were established with the Ming Emperor in China. By the 15th century, the Portuguese were exploring the coast. Before colonisation, approximately 90% of the peoples on the Kenya coast were enslaved. The colonial history of Kenya began with the establishment of a German protectorate over the Sultanate's possessions in 1885, followed by the Imperial British East Africa Company in 1888. Germany handed its coastal holdings to Britain in 1890.

The people of the country we call Kenya now experienced a hundred years of British colonial rule, beginning with the exploration and mapping of their land in the 1850s. On July 1st, 1895, the British government established direct rule of "British East Africa" through the East African

Protectorate, primarily as a way to open up the fertile highlands to white settlers. By the 1930s, 30,000 Europeans lived in Kenya, rising to 80,000 by the 1950s. The British established the education system.

In 1946, the Kenya African National Union (KANU) arose as an African nationalist organization that demanded access to white-owned land. The KANU was dominated by the Kikuyu, the African group most affected by the European presence and the most politically active of the groups. In 1947, Jomo Kenyatta, former president of the moderate Kikuyu Central Association, became president of the more aggressive KANU in order to demand a greater political voice for Africans.

From 1952 to 1959, a terrorist movement, known as the Mau Mau Uprising, shocked the world. Directed principally against the colonial government and European settlers, it was the largest and most success-ful such movement in Africa. Although intended to unite all the tribes of Kenya against the Europeans, the protest was mounted almost exclu-sively by the Kikuyu and it resulted in a bitter internal struggle among the Kikuyu themselves. Assassinations and killings on all sides reflected the ferocity of the movement and the ruthlessness with which the British suppressed it. Thousands of Kenyans died.

After suppressing the Mau Mau Uprising, the British provided for the election of six African members to the Legislative Council under a weighted franchise based on the level of education. The new colonial constitution of 1958 increased African representation but African na-tionalists began to demand a democratic franchise on the principle of "one man, one vote."

To support its military campaign of counter-insurgency, the colonial government embarked on agrarian reforms that stripped white settlers of many of their former privileges; for example, Kenyans were for the first time allowed to grow coffee, the major cash crop.

On December 12th, 1964, Kenya achieved self-government, with Jo-mo Kenyatta as its first prime minister. Kenyatta denied he was a leader of the Mau Mau but he had been convicted at trial and sent to prison in 1953, gaining his freedom in 1961. Kenya became a republic in 1964. During the Kenyatta regime (1963–1978), land that had been settled by Europeans was reclaimed and distributed among the Kenyan people. In many instances, land that had been the traditional territory of one tribal group was allocated to a different tribe. This practice caused widespread animosity among the tribes.

During the Moi regime (1978–2002), Daniel arap Moi concentrated power in the hands of the Kalenjin tribe. His governance was characterized by authoritarianism, ethnic favouritism, assassination, state repression, social inequality, graft, and brutality. The economy was in ruins and poverty increased exponentially. Chaos reigned. Worst of all, larceny and corruption drained the country of hope.

"Majimboism," a philosophy that emerged in the 1950s, is a Kiswahili word meaning federalism or regionalism. It was intended to protect local rights, especially regarding land ownership. Today, "majimboism" is code for certain areas of the country to be reserved for specific ethnic groups, fuelling the kind of ethnic cleansing that has swept the country from time to time. Majimboism has always had a strong following in the Rift Valley, the epicentre of violence, where many locals have long believed their land was stolen by outsiders.

The December 2007 referendum pitted today's majimboists, who campaigned for regionalism, against President Mwai Kibaki, who stood for the status quo of a highly centralized government that has delivered considerable economic growth but has repeatedly displayed the problems of too much power concentrated in too few hands, resulting in corruption, aloofness, favouritism and its flip side, marginalization. For example, in the town of Londiani in the Rift Valley, Kikuyu traders settled decades ago. In February 2008, hundreds of Kalenjin raiders poured down from the nearby hills and burned a Kikuyu school. Kikuyus quickly took revenge, organizing into gangs armed with iron bars and table legs and hunted down Luos and Kalenjins in Kikuyu-dominated areas such as Nakuru, where Moses Muthoki now resides.

## MOSES' STORY

The Rift Valley stretches for six thousand miles, from northern Syria to central Mozambique. This vast, arid trench, spanning the length of Africa and bounded on each side by forests and ridges, is visible from the moon. Where it runs through Kenya, the Rift Valley is a province known for its abundant crops and sheep. The mountain ranges framing the valley were still heavily forested when I was born there in 1977. All that has changed over the past thirty years.

Since the 1950s, the landscape of the Rift Valley has been severely modified by cultivation. Much of the natural grassland has been ploughed and reseeded to provide better grazing for sheep, leaving less natural habitat for the native bush pigs, waterbuck, buffalo, elephant, pelicans and grebes.

My home town, Molo, is a community of 20,000 people located in the Mau Forest, part of the Mau Escarpment that forms the western wall of the central Rift Valley. One of the coldest places in Kenya, the area around Molo is perfect for growing pyrethrum, a member of the chrysanthemum family which is a principal component in some insecticides and lice remedies.

My father, Geoffrey Muthoki Mbuthia, was born in 1947, just before the Mau Mau Uprising. When the colonial government issued a Declaration of Emergency, he was forced to move with his family back to Kiambu until the Declaration was lifted in 1960. At the age of twelve, my father moved to Molo, where his mother was a labourer on Taylor's farm. They lived as squatters, crowded in a village of mud huts.

My father was an exceptional student, moving through the forms (grades) quickly and earning money to raise the fees required. Eventually, he acquired a teaching certificate, purchased a parcel of land, and constructed the first stone house ever erected by a local.

In the spirit of Kenyanization under a program to take over land from the colonials, local people could come together, pool money in clearly defined proportions, purchase farms from white settlers, subdivide the land equitably and draw ballots for their allotment.

My boyhood home was located on the farm where my father had lived as a squatter's son. Our three-bedroom bungalow sat on two and a half acres bordering the 2300-acre Molo West indigenous forest. We had neither electricity nor running water, so we depended on a river that ran through the forest before my father sank a borehole in our shamba (plot of land).

From the age of seven, I spent most of my afternoons, weekends and school holidays grazing my father's two cows around the village paths, fields and empty farms. This was the most exciting of the family tasks shared among the five children and I was fortunate to be responsible for it because I was the last-born. While I was herding the cattle, my elder siblings toiled in our three parcels of land, cultivating potatoes, maize, peas and pyrethrum. Every other Saturday, we all had to pick pyrethrum flowers. I hated it because each of us was allocated a particular number of rows to pick. Since I was young and slow, I was often alone, weary, hungry, sun-baked and in tears, the others having completed their share of the work.

Whenever possible, I played and hunted hares with friends in the lush wheat and barley farms owned by the Agricultural Development Corporation. We loved to run and jump, bare-bottomed, into the cold highland waters of the same river where we fetched water for our homes downstream.

Circumcision, practised in different ways at around age 13, is a badge of honour in all Kenyan communities because that is when a boy becomes a man. One of my friends, Gathiru, became a hero at age nine after he plunged into the waters for a dip only to emerge bloody and shaking with a piece of wire jutting from his penis. Since Gathiru had been unexpectedly circumcised in this way, he had thus become an adult and was removed from our group.

Because both my parents were working teachers, my grandmother raised me before I began school. I gave her a difficult time as I ventured to discover the world. And I constantly bothered my older brothers as they did their school assignments. Due to my naughtiness and my naturally curious nature, I began school at the age of four – two years earlier than usual.

School held its fair share of terror, as we were often beaten by our teachers. When I was six years old, I was the youngest and smallest in the class, anxious and eager to learn. I distinctly recall the incident that caused that feeling to change.

I was called to the front of the class by the cane-wielding math teacher, Mr. Wilson. Mr. Wilson wanted me to say "30" in the Kikuyu language. I was unable to translate arithmetic terminology to my language, so I tried my best to change my long heavy Kikuyu accent by shyly saying *"thaaat."* Despite my best efforts, I could not manage the correct words – *mirongo itatu* – so Mr. Wilson's stick came down on my bottom. For each unsuccessful attempt, Mr. Wilson brought the stick down hard on me until I could not go on. Despite my cries, Mr. Wilson continued beating me.

From that day on, I hated school. However, unlike other pupils who simply stopped attending school, the fear of my father held me hostage at school and I remained at Mr. Wilson's mercy.

The Rift Valley province is a multi-ethnic region although the Kalenjin tribe calls it their ancestral home. I grew up and undertook my schooling among Kikuyu, Kisii, Luhya, Luo and Kalenjin in true friendship. We played together in the village and all suffered the same abuse from the teachers at school. Langat, a Kalenjin and the prefect in my class five, was a very close friend and on several occasions he rescued me from the claws of a teacher with a straight-faced lie, in spite of my obvious misbehaviour. But I was not always lucky and I rarely went home without a beating.

Nevertheless, I survived eight years of primary school and frequent caning to enter Molo Secondary School in 1990. From there, I went on to Kapsabet Boys High School, located in the northern part of the province and home to the Nandi, a Kalenjin sub-tribe known for excellence in athletics.

Of the 168 students in our class, only four of us were Kikuyus. In Kapsabet, I experienced tribal stereotyping for the first time. Kikuyus were openly taunted and called *chorindet,* which means thief. To other tribes, especially the Kalenjin, we were not trustworthy. We were obsessed with money. We spoke differently from the Kalenjin. These differences had all been acceptable, however, when we were boys going through school together.

During the two years prior to the 1992 general elections, public clamour for multi-party politics had been causing intense pressure on the Kenya African National Union (KANU) single-party government. Daniel arap Moi, the president, was determined to maintain the status quo but with the political temperature rising unbearably from disgruntled politicians, the civil society and the international donor community, Section 2A of the constitution was repealed and ushered the country into a multi-party democratic system.

I distinctly recall a photograph in a March 1992 edition of the *Daily Nation* newspaper of a Kikuyu man with an arrow lodged in his head. That disturbing picture remains etched in my mind.

Reports of skirmishes in Molo terrified me. Thoughts about the violence distracted me from my studies and my grades dropped dramatically. Everyone in the province was tense, with non-Kalenjin tribes fearing for their safety. At school, we experienced a new fear – fear of the unknown.

During that time, I had little access to accurate news, so I failed to understand how tribal violence was connected to land issues. The slow postal service was the only available channel of communication so I wrote home seeking news of my family. My brother's reply arrived two months after he sent it and I learned that they were even more worried about me.

When school closed for the April holiday in 1992, I had to travel from Kapsabet to Molo, a distance of over one hundred kilometres, through a region inhabited by the Kalenjins. The comparatively peaceful environment at school stood in stark contrast to the mayhem and killings in the villages we passed. There we saw vehicles with smashed windshields, houses on fire and hundreds of people huddled outside churches, schools, police stations and trading centres.

Organized groups of Kalenjin warriors armed with bows and arrows attacked Kikuyus, killing them and burning their houses. Striking at three o'clock in the morning, they looted, killed and burned houses, leaving death and destruction in their wake.

"Thank God for bringing you home safely," my mother cried, hugging me tightly. I also cried, clinging to her.

Protests sparked around the country as tribes demanded that the government restore peace. Media reports from the state-owned news agency could not be trusted so the population relied on the British Broadcasting Corporation (BBC) radio service and other international stations.

A Parliamentary Committee report, commissioned by the government in response to public pressure, unexpectedly verified that the attacks, far from being spontaneous, had been orchestrated by individuals close to the president. The report confirmed that the government had transported the warriors, who had been trained and paid for their acts of destruction.

After the violence abated, thousands had no choice but to trickle back to their farms in the killing fields. Many others swore never to return and sought to establish livelihoods away from the Rift Valley province.

Small urban areas hosting clash victims reeled under the strain of the sudden population expansion. The population of Molo more than tripled and our small town was overwhelmed by thousands of displaced people trooping in on foot, in lorries, on bicycles and donkeys. Prior to the clashes, sawmilling in Molo had caused alarm over the possibility of deforestation. After the unrest, jobless clash victims used the remaining fragments of forests to make charcoal. Within two years, the entire Molo West forest had been clear-cut.

I completed my secondary education amid changing ethnic and social circumstances. The psycho-social consequences of the tensions cannot be quantified. Though I said nothing, I viewed my Kalenjin classmates and teachers with suspicion because I never knew who might have participated in the violence. Too many Kenyans were left homeless, landless, destitute, orphaned, injured and abused.

My first posting as a teacher in 2005 was in Kuresoi, an area whose name was synonymous with violence. In 2006, teachers deserted their station to escape the mayhem and for three weeks all schools remained closed. To this day, Kenya continues to suffer from ethnic suspicions as evident in the atrocities in 2007. Emotions are so deep that a disagreement among students from different communities can spark violence. Tribal differences are still vented by killing people and torching houses.

## GOVERNANCE

Good governance is a process that takes time to learn and develop. For the past four decades as a republic, Kenya's culture of ethnic favouritism, nepotism, impunity, assassination and corruption has caused great suffering. Even basic social amenities such as paved roads, hospitals, schools, electricity and running water are lacking in many parts of the country. Government leaders deploy militia to intimidate their rivals. Bureaucrats use their power and authority over public resources to grab wealth for personal gain. Bribery and corruption are rampant. The peace, order and good government that form the foundation of governance are sadly lacking.

The values of traditional African society stand in direct opposition to the exploitation and oppression that now exist. African tribal cultures value sacrifice, patriotism, diligence, moral obligations, and community over self. Prior to independence, Elspeth Huxley, a Kenyan writer, said, "It is not possible to have a western-style democracy in a country divided deeply on racial, linguistic, cultural and religious lines." True to her prediction, traditional African values have been swept away by western influence and the centralization of power. The resulting loss of identity perpetuated the despotic neo-colonial rule.

The very antithesis of governance, that is, power and control run amok, has created inequity, disregard for the rule of law, self-aggrandizement over service, resistance to change, violation of rights, and politics over governance.

Lacking a precedent for progressive governance, Kenya is wedged in a retrogressive quagmire. Weak governance and institutional structures create feuding and acrimony in the quest for power. Though they might grumble about their lot in life, the populace knows nothing other than this.

What is the answer to this situation? We look to thoughtful citizens of the world for answers.


## REVIEW QUESTIONS

1.  How can Woodruff's seven non-negotiable elements required of the democratic state (see Girouard's essay) be achieved in Kenya?

2.  Which elements of governance should Kenya focus on in order to create harmony in its populace?

## REFERENCES

Maathai, Wangari. *The Challenge for Africa*. New York, NY: Pantheon (Random House), 2009.

## ENDNOTES

1    Ethnic groups: Kikuyu 22%, Luhya 14%, Luo 13%, Kalenjin 12%, Kamba 11%, Kisii 6%, Meru 6%, other African 15%, non-African (Asian European, and Arab) 1%.

# SECTION II

---

# DIMENSIONS OF SECURITY

---

# GENDER, STATE AND SECURITY: EXAMINING THE ISSUE OF VULNERABILITY FROM A GENDER PERSPECTIVE

LAURA BALBUENA GONZÁLEZ, PhD (Cand.)

## INTRODUCTION

In discussing security, we must include vulnerability. In the absence of good governance and security as a single concept, predators prey upon the vulnerable with impunity. In his opening chapter, Girouard proposes that the disenfranchised and vulnerable should be the focus of our humanitarian efforts if good governance and security are to be achieved. Even the most hardened business executives acknowledge that the absence of good quality of life (freedom from persecution of the disenfranchised and vulnerable) erodes stability and economic growth in the long term.

What are the attributes and circumstances that make a person vulnerable? How can nation-states not only protect these individuals from predators but empower them to become productive citizens of a nation-state? Are nation-states taking into account these aspects when creating policies on human rights? This chapter will discuss vulnerability from a gender perspective. As Hudson et al. assert, "Societal-based differences in gender status beliefs, reflected in practices, customs, and law have important political consequences, including consequences for nation-state security policy, and conflict and cooperation within and between nation-states."[1]

A gender lens shows us that security differs for men and women and it should therefore be treated differently by the nation-state. Our emphasis will be on security in relation to individuals rather than to states. In this sense, it would be easier for us to see the inequality that men and women face in terms of security. The chapter will first define the concept of gender and what it means as an analytical tool.

We use the term "gender" in a simple way because we are examining only women and their situation as the subject of our analysis. It is useful to limit the discussion by referring to men only in relation to women. The second section will examine the vulnerability of women on a daily basis, which requires the nation-state to look at their needs as different from that of men. The third and final part of the chapter discusses the role of the nation-state in ensuring women's security, not only in war but on a daily basis.

## EXAMINING GOVERNANCE AND SECURITY WITH A GENDER LENS

The connotations of "gender" include social expectations, roles, rights and the responsibilities for being born a certain sex. It requires acting in a certain way, having certain goals in life, being able to perform in the public sphere, being recognized by the nation-state as equal, *inter alia*. Being born a man or a woman in traditional societies makes a great difference in terms of being vulnerable during times of crisis or even peace. When discussing gender it is necessary to take into account its intersection with other discriminatory elements such as race, class, education, religion, age, ethnicity and rural/urban origin. All these elements affect access to political influence or power, decision-making and resources in a governance and security context.

A gender lens looks at how security affects men and women in a different way. It takes into account the fact that gender relations are hierarchical, constructed in institutions such as family, school, the legal system, the market and the media, among other situations that tend to place women in subordinate positions. We should not see gender relations as merely static and constantly violent; instead, they are dynamic and imply not only inter-gender cooperation or aggression between men and women but also between people of the same gender.

Why do we need to discuss gender when talking about security and governance for security? It is not enough to analyse important issues such as democracy, poverty, national identity or development when attempting to establish security. These problems are important for the security of nation-states in both the national and international arena. However, when examined alone, without a systems context, we lose sight of other integral aspects of freedom and quality of life that put a citizen at risk. If we agree that when discussing security we are talking about vulnerability, then we are looking at the vulnerability of a nation, a population or an individual.

As previously stated, when using a gender perspective in the context of human security, we have to turn from the nation-state to the individual where we can find the socio-biological reasons for the oppression of women and of men who do not comply with the general standards of masculinity. These inequalities are reinforced in the private sphere and rarely seen by the nation-state. For these reasons, the Beijing Platform requests that a gender lens should be included in all structures, programs, institutions and policies that nation-states create.[2]

## WHY ARE WOMEN MORE VULNERABLE?

The more traditional and patriarchal a society, the more likely their women are to be vulnerable. A traditional society sees women as inferior to men, with their place being in the household rather than the public sphere. Women are seen as the property of their husband or family, who have rights over their body and their life. This is the case of women who are stoned to death because they were unfaithful to their husband and, therefore, perceived to have dishonoured their family. At best, they are disfigured and cannot accept the courtship of other men or at worst, they are killed. They are raped because they are virgins and their rapists have contracted sexually transmitted diseases including AIDS and look to be "cured" by raping a virgin. They are sexually mutilated when they are little so they will never have sexual pleasure and their husbands can be assured that they will not cheat on them. Nation-states that adopt an "only-child" policy view girls as useless. Their parents prefer to have a son rather than a daughter, and seek abortions once they know the foetus is a girl.[3] In these nation-states, women are vulnerable for many reasons:

1. *Political:* Traditional culture places females in a position inferior to men. In some cultures, their testimony in court has half the value of that of a man. Women do not have full citizenship.

2. *Sexual:* Their bodies make them more vulnerable because the fear of sexual violence and the consequences of it (pregnancy) are particular to women.

3. *Economic:* Women cannot inherit or acquire property and, in some societies, are considered part of their husband's property and, for that matter, are part of the inheritance their brothers-in-law will receive if their husband dies. Women are the majority of informal workers and have no benefits or insurance. Even in some developed countries, women do not earn the same as men for the same work, and encounter a glass ceiling that prevents them reaching the top positions.

4. *Educational:* Women still make up the majority of the illiterate population in the world.

This inequity was addressed in the Beijing Platform, which states:

43. The advancement of women and the achievement of equality between women and men are a matter of human rights and a condition for social justice, and should not be seen in isolation as a women's issue. They are the only way to build a sustainable, just and developed society. Empowerment of women and equality between women and men are prerequisites for achieving political, social, economic, cultural and environmental security among all peoples.

46. To this end, governments, the international community and civil society, including non-governmental organizations and the private sector, are called upon to take strategic action in the following critical areas of concern:

• The persistent and increasing burden of poverty on women;

- Inequalities and inadequacies in and unequal access to education and training;
- Inequalities and inadequacies in and unequal access to health care and related services;
- Violence against women;
- The effect of armed or other kinds of conflict on women, including those living under foreign occupation;
- Inequality in economic structures and policies, in all forms of productive activities and in access to resources;
- Inequality between men and women in the sharing of power and decision-making at all levels;
- Insufficient mechanisms at all levels to promote the advancement of women;
- Lack of respect for and inadequate promotion and protection of the human rights of women;
- Stereotyping of women and inequality in women's access to and participation in all communication systems, especially in the media;
- Gender inequalities in the management of natural resources and in the safeguarding of the environment; and
- Persistent discrimination against and violation of the rights of the girl child.

## NEW INITIATIVES FOR GENDER EQUALITY

In recognizing that women are vulnerable to sexual violence and following the *Beijing Platform for Action,* nation-states have created places where women and girls can report sexual violence in a safe and confidential atmosphere. The UN *Model Strategies and Practical Measures on the Elimination of Violence against Women in the Field of Crime Prevention and Criminal Justice* urges nation-states to:

- Ensure that the applicable provisions of laws, codes and procedures related to violence against women are consistently enforced in such a way that all criminal acts of violence against women are recognized and responded to accordingly by the criminal justice system;

- Develop investigative techniques that do not degrade women subjected to violence and that minimize intrusion into their lives, while maintaining standards for the collection of the best evidence; and

- Ensure that police procedures ... take into account the need for the safety of the victim and others related through the family, socially or otherwise, and that those procedures also prevent further acts of violence.[4]

These safe places have been created on many continents and take different shapes. Family Support Units inside police stations allow women to report domestic violence. Examples of nation-states that have begun Family Support Units include Liberia, Sierra Leone and Afghanistan. Police stations have been established solely to report domestic violence and are another haven for women and men who are victims and want to report such crimes. The stations are staffed with policewomen who specialize in this type of violence and are located in countries of the so-called global south as well as Peru, Brazil, Argentina, Bolivia, Nicaragua, Uruguay, India, East Timor, Kosovo, Philippines, Sierra Leone, and Uganda.[5] Opening these centres does not ensure that the view of domestic violence will change in the particular society because the legal system in most countries is still "gender blind" and does not acknowledge the vulnerability of victims of domestic violence.

The Geneva Centre for the Democratic Control of Armed Forces tabled a report in 2007 that examined sexual violence perpetrated during armed conflicts. Key recommendations referred to gender violence in a society that was not engaged in inter- or intra-armed conflict.[6]

- **Coordination and cooperation** between security sectors' institutions and other entities of the government and of society are crucial in providing essential services to victims of gender violence and to those at risk. This entails a campaign of awareness about gender-based violence to educate civil society about this problem.

- Government security sectors' institutions should adopt a

gender-sensitive approach** at all stages of response to victims of gender violence. This involves **gender training** for all security sectors' personnel. As we have seen previously, it is important to have institutions such as special units in police stations that are dedicated to domestic violence. If these units are not staffed with trained personnel, the victims do not feel comfortable reporting their attacks. This initiative would involve changing legislation and the procedures used to certify the attacks because most victims come from a vulnerable position in society. This makes it difficult for them to have all the elements to prove their allegations.

- **The full and equal participation of women** in the security sector should be promoted. The victims will most likely confide in a woman (being the victims themselves) than in a man, especially in societies that have more traditional gender roles. This has been organized in various countries by creating a Secretary for Women and Children's issues who works on policies that promote the rights of women and children.

- Security sectors' institutions should develop **operational protocols and procedures** for assisting women and children who have been victims of gender violence. Such institutions must be sensitive to the needs of this vulnerable sector. In most cases, for a woman to report a sexual crime, she is required to submit to protocols or procedures that require her to relive a violent situation, without taking into account the nature of the crime.

- Security sectors' institutions should seek the **participation of civil society** in preventing domestic violence. As we have noted, society plays an important role in maintaining gender inequalities; therefore, it is crucial to engage society in preventing sexual and domestic violence.

## CONCLUDING OBSERVATIONS

In his book, *First Democracy*, Woodruff lists seven prerequisites for good governance and security in a democratic nation-state, one of which is freedom. In this chapter, freedom refers to individual security and freedom from the persecution of sexual exploitation, perpetrated by predators, upon the disenfranchised and vulnerable.

Good governance and security means freedom from abuse and release from being disenfranchised and vulnerable. As noted by Girouard, good governance is the crucible for choices. In combination with security, good governance is the construct that allows individuals to engage in personal growth and professional development. Good governance sets the parameters for a good quality of life, defended by nation-state security. Good governance and security provide the mandate to defend those standards on behalf of the most vulnerable.

Using a gender lens to look at security, we see vulnerabilities that are invisible to a more neutral approach. This latter perspective has recently been discussed by international monitoring organizations, making it a crucial tool for solving security problems for the most vulnerable, women and children. The investigations have demonstrated that security should not only be a concern for nation-states during times of inter-state conflict or of internal crisis, but must be a daily concern as long as women and children are not safe in environments where they should feel most protected, in their home and community.

The final word on a gender perspective of vulnerability is left with Girouard:

> Good governance is the hope of every citizen, a result of both wisdom and service. Governance is the human interface between a Nation's laws and its citizens. Applied with fairness, compassion and pragmatism, it is limited only by the energy, knowledge and imagination of its practitioners. Greed, paranoia and intolerance deliver the opposite end of the spectrum.

For the most vulnerable, hope is not about luxury; instead, it is about survival in an abusive society in a nation-state that supports violence overtly through its statutes and covertly through its tacit absence of action to defend the human rights of all segments of society. The human right to peace and the human potential for peace, as espoused by Douglas Roche and Douglas Fry, *inter alia*, mirror concepts presented in the chapter which call for action by all nation-states to defend whose who are sexually abused. Only through good governance and security can these most vulnerable members of society be protected and empowered.

## REVIEW QUESTIONS

1. Use the case of a war (current or past) and analyse the vulnerability of women in that scenario.
2. Think about your own vulnerability. What aspects of your current conditions make you vulnerable and what can authorities do about it?
3. What should the role of civil society be when examining security from a gender perspective?

## REFERENCES

Afkhami, M., et al. "Human Security: A Conversation." In The Status of Women in Developing Countries. *Social Research* 69, no. 3 (fall 2002): 657-673.

Bastick, M., et al. *Sexual Violence in Armed Conflict. Global Overview and Implications for the Security Sector.* Geneva Centre for the Democratic Control of Armed Forces, 2007.

Fry, D. P. *The Human Potential for Peace.* Oxford, UK: Oxford University Press, 2006.

Hudson, V. M. et al. "The Heart of the Matter: The Security of Women and the Security of States." *International Security* 33, no. 3 (Winter 2008/09): 7-45.

Ní Aoláin, Fionnuala. "Women, Security, and the Patriarchy of Internationalized Transitional Justice." *Human Rights Quarterly* 31, no. 4 (November 2009): 1055-1085.

Roche, D. *The Human Right to Peace.* Ottawa, ON: Novalis, St. Paul University, 2003.

Rodríguez A. *La Noción de "SeguridadHhumana:" Sus Virtudes y Sus Peligros.* Polis. Revista de la Universidad Bolivariana, Chile, 2005.

Sengupta, A. *Human Rights of Minority and Women's: Reinventing Women's Right.* New Delhi, India: Gyan Publishing House, 2005.

Woodruff, P. *First Democracy.* New York, NY: Oxford University Press, 2005.

Zeitlin, J., and D. Mpoumou. *No hay seguridad humana sin igualdad de género.* Women's Environment & Development Organization, WEDO. <http://www. catedradh.unesco.unam.mx/SeminarioCETis/Documentos/Doc_basicos/5_

biblioteca_virtual/3_d_h_mujeres/40.pdf> (Last accessed 4/20/2010).

## ENDNOTES

[1]  V. M. Hudson et al. "The Heart of the Matter: The Security of Women and the Security of States." *International Security* 33, no. 3 (Winter 2008/09): 12.

[2]  During the United Nation's Fourth World Conference on Women held in Beijing, China, in 1995, a platform for action was created. As its mission statement says, it is an agenda for women's empowerment. It aims at accelerating the implementation of the Nairobi Forward-looking Strategies for the Advancement of Women and at removing all the obstacles to women's active participation in all spheres of public and private life through a full and equal share in economic, social, cultural and political decision-making. This means that the principle of shared power and responsibility should be established between women and men at home, in the workplace and in the wider national and international communities. <http://www.un.org/womenwatch/daw/beijing/platform/plat1.htm>

[3]  For further information, look at the case of China or India. In India, as stated by Hudson, "The death toll of Indian women due to female infanticide and sex-selective abortion from 1980 to the present dwarfs by almost fortyfold the death toll from all of India's wars since and including its bloody independence." V. M. Hudson et al. "The Heart of the Matter: The Security of Women and the Security of States." *International Security* 33, no. 3 (Winter 2008/09): 8.

[4]  As cited in M. Bastick et al. *Sexual Violence in Armed Conflict. Global Overview and Implications for the Security Sector* (Geneva Centre for the Democratic Control of Armed Forces, 2007), 149.

[5]  As cited in M. Bastick et al. *Sexual Violence in Armed Conflict. Global Overview and Implications for the Security Sector* (Geneva Centre for the Democratic Control of Armed Forces, 2007), 150.

[6]  As cited in M. Bastick et al. *Sexual Violence in Armed Conflict. Global Overview and Implications for the Security Sector* (Geneva Centre for the Democratic Control of Armed Forces, 2007), 150.

# TRAFFICKING OF BOYS
# AND YOUNG MEN IN GUATEMALA

## MARÍA EUGENIA VILLARREAL, PhD

## INTRODUCTION

For more than a decade, the United Nations Organization has been voicing its concern about the trafficking of children, adolescents and women for slavery and exploitation, and the increase in the number of victims whose basic human rights are being violated. Trafficking in persons[1] is a means of perpetrating multiple illegal acts that range from irregular adoptions to the most aberrant forms of sexual or labour exploitation trade and trafficking of organs. This phenomenon has prompted the UN to promote the drafting and approval of protocols and conventions to combat these crimes and achieve the ratification and commitment of the states to their implementation. The adoption and enforcement of such protocols by some nation-states is an example of what Girouard refers to as mankind's successes in governance and security. The lack of adoption, or adoption with lack of enforcement, of these protocols and conventions, is an example of mankind's failures.

Trafficking in persons has been typified as a crime in the criminal codes of most of countries. It is a varied and complex social problem, as the objectives of this crime are sexual and labour exploitation (agricultural, domestic, manufacturing exploitation, and begging) pornography, etc., through sex tourism and trafficking in persons. Enforcement of the laws, through good governance and security, will determine the survival of a society, a nation, and mankind, as noted by Girouard. Enforcement will reflect the quality of life in a nation-state and the ability of the citizenry to achieve their potential.

Trafficking in persons is considered by nation-states to be a problem of security and of governance, as it is a transnational crime and is linked to organized crime. Traffickers transfer people from one country to another, from one region to another and from one continent to another for the purpose of exploiting them. Trafficking is a crime because there are networks inside the countries that recruit people in order to transfer them from rural areas to urban communities and from one city to another to sell them to centres that deal in the sexual or labour exploitation trade. But, above all, this is a crime and a problem of human rights because it disregards the dignity of people and violates their fundamental rights.

## MAGNITUDE OF THE PROBLEM

It is estimated that every year, worldwide, more than one million girls and boys are sucked into this net of sexual exploitation. These children are bought and sold for sex purposes or used in the child pornography industry. This is a multi-million dollar industry into which children and adolescents are enticed by force or deceit and are deprived of their rights, their dignity and their childhood. The sexual exploitation trade condemns them to one of the most dangerous forms of exploitation because it threatens their psychological, emotional and physical health.

Estuardo Figueroa Rodas, Guatemalan Vice Consul in Tapachula, Chiapas, Mexico has reported that Guatemalan children are victims of trafficking and exploitation in border cities in southeast Mexico. He says people who deal in trafficking visit the indigenous communities in the areas that border Guatemala with Mexico to buy children for the purpose of labour exploitation in Chiapas.

## TRAFFICKING IN CENTRAL AMERICA

Central America is a region that has become a corridor for trafficking in children, adolescents and women from Nicaragua, El Salvador and Honduras, who are transferred to Guatemala for their exploitation or sent to

Mexico, Belize or the United States. Guatemala is a country of destination, transit and of origin of trafficking in persons, where networks of traffickers use its territory to transfer Guatemalan and Central American children, adolescents and women to other places. Most international trafficking in persons takes place from Tecún Umán to Tapachula, Mexico. At the border areas in the department of La Libertad and into Belize and from Puerto Barrios, the victims are taken to Belize or Cancún, Mexico. Trafficking also takes place in the departments of Jutiapa (border with El Salvador) and Chiquimula (border with Honduras).

Investigations conducted by ECPAT Guatemala note that the main border areas where persons are interned in Guatemalan territory are: Las Chinampas or Valle Nuevo, department of Jutiapa, border with El Salvador; San Cristóbal, department of Jutiapa, border with El Salvador; Anguiatú, also known as Padre Miguel, road to Esquipulas, department of Chiquimula, border with El Salvador; Ciudad Pedro de Alvarado, department of Jutiapa, border with El Salvador; and Agua Caliente, Esquipulas, department of Chiquimula, bordering Honduras.

## A MAP OF THE BACK ROADS AND ALLEYS

Migrant children, adolescents and women are the most vulnerable to this crime. They start their voyage in search of work opportunities, to reunite with their family, or simply trying to flee from intra-family violence but on the way to their destination, they run the risk of falling prey to trafficking networks. Trafficking is a particularly alarming problem in the towns located along the borders. Migrant children and adolescents who cannot cross the border into Mexico frequently remain in the country and become victims of exploitation. Children and minor adolescents who have fallen prey to trafficking in persons have reported that immigration officials receive bribes from traffickers and that the officials force them to have sex in order to provide them with false identity documents and to allow them to cross the border.

# CAUSES AND CONTRIBUTING FACTORS – SOCIO-ECONOMIC AND GENDER

The main causes and contributing factors of trafficking in persons recognized by the authorities are, among others, poverty, migration, unemployment, indebtedness, and social factors such as intra-family violence and violence against women, gender discrimination in families, and the patriarchal and adult-centred culture. Other factors are derived from economic and social exclusion, expressed in low education levels, scarce job supply for adult persons, and the labour of young girls and boys who are introduced into income-generating activities. In many families, there is a history of sex abuse and ill treatment. Non-remunerated child labour, forcing children and adolescents to leave their communities for other regions of the country or to other countries as undocumented migrants in search of work opportunities, without the least notion of the risks such actions entail, contributes further to the problem.

## THE GENDER FACTOR

Trafficking in persons for the purpose of sexual exploitation is widely acknowledged as a gender factor because it involves men as the main actors and children and women as the victims. Underlying this fact are the social standards related to gender and the sexuality and dynamics of unequal power that reinforce it. Historically, research, programs and policies related to trafficking and sexual exploitation have dealt with the protection of young girls, adolescents and women. Unfortunately, they have paid little attention to the trafficking and exploitation of boys, male adolescents and young men; as a result, little is known about this latter segment of society, which is steeped in the morass of masculinity.

Many societies maintain a stronger taboo regarding the sexual exploitation of male children and adolescents, which means that these deeds remain hidden from view under the pretext of preserving the male status, male identity and the position of individual masculinity in a group. This problem includes the stigma of homosexual relations and the building of gender stereotypes from traditional male roles. Perhaps this is why the repercussions from the sexual exploitation of male children and adolescents can be complex. In addition to the consequences, male children and adolescents are violated in their sexual identity and bear the stigma of being considered homosexuals.

## DISEASE AND MALNUTRITION

Children and adolescents who are victims of sexual exploitation run a greater risk of sexually transmitted diseases, including HIV/AIDS, than adults. Given the fact that their bodies have not yet fully developed and they are vulnerable to disease due to poor nutrition, they are prone to lesions caused by physical abuse. It is important to point out that the same vulnerabilities exist in the sexual exploitation of girls. The underlying factors in the exploitation of both male and female children are related to the power and control relations of adults over children.

## SOCIAL NORMS

One of the characteristics of male sexual exploitation is that society accepts this problem and sees it as something natural, a social norm, which mainly occurs in the streets in the context of adult, homosexual and trans-sexual prostitution. In addition, some actors in the system of protection of children and adolescents focus their attention on girls and female adolescents but not on male children and adolescents. Even hotel personnel and National Police personnel see sexual exploitation of children in the streets as something natural. This idea of the problem being natural has permeated society, which also views adolescents involved in the sex trade in the streets as "normal." Unlike the exploitation of girls and female adolescents, the exploitation of male children and adolescents is not, in different contexts, a clandestine activity and in some instances is even carried out in broad daylight.

## DRUGS

Adolescents who consume drugs use the money gained from prostitution to buy drugs for themselves. Drug consumption is one of the precursors of sexual exploitation in males. When male children and adolescents are sexually exploited, this becomes a recurring scenario, with clients or friends introducing them to drug consumption. Once they become addicts, they are involved in a vicious circle, which makes it difficult for them to escape exploitation.

A huge problem in border areas is drug trafficking, which is directly related to sexual exploitation. Based on information provided by key informants and institutional sources, it is evident that drug-traffickers consistently exploit girls. Informants state, for example, that drug-traffickers on the Mexican and Guatemalan borders commission each other to find and transfer 10-12 year-old virgin girls for private parties.

PROSTITUTION

Another reason why children and adolescents find themselves being sexually exploited is the need to obtain resources to survive. In many cases, poverty and hunger is the motivating factor in getting clients who pay for sexual relations. It becomes a strategy of survival, which, in many cases, seems to be temporary but in fact becomes a torment for years. Exploiters take advantage of this condition of poverty and hunger to ensnare children and adolescents. Paid sexual relations are an option for survival offered by adults and by other adolescents who are already in this circle.

FAMILIES IN CRISIS

In the history of children and adolescents who are sexually exploited, families, which should provide the most protective space for children, have not performed their role. Dysfunctional, disintegrating and non-existent families do not generate support for the development of children and adolescents, and force them to survive by their own means. In some scenarios of child prostitution, the family is identified as the predator that pressures them into accepting paid sexual relations.

## THE SEX TOURISM FACTOR

The children and adolescents who live in the streets make up a group that is very vulnerable to the sexual exploitation trade. Foreigners seek out these male children and adolescents and offer them money for sex. Taxi drivers contact the adolescents and take them to the hotels where clients wait. In the street circuit, some children and adolescents are led or exploited by a pimp with whom they establish an affective link and/or who offers them protection from street violence. Many others experience a direct relation with the clients in a street setting.

## IMPUNITY FACTOR

Impunity is the *modus operandi* for those who traffic in and seek out children and adolescents as prostitutes because nobody dares to report them. Investigations into child prostitution note that mothers have been reporting this situation to the National Civil Police or to the justice of the peace verbally but do not dare file a formal report for fear of reprisals. As a result, no protection or criminal prosecution proceedings have been initiated.

## GOVERNANCE AND SECURITY SYSTEMS

Key government and security actors who should provide a system of protection for children and adolescents admit that their efforts, to date, have been oriented toward the protection of female children, adolescents and women; they had not considered that the problem also affects male children and adolescents. Because this problem is "invisible," there are very few reports of the sexual exploitation of young boys and adolescents. In addition, there have been few recorded attempts to rescue male victims or to conduct investigations of the criminals behind the sexual exploitation and trafficking of male children or adolescents. The idea that such nefarious activities are natural has been growing because this phenomenon occurs on a daily basis. Nothing has been done about it because, in society's mind, the sexual exploitation of males is just the norm. More recently, ECPAT Guatemala has investigated the problem in Guatemala City, Tecún Umán and on the border with Mexico. ECPAT was able to confirm that a considerable number of male children and adolescents are victims of trafficking for the purpose of sexual exploitation. Their ages range from 15-17. The victims detected were internal migrants who came from other departments in Guatemala or from El Salvador, Honduras and Nicaragua, or they were the children of migrants who had settled in the country. It was concluded that migration places male children and adolescents at high risk of being victims of trafficking and creates the demand factor of adult men who wish to have sex with them.

The Latin American Institute for Crime Prevention and Treatment of Offenders stated that the existing Free Transit Agreements (between Nicaragua, Honduras, El Salvador and Guatemala) has led to a lack of real immigration control of minors between these countries. The border areas with Mexico and Belize continue to be of prime concern due to the heavy flow of undocumented migrants who cross the borders, many of whom become victims of traffickers.

## CONCLUSION

In the absence of good governance and security in legislation and enforcement, trafficking of boys and young men in Guatemala has become epidemic. This problem indicates a dearth of protection measures for children and adolescents by this nation-state. Respect for the rights of children and adolescents has been deficient in all aspects of their lives. Basic social policies do not protect these children or any rights such as health, education or family, among others. When their family becomes unable to provide for their basic needs, especially due to conditions of poverty, there is no social assistance policy to strengthen the role of the family.

When governance and security do not protect the most vulnerable, they allow and even encourage sexual exploitation by perpetrators with impunity. There is an additional omission by the nation-states that border Guatemala relating to children and adolescents from other countries that are totally unprotected and at the mercy of traffickers. For this environment of exploitation of the most vulnerable, Girouard argues that if governance does not deliver, by default, freedom from exploitation, then it has failed the litmus test of democracy at the most fundamental human level.

Prevention, protection and care of young boys as victims or at risk are the responsibility of three main actors, the family, community and state, since it is a crime that violates all the fundamental rights of children. The first step in resolving this problem is recognizing this social phenomenon as a crime by the main actors and identifying risk factors and its different manifestations. It is the state's responsibility to develop programs and public policies for the protection of male children and the prosecution of the offenders. In addition, the family and the community have a key role to play in protection. Families and communities must endorse peaceful spaces where children and young people can be free from all forms of violence and exploitation.

Being committed to resolving this problem is the first step. The second step, deciding how, is a tougher challenge, according to Girouard. Good governance and security that supports change is a cultural process. When the culture views the trafficking of boys and young men as normal, sustainable change will be elusive. Change must begin at the grass roots in the attitudes, values and beliefs of all concerned. But this strategy is insufficient when examined out of context. When socio-economic conditions reinforce the status quo, the probability that change will take hold becomes infinitely small. Even if it does take hold, the probability that any change will be sustainable becomes equally small.

Good governance and security in a nation-state, with all it has to offer, is the hope of every citizen, especially the most vulnerable and those in need of protection. It establishes the parameters for the quality of life. When exacerbated by a weakness in governance, as is the case of Guatemala, it falls on others to intervene. Putting humanitarian issues aside, reinforcing good governance and security brings stability, which is good for business. Premising good governance on moral values and compassion is simply the right thing to do. Girouard concludes by arguing that the relationship with hope is that of delivering on it to those who most need it, not holding on to it. This is the immediate challenge that now falls on others to intervene because it is the right thing to do.

## REVIEW QUESTIONS

1. What attributes of governance and security within nation-states reinforce human trafficking?
2. How have traffickers used governance and security to assure success within their business of human trafficking?
3. What effect does human trafficking have on the victims and the victims' perception of governance and security?
4. Can victims of human trafficking influence governance and security to protect themselves and other potential victims from falling prey to traffickers?

### REFERENCES

ECPAT. *Report on Trafficking in Persons in Guatemala.* ECPAT-Guatemala (January 2004).

ECPAT. *Trafficking of Male Children and Adolescents for Purposes of Sex Trade in Guatemala: An Approximation.* ECPAT/Guatemala, August 2010.

INCEDES (Central American Institute for Social Studies and Development). *Report on Trafficking in Persons in El Salvador, Guatemala, Honduras and México, Global Rights.* Sin Fronteras, IAP, Asociación de Salud Integral (Integral Health Association), La Sala Project, Casa Alianza (Covenant House), Centro de Estudios Fronterizos y Promoción de los Derechos Humanos (Center for Border Studies and Promotion of Human Rights), A.C., "Fray Julián Garcés" Center for Human Rights and Local Social Development, A.C., Centro por la Justicia y el Derecho Internacional (Center for Justice and Internacional Law), Coordinadora Nacional de la Mujer Salvadoreña (National Coordinator for Salvadoran Women), Foro Nacional para Migraciones-Honduras (National Forum for Migrations-Honduras), Instituto Centroamericano de Estudios Sociales y Desarrollo. Washington, DC., 14 October 2005.

Pro-Democracy Office, Human Rights and Labour. *2008 Report on Human Rights Situation. Guatemala.* 25 February 2009.

U.S. State Department, Guatemala Section. *Ninth Annual Report on Trafficking in Persons.* , June 2009.

### ADDITIONAL REFERENCES

Far, K. *Sex Trafficking: The Global Market in Women and Children.* Richmond, UK: Worth Publishers, 2004.

Gallagher, A. T. *The International Law of Human Trafficking*. New York, NY: Cambridge University Press, 2010.

Mills, B. *Human Trafficking: Modern Day Slavery*. Victoria, BC: Trafford Publishing 2001.

Segrave, M., S. Milivojvic, and S. Pickering. *Sex Trafficking*. Devon, UK: Willan Publishing Ltd, 2004.

Shelly, L. *Human Trafficking: A Global Perspective*. New York, NY: Cambridge University Press, 2010.

## ENDNOTES

[1] "Trafficking in persons" is understood to be the holding, transport, transfer, sheltering or receiving of persons, by resorting to threats or to the use of force or other forms of coercion; the abduction, fraud, deceit, abuse of power or of a situation of vulnerability or the giving or receiving of payment or benefits to obtain the consent of a person who has authority over another, for the purpose of exploitation. This exploitation includes, as a minimum, the exploitation of the prostitution of a third party or other forms of sexual exploitation, forced labor or services, slavery or practices analogous to slavery, servitude or the extraction of organs. Article 3, clause (a) "Protocol for the Prevention, Repression and Sanctioning of trafficking in persons, especially women and children," that complements the UN Convention against Transnational Organized Crime.

# GOVERNANCE FOR SECURITY AND SECURITY FOR GOVERNANCE IN OUTLAW MOTORCYCLE GANGS

## TOM RIPPON, PhD

---

## GOVERNANCE AND SECURITY

In the opening chapter, Girouard asserts, "Governance is the means by which a State exercises its will and power. It is the process by which every social action is affected, whether by code or word of mouth." Governance comes in many forms, with security structures to enforce the rules. Governance and security exist in tandem to ensure that organizations and nation-states survive and, ideally, flourish. Sustainability is the manifestation of power that leaders exert through forms of governance and security in a network of economic, social and political relationships.[1]

Governance and security, as a singular theme, is familiar in all cultures, from loose associations with limited formal or informal rules, to bureaucracies with volumes of statutes, rules and regulations. It is important to note that the construct of governance and security is not the domain just of democracies. Dictators and anarchists have systems for governance with robust security structures that parallel executive and judiciary functionality found in democracies. Traditional clans and tribes have governance with forms of enforcement to achieve compliance based upon their cultures, which are not democratic by contemporary definition. In this construct, Girouard proposes that governance is the crucible for choices, for good or ill; governance requires security structures in order to confirm conformity with the choices.

---

There are degrees of democracy and gradations of governance. If the principal function of government, as Girouard suggests, "is the security of the State, the prime role of the civil service is the support of government through, traditionally, anonymous results." The security of the State, whether democratic or dictatorial, is achieved through social influence for voluntary compliance and through political coercion with the threat of the baton. Thus, governance is a function of the will and the power of those who choose to wear the mantle of leadership, directing security measures through a network of subordinate hierarchal structures to achieve their vision.

If governance requires networks and networks are the infrastructure of communities, then networks provide a structure for governance, the power to make and implement rules and regulations, and the security to enforce. The continuum defines the parameters of exclusive power-based structures and inclusive collaborative or collective structures.[2] The level of interaction between the rulers and the citizenry distinguishes dictatorships from democracies.[3] Increased interaction and transparency tends to decrease the need for more stringent forms of security and enforcement; conversely, decreased interaction and secrecy requires an increased need for security and enforcement.

For the purpose of this discussion on governance and security in outlaw motorcycle gangs, it is important to distinguish between the degrees of democracy and gradations of governance in gangs and the structure of security. To do so, one must first examine the genesis of gangs, which do not operate in isolation but in a systems matrix. The current *modus operandi* of gangs will be reviewed in terms of this matrix of systems theory.

## THE SYSTEMS MATRIX OF GANGS IN GOVERNANCE AND SECURITY

Outlaw motorcycle gangs operate regionally and nationally; some have evolved internationally and intra-nationally. The environment in which gangs operate is interdependent with financial markets, economic and commodity markets, and information markets although they have a clearly defined territory or turf, which they defend with a vengeance. All are perceived to be drivers of human security or insecurity depending on the confidence or threat they pose to individuals and those who govern nation-states.

Gangs, their governance and security, are phenomena in social evolution. Their roots are post-World War I but more clearly aligned with World War II and the United States. Some veterans had difficulty settling down to civilian life because of their anti-social behaviour associated with combat stress reaction, today referred to as post-traumatic stress disorder. They created loose associations or networks that developed into motorcycle clubs and eventually gangs, attracted by the ambiance of the brotherhood. Twenty-five years later, some servicemen who exhibited similar behaviour as a result of their tours of duty in the Vietnam War joined the ranks of motorcycle gangs. Where others in mainstream society did not understand them, brothers in the gangs did. Their motorcycle of choice was the Harley-Davidson, which had earned them a rebellious reputation akin to the *persona* of the riders.

Some ex-military gang members, who were not successful in the military because they rejected structure and discipline, ironically responded to the more draconian structure and discipline of the gangs. Other gang members who had not served in the military also exhibited difficulty following the norms of the larger structured society and, as a result, many served time in prison before and after joining gangs. Their criminal record helped raise their status to full-patch.[4] Yet, like the former group, they embraced gang rules and strict enforcement.

Gangs fill the social needs of the members and especially the need for acceptance and affiliation. Both create social bonding among members and this, in turn, establishes the basis of hierarchal governance and security. Although violent, gang discipline is perceived as a form of benevolence or tough love. Internally, gang members are faithful to one another. Advancement through the hierarchy is premised upon showing unquestionable trust and loyalty. Externally, however, gang members flaunt the laws of society at large and garner respect through collective criminal activities. The bonds between the band of brothers are reinforced by successive marauding engagements, each its own Agincourt.

Although perceived as being undisciplined outlaws, strict military-style decorum is maintained for the purpose of internal governance and security, commensurate with the dictates of gang protocol. Governance is achieved through a constitution and an executive structure with a president, vice-president(s), secretary-treasurer and sergeant-at-arms.[5] The latter is responsible for security and the enforcement of rules and dictates of the executive. Appointments to executive offices are top-down rather than democratically determined (bottom-up). The executive provides authority for security through the sergeant-at-arms, while the security permits the executive to function and the gang to maintain its internal integrity.

Gangs have written constitutions and bylaws stringently enforced by a sergeant-at-arms through blatant violence, the degree of which is determined by the level of severity of the infraction. They tend to have fewer rules than conventional lawful organizations, but enforcement is ubiquitous and immediate. This process, gang executives argue, contributes to the sustainability and integrity of the structure of the gang, unlike other businesses or nation-states that have failed. Today, the *modus operandi* of an increasing number of gangs is to remain as low-key as possible to avoid the undue attention of law-enforcement officers, while still flying their colours and riding for effect as they rule by fear and intimidation.

## GANGS AND LAW-ENFORCEMENT AGENCIES IN THE SYSTEMS MATRIX

Gangs have become sophisticated, strategic businesses with tentacles in global organized crime, facilitated by technology and globalization. Bremmer argues that technology has changed the world and the way business is conducted.[6] Indeed, gang business is now web-based and this fact is changing both gang and law-enforcement security protocols. Bremmer asserts:

> Technologies are not always instruments of democracy ... these tools are value-neutral; there is nothing inherently pro-democratic about them. To use them is to exercise a form of freedom,

but it is not necessarily a freedom that promotes the freedom of others.[7]

The state is also online promoting its own economic agenda, which includes efforts to curtail full transparency and monitor citizenry communications in cyberspace without threatening their political power base. Gangs have become acutely aware of this phenomenon, as have other criminal elements, while they electronically engage in illegal commerce that is a threat to lawful commerce.

In response, nation-states are expanding their respective definition of what constitutes threats to national security in the context of globalization and the global village.[8] Security discourse by law-enforcement agencies has migrated from a perception of gangs as a nuisance and a menace to local peace and good governance, to threats to the integrity of national and international infrastructures of state security. In some enforcement *lingua*, illegal gang activity is referred to as terrorist threats.[9] Motivation for managing this phenomenon has morphed from a micro approach of individual arrests to a macro strategy of infiltrating and incapacitating the governance and security of the gang structure. Engaging in the former without full comprehension of the capacity of the latter has, in some instances, created a greater challenge than the initial tactics were meant to resolve. Given the ostensibly superior technology available to law-enforcement agencies and the forays of enforcement into gang activities, how have gangs remained sustainable?

Systems theory asserts that gangs do not exist separately from other structures any more than do other organizations. Their cultures are particular, but are also sub-cultures and counter-cultures in nation-states and the global village. As such, gangs are influenced by their environment. They have positive and negative impacts on other organizational cultures, including the law-enforcement agencies that have been created and funded solely to prosecute the illegal and often nefarious activities of gang members. *Res Ipsa loquitur* – the fact speaks for itself. If gangs were eliminated, bureaucracies and the law-enforcement agencies created to prosecute them would also be eliminated. Without gangs, no resources would be needed.

Bureaucracies are self-sustaining; hence, it is not in the best interests of bureaucrats to work themselves out of employment by being highly effective. On the contrary, law-enforcement bureaucrats inflate structures in order to vie for and secure greater resources for their respective sustainability. This *modus operandi* assures job security for the entire bureaucracy. The challenge becomes one of marketing to the masses, the citizenry.

The uniform crime reporting (UCR) systems employed by law-enforcement agencies provide the means to report and manipulate the crime-related data. Creative data generation, tabulation and analysis have become their hallmark. In addition, associating gang members with known terrorists and declaring gang activities to be a terrorist threat to homeland security ensures almost endless resources allocated by politicians who have been mandated to protect the citizenry.

Politicians thrive on optics while law-enforcement agencies survive on statistics. The former want to be seen by the electorate as taking action that results in voter confidence from a sense of public perception of safety.[10] Being re-elected depends on this perception. Law-enforcement agencies need to justify the allocation of resources to their political masters in order to validate current budgetary expenditures and demands for future increases.[11] This bureaucratic behaviour to create and clandestinely promote hidden agendas for the purpose of controlling resources, Ghani and Lockhart argue, is unethical and impairs nation-state building. It undermines the integrity of good governance and security.[12]

Astute gang leaders are cognizant of this bureaucratic motivation and manipulation. They are also aware of the need to find a balance between not creating too much fear amongst the citizenry yet creating enough fear to guarantee their source of revenue. Creating too much fear would cause citizens to complain to politicians who would govern with directives and, if needs be, additional statutory authority to increase law enforcement under the mantle of national or regional security (optics). Gang revenue generation would suffer and power would erode. At the other end of the spectrum, *not* creating enough fear would cause gang wars to erupt as one gang perceived another gang to be weak and ripe for violent takeover; in management *lingua franca*, a business merger, acquisition or hostile takeover[13] would result in lay-offs and down-sizing.

A symbiotic business relationship, therefore, is sought by the security bureaucracies and law-enforcement agencies, on the one hand, and the gangs, on the other hand. Equilibrium exists by balancing fear and enforcement. In a related context, Goodman proposes that businesses can learn from organized crime.[14]

## RESPONSE TO PERCEIVED THREATS

Ferguson suggests that nation-states "operate somewhere between order and disorder on the edge of chaos."[15] When threatened, freedoms of democracy are waived in favour of security (through secrecy – the first casualty of war is truth) to protect the state and its citizenry. The governance continuum balances security and freedom; some citizenry give up certain freedoms for internal security while others defend freedom at the expense of internal security. Either perspective can be defended as fundamental to the public good, the goal of public good defined by Tierney as being "global stability and prosperity."[16] However, as perceived threats increase, a more informed, comprehensive understanding of the public good is overcome by images of terror-motivated chaos, resulting in the curtailment of freedom. In this context, the Us versus Them mentality is not in the public good for nation-states or outlaw motorcycle gangs.

George W. Bush suspended the rule of law after 9/11 because of an actual and perceived threat, ostensibly to protect the United States and the U.S. citizenry, in other words the dualistic "you are either with us or against us" proposition. One could argue that motorcycle gangs that have experienced and continue to perceive external threats to their survival from rival gangs or law-enforcement agencies respond in a similar manner. They are constantly adapting to dynamic changes in the environment (Us versus Them), including threats to their governance and security. Accordingly, they respond with violence to a state of siege. Gangs fail the litmus test of good governance when viewed through this lens; the public good is mute.

Reflecting upon the Bush Administration's response to 9/11, Glassner[17] and Furedi[18] propose that the culture of the U.S. is founded on fear, which causes a fear-based behaviour response. The U.S. is constantly adapting to dynamic changes in the environment, including perceived threats to its governance and security. In a similar context, Marsella asserts that U.S. obsession with "hegemonic economic, political and cultural control of the world" has created an internal culture of fear which is manifested in a culture of war: "An interlocking system of national meaning, beliefs, behaviours, institutions and identities that consider violence and war necessary and justifiable in pursuit of U.S. hegemonic global interests."[19] Marsella suggests that the U.S. has evolved toward a dictatorial form of governance with draconian security enforcement methodologies akin to the former U.S.S.R. during the Cold War. This trend has been motivated and manipulated by the culture of fear that it has created as a means of controlling its citizenry. Does the U.S. then also fail the litmus test of good governance when viewed through this lens of constant warring and violent behaviour, or is its behavioural response merely a logical lacuna? Is there global stability and prosperity? Is there a public good?

## OTHER LITMUS TESTS

Woodruff describes seven non-negotiable elements as a litmus test of good governance and security in democratic nation-states:

1. Harmony;
2. Rule of law;
3. Freedom;
4. Natural equality;
5. Citizen wisdom;
6. Reasoning; and
7. General education.[20]

Dictatorial nation-states and outlaw gangs do not meet these standards; some democratic states also fall short. Most criteria clearly place the emphasis on an enlightened and engaged electorate rather than politicians or bureaucrats who have been elected or appointed to govern. The engagement of an enlightened electorate has not been demonstrated in recent years, as exemplified by declining voting trends. In these jurisdictions, the citizenry is disengaged and disinterested. Gang members also tend not to be enlightened and yet they are more engaged and acutely aware of the governance and security of their gang-states.

Ghani and Lockhart propose a similar ten-factor litmus test to assess the degree of democracy and gradation of governance and security of the nation-state:

1.  Legitimate monopoly on the means of violence;
2.  Administrative control;
3.  Management of public finances;
4.  Investment in human capital;
5.  Delineation of citizenship rights and duties;
6.  Provision of infrastructure services;
7.  Formation of the market;
8.  Management of the state's assets (including the environment, natural resources, and cultural assets);
9.  International relations (including entering into international contracts and public borrowing); and
10. Rule of law.[21]

Commensurate with Woodruff's seven elements, dictatorial nation-states and outlaw gangs do not meet these standards either; some democratic states also fall short. As in gangs, governance and security in democracies is an arduous and often imperfect process. Contemporary morals and values become the guidance systems for decisions. Efficacy is based upon an enlightened citizenry that acknowledges the co-axial relationship between the two structures in the systems matrix and the constant need to strive for ethical integrity, the ability to steadfastly adhere to higher moral standards.

This ethos is the clear delineator, the litmus test that distinguishes good from bad governance and security. As noted by Girouard, "The world's Al Qaedas have no desire to improve the lot of the masses. The Taliban never worked to heal root causes but strove to dominate and subjugate, to dim their world into another Dark Age." Global stability and prosperity were not motivators of their actions; the public good was absent from their lexicon. Good governance and security has a series of checks and balances. When abrogated or allowed to erode with the curtailment of freedoms, the foremost being the freedom of speech, good governance and security are transformed into bad.

The litmus tests which Ghani and Lockhart[22] and Woodruff[23] present can be interpreted in the context of contemporary organizational behavioural literature. Research in these disciplines suggests that accelerating employee turnover is a constant challenge for leaders and managers; sustainability of the organization is stressed due to the high cost of training and development. The central causal factor is disengagement. The same employees who are disinterested and, as a result, disengage in the workplace tend to be the same citizens who are disinterested and disengaged in the political arena. Yet, turnover in gang organizations is very low; disinterest and disengagement are not constant challenges. Loyalty remains high; disengagement in the political arena in gangs is also high. Are the means by which governance and security are administered factors in the sustainability equation for gangs?

## SUMMARY OBSERVATIONS

This chapter presents a discussion of governance and security in outlaw motorcycle gangs. These gangs are not democracies, yet they have a form of governance and security that has contributed to their sustainability. Bankruptcy reports can attest to the fact that many organizations and businesses, and some supposedly democratic and dictatorial states, cannot boast of such sustainability. Failed and failing states are all too common and, as a result, pose a threat to the governance and security of all nation-states in the global village. What, then, distinguishes sustainability from un-sustainability? Neither the singular concept of governance and security nor sustainability is the sole prerogative of democracy. Is democratic governance, Girouard asks, the human interface between a Nation's laws and its citizens applied with fairness, compassion and pragmatism or is it limited only by the energy, knowledge and imagination of its practitioners? Greed, paranoia and intolerance deliver the opposite end of the spectrum.

The governance of outlaw motorcycle gangs falls at the opposite end of this spectrum. Internally, Queen argues that there is a sense of fairness, compassion and pragmatism in gangs; however, it is not extended universally.[24] Gangs recruit from a particular segment of the population and the selection process is strict and secretive in its scrutiny. Once accepted with full-patch status, few leave. Those who may wish to sever ties are subject to an equally arduous and violent exit process. Thus, relative internal stability is achieved through both positive and negative reinforcement, fulfilled needs and coercion.

Outlaw motorcycle gangs are not democracies. As counter-cultures, they were not created as democracies and have not evolved into democracies. They do, however, have governance and security structures. They have adapted to their environment, which Darwin would argue is the key to survival, and they have survived through acquisitions, mergers or hostile takeovers. For gangs, as with democratic and dictatorial states, governance is difficult and complex, and security equally demanding. In his conclusion, Girouard proposes:

> The prime function of the State and its apparatus is the protection of the borders and of the people. While acknowledging that in some regimes the emphasis is on the former more than the latter, the predominant approach for the modern state emphasizes the security of the people in a fairly broad context.

Gangs would argue that they protect their borders from external threats and that gang wars erupt in defence of tenacious turf. Gangs would assert that they protect their people (gang members), with greater loyalty than do many nation-states. In the latter, the security of the people, the citizens of the gang-state, *per se*, falls outside the broader definition.

Good governance is the citizenry. Girouard notes, "It speaks to a system where the machinery of government and the body politic become co-influencers, where a moral contract emerges among the politician, the bureaucrat and the citizen." As witnessed, most recently, with state security response to G8 and G20 protests by citizenry, co-influencing governance took a back seat to violent, draconian security measures. The balance between freedoms and security has tilted to the latter; the fulcrum has moved. In this regard, states appear not to have adapted to dynamic changes in the environment, including perceived threats, whereas gangs might have.

This chapter is entitled, "Governance for Security and Security for Governance in Outlaw Motorcycle Gangs." The attributes and applications of governance and security are seminal to the thesis. Peace, order and good government is a concept familiar to the enlightened and engaged citizens of Canada. Although not often articulated, there is an inherent understanding that governance can be achieved only when security structures become an integral part of the governance process to ensure stability. Good governance with a moral reflection requires ethical balance, another moral qualifier, as Girouard says, "A fact which demands judgment amongst those charged with delivering on the expectations raised by the tenets of peace, order and good government."

In the discussion on the governance processes of failed and failing states, the dearth of awareness and ethics was apparent in the balancing of governance and security decisions, *inter alia*. Other nation-states and gang-states that have not met the standards of peace, order and good government continue to function but not as isolated entities. Instead, they exist in the systems matrix, supported by and supporting other organizations in a symbiotic relationship. They govern for the security provided by co-emergence with the environment in the matrix, which seeks balance for their own self-sustainment. This, in turn, provides the security structures for governance. Nation-states and gang-states survive if they have situational awareness of this dynamic process and the strategic foresight to manoeuvre in this multi-dimensional matrix construct. Those that lack the awareness and the ability to adapt, fail. From a strategic, sustainability perspective, some governance and security models may be worth examining in a reconceptualised construct.[25]

Outlaw gangs have adapted their governance and security strategies to shifting variables in the environment of the systems matrix. Knowing is knowledge. Sustainability is about knowing when to adapt and having the ability to do so. Knowledge of the equilibrium in the multi-dimensional matrix ensures sustainability. Darwin is correct: adaptability is the key to survival and sustainability.

## REVIEW QUESTIONS

1. Comment on the proposition that the construct of governance and security is not the domain just of democracies. Dictators and anarchists have systems for governance with robust security structures that parallel executive and judiciary functionality found in democracies.

2. Is governance and security as a unitary concept necessary and sufficient to prevent nation-states from failing?

## REFERENCES

Bremmer, I. "Democracy in Cyberspace: What Information Technology Can and Cannot Do." *Internal Affairs,* (November/December 2010): 89-92.

Chomsky, N. *Failed States.* New York, NY: Metropolitan Books, 2006.

Ferguson, N. "Complexity and Collapse: Empires on the Edge of Chaos." *Internal Affairs,* (March/April 2010): 23-35.

Fischer, R., and K. Hanke. "Are Societal Values Linked to Global Peace and Conflict?" *Peace and Conflict: Journal of Peace Psychology* 15, no. 2 (2009): 227-248.

Furedi, F. *Culture of Fear.* New York, NY: Continuum, 2002.

Ghani, A., and C. Lockhart. *Fixing Failed States: A Framework for Rebuilding a Fractured World.* New York, NY: Oxford University Press, 2009.

Glassner, B. *The Culture of Fear.* New York, NY: Basic Books, 1999.

Goodman, M. "What Business Can Learn From Organized Crime." *Harvard Business Review.* November 2011. <http://hbr.org/2011/11/what-business-can-learn-from-organized-crime/ar/1?cm_mmc=email-_-newsletter-_-cant_miss_update-_-hbrcm111011&referral=01087&utm_source=newsletter_cant_miss_update&utm_medium=email&utm_campaign=hbrcm111011> (10 December 2011).

Gutberlet, J. *Recovering Resources: Recycling Citizenship.* Hampshire, UK: Ashgate, 2008.

Kirchner, E. J., and R. Dominguez, eds. *The Security Governance of Regional Organizations.* London, UK: Routledge, 2011.

Kooiman, J. *Governing as Governance.* London, UK: Sage, 2003.

Langton, J. *How the Outlaws, Hell's Angels and Cops Fought for Control of the Streets.* Mississauga, ON: John Wiles & Sons Canada, 2010.

Marsella, A. J. *The United States of America: A Culture of War*. Lifetime Achievement Award Address: International Academy of Intercultural Research (IARA), September 15, 2010, Honolulu, Hawaii. (In Press: International Journal of Intercultural Relations, Summer 2011.)

Pierre, J., and B. G. Peters. *Governance, Politics and the State*. New York, NY: St. Martin's Press, 2000.

Poulton, R. *Pale Blue Hope*. Winnipeg, MB: Turnstone Press, 2009.

Puranam, P., and B. S. Vanneste. Trust and Governance: Untangling a Tangled Web. *Academy of Management Review* 34, no. 1 (2009): 11-31.

Queen, W. *Under and Alone*. New York, NY: Ballantine Books, 2007.

Rippon, T. J., and B. Smith. *The Fear of Crime and the Public Perception of the Criminal Justice System*. Victoria, BC: Ministry of the Attorney General, British Columbia Police Commission, 1990.

Tierney, W. G. The Role of Tertiary Education in Fixing Failed States: Globalization and Public Goods. *Journal of Peace Education* 8, no. 2 (2011): 127-142.

Veno, A. *The Brotherhoods: Inside the Outlaw Motorcycle Clubs*. Crows Nest, NSW, Australia: Allen and Unwin, 2009.

Woodruff, P. *First Democracy*. New York, NY: Oxford University Press, 2005.

Woods, G., and T. J. Rippon. *Policing British Columbia in the Year 2001: Report of the Regionalization Study Team*. Victoria, BC: Ministry of Solicitor General, Province of British Columbia, 1990.

## ENDNOTES

[1] N. Ferguson. "Complexity and Collapse: Empires on the Edge of Chaos." *Internal Affairs,* March/April (2010): 26.

[2] J. Gutberlet. *Recovering Resources: Recycling Citizenship* (Hampshire, UK: Ashgate Publishing Ltd, 2008).

[3] J. Kooiman. *Governing as Governance* (London, UK: Sage Publications, 2003).

[4] W. Queen. *Under and Alone* (New York, NY: Ballantine Books, 2007).

[5] A. Veno. *The Brotherhoods: Inside the Outlaw Motorcycle Clubs* (Crows Nest, NSW, Australia: Allen & Unwin, 2009).

[6] I. Bremmer. "Democracy in Cyberspace: What Information Technology Can and Cannot Do." *Internal Affairs,* November/December (2010): 91.

[7] I. Bremmer. "Democracy in Cyberspace: What Information Technology Can and Cannot Do." *Internal Affairs,* November/December (2010): 87.

[8] N. Chomsky. *Failed States* (New York, NY: Metropolitan Books, 2006).

[9] W. Queen. *Under and Alone* (New York, NY: Ballantine Books, 2007).

10  T. J. Rippon and B. Smith. *The Fear of Crime and the Public Perception of the Criminal Justice System* (Victoria, BC: Ministry of the Attorney General, British Columbia Police Commission, 1990).

11  G. Woods and T. J. Rippon. *Policing British Columbia in the Year 2001: Report of the Regionalization Study Team* (Victoria, BC: Ministry of Solicitor General, Province of British Columbia, 1990).

12  A. Ghani and C. Lockhart. *Fixing Failed States: A Framework for Rebuilding a Fractured World* (New York, NY: Oxford University Press, 2009.

13  J. Langton. *How the Outlaws, Hell's Angels and Cops Fought for Control of the Streets* (Mississauga, ON: John Wiles & Sons Canada Ltd, 2010), 3.

14  M. Goodman. "What Business Can Learn From Organized Crime." *Harvard Business Review* November 2011. <http://hbr.org/2011/11/what-business-can-learn-from-organized-crime/ar/1?cm_mmc=email-_-newsletter-_-cant_miss_update-_-hbrcm111011&referral=01087&utm_source=newsletter_cant_miss_update&utm_medium=email&utm_campaign=hbrcm111011> (10 December 2011).

15  N. Ferguson. "Complexity and Collapse: Empires on the Edge of Chaos." *Internal Affairs,* March/April (2010): 23.

16  W. G. Tierney. "The Role of Tertiary Education in Fixing Failed States: Globalization and Public Goods." *Journal of Peace Education* 8, no. 2 (2011): 133.

17  B. Glassner. *The Culture of Fear* (New York, NY: Basic Books, 1999).

18  F. Furedi. *Culture of Fear* (New York, NY: Continuum, 2002).

19  A. J. Marsella. *The United States of America: A Culture of War*. Lifetime Achievement Award Address: International Academy of Intercultural Research (IARA), September 15, 2010, Honolulu, Hawaii. (In Press: International Journal of Intercultural Relations, Summer 2011), 1.

20  P. Woodruff. *First Democracy* (New York, NY: Oxford University Press, 2005).

21  A. Ghani and C. Lockhart. *Fixing Failed States: A Framework for Rebuilding a Fractured World* (New York, NY: Oxford University Press, 2009.

22  A. Ghani and C. Lockhart. *Fixing Failed States: A Framework for Rebuilding a Fractured World* (New York, NY: Oxford University Press, 2009.

23  P. Woodruff. *First Democracy* (New York, NY: Oxford University Press, 2005).

24  W. Queen. *Under and Alone* (New York, NY: Ballantine Books, 2007).

25  E. J. Kirchner and R. Dominguez (Eds.). *The Security Governance of Regional Organizations* (London, UK: Routledge, 2011).

# SECTION III

**PERSPECTIVES ON
RESOURCE SECURITY**

# ON ADAPTIVE WATER GOVERNANCE: PRODUCING AN EQUITABLE AND REFLEXIVE HYDRO-POLITICS OF SECURITY AND PEACE

## ERIC ABITBOL, PhD (Cand.)

## INTRODUCTION

Water has surfaced as a political domain of concern and deliberation in the 21st century. Leading global actors have been mobilizing in response to the possibility that water might become a prime factor in motivating or escalating contemporary social and armed conflicts. Debate has emerged on whether rights-based or commercial approaches to water governance are preferable in securing water and advancing peace. From a socio-political perspective, experiments continue to be pursued to assess the conflict and peace implications of citizen and stakeholder processes in water development, themselves dominated by engineering perspectives. If only hydro-political security and peace were as simple as ensuring that safe, clean and abundant water was made accessible to all human beings, regardless of their location, status and power.

Domestic use is only one of several areas demanding water. Agriculture is the planet's most intensive user of water, amounting to some 70% of all supply. Industry is another growing user in both the North and Global South, given the industrial development prerogatives of more recently established major economies such as China, India, Brazil and others. Water is used for hydropower generation, recreation and ecological services, as in the form of wetlands. In his introduction, Girouard proposes that to consider governance is to ponder how humanity makes things work; thus, the governance of water provision, allocation, development, sustainability and now production may be understood as a complex domain of political action. It draws together actors across sectors and throughout the global environment intent on shaping hydropolitical discourses and practices of security and peace.

## RIGHTS IN GOVERNANCE AND SECURITY OF FRESHWATER

During most of our known human existence and until fairly late in the 20th century, freshwater was a resource and patrimonial asset. In the natural world, there is no substitute for water. It cannot be replaced easily and it is unevenly distributed across the planet, thereby creating a host of global-equity-related challenges. In anthropocentric terms, water is both a basic human need and a recognized human right. After much popular and political mobilization across the planet over recent decades, and building on several UN Conventions (including the groundbreaking 1989 UN Convention on the Rights of the Child), on July 28, 2010 the United Nations General Assembly recognized water (and sanitation) as a human right. This recognition set in motion a state-based obligation to ensure the provision of safe and sufficient quantities of good quality water to all citizens and residents.

Natural freshwater includes groundwater, surface water, seasonal floodwaters and in some countries, rainwater. Going back to pre-modern and imperial times, the governance of such waters has been contextual, shaped by local circumstances and practices. For example, in the Middle Eastern region of the Ottoman Empire, families and clans (*hamulas*) were the principal managers of water, a resource that was understood to be part of their familial domain. Water was frequently made available, distributed and sold as "time at the well" rather than by volume, with concern for social standing and community responsibility. Today, in the same regions, water is largely (though still not entirely) managed by the state or state-like governing institutions. Its management is based principally on volume, with concern for human, environmental and state security as well as sustainable development. This example from the Levant reflects a tension that persists across the planet between traditional, local and/or communal forms of water governance and centralizing national institutions. As discussed below, the political ecology of water governance is made increasingly complex by the reach of globalizing agendas, processes and institutions.

## FROM NATURAL TO PRODUCED WATER

Freshwater resources have generally been understood and appreciated as relatively limited in most countries with related water stress experienced by human communities and water scarcity factored into economic planning. Recent technological developments promise to transform radically and paradigmatically this millennia-old human framing and experience of water, with governance implications discernable minimally at two levels. First, wastewater recycling and reuse is becoming a widespread practice, increasing water budgets substantially. Second, large-scale seawater desalination has created a seemingly limitless well of water, though one reliant on energy-intensive technologies. In the 21st century, the governance of water resources must now account for natural, recycled and produced water, raising different challenges and opportunities in the realms of security and peace.

While natural freshwater remains the primary source in today's water budgets, recycled and produced waters are quickly bringing up the rear. Wastewater recycling of grey and black water allows for water quality to be matched with water needs and requirements. Thus, the same water could be used for domestic purposes, notably drinking and food preparation. It could be reused for sanitation purposes. Finally, it could be recycled for irrigation. Technological innovations coupled with adaptive management practices alleviate water-related stress and increase the *productivity* of water, frequently generating economic, social and political dividends. Generally speaking, state or state-like institutions are the primary actors in governing such waters, intent on ensuring that both broadly defined human needs and rights to water are secured.

More innovatively, perhaps, large-scale seawater desalination is affecting the way we think about and govern water. Indeed, the concepts of water scarcity and stress are altered for those regions of the world that have a productive coastline. Seawater desalination is conjuring an *imaginaire* of limitless abundance and water security, a hydropolitical Shangri-La. It promises to offer a hydropolitical buffer against the uncertainties, erratic climatic events and lessened rainfall patterns associated with climate change in regions of the world such as the Middle East. As an *imaginaire* without water-related conflicts, desertification or hunger, it is a powerful organizing force, vindicating supply over demand-management and innovative *Soft Path* approaches to water governance. Like all promises apparently too good to be true, however, this one has its limitations and challenges. Desalination requires either direct access to a coast or indirect access through a neighbouring state with which one has peaceful relations. Desalination is based on access to innovative technology, frequently delivered along a Build-Operate-Transfer (BOT) model, requiring the willing participation of the private sector as profit-driven actors. Thus, seawater desalination is not likely to be successful in many countries without international development assistance, economic incentives or a maverick practice of corporate social responsibility. Environmentally speaking, its process relies largely on the burning of fossil fuels, thereby polluting the atmosphere while removing water from and thus affecting the seas. The haves, have-nots, have-lates and globalised have-wastes come sharply into relief through this analysis.

## PRIVATIZING WATER GOVERNANCE AND SECURITY?

In the modern era, a general though contested trajectory from traditional practices through to state governance and security over water resources has been discernable. With the rise of produced water, notably of large-scale seawater desalination, debate over water-governance arrangements has been vigorously renewed, raising fundamental questions. Who will pay for desalinated seawater? How shall the environmental impact be factored and controlled? How shall produced water be governed at local, national, regional and global levels? Ultimately, should natural, recycled and produced water be managed according to different values, rules and institutions? The debate frequently turns on the question of whether *all* water should be managed primarily as a public good or whether valid arguments can be made for water to be governed as a private good.

Since the creation of the World Water Council (WWC) in the mid-1990s, global discourse on water management has increasingly favoured multi-sectoral water governance, with the participation of the private sector. In the North, and with global inclinations, water governance is increasingly based on a public–private partnership model. Leading private actors include Thames Water (UK), Veolia and Suez (France), and to a lesser extent Aguas de Barcelona (Spain) and Saur International (France). With the support of national OECD country development agencies, export and development funding bodies, international development banks and the enabling force of hegemonic globalizing discourses, major corporations have pursued a politics of private-sector involvement in water governance across the Global South.

Far from ensuring that the basic human need for water has been delivered or that the right to water is respected, corporate involvement in water governance has catalysed counter-hegemonic popular resistance. In Bolivia and South Africa in the late 1990s, local populations flooded the streets in protest of rising water prices. The protests decried the restriction or denial of basic water-delivery services. They reflected popular fears associated with the relocation of governance authority to distantly managed, profit-driven corporations, the majority of whose shareholders possess little awareness of local reality. Academic research in the field of water management reveals few benefits from private water concessions. On the contrary, there is evidence of consistently rising water prices, of deteriorating service and of little consideration for the needs and rights of local populations.

## BRIDGING RULES OF WATER GOVERNANCE

Social movements around the world, such as those in Bolivia and South Africa, have influenced an evolving set of global rules of water governance attempting to bridge the many hydro-political chasms. Historically, the rules have been set out by government actors for the management of sovereign water resources and relations with co-riparians where water resources straddle boundaries. This is the case in some 263 major transboundary river basins across the planet. Today, such rules are the product of work undertaken by natural and social scientists and legal experts, as well as government and other actors.

Most recently, the Berlin Rules of Water Resources, adopted by the International Law Association (ILA) on August 21, 2004, put forward principles designed to accommodate possible governance arrangements including the likely participation of both public and private actors, as well as diverse stakeholder groups. The values and priorities conveyed by the Berlin Rules may be understood as:

- Privileging vital human needs over other uses;
- Recognizing inter-generational sustainability and ecological integrity;
- Establishing preference for shared Integrated Water Resources Management (IWRM) where waters are trans-boundary;
- Promoting the reasonable and equitable use of water resources;
- Requiring proper impact assessments for all proposed major developments;
- Advancing public participation in water development, noting corollary information and transparency requirements; and
- Prioritizing the resolution of water disputes through peaceful means, subject to arbitration or litigation that is both final and binding.

In reading these seven principles (themselves distilled from a richer framework, referred to below), one is led to appreciate the challenge of water-resource governance. Access to water for human consumption is a primordial need, the denial of which is a cause of conflict, notably where denial is not absolute but relative to other groups. In peacemaking processes today, the prevention of conflict would be premised, at least in part, on the construction of inter-generational sustainability and equity.

## DEVELOPING WATER, BUILDING EQUITY

Much of the accessible surface water and increasingly the coveted seawater of our planet are targeted for development. This trend entails major change in the hope of advancing fundamental, core and contemporary values. Development entails the securitized cultural transformation of human populations, with varying degrees of agency, benefits and hope. A cursory glance at two noteworthy moments in the trajectory of development provides insight into the production and location of security and peace.

From the 1950s onwards, water developments have frequently materialized as large-scale infrastructural projects, mainly in the form of hydro-electricity, irrigation and water-supply dams. Underpinned by a modernization agenda, large-scale water projects became the double-headed bête noir of the water-development sector. Such projects promised to deliver the benefits of modern development to all, notably in the form of electrification and sometimes irrigation water, aimed at bolstering national employment and wealth-generation. In practice, they saddled national governments with debts that were difficult to manage, while polarizing nations along the lines of empowered and marginalized communities.

The construction of the Kariba Dam on the Zambezi remains a notorious example as an initiative that further polarized the national population along racial, cultural and economic lines. According to a recent International Rivers study conducted by Dharmadhikary, a major push for Himalayan dam building is currently underway. Not unlike earlier projects, these efforts in India, Bhutan, Pakistan and Nepal are undertaking environmentally risky initiatives at the expense of local communities who are least likely to benefit.

At the same time, meaningful changes in water development and management practice since the 1950s are discernible. Perhaps most fundamentally, an expanded base of human experience is increasingly recognized as central to the development paradigm. Looking at areas of the world that aspire to, or indeed pursue IWRM, the practice of stakeholder engagement is apparent. In practice, populations likely to be affected by major water-development initiatives are being informed about project parameters and impacts, and consulted about fears, concerns and even aspirations associated with such projects.

It is promising to note that such processes are taking place in transboundary contexts, bringing together once hostile states, nations and communities in a process intent on shaping collective futures. For example, the proposed Red Sea–Dead Sea Conveyance (RSDSC) initiative in Jordan, Israel and the Palestinian Authority (PA), has been conducting a feasibility study that includes stakeholder consultations and a study to assess the conflict and peace dimensions of the proposed scheme. If managed well by eliciting the participation of concerned social and political actors, such processes may contribute to the development of human security. In this case it means that people are involved in shaping their future in something so fundamental as water. Introducing a note of caution, it should be recognized that the location of decision-making power is variable in large-scale development initiatives. It requires contextualized analysis, given that states are not always prepared to relinquish hierarchical authority, particularly in conflict environments. In practice, stakeholder consultations do not necessarily entail a meaningful or politically significant stakeholder engagement process.

In another respect, large-scale water development sometimes entails the physical transformation of territories, undermining antecedent land uses, transforming resource bases and undermining human communities. In eco-political terms, water development may violate agreements and principles from biodiversity to the concerns of aboriginal peoples. In a cautionary example close to home, decisions taken by the Gouvernement du Québec and its public and private partners to develop the James Bay region in the 1960s, without the consent of northern aboriginal communities, has had major implications for land, food security, aboriginal and governance issues in Canada.

The James Bay scheme provided massive hydropower supplies to the people of Québec for heating during frosty winters and cooling during humid summers and for sale to Americans south of the border. Northern communities, however, suffered a spike in reproductive abnormalities, cultural alienation from sacred land and other violence and human insecurity. Massive flooding from the development scheme resulted in large-scale mercury contamination of food supplies upon which northern aboriginal communities relied. In response, the James Bay Cree and the Inuit of Northern Québec negotiated a $225 million compensation and recognition package known as the James Bay and Northern Québec Agreement (JBNQA), which has also informed and contributed to structuring aboriginal governance approaches in Nunavik.

## GOVERNANCE AND SECURITY AS ADAPTIVE PRACTICE

Governing does not mean knowing or predicting every eventuality. There are far too many factors to take into consideration in a dynamic world. Governing means learning and developing the capacity for institutionalizing such learning. It entails the cultivation of adaptive practices, accounting for multiple framings and the diversity and frequently asymmetric power of concerned actors. It supports reflexivity, to mean the dynamic reconsideration and reformulation of practices against changing awareness of discursive meaning, force and effect. As a sociopolitical process, adaptivity is supported by management principles that include knowledge construction, information generation, targeted public circulation, public engagement, transparency and evaluation processes. Peace and security prerogatives entail that reflexive practices are institutionalized for the articulation, integration and reconsideration of "success," for fear of totalitarian centralization.

Without exception, water development is rife with actual and potential conflict, given that it is premised on change. Yet, conflict does not necessarily entail escalated violence. Effective water-governance systems are designed to solve conflicts through institutional mechanisms that resolve water disputes through peaceful means, as outlined in the Berlin Rules. Issues for consideration in the construction of such dispute-resolution mechanisms may include clarity of mechanism mandate, agreement on eligible issues, veto power of parties if any, composition of arbitrators, process for filing complaints, and the binding force of decisions. Like all institutions and mechanisms, the efficacy of this dispute-resolution mechanism in ensuring secure and peaceful development is premised on the confidence that relevant actors have in the mechanism.

## CONCLUDING THOUGHTS

The challenges of water governance are many, given that water seeps into so many aspects of biological, economic, technological, productive and political life. In consideration of security and peace as they relate to meaningful, participatory and sustainable water governance, it would seem the principles of grounded equity and adaptivity are trustworthy guides for development, evaluation and reflexivity. In his concluding remarks, Girouard states, "Depending on your place in the world order, hope can be luxury, vision, mirage or a singular thread by which one clings to survival." Water is the source of all life and survival. Thus, water governance and its inherent security is, as Girouard notes, "about those who have the will and the power and the vision, delivering on the hope of those around us in need."

People and communities around the world are politically motivated by their perception of injustice, notably related to human needs from water to security. Their mobilization assumes many forms. Water wisdom proposes that processes be structured into water-governance systems to create opportunities for meaningful engagement and for people to participate in shaping their future. Further, the principle of equity applies inter-generationally in relation to the cultural and eco-political foundations of human diversity.

Discursive and political resistance to the forms of water governance, discussed above, occurs throughout this chapter and book. There is persistent chimerical practice in the field of water governance, proclaiming one thing while developing another and rewarding narrow interests. There are practical obstacles to consider, rooted in ecological diversity and institutional limitations. Fundamentally, in ontological terms, security and peace as total systemic forms simply cannot exist.

Despite such challenges and limitations, the persistence of grounded, meaningful and visionary deliberation is essential, ideationally, institutionally and ultimately politically. One important insight to bear in mind is the awareness that water-governance practices and institutions that claim security and peace are inscribed discursively, at best producing particular forms of security and peace. Thus, whatever values such institutions and practices invoke and claim to advance must be scrutinized on the ground. Nonetheless, the prerogative of equitable water governance remains, so long as critical evaluation and political reflexivity infuse related practices and institutions with confidence and meaningful momentum.

## REVIEW QUESTIONS

1. What are some of the unique challenges of trans-boundary water-resources governance, both in general and in conflict regions?

2. What are the political implications of the recent production of water, in terms of human security and peaceful relations between national communities?

3. Who are the prime beneficiaries of both commercial and rights-based approaches to water management and development?

4. Does multi-sectoral governance favour the secure and sustainable management and development of water resources?

5. How do you understand "adaptive" water governance? Why and how is adaptivity significant in ensuring hydro-political equity and security?

### REFERENCES

Abitbol, Eric. "Developing Water and Marginalising Israel/Palestinian Peace: A Critical Examination of the Red Sea–Dead Sea Canal Feasibility Study Process." *Journal of Peacebuilding and Development* 5, no.1 (2009).

Abitbol, Eric, and Stuart Schoenfeld. "Adaptive Visions of Water in the Middle East: Lessons from a Regional Water Planning Initiative." Toronto, ON: York Centre for International and Security Studies (YCISS) Working Paper No. 50 (February 2009). http://www.yorku.ca/yciss/publish/documents/WP50-AbitbolandSchoenfeld.pdf (1 December 2010).

Adger, W. Neil, Katrina Brown and Emma L. Thompkins. "The Political Economy of Cross-Scale Networks in Resource Co-Management." *Ecology and Society* 10, no. 2 (2006).

Amnesty International. *Troubled Water – Palestinians Denied Fair Access to Water in Israel-Occupied Palestinian Territories*. London, UK: Amnesty International Publications, 2009.

Appadurai, Arjun. "Disjuncture and Difference in the Global Cultural Economy." In *Modernity at Large: Cultural Dimensions of Globalization*, edited by Arjun Appadurai. Minneapolis, MN: University of Minnesota Press, 1996.

Arendt, Hannah, and Jerome Kohn. *The Promise of Politics*. New York, NY: Schocken Books, 2005.

Azar, Edward E. "Protracted International Conflicts: Ten Propositions." In International Conflict Resolution: Theory and Practice, edited by Edward E. Azar and John W. Burton. Brighton, UK: Wheatsheaf, 1986.

Biswas, Asit K. "Integrated Water Resources Management: A Reassessment." *Water International* 29, no. 2 (2004): 248-256.

BRWR Website. *Berlin Rules of Water Resources*. 2004. < http://www.cawater-info. net/library/eng/l/berlin_rules.pdf> (10 November 2010).

Brandes, Oliver M., and David Brooks. May 2006. *The Soft Path for Water in a Nutshell*. Ottawa and Victoria: Friends of the Earth Canada and the Polis Project on Ecological Governance, University of Victoria, BC, November 2005.

Brooks, David, and Sarah Wolfe. "Water Demand Management as Governance: Lessons from the Middle East and South Africa." In *2nd Israeli-Palestinian-International Conference - Water for Life in the Middle East*, edited by Hillel Shuval and Hasan Dwiek. Antalya: IPCRI, 2004.

Buckles, Daniel, and Gerett Rusnak. "Conflict and Collaboration in Natural Resource Management." In *Cultivating Peace*, edited by Daniel Buckles. Ottawa, ON: International Development Research Centre in collaboration with the World Bank Institute/IBRD, 1999.

Burton, John W. *Conflict: Human Needs Theory*. Basingstoke, UK: Macmillan, 1990.

Bush, Kenneth D., and Robert J. Opp. "Peace and Conflict Impact Assessment." In *Cultivating Peace*, edited by Daniel Buckles. Ottawa, ON: International Development Research Centre in collaboration with the World Bank Institute/IBRD, 1999.

Davidson, Debra J., and Scott Frickel. (2004). "Understanding Environmental Governance: A Critical Review." *Organization & Environment* 17, no. 4 (2004): 471-492.

Dharmadhikary, Shripad. *Mountains of Concrete: Dam Building in the Himalayas*. Berkeley, CA: International Rivers, December 2008.

Downie, David Leonard. "Global Environmental Policy: Governance through Regimes." In *The Global Environment: Institutions, Law and Policy*, edited by R. S. Axelrod, David Leonard Downie and Norman J. Vig. Washington, DC: CQ Press, 2005.

Duffield, Mark. "Human Security: Linking Development and Security in an Age of Terror." Paper prepared for the GDI panel: *New Interfaces Between Security and Development*. 11th General Conference of the EADI. Bonn, Germany: EADI, 2005.

Ecomagazine Solar Website. *Solar-powered Desalination Plant Leads The Way.* <http://www.ecosmagazine.com/?act=view_file&file_id=EC134p4.pdf> (11 November 2010).

Escobar, Arturo. "Whose Knowledge, Whose nature? Biodiversity, Conservation, and the Political Ecology of Social Movements." *Journal of Political Ecology* 5 (1998): 53-82.

GLOWA JR Website. *GLOWA Jordan River*. <http://www.glowa.org/eng/jordan_eng/jordan_eng.php> (30 November 2010)

GWP. "A Handbook for Integrated Water Resources Management in Basins." Edited by INBO: *Global Water Partnership and International Network of Basin Organisations* 2009.

Homer-Dixon, Thomas F. *Environment, Scarcity, and Violence*. Princeton, NJ: Princeton University Press, 1999.

Kelly, Kevin. *Out of Control: The New Biology of Machines, Social Systems and the Economic World*. Don Mills, ON: Addison-Wesley Publishing Company, 1995/1994.

Khun, Thomas S. *The Structure of Scientific Revolutions* (3rd ed.). Chicago, IL: University of Chicago Press, 1996/1962.

Kramer, Annika. "Regional Water Cooperation and Peacebuilding in the Middle East." In *Initiative for Peacebuilding Regional Cooperation on Environment, Economy and Natural Resource Management Cluster*, 2008.

Lattemann, Sabine, and Thomas Höpner. "Environmental Impact and Impact Assessment of Seawater Desalination." *Desalination* 220 (2008): 1-15.

Lobina, Emanuele. "Problems with Private Water Concessions: A Review of Experiences and Analysis of Dynamics." *Water Resources Development* 21, no. 1 (2005): 55-87.

Lowi, Miriam R. *Water and Power: The Politics of a Scarce Resource in the Jordan River Basin*. Cambridge, UK: Cambridge University Press, 1993.

Medalye, Jacqueline (Lead Author); Jim Kundell (Topic Editor) "Water Governance." In *Encyclopedia of Earth*, edited by Cutler J. Cleveland (Washington, DC: Environmental Information Coalition, National Council for Science and the Environment). First published in the Encyclopedia of Earth 4 April 2008. <http://www.eoearth.org/article/Water_governance> (1 December 2010).

Mirumachi, Naho, and J. A. Allan. "Revisiting Transboundary Water Governance: Power, Conflict, Cooperation and the Political Economy." In *International Conference on Adaptive and Integrated Water Management.* Basel, Switzerland, 2007.

Murphy, Brian. "Beyond the Politics of the Possible: Corporations and the Pursuit of Social Justice" Paper prepared for the Forum Series: *Corporations as a Factor in Social Justice.* Summer Program of the Institute in Management and Community Development, Concordia University. Montreal, Canada, 2002.

OHCHR Website. <http://www.ohchr.org/en/NewsEvents/Pages/DisplayNews.aspx?NewsID=10240&LangID=E> (30 November 2010).

Prugh, Thomas, and Erik Assadourian. "What Is Sustainability, Anyway?" *World Watch Magazine* (September/October 2003): 9-21.

Rogers, Kevin H. "The Real River Management Challenge: Integrating Scientists, Stakeholders and Service Agencies." *River Research and Applications* 22, no. 2 (2006): 269-280.

Shani, Uri. *Letter Regarding the Amnesty International Report.* Tel Aviv: Israel Water Authority, 3 December 2009.

Shiva, Vandana. *Water Wars: Privatization, Pollution and Profit.* Cambridge, MA: South End Press, 2002.

Trottier, Julie. *Hydropolitics in the West Bank and Gaza Strip.* Jerusalem: PASSIA, 1999.

Trottier, Julie. "A Wall, Water and Power: The Israeli 'Separation Fence.'" *Review of International Studies* 33 (2007): 105-127.

Turton, A. R. "Water Scarcity and Social Adaptive Capacity: Towards an Understanding of the Social Dynamics of Water Demand Management in Developing Countries." In *MEWREW Occasional Paper No. 9,* edited by Water Issues Study Group. London, UK: School of Oriental and African Studies (SOAS), 1999.

Wolf, Aaron T., Annika Kramer, Alexander Carius, and Geoffrey D. Dabelko. "Managing Water Conflict and Cooperation." In *State of the World: Redefining Global Security 2005.* The WorldWatch Institute, 2005.

# INTELLIGENCE:
# THE UNSEEN INSTRUMENT OF GOVERNANCE

## ALAN BREAKSPEAR, BA, ndc

---

## INTRODUCTION

The introductory chapter to this volume offers three statements that constitute a definition of governance:

> "For the purposes of this discussion, governance is the complex and often murky construct of people, organization and rules that exist to run the nation-state."

> "Governance is the means by which State will and power is exercised."

> "Governance is about those who have the will and the power and the vision delivering on the hope of those around us who are in need."[1]

Only in the third of these statements, which appears in the final paragraph of Roger Girouard's opening chapter, does a hint of the forward-looking element of governance (foresight) appear. While I accept and generally endorse Girouard's discussion of governance, I find its inattention to foresight an important omission.

Governance is concerned with helping human society adapt to change. Whatever the form and expression of governance adopted by a nation-state, a corporation, a non-governmental organization, a professional association, a sports club or a debating society, the governance

---

structure must enable the organization to anticipate change in the external environment and thereby take advantage of and draw benefit from opportunities (positive change) or avoid the harmful effects of threats (negative change). The tools required are foresight and insight, formulated through intelligence in both its senses as learning and knowledge, and organizational decision support.

At the nation-state level, intelligence designates the organization that carries out the function, the process or function itself, or the product (the result of the function). This chapter is largely concerned with the process or function called intelligence and it addresses the questions: What is intelligence? What is its purpose? What are the expected and intended effects of intelligence activities?

## DISCUSSION

Dictionaries commonly cover both aspects of intelligence. The online *Oxford Dictionary*, for example, gives the following definitions for intelligence:

- the ability to acquire and apply knowledge and skills: *an eminent man of great intelligence;*
- a person or being with the ability to acquire and apply knowledge and skills: *extraterrestrial intelligences;*
- the collection of information of military or political value: *the chief of military intelligence;*
- people employed in the collection of military or political information: *British intelligence has secured numerous local informers;*
- military or political information: *the gathering of intelligence;*
- *archaic* information in general: news.[2]

The last element is a useful reminder of the old and generalized meaning of intelligence as information or news. The earlier elements juxtapose knowledge and skills against military or political information, which is a simplistic and almost archaic usage in light of the wide range of organizations and activities involved in intelligence work in the 21st century. The point, of course, is that intelligence is widely seen as an ability not only to think and learn but also to apply the learning.

A commonplace in English-language intelligence training manuals, books and articles about intelligence is a representation of the process by which intelligence is prepared as an iterative cycle, involving some five or six main stages: Requirements (or priorities), Collection (sometimes divided into collection plan and collection activity), Processing (or collation), and Analysis and Dissemination. This representation is of necessity simplistic, ignoring the need to move back and forth among these stages as a project unfolds. It is, nonetheless, a useful vehicle for teaching and discussion because of its very simplicity, which provokes discussion and explication.

Given the opportunity, I add labels to the cycle diagram that point to the fact that the first and last stages, Requirements and Dissemination, are a dialogue between those who carry out the intelligence function and the decision-making client, whether individual or group. The closer that dialogue comes to a real conversation, conducted face-to-face and in real time, the greater the likelihood of valuable intelligence being supplied. Too often, intelligence collectors and analysts receive their guidance about target requirements and priorities at several removes from the problems as seen by the decision-makers.

The term *dissemination* contributes to the distancing problem by suggesting that the results of intelligence analysis should always be distributed as widely as possible, consistent with the need to know. In fact, communication to the decision-maker(s) who identified the requirement (and thereby the problem that the intelligence product is intended to solve) is fundamentally more important than wide dissemination. The two must happen, indeed the two are often almost equally important, but communication should generally be regarded as the more important. Effective communication depends upon the presentation of the right content in the right form, at the right place and time. Getting any of these elements wrong may negate the value of the intelligence project.

## COMPETITIVE INTELLIGENCE

The practice of competitive intelligence in business makes the point strongly. In most business organizations, the distance between the decision-maker client of intelligence and the intelligence producers is far less (in terms of bureaucratic steps or levels) than in government. Thinking of Intelligence Requirements and Communication as part of an ongoing dialogue between producers and users is implicit in business but it is rarely seen that way in government, except perhaps at the most senior levels of the intelligence apparatus.

Too many scholars have examined intelligence activities, especially those of government agencies, without looking at the question of what intelligence is. What does it include or omit? How is it formulated and carried out? How should its effectiveness be judged and evaluated? Some have simply assumed that intelligence is what intelligence agencies do. This begs the question and downplays the appearance of intelligence activities in other domains besides government.

Business corporations, both large and small, became active users of intelligence in the last third of the 20th century, using the terms Competitive Intelligence and Business Intelligence. The second of these, Business Intelligence, has become associated with automated data processing. As used by software vendors in particular, it refers to the systematic processing of files and data banks available in a company and/or in its market segment (concerning sales, customer activities, production records, etc.) to produce indicators of company health and market strengths, for example.

The term *Competitive Intelligence* was adopted and championed by the Society of Competitive Intelligence Professionals (SCIP), which recently renamed itself Strategic and Competitive Intelligence Professionals. The term is representative of a substantive and professional intelligence discipline meriting serious consideration alongside the longer established intelligence disciplines practised in government. Many of the most successful practitioners of Competitive Intelligence learned their craft as intelligence analysts and/or collection managers in government,[3] but intelligence agencies in government rarely show interest in learning from the practice of Competitive Intelligence. As intimated earlier, intelligence scholars rarely do more than note the existence of Competitive Intelligence, while those who take a clinical and critical interest in Competitive Intelligence[4] find many points of interest that should constitute lessons worth considering in government practice.

(Within the competitive intelligence community, the term is often abbreviated to CI, but I hesitate to use the abbreviation here because it is too easily misread as counter-intelligence, or communications intelligence, or confidential informant, or any of a number of other terms in disciplines beyond intelligence – critical infrastructure, or community of interest, or counter-insurgency.)

## THE INTELLIGENCE COMMUNITY

The US intelligence community is the world's largest, with the biggest budget and the most widespread collection net. It is the community about which more is publicly known than any other and, therefore, the one to which others are most often compared. This does not mean that all others are similar to that of the USA. In recent years, scholars have begun to understand that the members of the important intelligence alliance that emerged from World War II now known familiarly as the Five Eyes (US, UK, Canada, Australia, NZ) in fact manage their intelligence activities more differently from one another than was previously assumed. Those differences deserve closer scholarly examination.

One aspect of US intelligence practice and policy has been pervasive and has long influenced public and media assumptions about intelligence in much of the English-speaking world. That aspect is the inclusion of covert action and counter-intelligence in the meaning of "intelligence." The author of one of the few books that come close to being a comprehensive and accessible standard text for teaching intelligence studies at the secondary and post-secondary level, Mark Lowenthal, states plainly, "Intelligence can be divided into four broad activities: collection, analysis, covert action and counter-intelligence."[5]

This unnecessary and confusing approach to the definition of intelligence influences the approach of US scholars to the issue of intelligence theory and serves as a useful marker in considering the intended purpose of intelligence.

Michael Warner's article, "Wanted: A Definition of 'Intelligence,'"[6] is a valuable and important contribution to intelligence theory. As he says, "Without a clear idea of what intelligence is, how can we develop a theory to explain how it works?"[7]

Warner's discussion focuses exclusively on government intelligence. His selection of definitions emphasizes the foreign targeting of intelligence, omitting the domestic security and business versions of intelligence. He suggests that secrecy is a "constitutive" element of intelligence, and he wholly endorses the assumption that intelligence includes covert action and counter-intelligence. His suggestion for the much-needed new definition of intelligence is: "Intelligence is secret state activity to understand or influence foreign entities."

As noted elsewhere in this chapter, secrecy is frequently attached to intelligence but should not, in my view, be considered a defining element. Intelligence is conducted by other actors besides the state. Influencing is the job of the policy-makers who are the clients and recipients of intelligence. It should not be the job of the intelligence agencies except in very special circumstances, by exception and under separate direction.

This might leave us, for now, with "Intelligence is an organizational activity to understand other entities." We will come back to this.

A British practitioner and scholar of intelligence, Michael Herman, wrote two books on intelligence, which, like Lowenthal's, come close to being a standard intelligence text.[8] He has also made available invaluable musings on the nature of intelligence, paraphrased here as:

> "Intelligence means knowing the target. Intelligence collects information about the target and develops expert knowledge about the target, using evidence from all sources."

> "Intelligence is about knowledge, and also about forecasting.... It must reach its clients in useable forms and in time. The key question is what use they make of it, which is rarely easy to establish."[9]

## THE DEVELOPING DEFINITION

Now we have three elements to add to our developing definition: forecasting target activities, timeliness of receipt and action by the recipient. In public discussion of intelligence, usually addressing it as an activity of the national government, too much is made of secrecy. Secrecy is not a necessary and defining characteristic of intelligence but rather attaches frequently to intelligence for one or both of the following reasons. One is the need to protect the source or means by which intelligence is collected or derived from collected information. The other is the need to avoid premature revelation of a decision taken on the basis of (or assisted by) the intelligence produced. Both reasons are transient, though the former can and often does lead to ongoing classification of intelligence records that lasts for decades.

## OPEN-SOURCE INTELLIGENCE

The value of open-source intelligence (OSINT) has long been recognized in the intelligence community and more recently in public and media discussion. Competitive Intelligence, almost by definition, relies heavily if not completely on OSINT and demonstrates that secret sources, processes and techniques are not a determinant of intelligence. Secrecy often attaches to the competitive intelligence findings that support a strategic business decision to maintain competitive surprise and advantage, but that secrecy is clearly recognizable as an attribute of the decision rather than of the intelligence that supported it.

## PROPOSAL

This chapter argues for understanding intelligence in modern governance as decision support. In this context, governance is inclusive of security; governance and security are a unitary concept, not separate entities. It goes further, suggesting that the decision support nature of intelligence will be better understood if a standard definition of intelligence were widely adopted. In its analysis thus far, the chapter has assembled a sequence of increasingly focused definitions of intelligence, which might be represented at this point as:

> Intelligence is conducted by governmental and other agencies as a means of better understanding other entities whose plans or activities might affect their interests, in order to better understand those entities and to forecast their actions in a timely manner, in support of decisions to be taken by those who receive the intelligence.

A 2007 publication from the US Joint Chiefs of Staff presents "fundamental principles and guidance for intelligence support to joint operations." The document provides an overview of the various intelligence-related disciplines from imagery to interrogation, and their employment in support of military operations. The document includes the following definition, which parallels the emerging definition pursued here:

> Intelligence allows anticipation or prediction of future situations and circumstances, and it informs decisions by illuminating the differences in available courses of action (COAs).[10]

These definitions remain less than satisfactory in their failure to generalize the kind of actions or situations that might be anticipated. The Joint Chiefs document talks of prediction, a slippery concept that risks derision rather than respect. Forecasting is more honest and pragmatic. It reflects an attempt to point at probability and to identify signs that can be watched for, which might give closer warning of the change at hand.

The proposed definition must provide for universality. Intelligence is not only an activity that might be done without secrecy, but it can also be undertaken by organizations in a wide range of sectors. These sectors include all levels of government, business and not-for-profit activities of all kinds. Any organization whose interests might be affected by external developments should arguably attempt to anticipate such developments and have plans ready to deal with them. That is, they should all conduct intelligence.

## A NEW DEFINITION

The following new definition is proposed:

> Intelligence is a corporate capability to forecast change in time to do something about it. The capability involves foresight and insight, and is intended to identify impending change that may be positive, representing opportunity, or negative, representing threat.

## BENEFITS

If and when this proposal is widely adopted, even as one element in an organization's definition of intelligence, it will permit clearer communication among intelligence practitioners, more effective audit and evaluation of intelligence functions in business and government, and better understanding of intelligence by the academics, media and the public. It will facilitate consistency of language, better communication among the clients (decision-makers), collectors, analysts, and managers of intelligence. It will also improve understanding among intelligence agencies, practitioners, educators, scholars, critics, members of the media and the public.

By pointing to the intended effects of the intelligence function, this definition will encourage effective audit and evaluation. It will assist intelligence managers and practitioners by concentrating on the importance of the requirements conversation. This conversation is the need to convey through successive layers of bureaucracy the nature of the policy problem for which intelligence is needed. It will lend emphasis and cogency to the need for intelligence findings to be communicated quickly to decision makers and then widely disseminated.

A definition applicable to intelligence is conducted in all sectors and spheres; therefore, the proposal will open the way to an appreciation of the lessons to be learned by intelligence practitioners, and managers and scholars across disciplines and sectors. It will include, for example, the lessons about collection management and opportunities as well as threats from Competitive Intelligence to Government Intelligence, the analytic techniques used in scientific foresight and medical research, and how these should be applied in criminal, military, foreign and economic intelligence; and so on.

The proposed definition should not be seen as sufficient in all settings. Those nations, notably the USA, that include actions taken to change or influence the target environment (such as counter-intelligence and covert operations) in the concept and definition of intelligence, will have the option of adopting the proposed definition as part of their national definition, and still gain the benefits foreseen here.

The proposed definition offers a means to clarify the support provided to decision-makers by the intelligence function and to separate intelligence from the action decisions made by its users and clients. Girouard asserts:

> We must differentiate between the aim, the implementation and the result. In the real world, all three are intertwined to be sure, guided and constrained by the checks and balances that are themselves a vital facet of the reality of governance.

Intelligence collection and analysis is increasingly carried out by non-human means (e.g., Unmanned Airborne Systems - UAS). The UAS carry in them the capability to exercise force (weapons systems carried in UAS alongside intelligence collection systems). Decision responsibility for action based on intelligence findings is separated from intelligence analysis by increasingly finer lines.

## REVIEW QUESTIONS

1. Intelligence analysts have sometimes been accused of politicizing their analysis, that is, of tailoring their findings to fit a conclusion apparently favoured by their decision-making client. How can this be avoided?

2. How important is it that intelligence analysts avoid suggesting or recommending a course of action to decision-makers?

3. What special risks attach to intelligence practice where it is defined as including the role of "influencing" a target's action plans, and therefore as including covert action and counter-intelligence?

What kinds of measures should be taken in the management and governance of intelligence to limit these risks?

4.  One of the undeveloped ideas underlying this chapter is that intelligence is increasingly practised in a range of sectors and disciplines, often under other names or terms. Identify some examples.

## REFERENCES

Oxford Dictionary. "Intelligence." <http://oxforddictionaries.com/definition/intelligence> (30 July 2011).

Lowenthal, M. M. Intelligence from Secrets to Policy (3rd ed.). Washington, CD: CQ Press, 2011.

Warner, M. "Wanted: A Definition of Intelligence: Understanding Our Craft." Central Intelligence Agency. Studies in Intelligence 46 no. 3 (2002) <http://www.cia.gov/csi/studies/vol46no3/article02.html (14 April 2007).

Warner, M. "Intelligence as Risk Shifting." In *Intelligence Theory: Key Questions and Debates*, edited by P. Gill, S. Marrin, and M. Phythian. Oxford, UK: Routledge, 2009.

Herman, M. *Intelligence Services in the Information Age*. Oxford & NYC: Frank Cass, 2001.

Herman, M. *Intelligence Power in Peace and War*. Cambridge University Press, 1996.

Herman, M. *Why Does Military Intelligence Matter?* Changing Character of War seminar, Oxford, 27 November 2007. <http://www.nuffield.ox.ac.uk/OIG2/herman%20paper%202007.pdf > (1 August 2011).

"Joint Intelligence." Joint Publication 2-0 (22 June 2007): ix. http://www.fas.org/irp/doddir/dod/jp2_0.pdf (13 August 2011).

## ENDNOTES

[1]   Roger Girouard, *On Governance and Security*. Feature essay.

[2]   Definition of Intelligence. <http://oxforddictionaries.com/definition/intelligence> (30 July 2011).

[3]   Prime examples are Jan Herring, who was recruited from CIA to set up Motorola's competitive intelligence function and Ben Gilad, who was introduced to intelligence in the Israeli military.

4    In the Competitive Intelligence community the term is often abbreviated to CI, but I hesitate to use the abbreviation here because it is too easily misread as counter-intelligence, or communications intelligence, or confidential informant, or any of a number of other terms in disciplines beyond intelligence – critical infrastructure, or community of interest, or counterinsurgency, etc.)

5    Mark M. Lowenthal. *Intelligence from Secrets to Policy*, 3rd ed. Washington, DC: CQ Press, 2011.

6    *Studies in Intelligence*, 46, No. 3, (2002). <http://www.cia.gov/csi/studies/vol46no3/article02.html>

7    Warner has provided further valuable discussion of the nature of intelligence in his chapter, "Intelligence as Risk Shifting," in *Intelligence Theory; Key Questions and Debates,* edited by P. Gill, S. Marrin, and M. Phythian. Oxford, UK: Routledge, 2009.

8    Michael Herman, *Intelligence Services in the Information Age*. Oxford & NYC: Frank Cass Publishers, 2001; and *Intelligence Power in Peace and War*, Cambridge University Press, 1996.

9    Oxford, Changing Character of War seminar, Oxford. 27 Nov 2007. *Why Does Military Intelligence Matter? Michael Herman.* <http://www.nuffield.ox.ac.uk/OIG2/herman%20paper%202007.pdf > (1 August 2011).

10   "Joint Intelligence," *Joint Publication* 2-0 (22 June 2007): ix. <http://www.fas.org/irp/doddir/dod/jp2_0.pdf> (13 August 2011).

# POLICING AND GOVERNANCE

## LES CHIPPERFIELD, BBA

## INTRODUCTION

Governance is all around us. While we normally associate the terminology with government institutions and business, it is literally everywhere. Families have their own governance structures. Service clubs, sports teams, religious groups and even friendships have rules. At differing levels, every society will have some sort of regulation. Whether popular or not, rules give some level of stability to their constituents. As noted by Girouard in his introductory chapter, "Governance is the crucible for choices, for good or ill, which touch virtually every part of our daily lives."

In any society constructed on models of good governance, the police are generally called on to ensure public rules are followed, thereby providing a level of public security. This is the essence of governance and security as a unitary concept. Commensurate with these models, structures are also in place to ensure the public police adhere to their own rules and regulations. How did the police force evolve in Canada and how is it governed? How has it become a model for emerging nation-states and for nation-states that have failed and look to the international community for guidance?

With most media networks looking for news to deliver 24/7 coupled with consumers' interest in staying abreast of current trends, police behaviour is often seen as interesting and perhaps slightly inflammatory. The police are the natural target of a protesting population. Due to the fact that they are constantly interacting with the public, for better or worse, the media seizes on particular interactions and generates news releases that they believe are of interest to consumers. In many instances, media reporting elicits a quick public response. The constant media and public interaction ensures that a story will live as long as it is meeting media expectations. When the next newsworthy event occurs, the media moves on.

In our electronic world, anyone with a cell phone has the ability to report on virtually anything they see. Images can be loaded onto Facebook, Twitter, MySpace, YouTube and various other social networking media sites in seconds, becoming immediately viral worldwide. This was evident with the death of Robert Dziekanski and the YouTube video taken by Gerry Rundle with his cell phone.[1] It was evident during the recent G20 meetings in Toronto and the numerous YouTube videos that were viewed around the world.[2] From the mass of information, the public can make instant judgments with limited information thus becoming *de facto* judge and jury. In many instances, media reporting and social networking information generate calls for more oversight of the police and demands for restrictions on what the police can and cannot do.

## THE POLICING ENVIRONMENT IN TRANSITION

Globally, the policing environment is in a constant state of flux. In the last 20 years, the police universe has been shifting from the command-and-control model to a mixture of contracting and networking.[3] The police force is increasingly contracting out services. In order to operate effectively, it is imperative that they develop and maintain networks in the public and private policing universes. This shift affects the relationship between communities and the police, with the police being situated between the public and the state, attempting to meet the interests of both.[4]

While many have an opinion about the police force and their powers, citizens rarely come into contact with the police. Other than public initiatives, the police deal mainly with crisis events and human issues. Something bad is occurring, has occurred or is about to occur for the police to be involved. Murray and Alvaro note:

They can be called on to do practically anything – and at any time of the day or night. They are the generalist social interveners who are constantly nudging society back onto the tracks of civility, order and safety. It is an essential role that no other group in society can fulfil.[5]

Adding to the complexity are the three levels of policing in Canada: municipal, provincial and federal. As an adjunct to the "real police," other organizations have various quasi-police or enforcement powers under municipal, provincial or federal legislation. There are various forms and levels of oversight or governance ascribed to those with enforcement powers, some being more stringent than others.[6]

## GOVERNANCE OF POLICING IN DOMESTIC OPERATIONS

Governance, in this milieu, is complex. As Girouard says, "[It is often] a murky construct of people, organizations and rules that exist to run the nation-state." Addressing governance requires an examination of internal professional management. Police unions and associations must be included because they affect the day-to-day operations and internal governance of any police department. Externally elected or volunteer governance through municipal councils and police boards must also be considered. Those involved in police governance must walk a fine line between oversight and involvement in actual police operations. "To be effective, police need to be independent when investigating crime and disorder; however, the police are unequivocally accountable for their actions at any level to the community."[7] From a governance perspective, oversight individuals or committees can give direction on what they want the police to do but they cannot direct the chief of police on how the task is to be accomplished. This would constitute an infringement on the right of the chief to conduct operations. In effect, the external governing body can task a chief of police with expected outcomes but they cannot direct the accomplishment of the outcomes. This concept appears to be understood by both sides, with minor disagreements from time to time.[8]

## GOVERNANCE OF POLICING
## IN PEACEKEEPING OPERATIONS

Canadian police have been involved in peacekeeping operations for over 40 years in Africa, the Balkan States, Haiti and Afghanistan, among others. Working in these environments with military and police officers from other nation-states brings many challenges. Not only are the training standards and operational policies different from country to country but the governance requirements may be widely different as well.[9]

## PARAMETERS OF THE CHAPTER

This chapter is not an exhaustive review of any of the foregoing elements. It will, however, provide sufficient information to provoke further research and examination. It will describe the foundational elements of policing in Canada and how it has developed, with minimal comparison to our neighbour to the south. Governance will be examined from internal and external perspectives followed by an assessment of the current and future directions for international policing.

## A BRIEF HISTORY OF POLICING – A BRITISH MODEL

Policing involves many diverse and interesting areas. In order to branch out and investigate the various tendrils of the profession, we must first establish a base of understanding by asking some questions. Where did our current policing system come from? How it is generally organized in our country? How it is governed?

Sir Robert Peel is generally recognized as the father of community policing, establishing the Metropolitan Police Force in London in 1829, the basis of our current system. In fact, he was responsible for two divergent models of policing. The Canadian system developed through rule of law and central control while the American system was politically based and controlled, at least initially, with senior police administrators being political appointees.[10] Both countries have evolved to more professional policing models but the election of sheriffs in the United States remains political.

From the beginning of American policing, the debate continues about who should oversee the police and enforce Peel's principles. At the outset, police appointments were political, with the New York police being controlled by the chief, the mayor and a city judge.[11] Policing in the United States has grown through various governance iterations to a current model that has greater citizen control over the police in their respective communities. "In order to take policing out of politics, the power to hire and fire the chief was given in whole or in part to the group of good citizens serving on police commissions."[12] Although Peel's model was the basis of policing in the United States, therefore, they were selective as to which parts they implemented. Irrespective of the developmental differences, it can generally be said that policing in both countries has evolved to a more professional model. In much of the world and certainly in Canada, the police are supported primarily through public funding. It is then incumbent on the chief to expend his financial resources in serving and protecting that same public who fund the police through their tax dollars. That is why it is essential, from an accountability perspective, for the chief of police to respond to the community, through a governance structure, informing them about financial resource allocations and accomplishments, as Walker mentioned in 1942.[13] While Walker's text was written seventy years ago, the premise remains as relevant to accountability and governance today as it was then.

A system of policing has been in place in England for hundreds of years, with the king and his officials being at the apex of the conservators of the peace. In AD 920, King Edward appointed the shire reeve (sheriff) as the earliest public official charged with keeping the peace. The roots of Canadian policing go back to the 1200s. At his time, constables were either members of local militias or had recently left the militia. In the early stages they were referred to as constables, a term derived from the military of the day. These early police officers had many duties and were responsible for maintaining relations between their community and other communities in the immediate vicinity. They were seen as "Conservators of the Peace," a term which continues in use today.[14] The position of village constable continued to evolve until the Industrial Revolution, 1750-1800s. During this period of social change, considerable pressure came to bear on government for some sort of established police presence.[15] By 1828, there were approximately 4,500 watchmen in London. They covered the metropolitan area and some local parishes. In addition, there were Bow Street patrols and some 450 Thames River Police. The cost of providing these services was 250,000 pounds, a large sum in those days and in fact the cost was the driving factor in moving to an integrated system of policing with the Metropolitan Police Act of 1829.[16]

While there is considerable information about the duties of the village constables, the enactment of Peel's legislation and the creation of the police force overshadowed the historical view of the community constable.[17] People were concerned about the powers of this new force and how its members might overstep their role. Another concern was that the police might resort to excessive force without some level of accountability. "Thus, the legislation introduced by Peel in 1829 was a compromise that strictly separated the job of the police from that of the judiciary, and narrowed the role of the police largely to the prevention and detection of crime."[18] Peel formulated a set of principles that made it clear that the police were to be accountable to the wider public of which they were a part.

The first police in London were called Bobbies while in Ireland they were called Peelers. As Sir Robert Peel, then Home Secretary, had been instrumental in having the legislation brought forward, these nicknames seemed fitting. Peel had developed a number of principles that were the foundation of policing in England and Ireland; they are still taught in all police academies in Canada today.[19]

THE PRINCIPLES OF SIR ROBERT PEEL

1. The basic mission of the police is to prevent crime and disorder.
2. The ability of the police to perform their duties depends on public approval of their actions.
3. The police must secure the cooperation of the public in voluntary

observance of the law in order to secure and maintain the respect of the public.

4. The degree of public cooperation with the police diminishes proportionately to the necessity of the use of physical force.

5. Police maintain public favour by constantly demonstrating absolutely impartial service, not by catering to public opinion.

6. Police should use physical force only to the extent necessary to ensure compliance with the law or to restore order only after persuasion, advice, and warning are insufficient.

7. Police should maintain a relationship with the public that is based on the fact that the police are the public and the public are the police.

8. Police should direct their actions toward their functions and not appear to usurp the powers of the judiciary.

9. The test of police efficiency is the absence of crime and disorder, and not the visible evidence of police action in dealing with them.

## CANADIAN MODEL OF POLICING

Both police academies and police executives across Canada still espouse Peel's principles as the core elements of the current service delivery model. While still in effect, the model has evolved differently in communities across Canada. The delivery of any community-based policing model is somewhat dependent on the complexities of each community. In general, Peel's points were meant to provide a context for the social interactions and behaviour of the public and the police. In general terms, in the United Kingdom, Ireland and Canada, a level of mutual respect exists between the public and the police.[20]

Early policing in Canada varied from area to area depending on population and ethnic mix. In regions that were primarily French, the traditional French system of captains of militia prevailed. In traditionally English areas, the policing system was based on common law with sheriffs, high constables, constables and justices of the peace.[21]

Canadian cities began to increase in size during the 1800s. With confederation, the responsibility for policing became part of the exclusive powers of the provinces.[22] In 1868, the federal government established a small police force called the Dominion Police. This force was initially organized to protect parliamentarians and government buildings following the assassination of Thomas D'Arcy McGee (one of the Fathers of Confederation and a Member of Parliament) in that year. That force continued to expand into other jurisdictions such as protecting the naval dockyards, operating the national fingerprint bureau, and coordinating the efforts of other police agencies during the First World War. The Dominion Police were absorbed into the Royal Canadian Mounted Police in 1920.[23]

As provinces and municipalities moved to incorporate some level of policing, the federal government established a central police force, which was given the name North West Mounted Police. This force was established to deal with whisky traders operating among the aboriginal people, primarily in Saskatchewan and Alberta. In May 1873, the first 150 officers were sent west to Manitoba; in July 1874, the now 275 mounted officers established permanent posts in southern Alberta and Saskatchewan. The force was almost disbanded in 1896 but with gold being discovered in the Yukon, it remained in existence, primarily to deal with the lawlessness that had erupted. The force entered into contractual arrangements with the provincial governments of Saskatchewan and Alberta from 1905 to 1916. These contracts were reinstituted in later years. Other provinces also entered into policing contracts so that by 1950 all provinces and territories with the exception of Quebec and Ontario were under contract. Today the force provides municipal police services to many municipalities under contract.[24]

The Parliament of Upper Canada at Niagara on the Lake made provision for the founding of a policing service in 1792. Initially, policing jurisdictions were limited to districts, townships and parishes. Policing in Ontario generally paralleled growth and development in the province. In 1877, the Constables Act extended jurisdiction throughout the province for designated officers. With the discovery of silver in northern Ontario, the Ontario Provincial Police was established as a province-wide entity. This initiative mirrored the expansion of the Royal Canadian Mounted

Police into the north during the gold rush as a response to lawlessness.[25] While the Royal Canadian Mounted Police and the Ontario Provincial Police had been delivering policing services in their respective jurisdictions, their futures were secured as a result of the discoveries of gold and silver. Québec, however, evolved in a different manner. In 1838, municipal forces were established for Montréal and Québec. A provincial force, the Québec Provincial Police was established for the rest of the province. It is interesting that rather than take an evolutionary approach by establishing a province-wide force in stages, the government of Quebec first chose to establish the provincial police. The name of the force was changed in 1968 to the Sûreté du Québec.[26]

Both provincial forces and the RCMP have contracts with municipalities of varying sizes depending on the provincial or federal legislation. Also of note is the fact that all three forces have a central control. While they provide services to provinces and municipalities, the officers delivering the service are ultimately responsible to a hierarchical structure outside their area of jurisdiction.

This central control has resulted in considerable governance unrest in some municipalities, much of which has nothing to do with the actual service delivery. In most cases, salaries, computer networks and other large-scale financial issues are negotiated with minimal if any input from the contracted municipality and, in some cases, provinces. These forces interact with the provincial and municipal authorities but local governance is not an issue with them. It should be noted that salary, one of the largest components of any policing budget, remains by statute the sole responsibility of the provincial government for the Ontario Provincial Police and the Sûreté du Québec, and of the federal Treasury Board for the Royal Canadian Mounted Police.

The police deliver primary services to the public but are ultimately responsible to a central authority. The Ontario Police Act is quite specific in requiring police boards to be in place. The board may deal only with local issues "but the board or joint board shall not establish provincial policies of the Ontario Provincial Police with respect to police services."[27] In essence, the commissioner may establish policies that conflict with those of a local area. The local policies are secondary to the provincial policies and are in effect nullified. In the past, the courts have been very clear that the RCMP do not fall under provincial police acts because they have their own act. It is for this reason that the RCMP has an external public complaints process whose mandate is to:

- Receive complaints from the public about the conduct of RCMP members;
- Conduct reviews when complainants are not satisfied with the RCMP's handling of their complaints;
- Hold hearings and carry out investigations; and
- Report findings and make recommendations.[28]

It is noteworthy that although the Public Complaints Commission has significant powers, in the end the chair can make only recommendations. The commissioner of the RCMP can choose to follow the recommendations or reject them. Governance is not easy to define for a large national organization with federal, provincial and municipal responsibilities.

## THE COMPLEXITY OF GOVERNANCE, OVERSIGHT AND ACCOUNTABILITY

The situation is similar if somewhat less complex for both the Ontario Provincial Police and the Sûreté du Québec. Issues that must be managed by individual municipalities with their own police force will be similar although exacerbated by the complexity and size of the one federal and two provincial organizations. As these large organizations are not the norm in Canada, a separate examination of their governance issues would be required.

McKenna suggests, "The effectiveness of any system of policing will hinge on the capacity of that system to have in place mechanisms or processes that ensure there is accountability for the delivery of this service."[29] What are governance, oversight or accountability mechanisms and how do they work in the general municipal policing universe? As in Peel's Principles, the police must work with the public to ensure continual approval. The community and the police are inextricably linked through governance, which is the bridge between community and the police.[30]

## THE PROFESSIONAL MODEL

The two primary public models are: first, a direct professional relationship through the city manager and, second, an elected or appointed relationship through a police services board or police commission. The direct governance approach emanates from the publicly elected mayor and council through the city manager. The city manager, a civic official, interacts directly with the chief of police on behalf of the mayor and council and their constituents, the community.[31] This is a professional-to-professional interaction that presumes that both individuals will be competent, well informed and have a thorough understanding of their respective areas of responsibility. This arrangement requires open and honest two-way exchanges of information between both professionals. Lynch notes:

> The police chief must understand the city manager's point of view – that is, what the city manager may expect from the police chief, what the city manager may expect from the council or commission, and finally what the commission or council usually expect from their city manager.[32]

The term "commission" can be equated with the police board because they function similarly. It is evident that there must be a good working relationship and trust between the city manager and the chief of police. They are both responsible for the entire city, albeit from different perspectives. It is important that they complement each other for the sake of community.

## THE POLICE COMMISSION OR POLICE BOARD MODEL

While the professional model[33] exists in many areas, the predominant choice is the police commission or police board. Boards or commissions are monitored to some extent in all provinces to ensure they are discharging their responsibilities properly and that their decision-making processes are sound. Murray explains: "While boards are monitored by the provincial authority, they are not subjected to the sort of scrutiny and accountability for their performance and decisions that police executives are."[34] There are a number of variations of this entity but it generally exists as the conduit between municipal government and the chief of police.

Everything about this relationship has to do with the exercise of power. Carter and Radelet point out, appropriately, that politics and administration are inseparable, just as power and politics are. Whether it be with a city administrator, a police commission or a police board, the chief's relationship requires skill in the exercise of the power and authority ascribed to the position. Chiefs must understand the needs of the public, city council, the police board, the police department and, within the department, the police union. Chiefs must be excellent communicators and strategists especially when moving into new areas.

Policing is no different from any organization faced with challenges. Not every innovative solution will work. In the corporate world, most failures are part of normal research and development. In the police world, however, failures become food for the media and bring criticism on the chief and sometimes the department. It takes a strong, knowledgeable person to lead any police organization.[35]

It is a time of increasing pressure on municipal budgets as the cost of policing services continues to rise. The Federation of Canadian Municipalities views increasing municipal cost being the "result of offloading by other orders of government."[36] It is generally recognized that policing falls within the provincial jurisdiction; nevertheless, the majority of police officers deliver their services to municipalities. The service is expensive and accounts for a major portion of any municipal budget. Although the debate on funding continues between the three levels of government, it is germane to this discussion to point out that policing is expensive. Police boards feel municipal budgetary concerns when interacting with the police chief, trying to balance community concerns and police department requirements against the municipal fiscal reality.

## CONTRACTING POLICE SERVICES
## TO PRIVATE ORGANIZATIONS

A new development for police executives and overseers is the contracting out of police services. Contracting to private organizations is becoming more prevalent and is being seen as a possible source of revenue for the department and, in some instances, for the municipality. In general, off-duty officers are contracted to provide police services at private events or for businesses. They wear their uniforms, use police vehicles and are completely indistinguishable from their on-duty compatriots. In addition, services such as alarm monitoring are becoming an area of revenue generation.[37] It is expected that this issue will see greater debate because contracting issues affect the normal delivery of police services.

## THE ROLE OF POLICE UNIONS

For many years, police unions and associations have concentrated their efforts on pay, benefits and working conditions. More recently, they are taking a much broader view of their responsibilities, not only to their members but to the community as well. "They are coming to regard themselves as a third element, together with the police chief and the police governing body in the decision-making and management of policing."[38] In the recent past, most union management issues have centred on wage increases. To show displeasure with results or inaction, the union may carry out a job action by failing to give traffic tickets and thus penalizing the municipality through revenue loss. Canadian police unions or associations have generally not been militant but that is changing. According to DeLord, Burpo, Shannon and Spearing, police unions in the United States have a long history of action. In fact, they have developed a tool they refer to as the Four Pillars of a Powerful Union – organizational power, political action, media involvement and confrontation.[39]

It is apparent that police unions in the United States have a basis for ensuring their goals are achieved. Canadian police agencies do not have a history of high levels of militant behaviour but this is changing.

Canadian police unions and associations have been taking advice from their counterparts in the United States.[40] As reported by Lafleche and Stepan:

> At the extreme is the Toronto Police Association, which has challenged the police chief on disciplinary matters, planned to endorse political candidates who supported their views on policing, hired private investigators to ensure the facts come out when police officers are accused of wrong-doing, and solicited funds from members of the public to support their efforts.[41]

In some provinces and municipalities, financial support for the police union is rewarded with a small decal that you can put inside your windshield. The perception by the public is that the visible evidence of support for the union might mitigate some future circumstance in which they may find themselves. While not encouraged by municipal officials, the police board or police management, the practice continues.

Police unions have learned how to use the media to best advantage. "For the most part, police executives are not practised managers of media relations."[42] In recent years, media-relations courses have been offered for senior police executives and they are improving but there is still a long way to go. It is essential for police executives to understand the media and how to deal with them. The media play a role in governance because they can pick and choose stories to use. In addition, they can keep the stories alive as long as they appear popular. The recent G20 Summit in Toronto is a good example of all sides making points through the media and keeping the issues in the forefront of the news.

As can be seen, the police, on a regular basis, try to show footage that backs up their actions and the stance they have taken. The advocates for an external review of police actions will have a press conference and expound their side of the issue. As an example, shortly after the G20 Summit, the Toronto chief of police stated that he was "offering no apologies for police tactics during the G20 Summit, including a controversial incident that saw hundreds detained at a downtown intersection in the soaking rain Sunday night."[43] The police then moved quickly into an investigative mode with all media interaction being directed to the investigation and away from any contentious issues that arose from the summit. To ensure the focus remained on the investigation, only the primary investigators appeared in the media on a regular basis and provided information or responded to questions about the investigation.

All levels of government appear to have distanced themselves from this media event with the hope that it will fade with time. In referring to the provincial government, the *Globe and Mail*'s Adam Radwanski states, "The message to police is clear – the current government couldn't care less how they do their jobs, even if they're doing them wrong."[44] Although the media are not a primary entity with respect to police governance, they are certainly in a position of influence. Over time, media coverage influences changes in public perception and in relationships between the police, the community and those involved in oversight.

## INTERNATIONAL POLICING INITIATIVES

Another area that is becoming more commonplace in the policing universe is the requirement for international policing initiatives. In fact, civilian police officers have been operating internationally since 1960 when they were first introduced in the Congo.[45] The Royal Canadian Mounted Police have been involved in international peacekeeping since 1989 when 100 officers were deployed to Namibia to help oversee country-wide elections.[46]

Other Canadian police officers have been involved with a number of United Nations initiatives but it was not until the Royal Canadian Mounted Police developed a position paper in 1993 that centralized control became solidified.[47]

> International policing is an essential part of post-conflict reconstruction and peace building and plays a crucial role in establishing stability in post-conflict societies. Irrespective of the breadth of the mandate, a successful police operation is necessary to ensure long-term peace in the mission country since the policing forces oversee the development of the public security forces – which often determines whether there will be peace or the resumption of conflict.[48]

Mobekk points out the five challenges to police operations: (a) the handling of the security gap, (b) the training and reforming of local police forces, (c) judicial reform, (d) penal reform, and (e) local justice issues and mechanisms. Much has been reported in the media about Canadian involvement in Afghanistan and our continuing efforts in all the areas Mobekk mentions in his report. In order to meet United Nations' expectations and apply international peacekeeping efforts in a constructive manner, the federal government approved a Canadian Police Arrangement in 1997 with revisions in 2006. This arrangement is the basic framework within which the partner organizations function. They include the Department of Foreign Affairs, the Canadian International Development Agency, Public Safety Canada and the Royal Canadian Mounted Police.[49]

In addition, because our military are usually involved in peacekeeping initiatives, the partners must interact with officials from the Department of National Defence. With US General David Petraeus as commander of military forces in Afghanistan, liaison took place with the government of the United States. For the Canadian government to determine whether our officers should be involved in an international policing mission, an analysis must take place to ascertain whether or not Canadian police officers should be involved in a United Nations' initiative. This process starts with the Department of Foreign Affairs and is measured against 12 factors:

1. *Canadian foreign policy interest:* What foreign and policy development interest would be served by Canadian participation in a mission?

2. *Official request:* Has an official request for civilian police been issued by a multicultural organization? The organization must have a mandate from its member states for regional and national security activities, or be in support of other international police operations as agreed to by the three signatory ministers.

3. *Authority:* Is the lead organization competent to support the operation? Is there clear and efficient division of responsibilities between civilian and military resources and are there agreed operating procedures?

4. *Mandate:* Does the mission have a clear and achievable mandate?

5. *Purpose:* What is the purpose of the civilian policing element within the mission? Is the mission likely to serve the cause of peace and lead to a political settlement and peace building in the long term?

6. *Agreement of the parties:* Have the principal antagonists agreed to a cease-fire and to Canada's participation? Is there commitment to a peace process?

7. *Role:* Is the role contemplated for Canadian police appropriate for their skills and the philosophy of Canadian policing?

8. *Expected results:* What are the expected results in furthering Canada's international peace and security objectives? To what extent will Canadian police be able to contribute to the successful implementation of the mission mandate?

9. *Safety and security:* Is the location where Canadian police will be living and working sufficiently safe (including health care, living conditions and legal system) and secure enough for them to accomplish their goals?

10. *Logistics and funding:* Is the mission adequately and equitably funded? Is there adequate Canadian and international logistical support?

11. *Capacity:* Will Canadian participation jeopardize other international commitments?

12. *Duration and exit strategy:* Are conditions for conclusion of the mission clear and measureable? What is the duration of the operation?[50] While not all of the factors will be satisfied with each deployment, they are all taken into consideration when a decision to deploy Canadian police resources is being made.

At present, there is one centralized selection process for Canadian police officers wishing to deploy to an international mission. However, each police agency may have its own internal selection process as well. Researchers such as LeBeuf are clear in the pre-mission and post-mission systems that must be put in place. These ensure that peacekeepers are properly trained and have the skills and knowledge required for the mission. Following the mission, returning peacekeepers will require time to decompress. They may require psychological assessment and should have the benefit of a structured and personalized reintegration plan.[51]

These points become more important once a police officer is actually on a mission. At present, there is no international policing standard. Each country and in some cases regions or states within countries have their own standards. "Confusion and friction can emerge among the various national contingents; each thinking their policing standard and methods are superior to the others."[52]

While in a foreign country, the local police force may have jurisdiction with the national police operating in an advisory capacity. Who has ultimate control and responsibility for the mission and the day-to-day operations? Is it the government of the country? Perhaps it is the United Nations or NATO if it is one of their missions. Is it the government of the country that supplied the police officers to the mission? While these questions may cause considerable concern and frustration for some governments deploying police resources, Canada has put the Royal Canadian Mounted Police International Policing Branch as the lead agency for Canadian police officers deployed on international missions.[53]

For the Canadian police officers on a peacekeeping mission, governance is relatively straightforward. The complexities are left to the contingent commander. If the commander is not the police mission commander, the link is to that commander. It should be noted that the RCMP are not always in command of the mission. The Canadian contingent commander may be an officer from another Canadian police department.[54] The police commander for the mission may well come from another country, as the selection is finalized by the United Nations. As an example, in Haiti, Major-General Gerardo Chaumont of Argentina was the commissioner of police for the United Nations Stabilization Mission in Haiti.[55] From a governance perspective, then, the Canadian contingent commander must liaise with the police commissioner while continuing communication with the Canadian international policing branch. This professional-to-professional approach appears to be working well.

More difficult is the ability of the mission commander to deal with disciplinary problems and criminal acts perpetrated by subordinate police officers. The United Nations has rules and regulations to which all international police officers must adhere. The problems arise when the rules or local laws are breached. In most cases, the perpetrators are either disciplined by their commanders or, in serious criminal cases, returned to their home country to be processed under their own judicial system. This has serious consequences for the police officers who remain and continue with the mission. The local population or victims have no input in the judicial process, which results in a perception that the international police are above the law; this opinion reduces the effectiveness of the mission. While it is recognized that most governments will not allow their nationals to be tried under local laws, "there must be established an international accountability structure, incorporating a feedback mechanism into the local community."[56] This approach would allow the community to see that there is accountability and it would strengthen the legitimacy of the mission.

One final issue is the notion of community policing while on peacekeeping missions. While we have a long history and principles from Robert Peel, the notion of our style of policing is unknown in most countries and in particular to those that have the benefit of United Nations' policing initiatives. This is a much larger issue that will have to be dealt with in terms of an international set of policing standards.[57]

International peacekeeping still has a long way to go. With the complexities of different governments, laws and policing agencies, any resolution of the issues will take time.

## CONCLUSION

This chapter has provided an overview of policing in Canada from a historical perspective. Governance as it applies to the RCMP, OPP and Sûreté has been emphasized although not thoroughly examined due to the complexities of their governance. The professional approach to governance, flowing from the mayor and council through city management to the police chief has been discussed and it is apparent that the use of police boards and commissions is the popular approach to police governance in Canada. Police unions and associations are not part of traditional or legal governance but they do have a strong effect on the police department, legal governing authority, mayor and council, and the citizens that they serve through their action and inaction. They have learned how to deal with the media to emphasize their issues. The media will always be involved with policing and, in particular, governance issues; anything involving the police is or can be made newsworthy. Finally, international policing has its own challenges with governance, areas of responsibility and chains of command during a mission. The clash of cultures, which contributes to conflicts in Canadian communities, becomes magnified at this international, global village level. In this larger context Girouard, in his summary comments, refers to the clash of civilizations and the need for governance and security as a unitary construct for policing.

While this chapter has examined the various elements of traditional government-fostered policing, there is a much larger issue to be addressed, that of private policing. The public police are regulated by various laws and are governed by various types of oversight boards. In addition, police unions or representatives continually inject their vision of the roles and responsibilities of their constituents. In short, the public police have considerable regulation and oversight. The question remains: Are they able to satisfy the growing public expectations for security?[58] From 2001 to 2006, private security in Canada grew at a rate of 15% compared with only 3% for the public police. In general, private security personnel are more evenly distributed across all age groups, have lower levels of education, have less training and receive less pay than the police force. Despite these facts, the growth of private police continues to escalate to the point that in the 2006 Census "there were three private security personnel for every two police officers."[59] This growth is expected to continue and it should be noted that the private security operators do not have the level of legislation, regulation or oversight as that of the public police force. Private security, therefore, is a business that requires a higher level of regulation and oversight. Exacerbating the private security argument is a worldwide proliferation of private security firms. Abrahamsen and Williams note:

> The world's largest PSC, Group4Securicor, currently operates in
> 115 countries, employs over 530,000 people, and ranks as one

of the London Stock Exchange's 100 largest corporations by capitalization. In 2007, it reported a turnover of $9 billion.[60]

## REVIEW QUESTIONS

1.  In the national and international context of security, what is the role of governance?

## REFERENCES

Abrahamsen, R,, and M. C. Williams. "Security Beyond the State: Global Security. Assemblages in International Politics." *International Policing Sociology* 3 (2009): 1-17 <http://www.didierbigo.com/students/readings/abrahamsenwilliamssecurityassemblageIPS.pdf (19 March 2012).

Bayley, D. H., and C. D. Shearing. *The New Structure of Policing: Description, Conceptualization, and Research Agenda.* 2001. <www.ncjrs.gov/txtfiles1/nij/187083.txt > (8 February 2008).

Biro, F., P. Campbell, P. McKenna, and T. Murray. *Police Executives Under Pressure: A Study and Discussion of the Issues.* Ottawa, ON: Canadian Association of Chiefs of Police, 2000.

Bruce, F. R. *Does Elected / Volunteer Oversight Versus Professional Oversight of a Police Service Affect Organizational Behaviour and the Impositions of Sanctions.* Diss: Wolfson College UK., 2010.

Canadian Association of Police Boards. *Best Practices – A Framework for Professionalism and Success in Police Board Governance.* August 2005. <http://www.capb.ca/FCKeditor/editor/fileCabinet/finalgovernancerpt.pdf>

Canadian Association of Police Boards Conference. *A Fine Balance: The Challenges of Police Governance in a Changing World.* 2009. <http://www.fcm.ca/english/View.asp?mp=1353&x=1368>

Canadian Constitution Act. 1867/1982. < http://laws.justice.gc.ca/en/const/index.html> (12 October 2011).

Carter, D. L., and L. A. Radelet. *The Police and the Community.* Scarborough, ON: Prentice Hall, 1999.

Commission for Public Complaints against the Royal Canadian Mounted Police. *Mandate.* Accessed from the <http://www.cpc-cpp.gc.ca/> (12 October 2011).

Critchley, T. A. *The History of the Police in England and Wales.* London UK: Patterson Smith, 1978.

Dantzker, M. L., and M. P. Mitchell. *Understanding Today's Police* (Canadian edition). Scarborough, ON: Prentice Hall, 1998.

DeLord, R., J. Burpo, M. Shannon, and J. Spearing. *Police Union Power, Politics and Confrontation in the 21st Century.* Springfield, IL: Charles C. Thomas, 2008.

Federation of Canadian Municipalities. *Towards Equity and Efficiency in Policing.* 2008. <http://www.fcm.ca/english/View.asp?mp=1353&x=1368>

Fleming, J., and R. Rhodes. *It's Situational: the Dilemmas of Police Governance in the 21st Century.* 2004. <http://www.adelaide.edu.au/apsa/docs_papers/Pub%20Pol/Fleming%20%20Rhodes.pdf> (6 September, 2009).

Forcese, D. *Policing Canadian Society* (2nd ed.). Scarborough, ON: Prentice Hall, 1999.

Grant, K. "Police Chief Offers no Apologies for G20 Tactics." <http://www.theglobeandmail.com/news/world/g8-g20/news/police-chief-offers-no-apologies-for-g20-tactics/article1621788/> (29 June 2010).

Griffiths, C. T., J. Verdun, and N. Simon. *Canadian Criminal Justice.* Toronto, ON: Harcourt Brace, 1994.

Griffiths, C. T., R. Parent, and B. Whitelaw. *Community Policing* (2nd ed.). Scarborough, ON: Nelson Thompson Learning, 2001.

Hewlett, S. A., L. Sherbin, and K. Sumberg. "How Gen Y & Boomers Will Reshape Your Agenda." *Harvard Business Review* (July-August 2009: 1-8.

Horrall, S. W. *History of the Dominion Police.* (n.d.). <http://www.thecanadianencyclopedia.com/index.cfm?PgNm=TCE&Params=A1ARTA0002348>

Juris, H. A., and P. Feuille. *The Impact of Police Unions: Summary Report.* Washington DC: Law Enforcement Assistance Administration, National Institute of Law Enforcement and Criminal Justice, 1973.

Kempa, M. *Research Towards Alternative Futures: Policing in Practice.* 2008. <http://www.policecouncil.ca/reports/Kempa2008.pdf>

Lafleche and Stepan (as cited in Biro Frederick, Campbell, Peter, McKenna, Paul and

Murray Tonita, *Police Executives under Pressure: a Study and Discussion of the Issues.* 2000, p. 15).

Law Commission of Canada. *In Search of Security: The Future of Policing in Canada.* Ottawa, ON: Law Commission of Canada, 2006.

LeBeuf, M. *Peacekeeping Missions and the Police in Canada: An Impact Study of Civilian Police Officers and Mounted Police,* 2004.

Li, G. *Private Security and Public Policing.* 2008. <http://www.statcan.gc.ca/pub/85-002-x/2008010/article/10730-eng.htm>

Lynch, R. *The Police Manager.* Cincinnati, OH: Anderson, 1998.

Marin, R. J. *Policing in Canada Issues for the 21st Century*. Aurora, ON: Canada Law Book, 1997.

McKenna, P. F. *Foundations of Policing in Canada*. Scarborough, ON: Prentice Hall, 1998.

McKenna, P. F. *Foundations of Community Policing in Canada*. Scarborough, ON: Prentice Hall, 2000.

Mobekk, E. *Identifying Lessons in United Nations International Policing Missions*. Geneva, Switzerland: Centre for Democratic Control of Armed Forces, 2005.

Moore, M. H., and D. W. Stephens. *Beyond Command and Control: The Strategic Management of Police Departments*. Police Executive Research Forum: Washington, DC, 1991.

Murray, G. *Civilian Governance and Social Responsibility: Safety, Community and Sustainability*. Canadian Association of Police Boards Conference Report, 2008.

Murray, T. *Developing a Framework for Cooperative Police Management*. Paper presented at the Canadian Association of Chiefs of Police Conference Saskatoon SK. Ottawa, ON: Canadian Police College Resource Centre, 2001.

Murray, T., and S. Alvaro. *A Profile of the Canadian Police Community*. Ottawa, ON: Canadian Association of Chiefs of Police, 2001.

Police Assessment Resource Centre. *Review of National Police Oversight Models for the Eugene Police Commission*. 2005. <www.parc.info/review_of_national_police_oversight_models.chtml>

Police Services Act of Ontario. R.S.O. 1990, Chapter P.15. http://www.e-  laws.gov.on.ca/html/statutes/english/elaws_statutes_90p15_e.htm

Public Complaints Commission - Commission for Public Complaints against the RCMP. http://www.cpc-cpp.gc.ca/prr/inv/index-eng.aspx

Ontario Provincial Police. *A Brief History*. Queen's Printer for Ontario, 2009. <http://www.opp.ca/ecms/index.php?id=129>

Ontario Provincial Police Collective Bargaining Act. 2006. <http://www.e-laws.gov.on.ca/html/statutes/english/elaws_statutes_06o35_e.htm>

Quebec Police Act. Éditeur officiel du Québec. R.S.Q., Chapter P3.1. Updated to 1 March 2012 http://www2.publicationsduquebec.gouv.qc.ca/dynamicSearch/telecharge.php?type=2&file=%2F%2FP_13_1%2FP13_1_A.htm

Radwanski, Adam. "McGuinty washes his hands of police mistreatment allegations." <http://www.theglobeandmail.com/news/politics/adam-radwanski/mcguinty-washes-his-hands-of-police-mistreatment-allegations/article1623731/>(29 June 2010).

RCMP Act. R.S.C., 1985, c. R-10 <http://laws.justice.gc.ca/eng/R-10/20100705/page-2.html?rp2=HOME&rp3=SI&rp1=royal%20canadian%20mounted%20police%20act&rp4=all&rp9=cs&rp10=L&rp13=50&rp19=2>

Royal Canadian Mounted Police. *The RCMP's History.* 9 July, 2007. <http://www.rcmp-grc.gc.ca/hist/index-eng.htm>

Royal Canadian Mounted Police. *2006-2008 Biennial Review. Canada's Police Community ... Working Together to Build a More Secure World.* Ottawa, ON: Royal Canadian Mounted Police International Peace Operations Branch, 2008.

Royal Canadian Mounted Police. *Haiti Update.* 2010. <http://www.rcmp-grc.gc.ca/news-nouvelles/2010/haiti/01-18-haiti-eng.htm>

Seagrave, J. *Introduction to Policing in Canada.* Scarborough, ON: Prentice-Hall, 1997.

Stansfield, R. T. *Issues in Policing a Canadian Perspective.* Toronto, ON: Thompson, 1996.

Stenning, Philip. *Governance and Accountability in a Plural Policing environment: The Story so far.* <http://www.policecouncil.ca/reports/Stenning_Governance2009.pdf> (8 February, 2009).

Swol, K. "Private Security and Public Policing in Canada." *Canadian Centre for Justice Statistics* (85-002-XIE) 18 (13). 1998. <http://dsp-psd.pwgsc.gc.ca/Collection-R/Statcan/85-002-XIE/0139885-002-XIE.pdf>

United Nations News Center. *Ban announces appointment of new UN police chief.* 2010. <http://www.un.org/apps/news/story.asp?NewsID=34005&Cr=police&Cr1>

YouTube. Gerry Rundel Testifies in Robert Dziekanski Tasering case. www.youtube.com/watch?v=NJAIb6yd344> (24 February 2009).

YouTube. G20 Protests Heat Up: Video of Police Car Fire in Toronto. <http://www.youtube.com/watch?v=32OW6cu4Ypk> (26 June 2010).

Villeneuve, G. *Quebec Provincial Police.* The Canadian Encyclopedia © 2010 Historica-Dominion. <http://www.thecanadianencyclopedia.com/index.cfm?PgNm=TCE&Params=A1ARTA0006600>

Walker, S. *A Critical History of Police Reform.* University of Nebraska at Omaha, NB: Lexington Books, 1942.

Whitelaw, B., R. B. Parent, and C. T. Griffiths. *Community-Based Strategic Policing in Canada* (2nd ed.). Scarborough, ON: Nelson, 2006.

ENDNOTES

1    YouTube. Gerry Rundel Testifies in Robert Dziekanski Tasering case. 24 February 2009. <www.youtube.com/watch?v=NJAIb6yd344>

2    YouTube. G20 Protests Heat Up: Video of Police Car Fire in Toronto. 26 June 2010. <http://www.youtube.com/watch?v=32OW6cu4Ypk>

3    J. Fleming and R. Rhodes, *It's Situational: the Dilemmas of Police Governance in the 21st Century.* 2004.<http://www.adelaide.edu.au/apsa/docs_papers/Pub%20Pol/Fleming%20%20Rhodes.pdf>

(6 September 2009).

4    F. R. Bruce, *Does Elected / Volunteer Oversight Versus Professional Oversight of a Police Service Affect Organizational Behaviour and the Impositions of Sanctions.* (Diss: Wolfson College UK. 2010).

5    T. Murray and S. Alvaro. *A Profile of the Canadian Police Community.* (Ottawa, ON: Canadian Association of Chiefs of Police, 2001).

6    M. Kempa, M. *Research Towards Alternative Futures: Policing in Practice.* 2008. <http://www.policecouncil.ca/reports/Kempa2008.pdf>

7    F. R. Bruce, Does *Elected / Volunteer Oversight Versus Professional Oversight of a Police Service Affect Organizational Behaviour and the Impositions of Sanctions.* (Diss: Wolfson College UK., 2010), 24.

8    M. H. Moore and D. W. Stephens, *Beyond Command and Control: The Strategic Management of Police Departments.* (Police Executive Research Forum: Washington, DC, 1991).

9    Royal Canadian Mounted Police. *2006-2008 Biennial Review. Canada's Police Community... Working Together to Build a More Secure World* (Ottawa, ON: Royal Canadian Mounted Police International Peace Operations Branch, 2008).

10   P. F. McKenna, *Foundations of Community Policing in Canada* (Scarborough, ON: Prentice Hall, 2000).

11   Police Assessment Resource Centre. *Review of National Police Oversight Models for the Eugene Police Commission.* 2005. <www.parc.info/review_of_national_police_oversight_models.chtml>

12   Police Assessment Resource Centre. *Review of National Police Oversight Models for the Eugene Police Commission.* 2005. <www.parc.info/review_of_national_police_oversight_models.chtml>

13   S. Walker, *A Critical History of Police Reform* (University of Nebraska at Omaha, NB: Lexington Books, 1942).

14   P. F. McKenna, *Foundations of Community Policing in Canada* (Scarborough, ON: Prentice Hall, 2000), 14.

15   J. Seagrave, *Introduction to Policing in Canada.* (Scarborough, ON: Prentice-Hall, 1997).

16   Critchley, 1978). T. A. Critchley, *The History of the Police in England and Wales.* (London UK: Patterson Smith, 1978).

17   P. F. McKenna, *Foundations of Community Policing in Canada* (Scarborough, ON: Prentice Hall, 2000).

18  Police Assessment Resource Center. *Review of National Police Oversight Models for the Eugene Police Commission.* 2005.www.parc.info/review_of_national_police_oversight_models.chtml p. 5.

19  C. T. Griffiths, R. Parent, and B. Whitelaw. *Community Policing* (2nd ed.). (Scarborough, ON: Nelson Thompson Learning, 2001), 7.

20  J. Seagrave, *Introduction to Policing in Canada.* (Scarborough, ON: Prentice-Hall, 1997).

21  C. T. Griffiths, R. Parent, and B. Whitelaw. *Community Policing* (2nd ed.). (Scarborough, ON: Nelson Thompson Learning, 2001), 7.

22  Canadian Constitution Act. 1867. < http://laws.justice.gc.ca/en/const/index.html>

23  S. W. Horrall, *History of the Dominion Police.* (n.d.). <http://www.thecanadianencyclopedia.com/index.cfm?PgNm=TCE&Params=A1ARTA0002348>

24  Royal Canadian Mounted Police, *The RCMP's History.* 9 July, 2007. <http://www.rcmp-grc.gc.ca/hist/index-eng.htm>

25  Ontario Provincial Police, *A Brief History.* 2009 <http://www.opp.ca/ecms/index.php?id=129>

26  G. Villeneuve, *Quebec Provincial Police.* 2010<http://www.thecanadianencyclopedia.com/index.cfm?PgNm=TCE&Params=A1ARTA0006600>

27  Police Services Act of Ontario, Sec. 9. R.S.O. 1990<http://www.e-laws.gov.on.ca/html/statutes/english/elaws_statutes_90p15_e.htm>

28  Public Complaints Commission - Commission for Public Complaints against the RCMP. http://www.cpc-cpp.gc.ca/prr/inv/index-eng.aspx

29  P. F. McKenna, *Foundations of Policing in Canada.* (Scarborough, ON: Prentice Hall, 1998), 109.

30  F. R. Bruce, Does *Elected / Volunteer Oversight Versus Professional Oversight of a Police Service Affect Organizational Behaviour and the Impositions of Sanctions* (Diss: Wolfson College UK., 2010), 24

31  R. Lynch, *Police Services.* Ottawa, ON: Royal Canadian G. *The Police Manager* (Cincinnati, OH: Anderson, 1998).

32  R. Lynch, *Police Services.* Ottawa, ON: Royal Canadian G. *The Police Manager* (Cincinnati, OH: Anderson, 1998), 248.

33  F. R. Bruce, Does *Elected / Volunteer Oversight Versus Professional Oversight of a Police Service Affect Organizational Behaviour and the Impositions of Sanctions* (Diss: Wolfson College UK., 2010).

34  T. Murray, *Developing a Framework for Cooperative Police Management.* Paper presented at the Canadian Association of Chiefs of Police Conference Saskatoon SK. (Ottawa, ON: Canadian Police College Resource Centre, 2001), 4.

35 D. L. Carter and L. A. Radelet, *The Police and the Community* (Scarborough, ON: Prentice Hall, 1999).

36 Federation of Canadian Municipalities.*Towards Equity and Efficiency in Policing*. 2008, p. 5. <http://www.fcm.ca/english/View.asp?mp=1353&x=1368>

37 D.H. Bayley and C. D. Shearing, *The New Structure of Policing: Description, Conceptualization, and Research Agenda.* 2001. <www.ncjrs.gov/txtfiles1/ nij/187083.txt> (8 February 2008).

38 F. Biro, P. Campbell, P. McKenna and T. Murray, *Police Executives Under Pressure: A Study and Discussion of the Issues* (Ottawa, ON: Canadian Association of Chiefs of Police, 2000), 14.

39 R. DeLord, J. Burpo, M. Shannon and J. Spearing, *Police Union Power, Politics and Confrontation in the 21st Century* (Springfield, IL: Charles C Thomas, 2008), 7-9.

40 F. Biro, P. Campbell, P. McKenna and T. Murray. *Police Executives Under Pressure: A Study and Discussion of the Issues* (Ottawa, ON: Canadian Association of Chiefs of Police, 2000).

41 Lafleche and Stepan (as cited in Biro Frederick, Campbell Peter, McKenna, Paul and Murray Tonita, Police Executives under Pressure: a Study and Discussion of the Issues. 2000 p 15.

42 F. Biro, P. Campbell, P. McKenna and T. Murray, *Police Executives Under Pressure: A Study and Discussion of the Issues* (Ottawa, ON: Canadian Association of Chiefs of Police, 2000), 15.

43 K. Grant, *Globe and Mail* article (29 June 2010).

44 Adam Radwanski, *Globe and Mail* article "McGuinty Washes his Hands of Police Mistreatment Allegations" (29 June 2010).

45 E. Mobekk, *Identifying Lessons in United Nations International Policing Missions.* (Geneva, Switzerland: Centre for Democratic Control of Armed Forces, 2005).

46 Royal Canadian Mounted Police. *2006-2008 Biennial Review. Canada's Police Community... Working Together to Build a More Secure World.* (Ottawa, ON: Royal Canadian Mounted Police International Peace Operations Branch, 2008).

47 M.-LeBeuf, *Peacekeeping Missions and the Police in Canada: An Impact Study of Civilian Police Officers and Mounted Police* (2004).

48 E. Mobekk, *Identifying Lessons in United Nations International Policing Missions.* (Geneva, Switzerland: Centre for Democratic Control of Armed Forces, 2005), 1.

49    Royal Canadian Mounted Police. *2006-2008 Biennial Review. Canada's Police Community... Working Together to Build a More Secure World.* (Ottawa, ON: Royal Canadian Mounted Police International Peace Operations Branch, 2008).

50    Royal Canadian Mounted Police. *2006-2008 Biennial Review. Canada's Police Community... Working Together to Build a More Secure World.* (Ottawa, ON: Royal Canadian Mounted Police International Peace Operations Branch, 2008), 9.

51    M.-LeBeuf, *Peacekeeping Missions and the Police in Canada: An Impact Study of Civilian Police Officers and Mounted Police* (2004).

52    E. Mobekk, *Identifying Lessons in United Nations International Policing Missions.* (Geneva, Switzerland: Centre for Democratic Control of Armed Forces, 2005), 18.

53    Royal Canadian Mounted Police. *2006-2008 Biennial Review. Canada's Police Community... Working Together to Build a More Secure World.* (Ottawa, ON: Royal Canadian Mounted Police International Peace Operations Branch, 2008).

54    Royal Canadian Mounted Police. *Haiti Update.* 2010. <http://www.rcmp-grc.gc.ca/news-nouvelles/2010/haiti/01-18-haiti-eng.htm>.

55    United Nations News Center. *Ban announces appointment of new UN police chief.* 2010. <http://www.un.org/apps/news/story.asp?NewsID=34005&Cr=police&Cr1>

56    E. Mobekk, *Identifying Lessons in United Nations International Policing Missions.* (Geneva, Switzerland: Centre for Democratic Control of Armed Forces, 2005), 22.

57    E. Mobekk, *Identifying Lessons in United Nations International Policing Missions.* (Geneva, Switzerland: Centre for Democratic Control of Armed Forces, 2005).

58    M. Kempa, *Research Towards Alternative Futures: Policing in Practice.* 2008. <http://www.policecouncil.ca/reports/Kempa2008.pdf>

59    G. Li, *Private Security and Public Policing.* 2008. <http://www.statcan.gc.ca/pub/85-002-x/2008010/article/10730-eng.htm>

60    Abrahamsen, Rita, Williams, Michael C. Security Beyond the State: Global Security Assemblages in International Politics. International Policing Sociology (2009) 3 1 – 17

# PRIVATE SECURITY
# AND MILITARY COMPANIES:
# SECURING THE PEACE?

SERGE VIDALIS, PhD (Cand.)

## INTRODUCTION

In the unitary construct of democratic governance and security, as defined by Girouard, the notion of security has different connotations to different people and cultures. What we can be sure of is that, as humans, our basic needs include security in conjunction with shelter and resources. To Westerners, security has transformed from a function of the state to an industrial apparatus created for economic opportunity and, most recently, to engage in quasi state-sponsored practitioners of "force." Until the 20th century, security services revolved around commercial, corporate and industrial entities aimed at protecting assets, intellectual property and providing safety to their personnel. By the end of the 20th century, the function of security included the protection of computer networks, protection against health pandemics, water security, environmental security and many other forms of protective strategies. What is certain is that by the beginning of the 21st century, the focus of security had changed.

Since the thaw of the Cold War and the eventual collapse of the Soviet Union, our global security has been diminished by the emerging threats from state and non-state actors. The latter became most evident in the events that unfolded on September 11, 2001, with the terror attacks on the United States by the now infamous terror group named al Qaeda. These attacks and several others that followed this pivotal point marked a radical change in how the security of our domestic and international interests would be pursued. Depending upon your national origin and/or place of residency, security measures may not have undergone any major changes because perceived threats may have been deemed negligible. In contrast, security measures implemented by the state and/or corporate bodies have intensified exponentially.

Corporate security functions in Western states and many other nations have undergone extensive refinements to combat the threat of terror in terms of both the domestic and international interests of their clients. This chapter presents the realities of today's governance of private security and military companies in areas of armed conflict, and raises questions about their role in promoting peace.

## THE PRIVATEERS

Prior to the formation of the modern state, the security of clans, tribes, villages and city-states existed as functions of its governance under one leader and alliances with fellow warriors. Their purpose was simple, to exercise authority and control over their population and to thwart the common enemy. The purpose was to provide protection for the people, resources and territory, whether in an agrarian or a commercial society. Progression from an allegiance to one governing leader required expanding the function of the security apparatus as communities grew and enemies strengthened. From these needs arose the paid armies who bore no allegiance to anyone but themselves in terms of looting and payment.

These warriors or privateers would today bear the name "mercenary," a term often looked upon with disapproval because of the association of taking up arms for the highest bidder. However, by the 17th century, these privateers affected the colonial pursuits of numerous European empires, establishing territorial claims on behalf of their state, often through the use of violence. Unfortunately, much of the history of colonialism and the negative effects on other peoples and cultures contributed to the current instability and threats in the West today. Cultures were repressed over years of Euro-centric violence and resource pilfering. The privateer has made a resurgence strongly resembling the days of colonialism.

## SECURITY AND THE MODERN NATION-STATE

It is suggested that the Treaty of Westphalia (1648) was a prelude to the formation of the modern nation-state as it established the foundations of diplomatic relations, yet most would agree that the French Revolution (ending in 1799) gave the world the first modern nation-state. This important event is noted for the creation of nationalism and the subsequent provision of the nation's security through a subservient armed force. No longer did privateers provide domestic protection but they would embark on the nation's defence and colonial pursuits, as discussed earlier.

Henceforward, the role of security would belong to a nation's armed forces, armed with emerging weaponry systems and manned by conscripts or aristocrats. The professional military would develop with the growth of paid servicemen, apolitical leaders and the development of doctrine. The Industrial Revolution (1750) would, in time, bring wealth to industrialised nations and conflicts of new proportions. Advanced weapons from rim-fired rifles to nuclear missiles meant the world has witnessed the death of millions during the last 100 years, followed by periods of global insecurity during the Cold War.

History documents numerous civil wars, rebellions and inter-state wars that were fought by uniformed forces pursuing the interest of the states they represented, whilst some contemporary conflicts bore the brutality of genocide and ethnic cleansing. Though efforts to mitigate armed conflict through international treaties and organizations gave hope to humankind, the reality is that the self-interest of many nation-states has voided their commitment to making or keeping the peace. The failure to intervene in a timely fashion or with vigour has resulted in the deaths of millions around the world and the virtual ineffectiveness of organizations such as the United Nations. These factors have demonstrated to would-be aggressors that they are free to kill and pillage without consequence and, worse, that the plight of victims will go unheard by interveners.

## DOMESTIC SECURITY

In many democratic nations, the function of domestic security and public safety has been delegated to the constabulary. In the 1800s, modern policing as created by Sir Robert Peel of the London Metropolitan Police provided nine principles of policing:

1. The basic mission for which the police exist is to prevent crime and disorder.
2. The ability of the police to perform their duties is dependent upon public approval of police actions.
3. Police must secure the willing co-operation of the public in voluntary observance of the law to be able to secure and maintain the respect of the public.
4. The degree of co-operation of the public that can be secured diminishes proportionately to the necessity of the use of physical force.
5. Police seek and preserve public favour not by catering to public opinion but by constantly demonstrating absolute impartial service to the law.
6. Police use physical force to the extent necessary to secure observance of the law or to restore order only when the exercise of persuasion, advice and warning is found to be insufficient.
7. Police, at all times, should maintain a relationship with the public that gives reality to the historic tradition that the police are the public and the public are the police; the police being only members of the public who are paid to give full-time attention to duties which are incumbent on every citizen in the interests of community welfare and existence.
8. Police should always direct their action strictly toward their functions and never appear to usurp the powers of the judiciary.
9. The test of police efficiency is the absence of crime and disorder, not the visible evidence of police action in dealing with it.

The purpose of establishing the nine principles of policing was to provide an organized response for crime prevention and public safety in contrast to the previous services of volunteer night watchmen. These principles are the foundation upon which many of today's police forces operate as a public service. From these principles, the birth of private security and detective services have grown with the creation of the Pinkerton Agency of Chicago, established by Allan Pinkerton in the 1850s.

## PRIVATE SECURITY COMPANIES AND ARMED CONFLICT

Modern security services arose to protect property and/or conduct investigative work relating to civil matters among the population. A clear divide existed between the mandate of the constabulary and security practices, yet the features shared by these two professions were in the realm of crime prevention. These are still the tenets of today's security practice with the exception that crime prevention has grown to keep abreast of technological developments and social, judicial and cultural change. With the exception of a modernized form of service, security in its root form reflects the same priorities that it held hundreds of years ago.

Reflecting on the mercenary role once taken by imperial forces or colonial privateers, the nature of today's private security company has, in some cases, regressed to those times, yet not in pursuit of sovereign expansion.

> Perhaps most surprising is that the authority transferred to privateers by European sovereigns in the 17th century has taken in a new and unexpected avatar. This occurred when President Bush invited privateers to assist the US government in its war on terror (post-September 11, 2001). Here was a very public rejuvenation of an old form of non-state license in the use of violence.[1]

Of the professional security firms practising around the globe, a limited number have ventured into the role of protective security services in combat zones such as Iraq and Afghanistan. Those that have assumed the role of modern-day privateers in both private security and military companies have been rewarded with lucrative contracts and salaries but many have paid dearly with the loss of life associated with the hazards of armed conflict.

## THE LEGITIMACY OF FORCE

The modern nation-state has characteristics that include the people, territory and borders, sovereignty, government, culture, language and the ability to use force. The function of force is legitimized for the enforcement of national laws and in defence of the nation by those who govern, either democratically elected or self-appointed. It stands to reason that the latter two applications of force have been performed by a nation's armed forces and/or constabulary pursuant to domestic and foreign policies, thereby legitimizing violence. The private security companies exercising force in countries such as Iraq and Afghanistan have done so. "Where states and businesses prove compatible, familiar forms of co-operation have emerged which at least echo the traits which characterized an era long past."[2]

The cause of such a rise in the use of force by private security companies is attributed to two international factors: (a) the end of the Cold War and the subsequent discharge of military personnel and sale of former military weapons, and (b) the decolonization of formerly held European nations' interests.[3] The ample supply of weapons and practitioners of force, and the inability of former territories and colonies to "establish effective national armed services" has "proved to be significant market drivers and created both a great supply and huge demand for violent services."[4]

The monopoly over the legitimized use of force, once held exclusively by nation-states, no longer exists because the compatible interests of state and business have merged to the extent that states have legislated the privatization for the use of force and defence. The contracting of private firms boomed during the first Gulf War in Iraq where the US government enlisted a multitude of private services and later inventoried those firms to determine which could offer direct support to US combat forces in the theatre of operations.

It is suggested that the legislated use of force by private security companies provides two political advantages. The first is to enable a corporate body to pursue state objectives by proxy. The second is for government to maintain arm's length relations when negative events occur. The most obvious example of such contracted services going wrong and exposing the questionable use of private security and military firms engaged in the use of force was that of US-based Blackwater USA, now known as Xe Services LLC. The incident in question occurred on September 16, 2007, when Blackwater guards shot and killed Iraqi civilians in Nisour Square, Baghdad. Reports by the US military indicate that Blackwater guards fired into a crowd of civilians without provocation and employed excessive use of force, killing 17 unarmed civilians. An investigation conducted by the Iraqi government and US Federal Bureau of Investigations deemed the shootings unjustified. This incident has raised questions about the control and accountability of private security and military companies operating in areas of armed conflict.

## DO PRIVATE SECURITY AND MILITARY COMPANIES PROMOTE PEACE?

The direct employment of private security and military companies to promote peace does not exist, certainly not under the authority of the United Nations. However, there have been numerous proposals about privatized security services engaging as Rapid Reaction Forces in support of peacekeeping operations because of their operational flexibility and capabilities. Again, the application of private security companies performing what has long been an international response by nation-states would be hypocritical in terms of the legitimate use of force when such legitimacy is associated with nation-states or, in this case, nations under the UN Charter.

From a practical perspective, the use of private security companies would, in many circumstances, eliminate or reduce the typical delays of deploying national peacekeeping forces that have often crippled peacekeeping missions and resulted in greater bloodshed. In light of the hypothetical employment of private contractors in peace operations, private security and military companies do provide services to organizations directly involved in humanitarian and reconstruction efforts.

In both the Iraq and Afghan wars, the employment of sanctioned non-government organizations (NGOs) has been widespread, as has the involvement of unsanctioned organizations. With regard to sanctioned NGOs operating in conflict zones, a number of these bodies such as CARE and the World Food Programme have employed the services of private security companies in order to provide protection for personnel and assets.[5] Though it is necessary to employ private security companies in conflict zones, it is not the desire of NGOs to do so, but rather a necessity. Most perceive a conflict of interest in hiring armed guards particularly when delivering aid or services to victims of conflict, while some prefer to develop in-house security capabilities. Unfortunately, the realities of warfare are that combatants often assess the mere perception of aid being provided to a population as a threat or an opportunity to commit criminal acts. Regrettably, numerous difficult lessons have been learned by NGOs failing to consider security services, at times costing the lives of innocent Samaritans who only wished to alleviate the pain and suffering of others.

## PRIVATE MERCENARY COMPANIES?

It is a mistake to think that private security and military companies will disappear as a result of mishaps, poor judgment and irresponsibility on the part of corporations and the authorities that employ them. The long history of privateers, mercenaries and now the "Use of Force" entrepreneurs means that domestic and international accountability and legal oversight is necessary to permit these companies to offer professional services.

The challenges of creating a regulatory body are as complicated as the diplomatic gamesmanship of the UN and the lack of enforcement capabilities of the International Criminal Court (ICC). Discussions on this issue have been held for some time but seldom include those who offer such specialized services. Despite this, a few countries have taken action in their jurisdiction to criminalize the mercenary profession with substantial consequences, contrary to the convention on mercenaries passed by the UN (International Convention against the Recruitment, Use, Financing and Training of Mercenaries, UN Resolution 44/34, 4 December 1989). In consideration of the importance of this resolution, the consequences of those alleged to have committed mercenary acts call for states "in whose territory the alleged offender is present shall, in accordance with its laws, take him into custody" to either begin criminal proceedings or extradition (Article 10).[6]

In 2006, the UN took further action to mitigate the growing concern of mercenary activities particularly as a result of the Iraq and Afghan wars. Through Resolution 61/151, *Use of Mercenaries as a means of violating human rights and impeding the exercise of the right of peoples to self-determination*, the General Assembly called on states to take action to prohibit mercenary activities. Of particular note, as referenced in Item 5, the Resolution requested:

> All States to exercise the utmost vigilance against any kind of recruitment, training, hiring or financing of mercenaries by private companies offering international military consultancy and security services, as well as to impose a specific ban on such companies intervening in armed conflicts or actions to destabilize constitutional regimes.[7]

At first glance, it would appear to those uninformed that the employment of private security and military companies in Iraq and Afghanistan is contrary to both UN Resolutions 44/34 and 61/151. One key element of Resolution 44/34, however, is that persons deemed to be mercenaries do not originate from states party to the conflict. This element has been circumvented by the fact that the primary employer of private security and military companies operating in Iraq and Afghanistan is the United States of America, a party to the conflict. Therefore, the legitimacy of non-US citizens or non-US private security and military companies operating in Iraq or Afghanistan is inconsistent with the legal framework established by the UN resolutions.

In terms of the spirit of these resolutions, it is suggested that the nature of armed services delivered by private companies is contrary to the intent of prohibiting mercenary activities as defined in Resolution 44/34, because private security guards are not members of a national military force. In consideration of these facts and the demand for private security and military company services, how best could they be incorporated into a framework that includes the values of good governance, accountability and oversight?

## ACCOUNTABILITY AND OVERSIGHT – IMPROVING FUTURE PRIVATE SECURITY SERVICES

The private security company apparatus employed to provide a protective service in conflict zones has lost credibility and the trust of many governments, organizations and the general public in the countries where they operate. Regardless of their necessary services, the damage caused by firms such as Blackwater has tainted their professionalism due to the absence of accountability and legal oversight. The security threats that exist in many regions of the globe, primarily in humanitarian and peacekeeping work (coupled with the diminishing human resources of international contributors) means that private security companies will still be in demand.

To mitigate the borderline illegalities associated with private security and military companies, it will be necessary not only to enforce the UN Resolutions on Mercenaries, but also to create good governance relating to the international security profession. This governance structure should include more robust international laws that delineate between acts of warfare (or mercenary-related work) and security work. Laws that exist without consequences are irrelevant and will alter neither the damage already done by private security companies nor the nations that employ them.

Various models in the international community regulate the activities of nation-states, industries and professions such as the UN Convention on the Law of the Sea, or the International Regulations for Preventing Collisions at Sea. These laws govern state responsibilities respecting national claims and jurisdictions, while the International Regulations reflect the internationally recognized regulation of ships operating at sea.

The emerging trends in terrorism, failing states, inter-state conflicts and the growth of aggressive non-state actors seeking power through armed confrontation mean the need to protect people and relieve suffering must be heard. Response must occur with accountability and legal oversight, attributes noted by Girouard in his introductory essay.

## REVIEW QUESTIONS

1. In consideration of the rapid pace of globalization with respect to markets, capital, labour and goods, the demands placed on securing the various related government and corporate assets and infrastructure networks has created the rise of private security and military companies (PSMC). Given this rapid pace of growth, what are the implications of sovereignty to nation-states? What are the implications to the legitimate use of force by nation-states?

2. The 21st century faces numerous challenges in promoting the security needed to combat the threats posed by non-state combatants. What are the implications to nation-states that choose to employ PSMCs where traditional military or constabulary forces were once applied?

3. The Treaty of Westphalia (1648) established the foundations of diplomatic relations of existing and emerging nation-states. What international treaties and or governing bodies provide a framework to regulate the PSMC industry? What remedies exist to ensure the compliance of International Law?

4. Given that the origins of private security services were founded on the commercialization of Sir Robert Peel's Principles of Policing to provide private security and detective services, is it conceivable that Private Constabulary Forces be created in lieu of PSMCs?

5. If a Private Constabulary Force were created and employed in international or intra-national conflicts, under what legal framework or governance model would they do so? Would such a force be more legitimate? Would such a force be acceptable? Why?

REFERENCES

Patterson, M. H.. *Privatising Peace, A Corporate Adjunct to United Nations Peace-keeping and Humanitarian Operations.* Hampshire, UK: Palgrave Macmillan, 2009.

Sheehy, B., J. Maogoto, and V. Newell. *Legal Control of the Private Military Corporation.* Hampshire, UK: Palgrave Macmillan, 2009.

United Nations. *International Humanitarian Law - Treaties & Documents,* 2005. International Committee for the Red Cross: <http://www.icrc.org/ihl.nsf/FULL/530?OpenDocument> (3 August 2010).

United Nations. *United Nations General Assembly, Resolution adopted by the General Assembly 61/151.* 14 February 2007. UNDEMOCRACY.com: <http://www.undemocracy.com/A-RES-61-151.pdf> (4 August 2010).

Vaux,T., C. Seiple, G. Nakano, and K. Van Brabant. *Humanitarian Action and Private Security Companies. Opening the Debate.* Unkn: International Alert, n.d.

ENDNOTES

[1]  M. H. Patterson. *Privatising Peace, A Corporate Adjunct to United Nations Peacekeeping and Humanitarian Operations.* (Hampshire, UK: Palgrave Macmillan, 2009), 89.

[2]  M. H. Patterson. *Privatising Peace, A Corporate Adjunct to United Nations Peacekeeping and Humanitarian Operations.* (Hampshire, UK: Palgrave Macmillan, 2009), 89.

[3]  B. Sheehy, J. Maogoto and V. Newell. *Legal Control of the Private Military Corporation* (Hampshire, UK: Palgrave Macmillan, 2009), 75.

[4]  B. Sheehy, J. Maogoto and V. Newell. *Legal Control of the Private Military Corporation* (Hampshire, UK: Palgrave Macmillan, 2009), 75.

[5]  T. Vaux, C. Seiple, G. Nakano and K. Van Brabant. *Humanitarian Action and Private Security Companies, Opening The Debate.* (Unkn: International Alert, n.d.), 15.

[6]  United Nations. *International Humanitarian Law - Treaties & Documents,* 2005. International Committee for the Red Cross: http://www.icrc.org/ihl.nsf/FULL/530?OpenDocument (3 August 2010).

[7]  United Nations. *United Nations General Assembly, Resolution adopted by the General Assembly 61/151.* 14 February 2007. UNDEMOCRACY.com: <http://www.undemocracy.com/A-RES-61-151.pdf> (4 August 2010).

SECTION IV

---

# STATES WITHIN STATES
# AND STATES OF CO-OPERATION

---

# LEADERSHIP DEVELOPMENT FOR FIRST NATIONS GOVERNANCE IN BRITISH COLUMBIA

SUSANNE THIESSEN, PhD (Cand.)

## INTRODUCTION

In his introduction, Girouard briefly proposes a theory of the Anastazi and their ultimate demise. He suggests, "Governance is not in and of itself rules ... rules are the enabler by which governance enacts and functions." Governance is a function of leadership; leaders with legitimacy govern. Governance cannot be sustainable without security for both the governors and the governed. Yet leaders vary in their respective methodologies, governance varies in its prescribed outcomes, and security varies in its application. Effective governance, Girouard asserts, is an amalgamation of the whole – an integrated system. Was the demise of the Anastazi an outcome of the leadership of this First Nation (FN) or were there intervening variables beyond the control of the Anastazi leadership, such as climate, that contributed to the disappearance of this developed and successful civilization? Was security too lax or too stringent?

This chapter will provide an overview of the present situation for FN government organizations and the challenges for elected leadership in balancing non-indigenous approaches to organization and management in a First Nations cultural context in British Columbia. It will determine a variety of desirable leadership competencies for elected First Nations leaders who work in FN government organizations, and recommend some appropriate strategies and an action plan for leadership development.

## FIRST NATIONS LEADERSHIP
## DEVELOPMENT PROCESSES

The majority of elected FN leaders have close cultural and family ties in their communities and the process of leadership development begins in childhood. Self-management and social capabilities are taught through informal teaching and mentoring and through formal rites of passage and ceremony. As adults, work facilitation capabilities are provided through formal academic training, and professional and personal development opportunities. Most of these learning opportunities take place outside the community but with other FN leaders who share similar issues. A large part of leadership learning is through experiential, social and developmental processes.

Elected First Nations government leaders must be competent in political, managerial and administrative areas and be strongly grounded in their own cultural identity if sustainable governance and security are to be achieved. A sustainable long-term strategy for First Nations leadership development will include all levels of the organization and governance, and extend to the community at large, including youth and elders. It will balance cultural practices and language with Western opportunities for leadership growth. In seeking Western forms of knowledge, the FN should seek programs where facilitators understand the cultural perceptions and values of FN people. Development opportunities should balance assessment, challenge, support and the recognition of achievement. Opportunities for development should include the traditional practices, values and methods that were present in the community prior to colonization and exposure to Western sources of knowledge.

## FIRST NATIONS' GOVERNMENT LEADERSHIP

In Canada, there are over 700 Indigenous communities that use a "First Nation" government organization created under the Indian Act[1] to administer government programs and services for their members. There are 203 First Nations government organizations in British Columbia that are organized by this structure. In FN communities in Canada, the elected chief councillor, Council members and their administration are the legitimate body of authority recognized by the Canadian federal government. The FN reports to Indian and Northern Affairs Canada (INAC) and administers annual payments received from INAC to its community programs and services. Health, housing, education and economic development are some of the portfolios managed by the chief and Council members in the context of governance and security for their respective communities.

Prior to colonization and still in some cases, tribes had their own distinct and complex systems of social and political organization and governance, which ensured the survival of that tribe; however, when the newcomers arrived in Canada, a federal system was imposed on indigenous tribes. This system set up a land reserve strategy with a rural system of municipal government but without a strong security construct to protect their culture and traditional forms of governance. The impact of this arrangement along with other assimilation policies enacted by the federal government has been devastating for indigenous people. A current movement has been instigated by indigenous leaders, scholars, activists, governments and others to recognize these injustices and try to reconcile the relationships between indigenous people and Canadian society through legal, social and economic mechanisms. Elected leaders, however, still grapple with the day-to-day management and administration of programs and services in their communities.

Although municipal government systems can be effective and their leadership respected, the disease that colonization has created for indigenous communities presents indigenous leaders with many challenges. Leaders in FN communities have political, managerial, administrative, and cultural responsibilities. Not only do FN leaders need to run their organizations and deal with the problems of any municipal government, but their concerns and leadership responsibilities are exacerbated by wider issues of transparency, accountability, legitimacy and competing value systems. Another factor is the trauma of colonization.

FN's relationship with INAC causes significant bureaucratic and legislative barriers. This leadership challenge is becoming even more critical in British Columbia as communities are directed towards treaty settlements with federal and provincial governments. In BC:

> First Nations will receive as much as $7 billion according to an economic analysis undertaken by Grant Thornton for the Treaty Commission. Total benefits from treaties, including increased investment, could be as high as $50 billion – $1 billion to $2 billion each year for the next 20-25 years.[2]

Such treaty settlements may mean the end of any federal system of support for the governance and security of many FN communities. In addition, these treaty settlements may have an even greater effect in assimilating indigenous societies by forcing them to engage fully in a capitalist economy without adequate leadership preparation in this arena.

Leadership is critical, given the history and the growing complexity of the issues that FN communities face as well as the importance of original identity for indigenous survival. "Understanding leadership means understanding indigenous political philosophy; conceptions of power and the primary values that create legitimacy and allow governments to function appropriately and effectively."[3] "Our Indigenous leaders need to make leadership development a priority like industry and mainstream government does for their leaders."[4]

## SCOPE, SOURCES AND PURPOSE

This chapter will draw from personal experience working with FN organizations in BC, public documents published by BC FN's organizations, and current scholarly articles and publications from indigenous and Western sources. It will seek to identify the relevant competencies needed by contemporary First Nations organizational leaders in British Columbia and describe some leadership development strategies that reflect indigenous culture and incorporate traditional indigenous methods of leadership development.

## BACKGROUND OF FIRST NATIONS
## GOVERNMENT ORGANIZATIONS

To appreciate the complex challenges for indigenous leaders in FN governments, it is important to understand the historical and current sources of leadership in FN communities. Prior to colonization, First Nations leaders were not elected but "emerged from the natural order and laws of nature as people who attracted followers, and traditional selection criteria."[5] In 1867, the "British North America Act, Canada's new constitution, made 'Indians and Lands reserved for Indians' a subject for government regulation, like mines or roads."[6] The resulting laws were codified in the Indian Acts of 1867, 1880, *inter alia*. One of these laws saw traditional government structures that had been in place in many nations for centuries replaced with a band council system. These laws took control of finances, imposed land tenure systems, and oversaw funding arrangements, membership, family matters and more. Many FNs have been working towards restoring their own vision of government. These systems take the form of several different models of government that include a "nation" model, a "public" model and an "urban" model. The models provide a framework in which indigenous communities can operate under Canadian law and, in some cases, reflect the traditional structures that existed prior to colonization.

As in Canadian municipal elections, FNs vote for their chief and councillors. Election rules and policies establish who can run for chief or council, how long they can serve, and who is allowed to vote for them, among other guidelines.[7] The organization is made up of a chief and councillors who are elected for a maximum term of two years to carry out business such as developing by-laws and administering community businesses and services. Members of the community (living on and off the reserve lands) have the right to vote for their chief and councillors. FN communities in BC have populations ranging between 250 and 18,000. Depending on the size of the community, the chief and Council members may lead from one to several portfolios. Larger communities have employees to deliver the programs and services or they may be employed in this role themselves.

First Nations governments in BC operate with varying levels of success in terms of efficiency, accountability and the ability to serve the needs of their communities. The measure of leadership success for a FN organization can be measured by the health and well-being of the people and the continuing strength of the nation as indicated by the preservation of traditional values.[8] A leader may ask herself several questions with respect to her leadership such as: Is the community happy, healthy and safe? Are cultural traditions and languages practised and protocols respected? Are people living in harmony with their environment?

One approach to measuring success in order to determine organizational goals, measures and leadership competencies is a balanced scorecard approach. As described by Robbins, "The balanced scorecard, developed by Kaplan and Norton, is an attempt to provide an integrated approach to measuring organizational effectiveness."[9] Though usually applied to very complex organizations, it fits the holistic approach to self and community development that is understood by indigenous people. In this context, the basic principles could be adapted. An example is shown in Figure 1, "The Balanced Scorecard – Measures that Drive Performance."[10]

There are several reasons for the ineffectiveness of FN leaders. They include the structure of the organizational system, the decision-making powers that legally bind the community and that still lie with INAC, the lack of technical skill or formal education of employees that the system demands, and the loss or disruption to hereditary systems of leadership development that existed in these communities. Some measures of success are presented above in order to emphasize the importance of balancing indigenous values with organizational strategy and culture, which give us a stronger idea of the necessary leadership competencies.

Leadership in FN communities must be approached in a "multidimensional way in order to take into account the individualist competitive ethos or a strong cooperative ethos that arises out of the local society."[11] Traditionalists will argue that a cross-cultural approach to leadership development in a FN community is a form of co-optation and will only further the assimilation agenda of colonial power. This statement may be accurate and FN leaders should consider those viewpoints.

However, we cannot ignore the fact that our communities are evolving and exist in a larger global context. Elected leaders and managers need to understand the multiple cultural approaches to leadership required to operate in a larger economy.

Figure 1. A Balanced Scorecard Perspective to a First Nations
        Government Organization

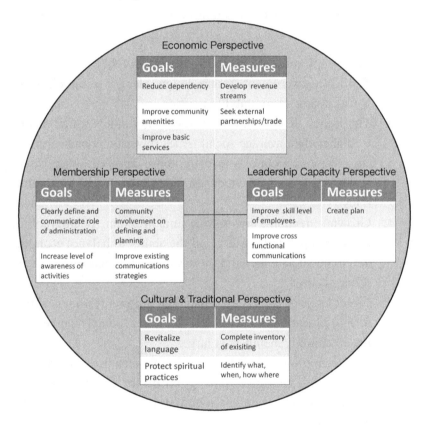

## LEADERSHIP CONTENT ISSUES

First Nations leaders who work in FN organizations are grappling with issues faced by all organizational or business leaders today. The issues include globalization, advances in technology, economic uncertainty, and environmental concerns. They affect daily operation directly or indirectly because of their impact on governance and security issues. Some leaders face extreme levels of political and social crisis in their communities. In exemplifying this position, Alfred asserts, "Without strong and healthy leaders committed to traditional values and the preservation of our nationhood, our communities will fail." These issues require appropriate leadership competencies because "it takes particularly strong leaders to guide people through uncertainty and rapid change."[12] The leadership situation is critical for most communities. The major issues are outlined as follows:

1. The complexities of and relationship with INAC;
2. The FN's government system design – length of appointment, voting issues, accountability issues;
3. The legacy of colonialism in the communities which has led to higher than average social issues (poverty, poor health, unemployment, alcohol and drug abuse, spousal abuse, lateral violence, a system of encouraged dependency and low literacy rates);
4. Growing demands for service and program (demographics) membership, family issues, and the ability to balance economic development activities and those values with social program and service delivery;
5. Lower levels of leadership capacity or follower readiness, skill or formal education of employees, chief and council members and the community members at large;
6. The assumption or belief by community members that the elected leadership can solve all the problems for the community;
7. Disagreement over direction and authority between hereditary and elected leadership in some communities; and
8. Balancing the participation in community economic development pursuits with traditional indigenous beliefs, culture and practices.

## LEADERSHIP COMPETENCIES

Before selecting appropriate methods for leadership development necessary for effectiveness in the context of a FN government organization, we will identify the desired leadership competencies. By competency we mean the "sets of behaviours a leader must display to perform the tasks and functions of their role with competence."[13] The FN leadership competencies stem from the type of organizational structures that FN governments follow and the issues described in the previous paragraphs.

Effective leadership in FN communities may require leaders to "discover and nurture all of the gifts they potentially possess."[14] To illustrate these possibilities, we will use a circle to show the connectedness of all aspects of leadership and corresponding archetypes (see Figure 2). Here, a leader is symbolized by four archetypes that relate to the four directions: teacher, healer, visionary and warrior. The four directions of north, south, east and west are based in an indigenous paradigm for relating oneself to the world and a way of approaching physical, emotional, intellectual and spiritual development. "In contemporary society, becoming an effective leader means developing these four aspects of personality."[15] "What is necessary for leaders to affect transformation today is to effect the regeneration of our minds, bodies and spirits. This is the ancient way of the warrior."[16] "Even though these four archetypes are emphasized in most shamanic traditions, it is important to understand that they are universal and easily accessed by all humans in a variety of different contexts, cultures, structures and practices."[17]

Table 1 categorizes the archetypes and the corresponding leadership competencies that relate to the leadership challenges mentioned previously. The columns to the right show a corresponding leadership model (Daniel Goleman's leadership repertoire from his research on emotional intelligence).[18]

These preferred leadership models all emphasize high relationship orientations with concern for people, respect and mutual trust preferred to task orientation.[19] They emphasize a move from a competitive style and related competencies to creating an environment that fosters collaboration and mutual support.[20] As organizational and political leaders,

First Nations leaders must ensure that their communities and their core values are aligned with their actions and their organizational leadership patterns. Indigenous philosophies are most closely aligned with what social psychologists call a "humanistic" philosophy. The central theme of a humanistic philosophy is that close personal relationships give meaning to life. According to Goleman, "Humanistic leaders gravitate toward leadership styles that emphasize interaction with others such as democratic, affiliative or coaching."[21]

Figure 2. First Nations Leader Archetypes

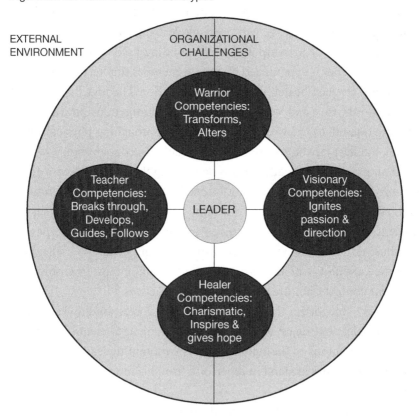

Table 1. First Nations Leader Competencies

| | | The Leadership Repertoire from "Primal Leadership" (Goleman, 2002) |
|---|---|---|
| Healer | • Crisis management skills<br>• Strong ability to empathise with people<br>• Spiritually connected to cultural traditions and ceremony<br>• Skill in traditional language<br>• Recognize importance of self-care and renewal | **Affiliative**<br><br>• Creates harmony by connecting people<br>• Heals rifts, motivates during stress, strengthens connections |
| Visionary | • Ability to lead and motivate a diverse work group (skill, education levels, ages) in their community<br>• Ability to inspire membership to work together – overcoming legacies of historical significance<br>• Emphasize collaboration over competition, break down boundaries between departments<br>• Ability to see the big picture | **Visionary**<br><br>• Moves people towards shared dreams<br>• When clear direction is needed |
| Teacher | • Embrace lifelong learning<br>• Demonstrate and foster an environment of learning – academic, professional, technical and cultural/traditional.<br>• Focus on empowerment and strengths<br>• Recognize value of mentorship in organization and community | **Coaching**<br><br>• Connects people to organizational goals<br>• Helps people build skills over the long term |
| Warrior | • Work to transform and or replace imposed colonial structures that are not effective – through policy, law and political savvy. Requires legal/technical/political leadership experience/skill<br>• Transformative leadership skills | **Democratic**<br><br>• Values input and participation from all members<br>• To build consensus |

# LEADERSHIP DEVELOPMENT PROCESSES

The FN concept of family is consistent with Girouard's assertion that, "governance as a theme is familiar to all cultures and regions." Hence, leadership in governance is also familiar. Although there is great diversity in regional, linguistic and cultural backgrounds, leaders "share common roles and responsibilities attributed to being an elected chief or council member trying to balance their Indigenous worldviews with Western organizational cultures."[22] Leaders are encouraged to run for chief or council positions by their community and family members because they are known to demonstrate strength or knowledge, or potential in some specific area(s) of community concern. In some cases, leaders are elected to ensure that family or community are granted priority access to FN funds, programs and services. This is a fault in a system that rewards members who manipulate the system that creates the "haves" and the "have-nots" in a community. The leaders are not necessarily elected because they will make the best community leaders but for self-serving reasons, leaving the FN community in a continued state of dependence, hopelessness and despair. When this situation occurs, we may see lower levels of leadership emerge without the political or organizational power to enact positive change. The emerging leaders and their development are just as important to the continued survival or revitalization of indigenous communities and should not be overlooked.

The process of developing leaders in a FN organization requires two important considerations: (a) FN leaders are typically born and raised in that community, so the nurturing of leadership that extends beyond the organization into the community and back again is important, and (b) indigenous learning is a holistic process that starts before birth and continues throughout life. Learning and teaching is a cyclical process and we are all learners and teachers at each point in our lives. The cyclical process of learning and leadership development is important to recognize when we are recommending appropriate strategies for leader development in FN organizations. Management and leadership education is typically an institutionalized form of learning. The indigenous view places equal value on learning that happens externally in a formal institutionalized program. According to Vaill, "Learning as a way of being is a whole mentality. It is a way of being in the world."[23]

Van Velsor and McCauley have identified three areas of capability that can be integrated in the holistic model for FN leader and leadership development.[24] These capabilities are identified as follows: self-management capabilities that enable leaders to develop positive and trusting relationships and to take initiative; social capabilities that enable meaningful connections to others; and work facilitation capabilities that enable them to facilitate accomplishments by others. The three areas are identified in the process below; they may overlap.

Figure 3. First Nations Leadership and Leader Development Processes

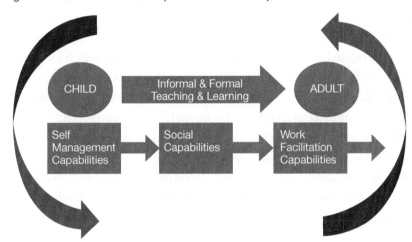

## LEADERSHIP DEVELOPMENT –
## SELF-MANAGEMENT AND SOCIAL CAPABILITIES

Leadership in and of itself was never a goal of indigenous education but rather a result of the way of living in communities and striving towards being complete.... Reciprocity, support, benefit, purpose and visions are combined with an ingrained love for one's people and orientation to act for the good of the people formed the foundation for the expression and development of leaders.[25]

Thus, "Leadership is not a position or a place in an organization, but a sense of responsibility."[26] In the context of governance, it is, as Girouard describes, "how parents seek to manage a home ... how a village elder oversees his or her small dominion ... how the multi-faceted elements of modern society, including nation-states [First Nations], consider and *choose*."

The process of leadership development for FN leaders begins in childhood, through informal teaching and mentoring and through formal rites of passage and ceremony. A major part of development is through listening and observing leadership events and actions while they are taking place. Children are included in development opportunities and elders take a large role in educating and mentoring children about leadership, life, cultural lessons and teachings. These processes are referred to by researchers as "social learning theory which recognizes that people learn by watching others"[27] and the process of "socialization which involves the transmission of cultural information and values."[28] For indigenous communities, the importance of developing children and community members is as important as providing organizational or professional development opportunities to employees. An indigenous approach to leader and leadership development means that everything is connected and development is cyclical. Leadership development leads to strong leaders and their continued development and ability to mentor children.

Prior to colonization, leadership development was critical to survival. Each person had a role, developed over their lifetime, which included technical and cultural teachings. There were leadership aspects to almost every role in the community. Because FN people have adapted to Western society, especially in the case of urban communities, many of the roles and the technical teaching that took place have been set aside and the technical teachings have been replaced with the technologies and theories learned through formal Western education. This does not mean that cultural teaching does not take place. In fact, the teachings, rites of passage and ceremony are still practised and are a large part of leadership development. McCauley and Douglas refer to the relationship-based learning that occurs in FN communities as "developmental relationships."[29] Relationships that develop over the course of a lifetime influence leadership and this process happens informally and formally.[30] In the case of FN development, relationships occur inside and outside the FN organizational context.

ISSUES

- It is important to provide children and adolescents with many different development opportunities but some communities lack the capacity (social or economic) to provide this. For these communities, aspects of health, culture and language must be restored as part of a process of leadership development for the community.
- When indigenous children enter the mainstream educational system, many of the culturally specific self-management and social capabilities are not recognized in that system. It is important for children to understand the value of their own culture and to celebrate their leadership aspirations in the community context.
- Some indigenous families do not place value on traditional systems. They may see life on the "reserve" as dysfunctional and, therefore, may not make connections to indigenous culture for their children. These children and potential leaders have no desire to explore their culture; they see being Indian as an impediment to their personal or professional development. FN leaders may try to find ways to include members living off the reserve in leader development activities.

## FORMAL LEADER DEVELOPMENT AND WORK FACILITATION CAPABILITIES

Prior to colonization, indigenous tribes did not participate in institutionalised formal education. "Education was not around in those days. They gathered all the elders and they would decide what the people would do, like for the winter, who will be going fishing who would be trapping and all that."[31] Today, the primary processes for development of work facilitation capabilities for most FN leadership are institutionalized post-secondary education programs, and similar professional and personal development opportunities. Most of these learning opportunities take place outside the community but in context with other FN leaders who share similar issues. Work facilitation capabilities include management skills, the ability to act and think strategically and creatively, and the ability to initiate change.[32] However, this area is not completely independent of the FN cultural context. Depending on the size of the community, the availability of training resources and the proximity to formal (Western) educational providers, the chief, council members and staff members have varying degrees of access and approaches to leadership training. Post-secondary education is not a prerequisite for getting elected or appointed to council. For a FN community, most leadership comes from that community and it is critical to develop that leadership from within. It is necessary to balance indigenous cultural teachings and indigenous identity with the technical teaching that now comes from Western sources. Both are equally important in leadership and leader development in FN organizations.

ISSUES

- Those who leave their community to gain a Western education are seen as an "apple" when they return; that is, they are indigenous on the outside but white in their ways of thinking and viewing the world. In the context of dysfunctional situations, "ethically challenged community leaders are uneasy about having their operation exposed to educated community members who may not agree with how budgets are being managed or not being managed or how resources are wasted."[33]

- Another reason for the rejection of the educated is because many community members see the importance of retaining cultural teachings. In terms of leadership, there is a sense of fear that a Western approach to leadership training may threaten the important teaching that comes from their own people and indigenous perspectives. However, in the organizational context, this leadership and management education is useful and valuable.

- It may be difficult to measure or assess leadership development for FN leaders. Institutional versus community goals and objectives need to be considered when selecting leadership development strategies.

- In some cases, hereditary leaders and their goals for the

community may be in direct conflict with elected leadership and its organizational mandate. An elected leader will need to seek value congruence before moving an organization or a community forward successfully.

- For most FN organizations, leaders are busy managing daily activities; leadership development is not part of a long-term strategy for the organization. Most take part in leadership development opportunities as they are offered.
- Most leaders have to travel long distance to attend formal leadership development workshops or seminars and their continued development is not supported once they return home.

## CONTEXTUAL ISSUES FOR FIRST NATIONS LEADERSHIP DEVELOPMENT

### INDIGENOUS CULTURE AND LEADERSHIP DEVELOPMENT TRAINING

The cultural fit of non-indigenous sources of leadership development for FN leaders needs to be considered.

When pursuing leadership development opportunities, certain values of non-Native North America produce difficulties for FN people in higher education organizations. The design, structure and curriculum, and methods of assessment are derived from the cultural tendencies within mainstream Canadian and U.S. society.[34]

For indigenous people, there is absolute meaning given to the teachings in their appropriate context. For example, cultural meaning can be misunderstood if a story is read in isolation or by someone unfamiliar with the culture. There are drawbacks to teaching leadership to an indigenous individual out of the context of their own culture.

Layers of meaning are exposed depending on the way a story is told, how it is told, who tells it and by listening to the whole story. This results in the interrelatedness of the word, thought, belief and action, and thus its holistic meaning.[35]

Traditional Aboriginal epistemologies consider that personal experience and the reflection upon this experience is essential in assembling a comprehensive understanding of something.[36] In this case, if the legitimate authority for leadership training, performance and assessment rests with Western institutional sources, leadership is not likely to be accepted by subordinates or community members. "A group's performance can suffer when goals and rewards are arbitrarily imposed from the outside."[37] Strategies that include culturally specific leadership development opportunities must always be balanced with other approaches. In addressing leadership development for non-North American cultures, Michael Hoppe asks, "In short, what should be done to successfully transfer U.S. leadership development models and practices to other cultures?"[38] A better question would be: How can FN cultural and leadership practices inform and improve Western leadership development approaches?

## LEADERSHIP DEVELOPMENT FOR COMMUNITIES IN CRISIS

Some FN communities in non-FN populations are struggling with far higher than average rates of poverty, alcoholism and drug abuse, domestic abuse, poor health and unemployment. Many are remote rural communities with limited opportunity for development contact. Because leadership comes from the community and their organizations are staffed by community members, it is difficult to pursue a leadership agenda, but probably more critical. In these cases, the cycle of daily crisis management is the norm. It is important for these leaders to look to appropriate external partners in reorienting the focus of the community or formulating crisis intervention strategies prior to or in conjunction with a leadership development strategy.

## STRATEGIES FOR FIRST NATIONS
## LEADERSHIP DEVELOPMENT

Based on the First Nations leader competencies identified earlier, the following table describes several strategies for developing leader capabilities in FN government organizations that overlap into leadership development for the community. The strategies will be different for every FN, depending on their cultural and social structures, background and goals. As mentioned previously, some communities recognize hereditary roles and these people hold elected positions. Other communities balance hereditary leadership with elected organizational leadership, while some look only to elected leaders as the source of leadership in their community.

The critical factor when choosing a leader development strategy is ensuring that the leader development goals are aligned with the goals and culture of that community, ideally reflected in the FN government organization. In addition, it is important that the leader can objectively assess, challenge and seek appropriate support for the particular leadership challenges.[39]

In Table 3, capabilities are identified as four archetypes associated with four indigenous leader capabilities: healer, visionary, teacher and warrior. Competencies associated with each archetype are adapted from Abbot Laboratories Leadership Competency model[40] and from Daniel Goleman's *Primal Leadership Competencies.*[41] Using this format, almost any competency model can be categorized as one of the four archetypes. Personal and professional strategies are outlined, which could be formal or informal processes for learning or understanding. For instance, in practising and learning one's traditional indigenous culture, elements of conflict or crisis management may also be taught. Some of the most important sources of leadership learning may exist in one's own community rather than come from external, formal, Western institutional sources. Communities will identify their own internal sources of cultural leadership learning.

In 2007, the Aboriginal Learning Knowledge Centre (ALKC) of the Canadian Council on Learning (CCL) released its models of *Holistic*

*Lifelong Learning* intended to measure learning progress in First Nations, Métis and Inuit communities.

These learning models were developed in response to the inadequacy of Western models of learning in addressing aboriginal learning needs, and are intended to provide alternate models that better reflect how aboriginal people in Canada conceptualize learning. The models assert that, to be most effective, aboriginal learning involves these characteristics[42] as follows:

- Holistic and multi-dimensional;
- A lifelong process;
- Experiential in nature;
- Rooted in aboriginal languages and cultures;
- Spiritually oriented;
- A communal activity, involving family, community and elders; and
- An integration of aboriginal and Western knowledge.

## ACTION PLAN

### STEP ONE

As a community, commit to a long-term vision of leadership that allows development across age and gender in each of the four competency areas identified: healer, visionary, teacher, warrior. The development opportunities may include formal and informal, indigenous cultural and Western sources, short- and long-term programs. They may cross age and gender boundaries. Programs or learning opportunities that are already in place in the community may be a part of this strategy. Development opportunities will include: youth, community at large, elders, organizational staff and managers, chief and council members.

Table 2. First Nations Leadership Development Strategies

| Capabilities | Competency | Personal Strategies Assess/ Challenge/ Support | Professional strategies Assess/ Challenge/ Support | Issues |
|---|---|---|---|---|
| Healer | Create a culture of open and honest communication, respect and knowledge sharing. Create harmony by connecting people together. | Learn/practice own language. Learn practice own culture and ceremony. Practice self care and personal renewal. Develop personal relationships with community members. Demonstrate and practice healthy choices and habits. | Learn crisis management skills. Learn effective conflict management skills. Learn and practice empathic listening. Develop meaningful relationships with employees. Create time to learn and reflect from own and others hardships. | First Nations leaders confirm that First Nations leadership is physically, emotionally, and intellectually demanding (Voyageur 2006, p. 5). Leaders must be mindful of the associated stress and burnout that they may experience in their roles. Burnout is "a unique type of stress syndrome, characterized by emotional exhaustion, depersonalization and diminished personal accomplishment" (Cordes et al., 1993, p. 621). FN leaders are no stranger to loss but the goal is to deal with loss in an effective and constructive manner. "By facing the loss and dealing with the adversity related to it, these challenges provide the opportunity to develop resilience" (Moxley, 2004, p. 185). |
| Visionary | Set vision and strategy. Create and deliver a vision for the future to maximize performance. Move people towards shared dreams. | Develop the ability to think and act strategically. Use positive and healthy informal opportunities to build relationships with organization and community members. | Develop the ability to think and act strategically. Learn to build cohesive and supportive teams. Learn/undergo western approaches to leader development and assessments. | While it may be useful for a FN leader to undergo some personal leadership assessments, some of the tools that are typically recommended for managerial leaders such as a 360 degree, may not be appropriate in the context of a FN community. "A history of mistrust, breach of confidentiality, ambiguity as to use of the data, or confrontational relationship may seriously undermine this practice (VanVelsor, 2004, p. 341). |

Table 2, *con't*

| | | | | |
|---|---|---|---|---|
| **Teacher** | Attract, develop, inspire and motivate people to maximize the collective skills of the community. Help people build skills over the long term. Set high goals for community success. | Find an appropriate mentor or role model. Participate in a coaching opportunity. Take opportunities to enhance personal development – interests and hobbies. | Find an appropriate mentor or role model. Learn how to teach or how to further develop and provide a continuous learning environment. Provide leadership support or mentorship to another. | Leaders must keep in mind that many of their members are dealing with social issues that may affect their ability to engage fully in learning opportunities. Higher levels of support or new approaches to learning must be created. Asking employees to develop or change may create additional stress, which may act to exacerbate social problems in some cases. The research says, "It is clear that for some portion of the population, stressful experiences at work increase the risk of problem drinking, substance abuse, and other adverse behavioural health outcomes" (Ducharme & Martin, 2000, p.225). From a stress perspective, "some workers may be more at risk than others for developing alcohol-related problems either because they are more sensitive and vulnerable to abuse-based stress, or because they are more willing to turn to alcohol as a means by which to cope with such stress" (Frone, 1999, p.288). |

## STEP TWO

Guide program and learning selections that align community and organizational goals with existing strengths and supplement areas that need further attention. Recognized leadership must take the primary role in participating in and supporting leadership development opportunities.

Ensure that opportunities are available to all members and that sufficient time and resources are available.

Ensure that activities have a component of assessment, challenge, support and celebration in each program area.

Table 2, *con't*

| Warrior | Understand the community needs, structure and limitations of the organization and all stakeholders. Build on participation from all members. Make good decisions in the obstacles of difficulties and challenges. Act decisively and courageously to change what is not working. | Develop comprehensive knowledge of community, history and background from internal and external perspectives. Understand historical relationship of community and with other governments. | Gain legal, policy development and related technical skills and knowledge. Develop organizational management skills. Understand role and uses of political and social activism. Develop strategic approaches to managing change and gaining sources of power. Develop strong time management skills. | A transformational leadership approach is relied on to enact change. According to Currie and Lockhart, transformational leaders "Motivate staff by creating high expectations, modelling appropriate behaviour, using symbols to focus efforts and providing personal attention to followers by giving respect and responsibility" (Currie & Lockett, 2007, p.344). Leadership relies on the readiness of followers. The ability to enact change will rely on a FN's leader's ability to create physically and culturally strong members. Some employees may not be ready to take on higher levels of responsibility and challenge. Transformational leadership within institutions is criticized as, "if current arrangements be challenged too strongly, and at an accelerated pace, then leaders may be attacked by their political overseers, or their subordinates, or both, because these groups do not agree with the direction their leaders are trying to take them" (Currie & Lockett, 2007, p.347). |

## STEP THREE

On a quarterly and annual basis, assess the effectiveness of each program area in relation to the areas the community decides are important to measure. Note that this will sometimes depend on external program funding. The community may decide to use its traditional patterns of marking time or seasons or cycles as the appropriate time to assess and plan new goals or activities. Each year, re-evaluate programs and opportunities and start the cycle over again.

CONCLUSION

Governance and security of First Nations poses challenges for the leaders who are required to balance their respective culture at the interface of FN and non-FN communities, organizations and governments. These conundrums reflect clashes of culture and, as Girouard notes, clash of civilizations. For the Anastazi, the unsuccessful resolution of similar clashes may have contributed to the premature demise of this FN culture. Today, leadership for sustainable governance and security of First Nations, by both FN and non-FN leaders, "needs to take into account the historical and cultural differences, seek out through clear curiosity their styles and strengths, ... and embed such elements into approaches and systems, even while seeking to exist in a modern and complex world."[43]

Based on the background, current issues and challenges that elected FN leaders in BC face in order to achieve sustainable governance and security, the following conclusions are drawn:

- Contemporary First Nations government leaders must be competent in political, managerial and administrative areas, and be strongly grounded in their own cultural identity in order to be effective community leaders.
- A holistic leadership competency model that allows development of four directions of learning and ways of being in the world is an appropriate model for FN leaders.
- A sustainable long-term strategy for First Nations leadership development will include all levels of the organization, extend to the community at large and include youth and elders. It will value and balance cultural practices and language with Western opportunities for leadership growth.
- The cultural fit with non-indigenous sources of leadership development for FN leaders is an issue. In most formal leadership development programs, the design, structure, curriculum and methods of assessment are derived from non-indigenous sources. These values may conflict with community leadership values.

## RECOMMENDATIONS

Supported by the analysis of the FN leadership context, indigenous development processes and the conclusions, the following recommendations are offered in an attempt to give FN leaders insight into developing a long-term leadership development strategy for their organization.

- A leadership development strategy should include chief and council, organizational staff at all levels, and the community at large. Some of these opportunities should be provided for specific groups and others should be opportunities for sharing across age and gender and community or organizational roles. Because FN community leadership comes from within, it important to allow youth and elders in leadership development to build on their self-confidence and ensure that they have the tools to help them succeed as future leaders.

- Each FN organization may start this process by identifying long- and short-term community goals. These goals may include the delivery of programs and services that support membership, community-driven economic goals, membership satisfaction and a leadership agenda. Once the community has identified these goals, the organization can then design a leadership development strategy.

- The previous section identifies a holistic approach to developing oneself as a leader in a FN context. It is a balanced approach to personal leadership development and one that is appropriate to indigenous leadership development. More specific personal and professional leadership development strategies are identified in Table 2.

- The term of the elected chief and council is two years; this short time frame may not be long enough for long-term leadership development to take place for an individual. An organizational strategy is necessary for leadership development that is part of a longer-term strategy, perhaps cyclical over time, through various levels of the organization and community.

- Because so much of FN leadership is learning from one's own culture, that aspect of development is critical and should be supported as a legitimate form of development.

- When selecting formal programs, FN should seek programs where facilitators understand the cultural perceptions and values of FN people.
- Formal mentoring programs that address the support component of development and that overcome geographic boundaries are important.
- McCauley and Van Velsor identify that all development opportunities should include the opportunity for assessment (by self or others), challenge and support.[44] A First Nation will need to find a balance in providing both indigenous and Western opportunities for leadership growth and finding culturally appropriate programs that balance assessment, challenge, support and the recognition of achievement.

## REVIEW QUESTIONS

1. What is the benefit to Western nations to integrating Indigenous competency models, given the multi-cultural dimensions of Indigenous and Western nations?
2. Can governance and security as a unitary concept be incorporated as a holistic model for all nations in the global village?
3. How can failed and failing states look to First Nations leadership for solutions to governance and security issues?

## REFERENCES

Aboriginal Learning Knowledge Centre, *First Nations Holistic Lifelong Learning Model.* 2007, <http://www.cclcca.ca/CCL/Reports/RedefiningSuccessInAboriginalLearning/RedefiningSuccessModelsFirstNations.htm> (10 May 2009).

Arrien, A. *The Four Fold Way.* San Francisco, CA: Harper, 1993.

Alfred, T. *Wasase: Indigenous Pathways of Action and Freedom.* Peterborough, ON: Broadview Press, 2005.

Alfred, T. *Peace, Power and Righteousness: An Indigenous Manifesto.* Don Mills, ON: Oxford University Press, 2009.

Bandura, A. *Social Foundations of Thought and Actions: A Social Cognitive Theory*. Upper Saddle River, NJ: Prentice Hall, 1986.

Bennis, W., J. Parikh, and R. Lessem. *Beyond Leadership: Balancing Economics Ethics and Ecology*. Oxford, UK: Blackwell, 1996.

Bopp, J., M. Bopp, and L. Brown. *The Sacred Tree: Reflections on Native American Spirituality*. Twin Lakes, WI: Lotus Light, 1989.

British Columbia Treaty Commission. *The Business Case for Treaties*. Vancouver, BC: BCTC, 2009.

Calliou, B. "Natural Resources Transfer Agreements, The Transfer of Authority, and the Promise to Protect the First Nations' Right to a Traditional Livelihood: A Critical Legal History" *Review of Constitutional Studies* 12:2 (2007): 173.

Calliou, B. "The Supreme Court of Alberta and First Nations Treaty Hunting Rights: Federalism and Respect for 'the Queen's Promises'." In *The Alberta Supreme Court at 100: History and Authority*. Edited by Jonathan Swainger. Edmonton, AB: University of Alberta Press and Osgoode Society, 2007.

Cajete, G. *Native Science: Natural Laws of Interdependence*. Santa Fe, NM: Clear Light, 1999.

Cordes, C. L., and T. W. Dougherty. "A Review and an Integration of Research on Job Burnout." *Academy of Management Review, 18*(4) (1993): 621-656.

Cranwell-Ward, J., A. Bacon and R. Mackie. *Inspiring Leadership: Staying Afloat in Turbulent Times*. London, UK: Cengage Business Press, 2002.

Currie, G., and A. Lockett. 2007, " A Critique of Transformational Leadership: Moral, Professional and Contingent Dimensions of Leadership Within Public Services Organizations." *Human Relations* 60, no. 2 (2007): 341-70.

Daft, R. L. *The Leadership Experience* (4th ed.) Mason, OH: Thompson Higher Education, 2008.

Ducharme, L. J., and J. K. Martin. "Unrewarding Work, Co-Worker Support, and Job Satisfaction: A Test of the Buffering Hypothesis." *Work and Occupations* 27, no. 2 (2000): 223-243.

Frone, M. R. "Work Stress and Alcohol Use." *Alcohol Research & Health: The Journal of the National Institute on Alcohol Abuse & Alcoholism* 23, no. 4 (1999): 284-91.

Giber, D., L. L. Carter and M. Goldsmith, eds. *Linkage Inc's Best Practices in Leadership Development Handbook*. San Francisco, CA: Jossey-Bass, 2000.

Helin, C. *Dances with Dependency, Indigenous Success Through Self-Reliance*. Vancouver, BC: Orca Spirit, 2006.

Hoppe, M. "Cross-cultural Issues in the Development of Leaders." In *Handbook of Leadership Development*. Edited by C. M. Velsor. San Francisco, CA: Jossey-Bass, 2004.

INAC. *Holding Band Council Elections*, Indian and Northern Affairs Canada, Canada, 2009, <http://www.ainc-inac.gc.ca/ai/scr/bc/proser/fna/bndelc/index-eng.asp.> (10 May, 2009).

INAC. *"Working with Aboriginal People."* Indian and Northern Affairs Canada, 2009. <http://nwt-tno.inac-ainc.gc.ca/yb/yb-A-eng.asp> (9 May 2009).

Irwin, N. *"Native Indian Leadership From Within."* Unpublished Master's Thesis. Edmonton, AB: University of Alberta, 1992.

Kaplan R., and D. Norton. "The Balanced Scorecard: Measures That Drive Performance." *Harvard Business Review* (Jan/Feb 1992): 71-9.

Kulchyski, P., D. McCaskill, and D. Newhouse. *In the Words of Elders; Aboriginal Cultures in Transition.* Toronto, ON: University of Toronto Press, 2003.

Newhouse, D. "Resistance is Futile: Aboriginal Peoples Meet the Borg of Capitalism." *The Journal of Aboriginal Economic Development* 2, no.1 (2001): 75-82.

McCauley, C., and C. Douglas. "Developmental Relationships." In *Handbook of Leadership Development.* Edited by C. M. Velsor. San Francisco, CA: Jossey-Bass, 2004.

Mckee, A., D. Goleman, and R. Boyatziz. *Primal Leadership, Learning to Lead With Emotional Intelligence.* Boston, MA: Harvard Business School Publishing, 2002.

Mihesuah, D. A., and A. Cavender. *Indigenizing the Academy: Transforming Scholarship and Empowering Communities.* Lincoln, NE: University of Nebraska, 2004.

Moxley, R., and M. Pulley. "Hardships." In Handbook of Leadership Development. Edited by C. M. Velsor. San Francisco, CA: Jossey-Bass, 2004.

Ottman, J. *First Nation's Leadership Development.* Calgary, AB: University of Calgary, 2005.

Robbins, S. P., and N. Barnwell. *Organization Theory; Concepts and Cases.* Australia: Pearson Education, 2002.

Royal Commission on Aboriginal Peoples. *People to People: Nation to Nation.* Ottawa, ON: Ministry of Supply and Services, 1996.

Stogan, V. "Musqueum First Nation, British Columbia." In *In the Words of Elders, Aboriginal Cultures in Transition.* Edited by P. Julchyski, D. McCaskill, and D. Newhouse. Toronto, ON: University of Toronto Press, 1999.

Wood, J., R. M. Zeffane, J. Fromholtz, and J. Fitzgerald. *Organizational Behaviour: Core Concepts and Applications* (1st Australian ed.) Milton, QLD: John Wiley & Sons, 2006.

Woodruffe, C. "Competent by any Other Name." *Personnel Management* 23, no. 9 (September 1991): 30-3.

Vaill, P. *Learning as a Way of Being: Strategies for Survival in a World of White Water.* San Francisco, CA: Jossey-Bass, 1996.

Van Maanen, J., and E. Schein. "Toward a Theory of Organizational Socialization." In *Research in Organizational Behaviour* (Vol. 1) Edited by B. Staw. Greenwich, CT: JAI Press, 1979.

Van Velsor, E., and C. McCauley. "Our View of Leadership Development." In *Handbook of Leadership Development.* Edited by C. M. Velsor. San Francisco, CA: Jossey-Bass, 2004.

Yukongdi, V. MGT8030 Leadership Development: Study Book. Toowoomba, QLD: University of Southern Queensland, 2008.

Voyageur, C., and B. Calliou. "Aboriginal Leadership Development: Building the Capacity for Success." *Journal of Aboriginal Management.* Aboriginal Financial Officers Association of Canada, Ottawa (2007): 8-15.

## ENDNOTES

[1] *The Indian Act*: Canadian federal legislation *("An Act Respecting Indians")* first passed in 1876 and amended several times since. It sets out certain federal government obligations and regulates the management of Indian reserve lands, Indian moneys and other resources.

[2] British Columbia Treaty Commission. *The Business Case for Treaties* (Vancouver, BC: BCTC, 2009).

[3] T. Alfred. *Peace, Power and Righteousness: An Indigenous Manifesto* (Don Mills, ON: Oxford University Press, 2009), 47.

B. Calliou, "Natural Resources Transfer Agreements, The Transfer of Authority, and the Promise to Protect the First Nations' Right to a Traditional Livelihood: A Critical Legal History" (2007) 12:2 Review of Constitutional Studies, 173.

[4] B. Calliou. "The Supreme Court of Alberta and First Nations Treaty Hunting Rights: Federalism and Respect for 'the Queen's Promises'" *The Alberta Supreme Court at 100: History and Authority,* edited by Jonathan Swainger (Edmonton, AB: University of Alberta Press and Osgoode Society, 2007), 133.

[5] N. Irwin. *Native Indian Leadership From Within.* Unpublished Master's Thesis (Edmonton, AB: University of Alberta, 1992), 10.

[6] Royal Commission on Aboriginal Peoples. *People to People: Nation to Nation* (Ottawa, ON: Ministry of Supply and Services, 1996), 10.

[7] INAC. *Holding Band Council Elections*, Indian and Northern Affairs Canada, Canada, 2009, <http://www.ainc-inac.gc.ca/ai/scr/bc/proser/fna/bndelc/index-eng.asp.> (10 May, 2009).

8  T. Alfred. *Peace, Power and Righteousness: An Indigenous Manifesto* (Don Mills, ON: Oxford University Press, 2009), 140.

9  S. P. Robbins and N. Barnwell. *Organization Theory: Concepts and Cases* (Australia: Pearson Education, 2002), 82.

10  R. Kaplan and D. Norton. "The Balanced Scorecard: Measures That Drive Performance." *Harvard Business Review*, vol. Jan/Feb (1992): 71-9.

11  W. Bennis, J. Parikh and R. Lessem. *Beyond Leadership: Balancing Economics Ethics and Ecology* (Oxford, UK: Blackwell, 1996), 166.

12  T. Alfred. *Peace, Power and Righteousness: An Indigenous Manifesto* (Don Mills, ON: Oxford University Press, 2009), 7, 11.

13  C. Woodruffe. "Competent by any Other Name." *Personnel Management,* vol. 23, no. 9, September (1991): 30-3.

14  J. Bopp, M. Bopp and L. Brown. *The Sacred Tree: Reflections on Native American Spirituality* (Twin Lakes, WI: Lotus Light, 1989): 33.

15  A. Arrien. *The Four Fold Way* (San Francisco, CA: Harper, 1993), 15.

16  T. Alfred. *Wasase: Indigenous Pathways of Action and Freedom* (Peterborough, ON: Broadview Press, 2005), 278.

17  A. Arrien, *The Four Fold Way.* (San Francisco, CA: Harper, 1993), 15.

18  Daniel Goleman 2002, 55.

19  R. L. Daft. *The Leadership Experience,* 4th ed. (Mason, OH: Thompson Higher Education, 2008), 67.

20  R. L. Daft. *The Leadership Experience,* 4th ed. (Mason, OH: Thompson Higher Education, 2008), 10.

21  Goleman, 2002, p. 123

22  J. Ottman. *First Nation's Leadership Development* (Calgary, AB: University of Calgary, 2005), 19.

23  P. Vaill. *Learning as a Way of Being: Strategies for Survival in a World of White Water* (San Francisco, CA: Jossey-Bass, 1996), 51.

24  E. Van Velsor and C. McCauley. "Our View of Leadership Development." In *Handbook of Leadership Development,* edited by C. M. Velsor (San Francisco, CA: Jossey-Bass, 2004), 12-15.

25  G. Cajete, G. *Native Science: Natural Laws of Interdependence* (Santa Fe, NM: Clear Light, 1999), 90.

26  J. Cranwell-Ward, A. Bacon and R. Mackie. *Inspiring Leadership: Staying Afloat in Turbulent Times* (London, UK: Cengage Business Press, 2002), xxiii.

27  A. Bandura. *Social Foundations of Thought and Actions: A Social Cognitive Theory* (Upper Saddle River, NJ: Prentice Hall, 1986).

28  J. Van Maanen and E. Schein. "Toward a Theory of Organizational Socialization." In *Research in Organizational Behaviour* vol. 1, edited by B. Staw (Greenwich, CT: JAI Press, 1979).

29  C. McCauley and C. Douglas. "Developmental Relationships." In *Handbook of Leadership Development,* edited by C. M. Velsor (San Francisco, CA: Jossey-Bass, 2004).

30  C. McCauley, C., and C. Douglas. "Developmental Relationships." In *Handbook of Leadership Development,* edited by C. M. Velsor (San Francisco, CA: Jossey-Bass, 2004).

31  Kulchyski, 1999, p. 448.

32  E. Van Velsor and C. McCauley. "Our View of Leadership Development." In *Handbook of Leadership Development,* edited by C. M. Velsor (San Francisco, CA: Jossey-Bass, 2004), 15.

33  C. Helin, C. *Dances with Dependency, Indigenous Success Through Self-Reliance* (Vancouver, BC: Orca Spirit, 2006), 194.

34  Misesuah, 2004, p. 53

35  T. Alfred. *Peace, Power and Righteousness: An Indigenous Manifesto* (Don Mills, ON: Oxford University Press, 2009), xvii.

36  (Newhouse, 2001, p. 75).

37  J. Wood, R. M. Zeffane, J. Fromholtz and J. Fitzgerald. *Organizational Behaviour: Core Concepts and Applications.* 1st Australian ed. (Milton, QLD: John Wiley & Sons, 2006), 199.

38  C. McCauley and C. Douglas. "Developmental Relationships." In *Handbook of Leadership Development,* edited by C. M. Velsor (San Francisco, CA: Jossey-Bass, 2004), 332.

39  E. Van Velsor and C. McCauley. "Our View of Leadership Development." In *Handbook of Leadership Development,* edited by C. M. Velsor (San Francisco, CA: Jossey-Bass, 2004).

40  D. Giber, L. L. Carter and M. Goldsmith (eds.). *Linkage Inc's Best Practices in Leadership Development Handbook* (San Francisco, CA: Jossey-Bass, 2000).

41  Goleman, 2002.

42  Aboriginal Learning Knowledge Centre, *First Nations Holistic Lifelong Learning Model.* 2007, <http://www.cclcca.ca/CCL/Reports/RedefiningSuccesssInAboriginalLearning/RedefiningSuccessModelsFirstNations.htm> (10 May 2009).

43  Girouard, concluding remarks.

44  E. Van Velsor and C. McCauley. "Our View of Leadership Development." In *Handbook of Leadership Development,* edited by C. M. Velsor (San Francisco, CA: Jossey-Bass, 2004).

# GOVERNANCE AND
# THE CREATION OF PEACE SYSTEMS

## DOUGLAS FRY, PhD

## INTRODUCTION

Approximately 50 years ago, US President John F. Kennedy delivered a commencement address at the American University, Washington, DC in which he stated:

> I do not deny the value of hopes and dreams, but we merely invite discouragement and incredulity by making that our only and immediate goal. Let us focus instead on a more practical, more attainable peace – based not on sudden revolution in human nature but on a gradual evolution of human institutions.[1]

In agreement with President Kennedy, hopes and dreams can be important but human institutions have a critical role to play in assuring lasting peace and security. However, also implicit in Kennedy's words is the implication that human nature somehow works to the detriment of peace. In light of research developments unfolding in various fields, contrary to President Kennedy's assumption, human nature and human institutions carry potential for promoting peace and security. This chapter will consider peace systems and how both human nature and human institutions have roles to play in achieving peace and security.

## THE NEW PERSPECTIVE ON HUMAN NATURE: IMPLICATIONS FOR PEACE AND SECURITY

The dominant perspective in the evolutionary sciences has long been that competition, often expressed through aggression, is the norm.[2] However, we may be at the threshold of a paradigm shift away from the dominance of "nature, red in tooth and claw," as Tennyson expressed it, toward a perspective which acknowledges that cooperation, sharing, helping, conflict resolution, restraint and reconciliation have strong evolutionary bases and are critically important in the behavioural repertories of social species such as humans.[3] This shift in focus toward acknowledging the strong human potential for peace is reflected across a variety of topics and research fields, both in the types of research question now being asked and in the answers that are emerging.

The origin of war, for example, has long been assumed to be ancient, perhaps even predating the genus *Homo*,[4] but as part of the new paradigm this presumption is now being questioned and evidence re-evaluated.[5] Correspondingly, a great deal has been written about chimpanzee lethal aggression with extrapolations sometimes being made to humans and their ancestors.[6] In accordance with the new paradigm, however, a recent rejoinder[7] that considers peaceable bonobos as well as chimpanzees, suggests that ancestral intergroup conflict may have been more bonobo-like – that is, lacking lethal raiding – than chimp-like. One piece of evidence in support of this view is that the 4.4 million year old *Ardipithecus ramidus* described by White and his colleagues, in contrast to chimpanzees, had non-projecting small-sized canines and minimal sexual dimorphism in body size – anatomical features that tend not to be associated with overly aggressive behaviours. In a similar vein, the long-standing presumptions of predatory predilections in the human evolutionary line are being re-evaluated; Hart and Sussman review the evidence and conclude that instead of "man the hunter," ancestral humans deserve the moniker "man the hunted," clearly having been preyed upon in prehistory by a plethora of predators.

Even the widely propagated proposition that warriors and other killers have higher reproductive success than non-killers, a view stemming from one article on the Yanomamö[8] has recently been re-evaluated theoretically, mathematically, and empirically to suggest that in fact the opposite is the case.[9] For example, a mathematical re-analysis of the data on the Yanomamö men in the original study revealed that those reported to have killed averaged more offspring in part because they were more than 10 years older than the men who had never killed anybody.[10] Older men in Yanomamö society tend to average more offspring than younger men simply because they have had more years to reproduce. Additionally, research using data from two different cultures – the Cheyenne and the Waorani – not only failed to replicate the original findings, but, on the contrary, found fitness to be negatively correlated with killing.[11] These findings are in concordance with game theoretic analyses of animal conflict, and much data on intraspecific agonism in mammals, that draw attention to the dangers to life and limb associated with engaging in severe forms of aggression.[12]

Further evidence for an emerging paradigm that acknowledges the importance of cooperation, pro-sociality, and peaceable behaviour comes from many fields.[13] From ethology, the research documents cooperation, empathy, and conflict resolution in various animal species.[14] Pan-mammalian patterns of agonism – in correspondence with game theoretic simulations[15] – reveal that escalated fighting among same-species rivals is very rare compared to the widespread use of non-contact displays and ritualized contests that make serious injuries or death unlikely. Across the primate order, physical aggression constitutes only a minute portion of all behaviour,[16] and aside from the special case of infanticide, conspecific killing is uncommon. The new paradigm points to how restraint characterizes much human conflict behaviour.[17] If clocking hours of observation time, the overwhelming majority of human behaviour in any society is non-violent, and the overwhelming majority of conflicts are managed non-violently, depending on culture and circumstance, through withdrawal, toleration, discussion, reprimands, withholding support, negotiation, payment of compensation, mediation, adjudication, sulking, apologizing, forgiving, reconciling and so forth.[18] As Fuentes quipped, "It's not all sex and violence."[19] In fact, contra Hollywood films, it is very rarely violence.

The landmark work of de Waal[20] and his colleagues[21] shows that non-human and human primates readily cooperate and reconcile after aggression, especially when their valuable social relationships are involved.[22] Thus an evolved capacity to work together is older than humanity. A new take on nomadic forager data notes the ubiquity of cooperation, helping, and sharing in these societies. It points out that of most disputes – whether lethal or non-lethal – reflect interpersonal, not intergroup, motivations stemming from, for example, jealousy or rivalry between two men over a woman.[23] Such disputes cannot be considered war. Such observations about the overwhelming predominance of sharing and caring, helping and being helped, in all human societies, tend to have been ignored or considered unimportant by the many writers who have focused their attention almost exclusively on the violence.[24]

My own work has shown that warfare is typically rare-to-absent at the ancestral nomadic band level of social organization – the type of social existence over many millennia of human evolution.[25] Neurobiological research shows that humans receive an immediate biochemical reward in oxytocin – one of the "feel good" hormones – after cooperating, and this may be part of an evolved brain-reward system in humans related to cooperation, trust and altruism.[26] Finally, findings from military science show that it is more difficult to get men to kill in combat than commonly assumed under the traditional paradigm's overemphasis on the "struggle for existence," the "survival of the fittest," "original sin," or "demonic males." A resistance to killing the enemy has been documented in soldiers in various wars from different time periods and different cultural settings.[27] If killing were so natural, why do so many combat soldiers suffer from post-traumatic stress disorder for the rest of their lives?

In sum, the traditional focus in many fields has been on competition, self-interest, violence and war.[28] When President Kennedy alluded to human nature in his 1963 speech on peace, he presumably had some of these conflict-oriented human capacities in mind. However, there is bountiful evidence from numerous sources that human nature may actually incline us toward getting along with each other without violence, showing restraint against lethal aggression, cooperating toward shared goals, feeling empathy towards others, and resolving disputes peaceably, often with reconciliation and forgiveness as part of the relationship-mending process. These behaviours occur to a much larger degree than has been assumed by presidents and non-presidents alike. In proposing that we are seeing a paradigm shift toward a greater appreciation of cooperation, peacemaking, empathy and sharing, the point is not to deny the obvious human capacity to engage in war, but rather to balance this traditional emphasis on competition and violent human conflict behaviour with a growing body of findings which substantiate a new less red-toothed and bloody-clawed interpretation of human nature.[29] As Tennyson wrote, "The old order changeth, yielding place to new." Our understanding of our own nature thus changeth too.

This paradigm shift, the new perspective that balances competition and cooperation, selfishness and sharing, warring and peaceablity, has implications for security in the geopolitical world. The new perspective highlights the evolved capacity of humans and other animals to get along with each other, to work together pro-socially, and to resolve disputes and differences without bloodshed. Such behaviours have been important over the course of human evolution and are necessities in the 21st century. Competition does play a central role in Darwinian evolutionary thinking, and rightly so, but the new perspective resting solidly on empirical evidence shows that sometimes the best competitive strategy in a fitness-enhancing sense is to be cooperative in a behavioural sense. Similarly, aggression is dangerous, and so evolution has clearly selected for the judicial use of aggression rather than for the unleashing of unbridled fury.

One's view of humanity affects one's views about how best to seek security. Perceptions that humans are naturally selfish, competitive and aggressive lead to fear of others, distrust and a reluctance to cooperate. These perceptions may also lead to pessimism about ending the institution of war or preventing particular wars. If human nature is nasty and aggressive it follows that there may be only a slim chance of achieving a more peaceful and secure world. In any case, the way to seek security is to keep up one's guard, keep the powder dry and remain suspicious of the intentions of others. On the other hand, perceptions that humans can be cooperative as well as competitive and peaceful as well as warlike open the door to a different type of security strategy. Perhaps the abolition of war would be possible and disputes could be handled justly without violence. President Kennedy suggested, "Every thoughtful citizen who despairs of war and wishes to bring peace should begin by looking inward – by examining his own attitude toward the possibilities of peace." The new paradigm offers hope that human nature does not stand in the way of peace. This is a very important real-world implication.

## THE MALLEABILITY AND IMPORTANCE OF HUMAN INSTITUTIONS

As Kennedy emphasized nearly fifty years ago, human institutions have a crucial role to play in creating and maintaining peace. Human institutions evolve. Additionally, existing institutions for resolving conflicts and providing justice at one social level can be applied at higher orders of society to achieve the same ends. We will consider some examples of how this has been done. Kennedy was optimistic along these lines:

> Peace is a process – a way of solving problems. With such a peace, there will still be quarrels and conflicting interests, as there are within families and nations. World peace, like community peace, does not require that each man love his neighbour – it requires only that they together in mutual tolerance, submitting their disputes to a just and peaceful settlement.

Interestingly, President Truman held similar views about the possibility of applying judicial institutions at higher social levels:

> When Kansas and Colorado have a quarrel over the water in the Arkansas River, they don't call out the National Guard in each state and go to war over it. They bring suit in the Supreme Court of the United States and abide by the decision. There isn't a reason in the world why we cannot do that internationally.[30]

Today's world is divided into nation-states, but nation-states are not really very old. Alternative institutions and levels of governance can be visualized. This chapter will consider the idea of adding one or more tiers of supra-national governance to achieve peace and to facilitate international cooperation. We will begin by considering how higher levels of governance – new institutions – can bring about peace and security among previously disparate social units. Girouard proposes such a possibility in pondering "how humanity makes things work."

Surveying the types of human society that exist around the globe, we observe that some are politically acephalous whereas others are not.[31] For most of humanity's existence, the only form of social organization – the nomadic forager band – was acephalous, lacking authoritative political leadership. This feature plus an emphasis on egalitarianism and individual autonomy are hallmarks of this ancestral form of socio-political organization.[32] Tribal peoples tend to lack authoritative central leadership. With the rise of chiefdoms within the last 12,000 years or so, humanity began a major socio-political shift toward centralized leadership and strong political authority.[33] As the first civilizations arose, a mere 5,000 to 6,000 years ago, the state was born. Nation-states are their current incarnations. Chiefdoms, kingdoms, ancient civilizations and modern nation-states have social hierarchies with decision-makers at the top and slaves or workers at the bottom.[34]

So, even though today a global system based on nation-states is taken for granted, there is nothing sacred or even very old about this form of governance. Politically speaking, it has not always been this way and, conceptually, it certainly does not always have to be this way – other forms of governance are possible. Alternative types – for instance, supranational institutions – can be conceptualized in place of a global system based on national sovereignty. In fact, as we will consider shortly, supranational governance already co-exists along with national governance in today's world in cases such as the European Union.

One important general lesson is that the unification of independent social units may reduce hostility among them. This principle has been demonstrated repeatedly.[35] Unification can be voluntary or imposed. Empires can bring peace by outlawing fighting among the peoples they dominate, as illustrated by the *Pax Romana* and *Pax Britannica*. But this is only one model.

Nadel described the socio-political transition from acephalous to cephalous institutions among the Otoro Nuba of Africa. In this cultural case, one leader announced that no longer would feuding between factions be tolerated.

> The first aims of the chieftainship which arose in Otoro were to eliminate this open test of strength between the component segments of the group. It attempted to establish a unity which would supersede the segmentary structure. It assumed the prerogative of using force as a means of maintaining internal peace.[36]

Under the new system, the chief and his administrators delivered justice and the people began to bring their grievances to court for resolution. Consequently, the chief's law replaced the previous self-redress violence of individual against individual or of one kin group against another. This institutional shift in Otto Nuba society illustrates how the imposition of a higher authority over social entities can reduce fighting among them. The Otoro Nuba underwent a transformation from weak governance toward a stronger form of supra-ordinate governance, a chiefdom, which was able to substitute adjudication for the violence of self-redress.

Another example of the pacifying potential of supra-ordinate sociopolitical institutions, this time more democratic in nature, is provided by the Iroquois confederacy. Prior to the second half of the 15th century, the Cayuga, Mohawk, Oneida, Onondaga, and Seneca tribes raided and warred with each other on a regular basis, and many lives were lost.[37] With the creation of their confederacy, they took a familiar institution for conflict resolution, the village and tribal councils, and raised this dispute resolution institution to a higher social level, forming an intertribal Council of Chiefs that represented all five of the uniting tribal nations.[38] The Iroquois brought an end to the feuding and warfare within their confederation.[39]

Dennis wrote:

> Initiating new rituals and practices, and inventing new social and political institutions, the prophet Deganawidah and those who followed his teachings found ways to assure domestic

concord, to extend the harmony within longhouses, lineages, and clans to wider domains, and to confront the ever-present threats to stability, reason, and peace. [40]

Attaining peace and security were concurrently the driving object-ive and the remarkable result of adding a new level of governance, the intertribal Council of Chiefs. It developed a wider social identity, with the effect that former enemies were transformed into relatives and neigh-bours "who found shelter, security, and strength under the branches of the Great Tree of Peace."[41]

## THE CREATION AND MAINTENANCE OF PEACE SYSTEMS

International relations in the 21st century are in some ways similar to those of the Iroquoian peoples before they created their confederacy. As among the Iroquois prior to the formation of their confederacy, the 21st century people of the planet are not truly secure in a global system that accepts the waging of war as the sovereign right of any nation-state – some possessing nuclear weapons. The security challenge faced by people worldwide in the 21st century is remarkably similar to that encountered by the Iroquoian tribes before the 15th century: How can the spectre of war be eliminated? How can a social system where bloodshed and mass destruction remain an ever-present danger be replaced by a social uni-verse in which peace and security are not merely dreams for the future but become the new social and political realities of the present?

A consideration of peace systems provides insights relevant to an-swering these questions.[42] Peace systems can be defined as groups of neighbouring societies that do not make war on each other or usual-ly with outsiders either. Kupchan (2010) called them "zones of stable peace." Besides the Iroquois confederacy, ethnographic examples of peace systems include the ten tribes of the Upper Xingu River Basin in Brazil, the societies of the Nilgiri Hills and Plateau in India, the Orang Asli peoples of Peninsular Malaysia, the Aborigines of the Australian Western Desert and, as we will consider shortly, the European Union.[43]

The tribes that make up the Upper Xingu River peace system,

representing four different language groups, hold a unified identity in addition to their own particular tribal identities.[44] Shared rituals, inter-marriage and trade partnerships reinforce the perception that each person from any tribe is a member of a larger, peaceful society. Likewise, the peoples of the vast Western Desert in Australia transcend local band membership and language dialect.[45] The Western Desert peoples belong to "one country." They see the landscape as boundary-less, and include all inhabitants of this region in one unifying kinship system.[46]

Some peace systems may be termed passive, meaning that they consist of neighbouring non-warring societies lacking a clearly formed over-arching authority.[47] The peoples of aboriginal Malaysia, referred to collectively as Orang Asli, illustrate a passive peace system. A long-standing tradition of Orang Asli non-violence among neighbours makes the idea of engaging in warfare alien to the Batek, Semai, Chewong, Jahai, and other indigenous neighbours.[48] Sluys noted, "The Jahai are known for their shyness toward outsiders, their non-violent, non-competitive attitude, and their strong focus on sharing.... In times of conflict, the Jahai withdraw rather than fight."[49] Howell noted that peaceablity is an Orang Asli trademark, and that they lack "any history of warfare, and overt acts of aggression are very rare."[50] The peace system and internal non-violence of these Orang Asli societies are reflected not only in the absence of feuds and war among the tribes, but also historically by their shunning of armed resistance to slave raiders.[51]

The second kind of peace system can be called active. Active peace systems have developed unifying, identity-expanding, social and political institutions that promote and maintain peace and security within the system. The Iroquois confederacy, which was also known as the Iroquois Great League of Peace, is a good example of an active peace system.[52]

The creation of the Iroquois peace system entailed not only a shift in values toward peace, an elaboration of kin-relations to include members of other groups, a creation of new inclusive rituals, ceremonies and symbols to galvanize peaceful interaction, but also a new governing body – a new institution – that consisted of some fifty chiefs.[53] This Council of Chiefs convened regularly as a newly created political entity. One concrete shift in Iroquois judicial thinking was the abandonment of blood revenge in response to violence and the inauguration instead of a compensatory approach to providing justice. Although living on different continents, the Otto Nuba and the Iroquois thus discovered the same judicial principle: self-redress vengeance can be phased out and replaced by a legal system based on compensation.[54]

Thus far we have considered how a new evolutionary paradigm presents a less violent view of human nature, a shift in thinking that holds important peace-promoting potential, and how human institutions can be created and applied at higher social levels in the interest of peace. In the remainder of the chapter, we will consider some of the processes that may be important for the creation of security through peace systems: (1) developing a visionary goal, (2) creating interdependence, and (3) expanding social identity to encompass a larger social amalgam.

## THE IMPORTANCE OF VISION

President Kennedy was a visionary. When he announced his agenda for achieving a more peaceful world, one cannot help but be aware that during the Cuban missile crisis some months before, this leader had stared Armageddon in the face. As a combat veteran of World War II, he understood firsthand the horrors of war and realized that in the nuclear age "total war made no sense." President Kennedy was the father of two young children and on a rainy day in the Oval Office had asked an advisor what became of the nuclear fallout from above-ground atomic testing. He was disturbed by the answer that the radioactivity disperses and eventually finds its way into the air, the soil, and the water – in the rain falling outside his window. In his 1963 speech, he announced the beginning of high level discussions in Moscow for the purpose of creating a comprehensive test ban treaty, and the first concrete result was the enactment of the Partial Nuclear Test Ban treaty later the same year, which stopped atmospheric testing by the USSR and the USA. The visionary thinking of President Kennedy comes through at many times during his speech, as follows:

> I am talking about genuine peace, the kind of peace that makes
> life on Earth worth living, the kind that enables men and nations

to grow and to hope and to build a better life for their children – not merely peace for Americans but peace for all men and women – not merely peace in our time but peace for all time.

President Kennedy was not only a dreamer but also a doer. The rapid enactment of the Partial Nuclear Test Ban treaty in 1963 is an example. Recall that he also set the ambitious goal of travelling to the moon within a decade and set in motion the processes to achieve that objective.

President Kennedy's ability to conceive and express a far-reaching vision is exceptional among leaders. In fact, the importance of having a clear and comprehensive vision is overlooked in many discussions of peace and security. A common assumption seems to be that a significant social transformation away from war simply would not be possible, that it is unrealistic, that only a handful of naïve poets and musicians can "imagine all the people living life in peace." Widespread fatalism easily results in a self-fulfilling prophecy. President Kennedy did not fall into that pessimistic mind-trap:

> Our problems are manmade – therefore they can be solved by man.... No problem in human destiny is beyond human beings.... We shall also do our part to build a world of peace where the weak are safe and the strong are just.

*Having a vision of a world without war is the first step toward creating such a world without war.*

Prior to the development of their peace system, the tribes that were to form themselves into the Iroquois confederacy lived in constant fear of attack from each other. The archaeological evidence shows that they constructed stockades around their villages. Excavations near Elbridge, New York revealed that the early Onondagas, for instance, had excavated trenches and constructed a three-meter high wall to protect their village.[55] The social construction of the Iroquois Great League of Peace in large part ended the fear of attack. In Iroquois legends, the visions of one man named Deganawidah were pivotal for transforming a war system into a peace system within the confederacy. In the epic tale, Deganawidah and his companions planted a Great Tree of Peace, whose roots extended in four directions symbolizing the spread of peace beyond the Great League of Peace, ultimately to encompass all humanity. Dennis explained:

> Deganawidah and the chiefs then uprooted a great and lofty pine, exposed a chasm, and discarded their weapons of war. A swift current of water swept them away, they replanted the tree, and they proclaimed "Thus we bury all weapons of war out of sight, and establish the 'Great Peace.' Hostilities shall not be seen nor heard of any more among you, but 'Peace' shall be preserved among the Confederated Nations."[56]

Deganawidah, the visionary, saw a new social world where neighbouring peoples conceived of each other not as enemies but as kinfolk, expanded their identities beyond that of a particular village or tribe, and addressed the disputes that invariably arise in social life not through violence but through council meetings. According to legend, Deganawidah advocated a new mindset that held peace and unity at its core, with the explicit goal of abolishing war among the former enemies united under the Iroquois Great League of Peace.

Like President Kennedy and Deganawidah, Jean Monnet – the father of Europe – was a visionary. And like the other two, Monnet was effective at inspiring social change. The birth of the European Union provides another illustration of the importance of having a vision. Former German Chancellor Konrad Adenauer said that Monnet has been sent by God. He gave to the political leaders not only an image but also a plan for how to avoid the next war in Europe.[57] Part of Monnet's insight was to comprehend that the centuries of warfare in Europe – and he had experienced World Wars I and II in his own lifetime – fundamentally stemmed from unrestrained national sovereignty in a political system without supra-national institutions. This is exactly the same problem that the Otoro Nuba had experienced, but on a smaller scale, with feuding and violence between independent lineages until a court of law was established by the chief to resolve disputes without bloodshed. To abolish warfare in Europe, Monnet envisioned a new socio-political order with centralized, supra-national institutions. Like Deganawidha, Monnet was a prophet with a vision of how to create a lasting peace, and like

Deganawidah, Monnet understood the necessity of unifying nations, not just formulating treaties among them. The key to unification and the end of war was to develop a higher level of governance, a new broader social identity, and a new unity of purpose. EU Commissioner Jose Manuel Barroso recalled how President Kennedy once praised Monnet:

> In just 20 years, Jean Monnet did more to unite Europe than a thousand years of conquerors. Monnet's vision transformed a whole continent and forged *an entirely new form of political governance.*[58]

President Kennedy spoke broadly of a planet at peace – of "world peace" – and also mentioned "world law" and "world disarmament." Might he have had in mind, as long-term visionary goals, *"an entirely new form of political governance"* based on law at the planetary level?

## INTERDEPENDENCE

The EU provides a modern-day example of how interdependence can purposefully be augmented as part of a deliberate plan to create a new level of political governance. It is sometimes forgotten that a major impetus behind the multi-stage process of European integration was to eliminate the threat of war in the region.[59] In post-war Europe, as the horrific memories of widespread death, bombings and blackouts, food rationing and hunger, concentration camps and mass graves were still fresh in the minds of the survivors, the motivation was very strong to devise a way to prevent future European wars.

> Amid the misery and ruin left behind by the twentieth century's two lethal world wars, a group of Europeans set out to create a lasting peace on the continent and a shared economy. They did not aim low. Their dream was to produce, once and for all, an end to war on the continent, and an end to poverty.[60]

In Zurich in 1946, Winston Churchill proposed that a pan-European peace could be forged through the creation of strong trade relations. He called for the creation of the United States of Europe.[61] A number of leaders such as French Foreign Minister Robert Schuman and Germany's Chancellor Konrad Adenauer readily adopted Churchill's and Monnet's vision of Europe as an interdependent union that would once and for all put an end to war.[62] In 1953, Monnet in an interview on CBS television explained what he saw as the sentiment in Europe at the time:

> I don't think there is anyone in Europe, who has lived the last fifteen years, who at a certain moment has not realized that a great deal of the reason for the catastrophe we have experienced comes from the fact that those nations had been separated by national sovereignty; and they see in this effort of unifying the people a hope and an assurance that that is the greatest contribution to peace that can be made; and they see in it, at the same time, the creation of a big market and, therefore, prosperity *and* peace.[63]

The approach of these founding fathers was to increase interdependence among the national economies to make Europe progressively more integrated.[64] They began in the early 1950s by placing coal and steel – critical resources in times of peace and war – under supra-national control. Thus began, over a series of concrete steps, a pattern of multilateral cooperation and unification that continues to this day.[65]

Remarkably, the EU is a deliberately created peace system. Reid commented:

> The EU, after all, is a cooperative community that has been an historic success at its main goals, preventing another war in Europe and giving European nations new stature on the world stage.[66]

There are important lessons for the entire world in this age of global interdependence. Using interdependence to create peace cooperatively and deliberately is a remarkable achievement! War between EU members has become unthinkable.[67] This change in thinking represents a monumental shift from the first half of the 20th century when World War I and World War II ravaged Europe. In a peace system, or what Kupchan called a zone of stable peace:

Its member states let down their guard, demilitarize their relations, and take for granted that any disputes that might emerge among them would be resolved through peaceful means.[68]

The creation of peace systems has occurred many times historically and ethnographically, but not yet to provide safety and security at the global level.[69] Perhaps it is time to try this approach.

## CREATING OVERARCHING SOCIAL AND POLITICAL IDENTITY: EXPANDING THE US

Gandhi was a champion of what I like to call "Expanding the Us to include the Them" when he stated that he was a Hindu, a Muslim, a Buddhist, a Christian, and a Jew. Charles Darwin understood the peacemaking potential of Expanding the Us when he reflected:

As man advances in civilization, and small tribes are united into larger communities, the simplest reason would tell each individual that he ought to extend his social instincts and sympathies to all the other members of the same nation, though personally unknown to him. This point being once reached, there is only an artificial barrier to prevent his sympathies extending to the men of all nations and races.[70]

The ten tribes of the Upper Xingu River basin, the Iroquois and the Aborigine bands of the Western Desert show that clusters of neighbouring societies can Expand the Us and get along peacefully as members of a larger peace system.[71]

Anthropological and psychological research suggests that there are many ways to Expand the Us to develop higher level social identity. First, cross-cutting ties can be developed among groups, for example, through trade relationships, intermarriage, interlinking friendships, and taking part in common rituals and ceremonies.[72] People from the Xingu tribes form trade relationships with people from other groups, a practice that helps to Expand the Us identity across the entire social system.[73] Intermarriage contributes to Expanding the Us as shown by a Xingu man's gesture, which marked from head-to-toe his body's midline as he pronounced: "This side…Mehinaku. That side is Waurá."[74] Second, working together to achieve super-ordinate goals may contribute to the development of a higher-level social identity.[75] Psychological studies show that participating in cooperative activities enhances trust, friendship, positive relations and a common identity among groups.[76]

Returning to the EU case, a new higher-level European identity is emerging, not to replace national identities, but rather as a new overarching level of social identity. As Kupchan[77] pointed out, this formation of a higher level of identification takes time. Evidence of the emerging European identity is numerous and diverse: an EU flag, a common currency (for most member countries), EU passports and the opening of borders for the free movement of people, democratic elections for EU parliamentarians, and so on.[78] In short, the ongoing shift is to add to national identities a new layer of social identification, a pan-European identity, which parallels how the Western Desert Aborigines, the Upper Xingu peoples, and the Iroquois developed an additional social identity as members of an overarching peaceful social system.

## CONCLUSION

President Kennedy was ahead of his time in realizing that nuclear weapons linked the fate of all people on the planet. The use of nuclear weapons makes no sense:

> In an age when the deadly poisons produced by a nuclear exchange would be carried by wind and water and soil and seed to the far corners of the globe and to generations yet unborn…. Our most basic link is that we all inhabit this small planet. We all breathe the same air. We all cherish our children's future. And we are all mortal.

With the largest military on the planet, a half-century after Kennedy spoke of the need to develop a "world security system – a system capable of resolving disputes on the basis of law, of insuring the security of the large and the small, and of creating conditions under which arms can finally be abolished," many US leaders seem to think that safety and security can be achieved unilaterally through the barrel of a gun or an arsenal of nuclear weapons. But competitive military-based strategies are no longer viable in an interdependent world facing common challenges to safety and security.[79] US military strength can do nothing, for example, to halt and reverse global warming. The only manner to meet this planetary problem and to achieve security is through international cooperation.

International cooperation is possible. One example that proves this point is the successful protection of the Earth's ozone layer. In the late 1980s, the countries of the world negotiated and implemented the Montreal Protocol on Substances that Deplete the Ozone Layer and have worked together to phase out ozone-destructive chemicals such as CFCs worldwide.[80] Since the elimination of global CFCs and other ozone-depleting substances, the Earth's ozone layer has been replenishing itself. Sachs pointed out that through international cooperation "the world quickly, indeed almost painlessly, headed off a major man-made threat."[81] So, international cooperation even at the global level is possible.

There will always be naysayers – those that ask the question "Why?" instead of the more visionary "Why not?" In the 21st century, humanity can naysay itself into oblivion or, alternatively, engage in visionary thinking followed by action. Why not actively create a global peace system and abolish war from the planet? After all, the people of the Earth today face some of the same challenges that Europeans solved following World War II. First, the world's people, like the citizens of post-war Europe, face challenges about how to create peace and prosperity. Additionally, the people of today must figure out how to solve shared challenges like global warming, oceanic pollution, and ecosystem degradation that threaten not merely some areas of the planet but endanger human survival. Can we glean some inspiration from visionaries like President Kennedy, Deganawidah and Monnet?

The fact that people have created and maintained non-warring peace systems in various quarters of the globe demonstrate that alternatives to the current-day war system are in fact possible. Ethnographic examples of peace systems in conjunction with the regional EU peace system should combine to stimulate our imagination to create a global peace system. And the example of the Montreal Protocol shows that the nations of the world *can* work together when faced with common threats. There are several take-home messages based on what we have been discussing in this chapter. Of centrality, creating an overarching level of governance contributes substantially to peace within the constituent social units. This principle is well established.[82] How can overarching levels of governance be developed?

First and foremost, there must be the vision followed by concrete steps to transform the vision into the new reality. Second, understanding that interdependence exists (and can be augmented) is critically important. Interdependence provides the rationale for why cooperation and new institutions of governance are necessary to meet common concerns such as global warming and climate change. Safety and security in an interdependent world require joint action among all the parties. This principle of interdependence clearly applied in the creation of the EU and helps to maintain other peace systems as well.[83] The concerted cooperative effort to save the Earth's common ozone layer with the Montreal Protocol illustrates that an understanding of interdependence leads to cooperative action.[84] The new evolutionary paradigm and its concordant view of human nature as not so nasty after all document the long-standing importance of cooperation in humans and other social animals.[85] In fact, cooperation is a hallmark of human beings.[86] Third, as we think about our social identities, we must Expand the Us to include a common identity of humanity as a whole. The Iroquois turned enemies into kin, established unifying rituals and ceremonies, and created myths and symbolism to reinforce the values of peace. They Expanded the Us. The EU seems headed in the same direction in Europe.

Human survival requires that nation-states give up the institution of war and replace it with a cooperative global peace system for the safety and security of all people everywhere. This is consistent with Girouard's reference to the recurring theme of governance. Constructing a peace system for the entire planet involves many synergistic elements, including the transformative vision that a new peace-based global system is possible, the creation of new political institutions at a supra-national level, the understanding that interdependence and common challenges require cooperation, an expanded perception of social identity along the lines that Darwin envisioned and finally, the development of values, symbolism, expressive culture and ceremonies that reinforce peace. The Great Peace of the Iroquois illustrates how peace is an active process that must be created and re-created through vision, cooperation, socio-political institutions, expanded identity, values, symbols, rituals and other cultural channels. Could a global peace system really be created? I suspect that the Xinganos, Iroquois, and founders of the EU would say, "Yes" for they have already created their own peace systems. German philosopher Arthur Schopenhauer (1788-1860) is credited with saying:

> All truth passes through three stages. First, it is ridiculed. Second, it is violently opposed. Third, it is accepted as being self-evident.

## REVIEW QUESTIONS

1. How can a higher order level of governance and security bring about peace between previously desperate and hostile social entities through a new common identity as envisioned by Jean Monnet?
2. The unification of desperate social units reduces hostility among them; the unification can be voluntary or imposed. Compare and contrast this concept of unification – the expanding of us, as occurred during the eras of Pax Romana, Pax Britannica, and modern-day European Union.
3. Discuss the law of force and the force of law as manifestations of peaceful governance and security.

## REFERENCES

Aronson, E., N. Blaney, C. Stephan, J. Sikes, and M. Snapp. *The Jigsaw Classroom.* Beverly Hills, CA: Sage, 1978.

Aureli, F., and F. de Waal. *Natural Conflict Resolution.* Berkeley, CA: University of California Press, 2000.

Barroso, J. M., and J. Monnet. <http://www.time.com/time/magazine/article/0,9171,1552584,00.html> (2006).

Beckerman, S., et al. "Life Histories, Blood Revenge, and Reproductive Success Among the Waorani of Ecuador." *Proceedings of the National Academy of Sciences* 106 (2009): 8134-8139.

Bekoff, M., and J. Pierce. *Wild Justice*. Chicago, IL: University of Chicago Press, 2009.

Bellier, I., and T. Wilson. "Building, Imagining, and Experiencing Europe: Institutions and Identities in the European Union." In *An Anthropology of the European Union*, edited by I. Bellier and T. Wilson. Oxford, UK: Berg, 2000.

Bertens, J.-W. "The European Movement: Dreams and Realities." Paper presented at the seminar *The EC after 1992: The United States of Europe?* Maastricht, The Netherlands, 1994, January.

Boehm, C. *Hierarchy in the Forest*. Cambridge, MA: Harvard University Press, 1999.

Brosnan, S. "Conflicts in Cooperative Social Interactions in Non-human Primates." In *War, Peace, and Human Nature*, edited by D. P. Fry. New York, NY: Oxford University Press, in press.

Chagnon, N. "Life Histories, Blood Revenge, and Warfare in a Tribal Population." *Science* 239 (1998): 985-992.

Coleman, P., and M. Deutsch. "Introduction." In *The Psychological Components of a Sustainable Peace*, edited by M. Deutsch and P. Coleman. New York, NY: Springer, in press.

Darwin, C. *The Descent of Man*. New York, NY: Prometheus Books, 1871/1998.

Dennis, M. *Cultivating a Landscape of Peace*. Ithaca, NY: Cornell University Press, 1993.

Dentan, R. K. "Cautious, Alert, Polite, and Elusive: Semai of Central Peninsular Malaysia." In *Keeping the Peace: Conflict Resolution and Peaceful Societies Around the World* (pp. 167-184), edited by G. Kemp and D. P. Fry. New York, NY: Routledge, 2004.

Dentan, R. K. *Overwhelming Terror: Love, Fear, Peace, and Violence Among the Semai of Malaysia*. Lanham, MD: Rowman & Littlefield, 2008.

Deutsch, M. "Cooperation and Competition." In *The Handbook of Conflict Resolution* (pp. 23-42), edited by M. Deutsch, P. Coleman, and E. Marcus. San Francisco, CA: Jossey-Bass, 2006a.

Deutsch, M. "Justice and Conflict." In *The Handbook of Conflict Resolution* (pp. 43-68), edited by M. Deutsch, P. Coleman, and E. Marcus. San Francisco, CA: Jossey-Bass, 2006b.

de Waal, F. *Peacemaking Among Primates*. Cambridge, MA: Harvard University Press, 1989.

de Waal, F. *The Age of Empathy.* New York, NY: Harmony Books, 2009.

Elliott, M. "The Decline and Fall of Rome." *Time* (European Edition) 165 no. 24 (2005): 20-21.

Ember, C. "Myths About Hunter-gatherers." *Ethnology* 17 (1978): 439-448.

Endicott, K. M. "The Effects of Slave Raiding on the Aborigines of the Malay Peninsula." In *Slavery, Bondage and Dependency in Southeast Asia* (pp. 216-245), edited by A. Reid. New York, NY: St. Martin's Press, 1983.

Endicott, K. M. "Peaceful Foragers: The Significance of the Batek and Moriori for the Question of Innate Human Violence." In *War, Peace, and Human Nature,* edited by D. P. Fry. New York, NY: Oxford University Press, in press.

Endicott, K. M., and K. L. Endicott. *The Headman was a Woman: The Gender Egalitarian Batek of Malaysia.* Long Grove, IL: Waveland, 2008.

Ferguson, R. B. "Introduction: Studying War." In *Warfare, Culture, and Environment* (pp. 1-81), edited by R. B. Ferguson. Orlando, FL: Academic Press, 1984.

Ferguson, R. B. "Born to Live: Challenging Killer Myths." In *Origins of Altruism and Cooperation* (pp. 249-270), edited by R. W. Sussman and C. R. Cloninger. New York, NY: Springer, 2011.

Ferguson, R. B. "The Prehistory of War and Peace in Europe and the Near East." In *War, Peace, and Human Nature,* edited by D. P. Fry. New York, NY: Oxford University Press, in press.

Fry, D. P. *The Human Potential for Peace: An Anthropological Challenge to Assumptions About War and Violence.* New York, NY: Oxford University Press, 2006.

Fry, D. P. *Beyond War: The Human Potential for Peace.* New York, NY: Oxford University Press, 2007.

Fry, D. P. "Anthropological Insights for Creating Non-warring Social Systems." *Journal of Aggression, Conflict and Peace Research* 1 no. 2 (2009): 4-15.

Fry, D. P. "Human Nature: The Nomadic Forager Model." In *Origins of Altruism and Cooperation* (pp. 227-247), edited by R. W. Sussman and C. R. Cloninger. New York, NY: Springer, 2011.

Fry, D. P. "Life Without War." *Science* 336 (2012): 879-884.

Fry, D. P., B. D. Bonta, and K. Baszarkiewicz. "Learning from Extant Cultures of Peace." In *Handbook on Building Cultures of Peace* (pp. 11-26), edited by J. de Rivera. New York, NY: Springer, 2009.

Fry, D. P., G. Schober, and K. Björkqvist. "Non-killing as an Evolutionary Adaptation." In *Non-killing Societies* (pp. 101-128), edited by J. Evans. Honolulu, HI: Center for Global Nonkilling, Honolulu, 2010.

Fry, D. P., and A. Szala. "The Evolution of Agonism: The Triumph of Restraint in Non-human and Human Primates." In *War, Peace, and Human Nature*, edited by D. P. Fry. New York, NY: Oxford University Press, in press.

Fuentes, A. "It's Not All Sex and Violence: Integrated Anthropology and the Role of Cooperation and Social Complexity in Human Evolution." *American Anthropologist* 106 (2004): 710-718.

Fuentes, A. "Cooperation, Conflict, and Niche Construction in the Genus *Homo*." In *War, Peace, and Human Nature*, edited by D. P. Fry. New York, NY: Oxford University Press, in press.

Gregor, T. "Uneasy Peace: Intertribal Relations in Brazil's Upper Xingu." In *The Anthropology of War* (pp. 105-124), edited by J. Haas. Cambridge: Cambridge University Press, 1990.

Gregor, T., and C. A. Robarchek. "Two Paths to Peace: Semai and Mehinaku Nonviolence." In *A Natural History of Peace* (pp. 159-188), edited by T. Gregor. Nashville, TN: Vanderbilt University Press, 1996.

Grossman, D. *On Killing*. New York, NY: Little Brown, 2009.

Hart, D., and R. W. Sussman. "The Influence of Predation on Primate and Early Human Evolution: Impetus for Cooperation." In *Origins of Altruism and Cooperation* (pp. 19-40), edited by R. W. Sussman and C. R. Cloninger. New York, NY: Springer, 2011.

Howell, S. "'To be angry is not to be human, but to be fearful is:' Chewong Concepts of Human Nature." In *Societies at Peace: Anthropological Perspectives* (pp. 45-59), edited by S. Howell and R. Willis. London, UK: Routledge, 1989.

Hrdy, S. B. *Mothers and Others*. Cambridge, MA: Harvard University Press, 2009.

Hudgens, T. *We Need Law*. Denver, CO: BILC Corporation, 1986.

Hughbank, R., and D. Grossman. "The Challenge of Getting Men to Kill: A View from Military Science." In *War, Peace, and Human Nature*, edited by D. P. Fry. New York, NY: Oxford University Press, in press.

Kelly, R. *Warless Societies and the Origin of War*. Ann Arbor, MI: University of Michigan Press, 2000.

Kennedy, J. F. Commencement address at American University. <http://www.jfklibrary.org/Research/Ready-Reference/JFK-Speeches/Commencement-Address-at-American-University-June-10-1963.aspx/ > (10 June 1963).

Kupchan, C. *How Enemies Become Friends*. Princeton, NJ: Princeton University Press, 2010.

Maynard Smith, J., and G. Price. "The Logic of Animal Conflict." *Nature* 246 (1973): 15-18.

Miklikowska, M., and D. P. Fry. "Values for Peace." *Beliefs and Values* 2 (2010): 124-137.

Miklikowska, M., and D. P. Fry. "Natural Born Nonkillers: A Critique of the Killers-have-more-kids Idea." In *Nonkilling Psychology* (pp. 43-70), edited by D. Christie and J. Evans. Honolulu, HI: Center for Global Nonkilling, 2012.

Moore, J. "The Reproductive Success of Cheyenne War Chiefs: A Contrary Case to Chagnon's Yanomamö." *Current Anthropology* 31 (1990): 322-330.

Myers, F. R. *Pintupi Country, Pintupi Self. Sentiment, Place and Politics Among Western*

*Desert Aborigines.* Berkeley, CA: University of California Press, 1986.

Nadel, S. F. *The Nuba.* London, UK: Oxford University Press, 1947.

Nowak, M., with R. Highfield. *SuperCooperators.* New York, NY: Free Press, 2011.

Ostrow, M. *Race to Save the Planet: Now or Never* (episode 10). Annenberg, PBS series. (1990)

Pinker, S. *The Better Angels of Our Nature.* New York, NY: Viking, 2011.

Reid, T. R. *The United States of Europe: The New Superpower and the End of American Supremacy.* New York, NY: Penguin, 2004.

Reyna, S. P. "A Mode of Domination Approach to Organized Violence." In *Studying War: Anthropological Perspectives* (pp. 29-65), edited by S. P. Reyna and R. E. Downs. The Netherlands: Gordon & Breach, 1994.

Rilling, J. "The Neurobiology of Altruism and Cooperation." In *Origins of Altruism and Cooperation* (pp. 295-306), edited by R. W. Sussman and C. R. Cloninger. New York, NY: Springer, 2011.

Rubin, J., D. Pruitt, and S. Kim. *Social Conflict: Escalation, Stalemate, and Settlement.* New York, NY: McGraw-Hill, 1994.

Sachs, J. *Common Wealth: Economics for a Crowded Planet.* New York, NY: Penguin Press, 2008.

Sherif, M., O. Harvey, B. White, W. Hood, and C. Sherif. *Intergroup Conflict and Cooperation: The Robbers Cave Experiment.* Norman, OK: University of Oklahoma Press, 1961.

Sluys, C. M. I. van der. "Jahai." In *The Cambridge Encyclopedia of Hunters and Gatherers* (pp. 307-311), edited by R. B. Lee and R. Daly. Cambridge: Cambridge University Press, 1999.

Smith, D. C. *Jean Monnet: The Father of Europe.* Documentary film available at: <http://www.law.du.edu/index.php/jean-monnet-father-of-europe/documentary> (2011).

Staab, A. *The European Union Explained: Institutions, Actors, Global Impact.* Bloomington, IN: Indiana University Press, 2008.

Staub, E. "The Psychological and Cultural Roots of Group Violence and Creation of Caring Societies and Peaceful Group Relations." In *A Natural History of Peace* (pp. 29-155), edited by T. Gregor. Nashville, TN: Vanderbilt University Press, 1996.

Sussman, R., and C. R. Cloninger. *Origins of Altruism and Cooperation.* New York, NY: Springer, 2011.

Sussman, R. W., and P. Garber. "Cooperation and Competition in Primate Social Interaction."

In *Primates in Perspective* (pp. 636-651), edited by C. Campbell, A. Fuentes, K. C. MacKinnon et al. New York, NY: Oxford University Press, 2007.

Tonkinson, B. "Resolving Conflict Within the Law: The Mardu Aborigines of Australia." In *Keeping the Peace* (pp. 98-105), edited by G. Kemp and D. P. Fry. New York, NY: Routledge, 2004.

United Nations Environmental Program. *The Montreal Protocol on Substances that Deplete the Ozone Layer.*

< http://www.unep.org/ozone/pdfs/montreal-protocol2000.pdf >

<http://www.unep.org/themes/ozone/?page=home> (2000)

Verbeek, P. "Peace Ethology." *Behaviour* 145 (2008): 1497-1524.

Verbeek, P. "An Ethological Perspective on War and Peace." In *War, Peace, and Human Nature*, edited by D. P. Fry. New York, NY: Oxford University Press, in press.

Wallace, P. *White Roots of Peace.* Santa Fe, NM: Clear Light, 1994.

White, T., et al. "*Ardipithecus ramidus* and the Paleobiology of Early Hominids." *Science* 326 (2009): 75-86.

Wrangham, R., and D. Peterson. *Demonic Males.* Boston, MA: Houghton Mifflin, 1996.

## ENDNOTES

[1]   J. F. Kennedy, 1963

[2]   See Bekoff & Pierce, 2009; Fuentes, 2004, *in press*; Fry, 2012; Nowak, 2011; Sussman & Cloninger, 2011

[3]   de Waal, 2009; Fry et al., 2010; Fuentes, 2004, *in press*; Hrdy, 2009; Verbeek, 2008

[4]   Ember, 1978; Wrangham & Peterson, 1996

[5]   Fry, 2011; Ferguson, 2011, *in press*; Kelly, 2000

[6]   e.g., Wrangham & Peterson, 1996

[7]   e.g., de Waal, 2009; Ferguson, 2011

[8]   Chagnon, 1988

[9]   Beckerman et al., 2009; Ferguson, 2011; Fry, 2006; Miklikowska & Fry, 2012

[10]  Fry, 2006

[11]  Beckerman et al., 2009; Moore, 1990

[12]  Fry & Szala, *in press*

[13]  Fry, 2012

[14]  Bekoff & Pierce, 2009; de Waal, 1989, 2009; Verbeek, *in press*

[15]  Maynard Smith & Price, 1973

[16]  Sussman & Garber, 2007

[17]  Fry, 2006; Fry et al., 2010; Fry & Szala, *in press*

[18]  Fry, 2006

[19]  Fuentes, 2004

[20]  e.g., 1989, 2009

[21]  e.g., Aureli & de Waal, 2000; Brosnan, *in press*

[22]  Aureli & de Waal, 2000; de Waal, 1989, 2009

[23]  Fry, 2011

[24]  e.g., Wrangham & Peterson, 1996

[25]  Fry, 2006; 2011; contra Ember, 1978; contra Pinker, 2011

[26]  Rilling, 2011

[27]  Grossman, 2009; Hughbank & Grossman, *in press*

[28]  Fuentes, 2004; Nowak, 2011; Sussman & Cloninger, 2011

[29]  de Waal, 2009; Ferguson, 2011; Fry, 2006; Hart & Sussman, 2011; Nowak, 2011

[30]  Hudgens, 1986, p. 12

[31]  Reyna, 1994

[32]  Boehm, 1999; Fry 2006, 2011

[33]  Fry, 2006

[34]  Reyna, 1994

[35]  Ferguson, 1984; Fry, 2006

[36]  Nadel, 1947, p. 163

[37] Dennis, 1993; Kupchan, 2010

[38] Dennis, 1993

[39] Fry, 2012).

[40] Dennis, 1993, p. 77

[41] Dennis, 1993, p. 109

[42] Fry, 2009; 2012; see also Kupchan, 2010

[43] Fry, 2006, 2009, 2012; Miklikowska & Fry, 2010

[44] Fry, 2006, 2009, 2012

[45] Myers, 1986

[46] Myers, 1986; Tonkinson, 2004

[47] Fry, 2012

[48] Dentan, 2004, 2008; Endicott & Endicott, 2008; Endicott, *in press*

[49] Sluys, 1999, pp. 307, 310

[50] Howell, 1988, p. 150

[51] Endicott, 1983, p. 238; Dentan, 2004

[52] Dennis, 1993; Fry, 2012; Kupchan, 2010; Wallace, 1994

[53] Wallace, 1994

[54] Fry, 2006, 2007

[55] Dennis, 1993, p. 54

[56] Dennis, 1993, pp. 94-95

[57] Harryvan interview in Smith, 2011

[58] 2006; emphasis added

[59] Bellier & Wilson, 2000, p. 15; Reid, 2004; Staab, 2008, p. 144

[60] Reid, 2004, p. 25

[61] Elliott, 2005, p. 20

[62] Reid, 2004; Smith 2011

[63] Monnet, 1953, in Smith, 2011

[64] Fry, 2009; Reid, 2004

[65] Staab, 2008

[66] Reid, 2004, p. 193

[67] Bertens, 1994; Smith, 2011

[68]  Kupchan, 2010, p. 2

[69]  Fry, 2009, 2012; Kupchan, 2010

[70]  Charles Darwin (1871/1998) pp. 126-7

[71]  Fry, 2009; Miklikowska & Fry, 2010

[72]  Coleman & Deutsch, *in press;* Fry, 2006, 2009, 2012; Rubin, Pruitt, & Kim, 1994; Sherif et al., 1961

[73]  Gregor, 1990

[74]  Gregor & Robarchek, 1996, p. 173

[75]  Sherif et al., 1961

[76]  Aronson, Blaney, Sikes, & Snapp, 1978; Deutsch, 2006a, 2006b; Sherif et al., 1961

[77]  Kupchan, 2010

[78]  Bellier & Wilson, 2000; Fry, 2009; Reid, 2004

[79]  Fry, 2006, 2007

[80]  Ostrow, 2000; United Nations Environmental Program, 2000

[81]  Sachs, 2008, p. 113

[82]  e.g., Dennis, 1993; Ferguson, 1984; Fry, 2006, 2007; Nadel, 1947; Smith, 2011

[83]  Fry, 2009; Fry, Bonta, & Baszarkiewicz, 2009

[84]  Fry, 2006; Rubin, Pruitt, & Kim, 1994; Sherif et al., 1961

[85]  Bekoff & Price, 2008; de Waal, 2009

[86]  Fuentes, *in press*; Hrdy, 2009; Nowak, 2011; Sussman & Cloninger, 2011

SECTION V

---

# RULES TO ENSURE
# GOOD GOVERNANCE AND SECURITY

---

# GOOD GOVERNANCE AND A MORE SECURE WORLD – NATURAL BEDFELLOWS

## ROY CULLEN, PC, BA, MPA

## INTRODUCTION

The evidence is clear that stable and sound government institutions are more important to good governance than good economic policy or geography.[1] In fact, the latter do not even come close to the impact of governmental institutions that promote political stability, property rights, legal systems and patterns of land tenure on the rate of growth in poor countries. An effective barometer of good governance in any society is the degree of corruption that permeates the society, like a sickness causing havoc in its wake.

The poverty of the world's poor nations is exacerbated by bribery and corruption. In my book, *The Poverty of Corrupt Nations*, I identified a very high correlation (.86) between a country being corrupt and being poor. The problems of income distribution amongst the political elites, the working poor, and the poverty-stricken become more exaggerated and sap hope. Corruption leads to political instability, donor fatigue, and the disappearance of much-needed investment capital in the affected countries, although which factor is the cause and which the effect is not easily identified. Are countries corrupt because they are poor or are countries poor because they are corrupt? Notwithstanding this intellectual dilemma, it is my considered view that reducing the incidence of global corruption will move many people from the ranks of the poor. My thesis is that the reduction of global poverty will increase political stability and make our world a safer place in which to live.

## CORRUPTION AND ECONOMICS LINKAGE

Girouard argues that governance is "the process by which every social action is affected." It is the "human interface between a nation's laws and its citizens." This interface spans the spectrum from ethical to corrupt. We know that disparities between the rich and poor nations are not just a function of corruption alone. In fact, corruption is not unknown in the so-called developed world. There is a strong correlation between poverty and geography, and poverty and conflict, but corruption is the major problem to be solved. The Global Organization of Parliamentarians Against Corruption (GOPAC) was established to build the political will to improve global governance. Its methods are to reduce and minimize the negative effects of global corruption and money laundering. As a director of GOPAC, I lead the anti-money-laundering global task force.

Corruption diverts scarce public resources from worthwhile projects that would assist in lifting citizens out of poverty. Corruption skews economic decision-making in favour of projects where the opportunities for corruption are greatest. In other words, corruption causes scarce public resources to be misallocated and misused. As Girouard asserts, corrupt governance determines gridlock, penury, conflict, illness and arrested development.

Corruption limits economic growth because it adds to the economic cost of doing business. Corruption reduces the flow of investment, both public and private, into countries where it is rife. The economic benefits of foreign direct investment are, therefore, diminished. Corruption undermines faith in public institutions and public officials, and encourages people to become cynical about the political process. As a result, citizens tend to disengage from politics and are disinclined to exercise their democratic rights.

## CORRUPTION AND DESTABILIZATION LINKAGE

Bribes paid to officials may introduce greater risks in health, safety, and environmental concerns when rules are ignored after money has changed hands because bribes are often paid to relax rules and regulations meant to protect the public. In September 2002, I accepted an invitation from NATO to address a group of Eastern European parliamentarians in Kiev, Ukraine, on the topic "Money Laundering and Corruption as New Threats to National Security." The choice of topic surprised me but the more I thought about it, the more easily I began to make sense of it. Corruption results in the destabilization of society while money laundering compromises international financial markets. In that sense they are both threats to national and international security. In addition, those in a corrupt military are more easily persuaded to sell weapons of mass destruction to unstable states and/or terrorists. This possibility is a concern with respect to the Russian military after the break-up of the former Soviet Union, especially given Russia's nuclear weapons capability and its corrupt military.

## CORRUPTION AND STATE SECURITY LINKAGE

Corrupt officials and law enforcement officers are susceptible to turning a blind eye to drug trafficking, trafficking in human beings, and to the production and distribution of counterfeit and pirated goods. It has been shown that terrorist groups have been funded through money laundered from these illegal acts. In 2004, the secretary-general of Interpol told reporters in Brussels that there is "a significant link between product counterfeiting and terrorism in locations where there are entrenched terrorist groups." Interpol found that some of the suspects involved in the sale of fake car brakes in Lebanon had links with terrorist groups. Militants in Northern Ireland and Colombia have been linked to counterfeiting, according to Interpol.[2]

## CORRUPTION AND TERRORISM LINKAGE

The linkage between money laundering, international development assistance and terrorism is complicated. US Congressman Barney Frank told a Parliamentary Network of the World Bank conference (May 2003) that it is a mistake to justify more foreign aid using the security argument that more aid will make for a safer world. He suggested that this rationalization could attract a "belligerent rather than a benevolent response" from donor countries like the United States. The point that Congressman Frank was making, I believe, is that we need to solve the underlying problems associated with terrorism; simply throwing money at the problem will not work. It is reasonable to assume that development assistance from donor countries may be diverted to terrorist activities if the recipient countries harbour resentment and hatred towards those donor countries. I would strongly suggest that events such as September 11th, 2001 show the financing of terrorist activities and related money-laundering activities threaten the peaceful co-existence of countries and people around the world.

The nature of the linkage between poverty and terrorism is unclear. However, the terrorist attacks that targeted innocent Americans and others by Muslim extremists on September 11th, 2001 cannot be justi-fied by any reasonable criteria. While the immediate and medium-term response must be an outright attack on terrorism, we should be ask-ing ourselves: What are its causes? What motivated the perpetrators to commit themselves to certain death? What motivated them to make that ultimate sacrifice? Commentators and experts have advanced various hypotheses. Some argue that these people are Islamic fundamentalists who are determined to destabilize the United States for political reasons while others argue they are individuals responding to the call for a Jihad against the impure and against the excesses of Western society. As Yossef Bodansky suggests:

> Followers of the Ayatollah Khomeini in Iran view the United States as a land preoccupied with the adulation and worship of money, and Majid Anaraki, an Iranian who lived for several years in Southern California, described the United States as a "collection of casinos, supermarkets, and whore-houses linked together by endless highways passing through nowhere, all dom-inated and motivated by the lust for money."[3]

Other commentators speculate that the motivation was to draw attention to the plight of the Palestinians. In this context but focused on a previous struggle, Mahatma Gandhi noted that poverty is the worst form of violence. An argument can be made that terrorism is a violent response to terrible poverty. However, in his book, *Cold Terror*, Stewart Bell argues:

> The root cause of Islamic terrorism is not poverty, nor is it, as former Canadian Prime Minister Chrétien has also suggested, Western arrogance and greed – it is a group of fanatics who want to convince Muslims that theirs is the one true faith and that it is their duty and right to take over the world by force.[4]

"Europeans prefer to say that the root cause of terrorism is poverty – or the unresolved conflict in Palestine, which they accuse former US President George W. Bush of having dangerously neglected during his first term."[5] President Bush argues to the contrary that the primary cause of terrorism is the failure of democracy to take root in the Middle East.

## THE POVERTY – THE POOL
## OF THE DISENFRANCHISED

While we may never know the real motivation for such terrorist actions (indeed the individuals involved may not know clearly why they did what they did), in my view, the reasons for this type of behaviour are more fundamental. It has to do with the growing impatience and frustration of those who "don't have," with the gap between the realities of their own lives and the lives of those who "have." I believe it is derived from the classical "have/have not" tension. While terrorist leaders may be driven by ideology, they are able to draw on a large pool of disenfranchised, forgotten and demoralized individuals to fight their war.

In his autobiography, *My Life*, former US President Bill Clinton asserts that one of the five priorities that the United States should be pursuing is to "make more friends and fewer terrorists by helping the 50 per cent of the world not reaping the benefits of globalization to overcome poverty, ignorance, disease and bad government."[6]

We know intuitively that where there is no hope, people will turn to desperate acts. They consider they have nothing to lose and, perhaps, something to gain. There are some, however, who are motivated to become suicide bombers based exclusively on ideology. As Lieutenant-General Roméo Dallaire so aptly put it in his book, *Shake Hands with the Devil*, following his experience in Rwanda:

> If September 11th taught us that we have to fight and win the "war on terrorism," it should also have taught us that if we do not immediately address the underlying (even if misguided) causes of those young terrorists' rage, we will not win the war. For every al-Qaeda bomber that we kill there will be a thousand more volunteers from all over the earth to take his place .... Human beings who have no rights, no security, no future, no hope and no means to survive are a desperate group who will do desperate things to take what they believe they need and deserve.[7]

Former US Secretary of State, Colin Powell, reiterates this sentiment: "We have to go after poverty. We have to go after despair. We have to go after hopelessness."[8]

## THE SEGUE TO GLOBAL CORRUPTION

This brings us back to the extent of global corruption. Estimates of the scale of global corruption abound but, being a clandestine activity, precision is not possible. An IMF estimate in 1998 placed the value of global money laundering, including the laundering of corrupt funds, at between $800 billion and $2 trillion annually. Nigeria's anti-corruption commission reported that their previous rulers had stolen or misused $500 billion (equal to all the Western aid to Africa in four decades!). In Africa, from estimates derived by the African Union itself, some $148 billion is lost every year to corruption and Africa is the continent with the greatest number of people living in poverty.

In contrast and ironically, Africa is a continent rich in natural resources with 50 per cent of the world's gold, 98 per cent of its chromium, 90 per cent of its cobalt, 64 per cent of its manganese and 33 per cent of its uranium. A recent World Bank survey on Africa claims, "The amount stolen and now held in foreign banks is equivalent to more than half of the continent's external debt."[9]

Corruption is not limited to Africa. It is estimated, for example, that in China, corruption accounts for 15 per cent of the country's GDP and regrettably, the list goes on as one crosses the world. We in the developed economies should not feel "holier than thou" on the issue because we are not immune from corruption ourselves. After the uncovering of a corruption scandal in Canada related to the so-called sponsorship program, we slipped in the worldwide Transparency International ranking to 12th place (i.e., the 12th least-corrupt country) on a list of 146 countries.

Transparent and accountable political systems, like those we have in Canada, flushed out the workings and abuse of the sponsorship program and held the responsible officials accountable. Institutional safeguards such as the Auditor General of Canada together with a free and independent media and parliamentary overseeing produced the intended result – a result I respected notwithstanding the negative consequences for the political party I serve.

It is an example of good governance in the face of corruption but these independent mechanisms of overseeing and accountability do not exist in many countries, in particular in developing and emerging economies. As a result, corruption and money-laundering activities are often hidden from public view or tolerated and accepted because of the cynicism associated with political systems that lack this transparency and accountability. It is this tragic and damaging phenomenon that we need to change.

## FUTURE DIRECTION

Before we do, we should ask: Why should those of us in the developed world be concerned? Our sense of what is right and wrong should start ringing a few bells. The huge disparities between the rich and the poor should cause us to reflect on whether this is fair and just. However, there are more pragmatic reasons. If we do not help the poor to help themselves, this disparity will foster continued discontent and instability in the world. Those who are impoverished and believe that they are oppressed and those without hope will eventually try to take by force what they feel is their fair share (the Palestinians in search of a secure homeland, and the Somali pirates in search of an acceptable standard of living). We return to this issue of international security and terrorism.

Second, it is important that we distinguish between grand or big-ticket corruption and petty bribery. In many countries, government officials are frequently paid a wage or salary that is insufficient to live on and, as a result, they are expected to demand and receive bribes so that they can support themselves and their families. This type of bribery, which is problematical, needs to be distinguished from the grand larceny perpetrated by various world leaders and ruling elites.

Transparency International recently identified the Top 10 most corrupt contemporary political leaders. Collectively, these ten individuals embezzled between them $32 billion-$58 billion.

Table 1. Transparency International's Report of the Ten Most Corrupt Leaders

| Despot | Country | Embezzled (est.) |
|---|---|---|
| President Suharto 1967-98 | Indonesia | $15-$35 billion |
| Ferdinand Marcos 1972-86 | Philippines | $5-$10 billion |
| Mobuto Sese Seko 1965-97 | Zaire | $5 billion |
| Sani Abacha 1993-98 | Nigeria | $5 billion |
| Slobodan Milosevic 1989-2000 | Yugoslavia | $1 billion |
| J.-C. Duvalier 1971-86 | Haiti | $300-$800 million |
| Alberto Fujimori 1990-2000 | Peru | $600 million |
| Pavlo Lazarenko 1996-97 | Ukraine | $114-$200 million |
| Arnoldo Aleman 1997-2002 | Nicaragua | $100 million |
| Joseph Estrada 1998-2001 | Philippines | $78-$80 million |

Source: Transparency International 2004 Report.

Suharto of Indonesia who stole $15-$35 billion and Marcos of the Philippines who embezzled $5-$10 billion, are the two worst. It is not difficult to imagine how many hospitals and schools could have been built, how many doses of HIV/AIDS vaccines administered, or the countless other ways the US $32–$58 billion stolen by these leaders could have been spent to reduce poverty and improve the lives of their citizens. If we take the mean in the range of the amounts stolen by these leaders of $32-$58 billion (i.e., $45 billion) and use World Bank and United Nations program cost estimates, we can calculate that this money could have been used in the developing world, for example, to:

- Provide 112 million households with water;
- Build 108,000 kilometres of road (this would circumnavigate the world almost three times); and
- Treat 270 million people living with HIV/AIDS.

It may be noted that many of these countries are involved in the business of natural resource extraction and this more than any other business lends itself to political corruption. International NGOs such as Extractive Industries Transparency Initiative, Publish What You Pay Coalition, and Revenue Watch Institute have recognized the great level of corruption that attaches itself to natural resource exploitation. They refer to it as the "resource curse."

Although there are no magic solutions to deal with the rampant corruption that contributes to poverty and the feelings of despair, it is imperative to give this problem serious thought. In his book, *The Bottom Billion*, Paul Collier speaks about the four development traps facing the abject poor worldwide:

- The conflict trap;
- The natural resources trap (*resource curse*);
- Being landlocked with bad neighbours; and
- Bad governance in a small country.

In my work with GOPAC (with 700 members worldwide), I have had the opportunity to meet many parliamentarians who are committed to the fight against corruption, some at great personal risk and cost. Many have argued that they view money laundering as inextricably linked to the challenge of reducing or eliminating corruption. The proceeds from corruption and other crimes are laundered to make the funds more accessible to the perpetrators; thus, corruption is increasingly associated with organized crime as well as terrorism. GOPAC members have decided that we need to fight corruption. At the same time and on a parallel track, we must attack the laundering of corrupt money. This initiative includes enhancing the collective ability to recover stolen assets and to repatriate them to the countries where they were illegally derived, for the benefit of all their citizens.

We believe the institution of parliament has a key role to play in fighting corruption. Parliamentarians can hold an executive branch of government to account for their spending and administrative actions. This important role can be achieved in a number of different ways:

- Through debates and questions in the legislature itself;
- Through the work of an auditor general or accounts chamber that reports directly to parliament; and
- By enquiry and investigative work by a public accounts committee of parliament.

## CONCLUDING OBSERVATIONS

In his summary, Girouard notes:

> Depending on your place in the world, hope can be luxury, vision, mirage, or a singular thread by which one clings to survival. Good governance is about those who have the will and the power, and the vision delivering on the hope of those around us in need.

There is also the reality of hope. We realize that there are no magic bullets or instant solutions and that realistically, corruption and money laundering will never be completely eliminated. However, with dedication and hard work in the fight against global poverty, the problem can be contained if we reduce the incidence of corruption. To do this, we need the courage and foresight to look at new ideas and we must dedicate ourselves to new solutions to these serious problems. Some of the ideas I have been promoting to improve governance and fight poverty fall in the following three categories:

**A. Discourage dependence on Official Development Assistance (ODA) to alleviate donor fatigue and cynicism:**

- Encourage the formation of domestic savings and capital pools in developing countries;
- Expand micro-credit – especially to women;
- Unlock trapped capital in developing countries (the Hernando de Soto model); and
- Facilitate share ownership by employees.

**B. Enhance the role of parliaments to oversee the executive branch, and enhance transparency and accountability:**

- Promote an independent judiciary, an independent auditor-general or its equivalent, freedom of speech and freedom of the press, and an adequately resourced anti-corruption agency;
- Pass effective laws that sanction individuals and corporations that pay bribes to public officials;
- Reform the civil service in developing countries and reduce the culture of corruption by paying public servants a fair wage and penalizing those who accept bribes;
- Reduce unnecessary red tape in governments to encourage entre-preneurship and reduce the temptation to expedite decisions through bribes;
- Require the mandatory disclosure of income and assets of pub-lic officials;
- Foster freedom of speech and freedom of the press so that the media can focus attention on corruption; and
- Encourage the involvement of the private sector in development initiatives, including public/private partnerships.

**C. Other initiatives**

- Reward and support jurisdictions that practise good governance (e.g., Ghana);
- Reduce the debt loads of poor countries that are committed to good governance and fighting corruption;
- Remove trade barriers so that developing economies can partici-pate more fully in the global economy; and

- Educate the public worldwide about the costs and negative effects of bribery and corruption.

The challenge is before us. President Obama recently asserted that change would not come if we wait for some other person or some other time. We are the ones we've been waiting for. We are the change that we seek. This statement reflected Mahatma Gandhi's adage: "Be the change you want to see in the world." Good governance and security are not built on a foundation of corruption, whether individual or institutional.

## REVIEW QUESTIONS

1. Why should we fight corruption? The problem is so large and endemic that we will never succeed.
2. Global corruption is a huge problem, but what about governance issues right here at home in Canada (First Nations, Province of Quebec, etc.). Shouldn't we focus on these problems first?
3. Who are some of the newer top ten most corrupt world leaders (e.g., Gadhafi, Mubarak, etc.) to add to the Transparency International list?

## REFERENCES

Cullen, R. *The Poverty of Corrupt Nations*. Toronto, ON: Blue Butterfly Book, 2008.

Ghani, A., and C. Lockhart. *Fixing Failed States: A Framework for Rebuilding a Fractured World*. New York, NY: Oxford University Press, 2009.

Homer-Dixon, T. *The Upside of Down*. Washington, DC: Island Press, 2006.

Kupelian, D. *The Marketing of Evil: How Radicals, Elitists, and Pseudo-experts Sell Us Corruption Disguised as Freedom*. Nashville, TN: WND Books, 2005.

McCandless, H. E. *A Citizen's Guide to Public Accountability: Changing the Relationships Between Citizens and Authorities*. Victoria, BC: Trafford, 2002.

Moghaddam, F. M. *How Globalism Spurs Terrorism*. Westport, CT: Praeger, 2008.

Pinto, J., C. R. Leana, and F. K. Pil. "Corrupt Organizations or Organizations of Corrupt Individuals? Two Types of Organization-level Corruption." *Academy of Management Review* 33, no. 3 (2008): 685-709.

Pfarrer, M. D., K. A. DeCelles, K. B. Smith, and M. S. Taylor. "After The Fall: Re-integrating the Corrupt Organization." *Academy of Management Review* 33, no. 3 (2008): 730-749.

## ENDNOTES

[1]  "Tropics, Germs and Crops: How Endowments Influence Economic Development." (Cambridge, Mass: National Bureau of Economic Research (NBER) Working paper 9106 (William Easterly, Ross Levine).

[2]  Margaret E. Beare and Stephen Schneider. *Money Laundering in Canada: Chasing Dirty and Dangerous Dollars* (Toronto, ON: University of Toronto Press, 2007).

[3]  Yossesf Bodansky. *Bin Laden: The Man Who Declared War on America* (New York, NY: Prima Publishing, 1999), xiii–xiv.

[4]  Stewart Bell. *Cold Terror* (Toronto, ON: John Wiley & Sons, 2004).

[5]  The Economist (February 19, 2005), 11.

[6]  Bill Clinton, *My Life (The Presidential Years)* (New York, NY: Vintage Books, 2005).

[7]  Lt.-Gen. Roméo Dallaire, *Shake Hands with the Devil* (Toronto, ON: Random House, 2003).

[8]  John C. Polanyi. Toronto Star (June 16, 2003).

[9]  World Bank Survey.

# FROM SECURITY STRATEGY
# TO PROJECT GOVERNANCE

## DALE CHRISTENSON, PhD

## INTRODUCTION

Well-intentioned and well-planned projects continually get stuck in a quagmire that holds progress in abeyance until necessary decisions are applied to free them. Recent research has shown that project success depends on certain conditions and factors. An outlier of this research was the attribute of project governance. Upon further reflection, it became the case of the glaringly obvious, as projects were getting stuck because they did not have the decision-making structures in place to provide timely decisions. So spawns the genesis of this chapter as a reflective examination of project governance and its importance to the success of security projects.

Girouard defines governance in the introductory chapter of this book as "the complex and often murky construct of people, organization and rules that exist to run the nation stated." This definition is relevant, consistent, and can be unilaterally applied to the definition of project governance, which is no less critical for the success of a nation than for the success of a project. A more colloquial definition might suggest governance is defined as "who gets to decide what and when." The latent power of project governance is embodied in the will and power of the host organization. Nevertheless, governance personified has a culture complete with morals, values and even attitudes that reflect the host organization. Governance can be the beauty or the beast in terms of social constructs controlling the selection and execution of project activities to meet organizational and project objectives. It can be the beauty that facilitates project success or the beast that acts as an impenetrable barrier to success.

Governance and security are constructs that can be viewed at either an international or local level. Modern project management was born in the mid 1940s from a need to maintain national security when the Manhattan Project was conceived, planned and implemented. Project management has not been used only for security-related projects in the military realm but is often used for international security projects such as foreign aid projects where governance and security structures are integral to the effective delivery of the aid in highly volatile and dangerous arenas. Project management governance is no less important to local security projects such as the projects that attempt to increase public safety for citizens. We will review such a project as a case study to emphasize the necessary governance conditions required for security projects or indeed any project's success.

## PROJECT GOVERNANCE AND SECURITY

Project governance emerged in the literature in the early 2000s and has reached increasing prominence in the last decade. First, a review of the critical success factors by Christenson in 2007 revealed "governance" as a critical factor both as a separate social construct and as a mechanism to establish other critical success factors for projects to increase their likelihood of success. Before this time, projects relied on traditional governance structures in the host organization. These structures were inadequate in terms of providing the necessary focus on project requirements to support success. Second, there has been growing recognition that the form of project governance must match the culture, size, and complexity of the projects it is governing in order to be effective. An over-development of governance on simple projects in mature organizations would slow projects down. Inadequate project governance on complex projects or in an environment with low project maturity would find projects stuck.

Project governance has a continuum of perspectives from pure oversight to pure support. Each perspective forms and shapes the governance structures of the project based on the managers' perceived understanding of the environment and complexity of the project at hand. Third, the null perspective is where governance is lacking. Projects that are being managed within desired budgets and schedules will typically have a longer-term horizon and provide a support context. This context will advocate on behalf of the projects to ensure timely decision-making and adequate resourcing for the project. Projects that are not being managed within budgets or schedules will typically have shorter-term horizons and focus on the here and now. This myopic view can be a considerable risk point for the project because the environment changes and catches the project manager unaware.

Governance needs to ensure that the organization is doing both "the right project" and "getting it done the right way." This is often an evolution of project maturity in the host organizations that has developed from doing projects the right way and then ensuring they are doing the right project. This process is clearly backwards and risks doing the wrong projects right. However, doing it right has recently become more complex in the private and public sectors with the introduction of Sarbanes Oxley laws and legislated transparency requirements (i.e., the Transparency and Accountability Act), respectively.

## CRITICAL SUCCESS FACTORS

Project critical success factor research[1] identified a number of critical factors that are under the jurisdiction of an effective governance system regardless of its form. Governance structures, as stated above, must select the right project and ensure it is completed in the right way. In order to influence these requirements, the governance system must first determine what it is they want the project to accomplish; they must be able to state the need for the project and the preferred future end state or vision. One needs to determine the "Where" and the "Why Now" to create a sense of urgency and a call to action. The "Where" and "Why Now" will influence the selection of "What" project should be completed. Now the governance system needs to have input into the "How" we will achieve the project's objectives that flow from the need. Governance is often the foundation upon which action is taken and it addresses these very simple questions of why, what, where and how. The project management critical success factors identified by Christenson[2] clearly show the critical nature of senior management support, a clear understanding of the need (why), a shared vision (where) and a shared understanding of the project framework (how).

Critical success factor research[3] clearly shows the a priori nature of senior management support for any project to be successful. This senior management support is often transferred to the project by a project sponsor. Therefore, this role is critical and cannot be overlooked. In addition, appropriate delegation of the host organization's power to the temporary organization (project) via a project sponsor shows organizational maturity and understanding of the importance of the strong organizational governance of projects. In order to be successful, a project must have its solution (project) aligned to its need. Without a clear definition of the need, the selection of the "right" project is haphazard and unlikely to meet the need fully or successfully.

Critical success factor research identifies the need for a project management framework that allows understanding of how the project will be completed from concept to cash. This framework is instrumental in the formation of the processes used to complete the project. It is a vital construct for the governance system of the project. Without this framework, endless decisions would compete with each other due to a loss of form and structure at the process level.

Without a structure, organizations may end up doing the wrong project right or the right project in the wrong way. Either combination is ineffective and prone to project failure or inordinate delays and cost overruns. When security is at stake, this inefficiency is untenable and we are negligent when we have the knowledge to perform more effectively.

## CASE EXAMPLE: JIMS

### THE NEED

It is not uncommon among local justice jurisdictions that individual communities or districts maintain their own records, have poor data quality and lack effective systems to share information in a timely manner, if at all. If protocols or effective systems are not shared, each jurisdiction is left on its own to learn critical information about each offender. Even when sharing does occur, the quality of data is often problematic.

All too often prosecutors learn after the fact that they have voluntarily released highly dangerous offenders back into the community who may not appear for subsequent court dates. The data access issue is further eroded by simple recording and data entry errors. Access to accurate information to increase public safety is a critical need of one local justice jurisdiction. The solution to the issue came in the form of the JIMS project whose vision was based on the need for public safety. It was in itself a vision of a preferred future end state that would result in safer communities. While the project had the typical issues one expects when managing highly complex projects, it was successful in part because of a strong governance structure.

### THE PURPOSE OR SOLUTION

JIMS had its beginnings in the early 1990s to meet the business need described above and to create an integrated application in the various justice agencies. The idea was to create a central repository of information involving four interrelated elements of a justice system in which data would be gathered and shared (subject to strict privacy and confidentiality arrangements) to improve information management.

The project is typical of the need in service organizations that have many interlinked but separately operating entities. The need involves sharing vital authorized information to avoid duplication, incorrect information entry or maintenance errors. The purpose is to avoid wasting management energy in establishing duplicated information systems. The original mission of JIMS was to develop a simple centralized case management database system that would achieve a grander vision of public safety. A JIMS participant stated the purpose more broadly:

> The purpose of the JIMS Project is to try to provide an integrated system for the province, incorporating the major stakeholders that are engaged in the criminal justice process, namely the police, the Crown, the courts, the judiciary and corrections people. Basically it is to provide an integrated system that would, theoretically and practically remove silos of information, and silos of jurisdiction of independence and provide a way in which criminal information could be readily shared within some kind of jurisdictional authority.

Given the complexity and multiple stakeholders involved in this project, the governance and structure became very important.

## THE PROJECT STRUCTURE

Over the five-year history of this project, a need for greater governance evolved, requiring more formal structures and greater rigidity of decision-making. This came at a price. There was less creativity in problem-solving and ultimately an advocacy positioning of stakeholders. The evolution and decision-making structure was well stated by one participant:

> The governance evolved over time, but generally there was a project steering committee, and that steering committee included Assistant Deputy Ministers from the various branches, Corrections, Court Services, Criminal Justice Branch as well as directors of Judicial Administrations, the judiciary were represented on the project, as well as senior RCMP and municipal police. Under the steering committee there was a project management committee which included project directors from all of the various respective branches. And then there were a number of working groups, for training development and requirements and planning.

The formal project management structure comprised a Steering

Committee and various sub-committees (business change council, change request, configuration and training). The chairperson of JIMS Steering Committee, a senior executive from one of the core agencies, acted as the executive sponsor. (Note: A core agency represents one of the major internal stakeholders who has stewardship over a portion of the data in the information system.) A full-time project manager was assigned from the ranks of the Information Technology Division, a central agency providing technology support to all government branches. Key stakeholders were represented on all committees and subcommittees. Project managers were selected for each core agency and designated as representative key stakeholders. Those selected to be project managers, however, had no formal training to meet their new responsibility and title. Their authority was uncertain in their respective agencies and dubious in the context of the project management structure. It appeared that the executive members of the individual agencies retained power over decision-making and resource allocation, leaving only routine management functions to the project managers. Figure 1 illustrates the stakeholder relationship of these individual groups to the leadership committee and structure.

Figure 1. Stakeholder Relationships

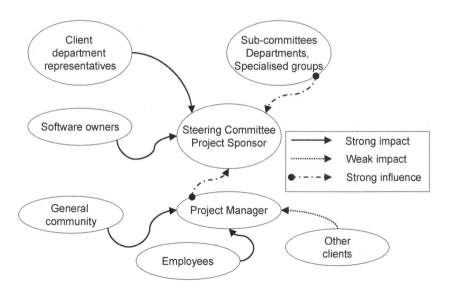

STAKEHOLDERS

One respondent noted: "It is like a pyramidal structure where the hierarchal thing is to try to have everybody represented." From this high-level structure, individual stakeholder organizations created their own representative committees as described by the same JIMS respondent:

> And then you have got the management committees that would manage their own change process or whatever process is required to make the project work. So if you imagine it as a pyramidal structure then you can see all these nodes filtering right down to the grassroots level, where each individual location that will be affected will have their respective project committee.

PROJECT SUCCESS

It should be noted that the project (despite not fully meeting all the needs of all stakeholders) was judged highly successful by the remaining core stakeholders and the sponsoring government ministries as reported by many of the research participants. It was a success in that it delivered what it had to deliver. It has now been fully implemented across the province for over five years. It is in 450 office locations with approximately 4,000 users, delivering systems for the police, the Crown, the courts and corrections.

Integration projects often seem to be a puzzle that, when completed, create the whole picture. Many pieces are needed to fit together in order to create success; governance can certainly be viewed as the glue that holds it all together.

FINDINGS

There is much rhetoric in the public sector about "busting silos" and "working horizontally." Working horizontally in an organization has considerable appeal because working together should reduce redundancy and leverage one another's knowledge, processes and systems. Experience proves that doing so is difficult. While it is hard to argue against a "two heads are better than one" perspective, in practice the effective governance of such horizontal structures has proven problematic. Regardless of this and other difficulties, it is essential to deal with this issue in multi-stakeholder projects that cross traditional and functional boundaries. This was the case with the JIMS project described above. A multi-stakeholder project framework included a steering and sub-committee structure with representation by all stakeholders. The common bond was both philosophical and functional, as everyone believed in public safety.

Achieving greater public safety required working differently, not just in the case of practices and systems but horizontally as an integrated process, as related by this participant:

> So in the case of JIMS, that is from that silo paper-based model to an electronic integrated justice model so that includes everything from assessing change readiness from a cultural, HR perspective, to a outside training and different ways of delivering training, right down to potential different organizational models and job descriptions and so on and so forth.

Without exceptional project governance, such changes in a multi-stakeholder environment would have been impossible.

## CONCLUSION

Governance can be either the oil that greases the wheel or the sludge that eventually grinds the project to a halt. Whether dealing with international or local security projects, the governance and security structure of a project needs to ensure the right project is being completed in the right way. To do this, the governance structure needs to determine the need for the project and select the correct solution (i.e., the project to address this need). It needs to set the vision of a preferred future end state that everyone knows and understands. Following these fundamental decisions, the project's governance and security structures influence the successful completion of the project through its decision-making structure.

Without an appropriate and effective governance structure, the success of security projects is mere happenstance.

## REVIEW QUESTIONS

1. What are some of the implications of setting up governance structures after project selection?
2. Discuss the duality of the governing role from the perspective of both the host (permanent) organization and the project (temporary) organization.

### REFERENCES

Beecham, R. *Project Governance: The Essentials*. Cambridge, UK: IT Governance Ltd, 2011.

Christenson, D. *The Role of Vision as a Critical Success Element in Project Management*. Royal Melbourne Institute of Technology University School of Property, Melbourne, Australia, March 26, 2007.

Crawford, L., C. Bredillet, and R. J. Turner. *Project Governance: Integrating Corporate, Program and Project Governance*. London, UK: Routledge, 2010.

Dinsmore, P. C., L. Rocha, and D. L. Pells. *Enterprise Project Governance: A Guide to the Successful Management of Projects Across Organizations*. New York: AMACOM, 2012.

Kerzner, H. *Project Management Best Practices*. Hoboken, NJ: John Wiley & Sons, 2010.

Kerzner, H., and F. P. Saladis. *Value-driven Project Management*. Hoboken, NJ: John Wiley & Sons, 2009.

Muller, R. *Project Governance*. London, UK: Ashgate, 2009.

Thomas, J., and M. Mullaly. *Researching the Value of Project Management*. Richmond, VA: Project Management Institute, 2008.

### ENDNOTES

[1]  D. Christenson. *The Role of Vision as a Critical Success Element in Project Management*. (Melbourne: Royal Melbourne Institute of Technology, 2007).

[2]  Christenson, 2007.

[3]  Christenson, 2007.

**SECTION VI**

# CHALLENGES TO ASSURING SECURITY

# GOVERNANCE FOR PEACE AND DEVELOPMENT

## MICHAEL CANARES, MSc

---

## INTRODUCTION

Peace is largely understood as an absence of violence, dissension or war.[1] As a human aspiration, it normally refers to the cessation of atrocities, the end of ruthless hostility and the flourishing of concord between enemy camps. Like good governance, as Girouard proposes in his introductory chapter, peace is a theme familiar to all cultures and regions; like good governance, peace has not been universally achieved.

Peace as a concept is beyond simply an accord between enemy camps. It may mean harmony, which does not only denote a state of non-violence but more importantly a state of agreement, social order or accord. It may not be taken only in a social context, but also on the individual level where a person is "at peace" though s/he exists in a chaotic environment. Further, peace may be seen in a physical sphere and also in the moral, psychological and the intellectual sphere. Even when people seem to be in accord, peace may be considered absent because violence against persons through wilful and deliberate discrimination still exists.

Indeed, although peace as a goal is universally accepted or at least agreed to by many, peace as a concept is a multi-layered or multi-dimensional idea on which theorists, researchers and advocates rarely reach agreement. Like governance, it is a complex and murky construct and the crucible for choices as described by Girouard. John Galtung emphasized that nobody has a monopoly on defining peace. In his seminal work, the concept of peace has evolved from a narrow definition of absence of (inter-state) wars between symmetric powers to a larger concept of structural violence.[2]

This chapter takes a rather simplistic view of peace – that it is indicated by only a few variables. Thus, governance for peace and development is seen from a similar viewpoint. The understanding is limited in order to facilitate the generation of meaningful conclusions based on study results. In this chapter, peace is indicated by the reduction or absence of rebellious and insurgent activities, increased resettlement in communities, and the increased number of rebel returnees. The choice of variables mirrors the different concepts of peace (the absence of physical violence, the presence of harmony and accord, and the weakening of rebel forces due to people's growing confidence in institutions) in governance and security for peace and development.

This chapter is structured in four parts. The first section sets the study in the Philippines where peace as a condition differs across regions and contexts, and how thinking on peace and development has evolved over the years. The second part presents the poverty-reduction program of the study locale, the Province of Bohol, where a decrease in poverty and insurgent activities was claimed. The third part scrutinizes claims of attribution. It emphasizes that beyond a poverty-reduction governance program are institutional arrangements that have made these achievements possible through (amongst other variables) security measures to assure sustainable governance. The final section suggests that focusing intervention on institutional structures (where access to economic, social, and political opportunities is assured) is the more sustainable way of achieving both poverty reduction and peace. It is a criterion of the litmus test for good governance as proposed by Girouard.

## A LANDSCAPE OF DIFFERING PEACE CONTEXTS

The Philippines is a land of many contrasts. Its 7,107 islands are inhabited by roughly 80 million people who speak 12 main languages. The majority of Filipinos are Christians although the southern regions on the island of Mindanao are predominantly Moslem. The country boasts of being Asia's oldest democracy but corruption and instability have characterized its fledgling political history; communism is still a thriving political ideology. Through the years, it has struggled to unite its culturally diverse citizenry while a few secessionist groups clamour for independence.

Despite problems of political stability, the country may be considered relatively peaceful. Insurgency is largely concentrated in the Moslem south in remote areas where the New People's Army (NPA) of the Communist Party of the Philippines (CPP) has strong base of operations and local support.[3] From time to time, the national government in the capital city of Manila has been threatened by numerous but failed coup attempts since 1986 when democracy was re-established in a non-violent uprising. Crimes against persons and property are minimal and not of cataclysmic proportions when compared to other developing countries.

National security problems are met with the conventional solution of deploying military troops in conflict areas to restore and maintain peace and order. In response to the global call to fight terrorism under the "with us or against us" mandate, the country welcomed American troops through the Visiting Forces Agreement (VFA), more particularly in Mindanao. It was rationalized by the government as a way of professionalizing and enabling the services of the Philippine Armed Forces. In the last five to ten years, however, the realization has been growing that this was not enough; indeed, it was sometimes entirely misplaced. It led not only to the destruction of the rule of law but also the alienation of affected communities.[4]

An influential document reinforced the notion that militarization was necessary but insufficient. It was the report of the National Unification Commission, a forerunner of the Office of the Presidential Adviser for Peace Process (OPPAP) of then President Fidel Ramos in 1993. It sought to identify, among other things, the causes of "unpeace" in the country (see Figure 1), the primary cause being the massive poverty and inequity in the countryside.[5]

Figure 1. Causes of the State of Unpeace in the Philippines
(NUC as cited in Polestico, 2001)

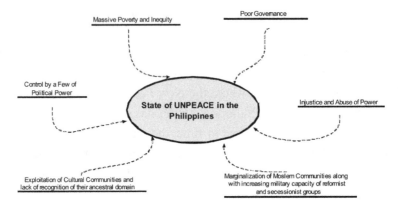

But is this really the case? Is poverty the cause of unpeace, or its effect? This is a strategic question for countries facing internal conflicts and pervasive deprivation. For example, in achieving peace (by minimizing, if not eradicating violence), what should governments do? Will solving poverty be a priority action over and above maintaining the rule of law? Or will government focus its efforts on maintaining a monopoly of power in the hands of the state to ensure that violence can be contained, if not eliminated? What will be necessary to achieve peace in conflict areas – poverty alleviation or aggressive militarization?

These questions are critical because the answers influence the governance of peace and security at the national and local levels. The national government, for example, indicated in its Medium-term Philippine Development Plan for 2004-2010 that in order to address issues of peace and order, the government needs to ensure "effective and credible law enforcement jointly executed by a trilateral partnership between the local executive, the police and the community; professionalization of the PNP; and continuous and intensified operations to neutralize terrorism and other organized crime groups."[6]

# BOHOL'S POVERTY ALLEVIATION AND PEACE PROGRAM

## THE RATIONALE OF THE PROGRAM

The interest in Bohol as a case study through which to explore these questions stems from two reasons. First, Bohol is one of the few provinces in the Philippines with a clearly defined peace and development program, whose goal is two-fold: (a) to decrease poverty incidence, and (b) to promote peace and order. Second, the province has been cited on various occasions and received many awards for its efforts in governance of the environment, investment promotion, peace and order, and poverty reduction.

The island province of Bohol is in the heart of Central Visayas in the Philippines and comprises 48 municipalities (towns) with 15, 14, and 19 municipalities composing the first, second, and third congressional districts, respectively. The productive force of Bohol is almost 58% of the total population as of 2005, of which around 89% are engaged in farming and fishing. Agriculture remains the biggest sector in the province in terms of working population and land use.[7] Tourism is the primary service sector in the province because Bohol is a major tourist destination in the country.

In 2000, poverty incidence was very high in the province at 50.2% in terms of population and 47.3% in terms of families,[8] affecting mostly farmers and fisherfolk.[9] In the same year, the province was one of the poorest 20 in the country (18th out of the 82 provinces) using monetary measures as criteria.[10] The alarming thing was that the poverty incidence had increased by 27% compared to the 1997 base figures. The United Nations Development Program ranked Bohol as the 7th in its list of 20 poorest provinces in 2001.[11] At the same time, Bohol contained four armed fronts of the New People's Army (the armed rebel group of the Communist Party of the Philippines) whose main goal is to establish a communist government as an alternative to its current democratic form.[12] Bohol housed the regional headquarters for Visayas of the rebel group.

In responding to the increasing poverty and the threat of insurgent activities, the provincial government embarked on a novel initiative of crafting a poverty-reduction and management program. The program would serve as its definitive strategy in reducing poverty incidence to 23% by 2015. The Bohol Poverty Reduction and Management Office (BPRMO) of the Provincial Planning and Development Office (PPDO) was created in 2001 with the mandate to implement the program.

Because resources were limited, the program adopted a targeting policy frame where those requiring urgent and immediate attention were identified and received the intervention. Interestingly, however, one of the first poverty maps produced in relation to the province's poverty-reduction efforts was an insurgency map (see Figure 2). As indicated in Figure 2, barangays[13] were classified as:

- *Influenced* (where 50% or more of the inhabitants support the rebel cause and where local legal organizations are formed to support the armed groups);
- *Infiltrated* (where at least 25% support the cause and where local leaders were recruited); and
- *Threatened* (where there were sightings of armed rebels but the area only served as passageway to other villages).[14]

Figure 2: One of the First Poverty Maps

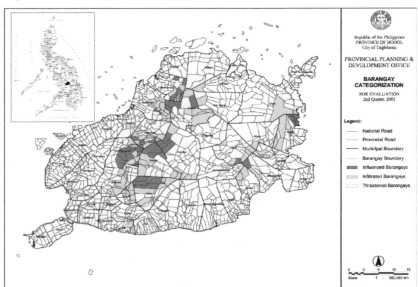

The poverty-reduction program sought to reduce poverty in 20 towns where insurgency was most pronounced. This was grounded on the assumption (a) that poverty was the primary reason for joining the CPP-NPA, and (b) the realization that long years of militarization has had little effect on the problem of insurgency in the province. Poverty reduction, then, was considered not just a goal for human development but an anti-insurgency policy, a primary concern not only of BPRMO but also of the Provincial Peace and Order Council (PPOC). It was undertaken in close partnership with the military's Special Operations Team (SOT).

The provincial government embarked on a comprehensive poverty-mapping exercise to identify the poorest municipalities based on a set of minimum indicators:

- Health (e.g., malnutrition, access to potable water, sanitary toilet); and
- Education (e.g., school participation rate, dropout rate) in 2003.

The resultant map mirrored the provincial poverty map developed by the National Statistics Coordinating Board (NSCB) using the monetary cost-of-basic-needs approach. This gave the provincial government confidence in the use of the proxy welfare indicators as an initial gauge in identifying the high-priority municipalities.

## THE PROGRAM INTERVENTIONS

The province's poverty-reduction program embarked on a twelve-point agenda (illustrated in Figure 3 below) with two primary strategies:

- It sought to increase access to services and the participation of disadvantaged people and communities; and
- It intended to achieve pro-poor economic growth through investments in preferred areas such as agricultural development and eco-tourism.

Figure 3. The Bohol Poverty Reduction Framework (PPDO, 2001)

Figure 3 shows the many initiatives that the program wanted to cover. It should be noted that this menu of interventions was not carried out on a province-wide scale but in select barangays only. When the program started in 2001, there were only 41 barangays covered by the program in 20 different municipalities.

Program interventions were based on local livelihood creation. The 2005 funding profile of BPRMO, for example, reports 90% utilization of 10-million peso[15] program funds for livelihood projects (BPRMO 2006). The approach of the program is influenced by community-organizing principles that involved communities in the assessment of their needs and letting them decide the type of livelihood project they would like to embark on. After they decided on a project proposal, technical training was undertaken, farm input and machines were provided, financial assistance was released and links were made with buyers in and outside the city. To manage program funds, cooperatives were organized and registered.

It is evident that while the program framework (Figure 3) involved many initiatives such as infrastructure, education, population management, governance and health, these were not captured by the interventions of BPRMO on the ground. A review of BPRMO project reports revealed that activities were geared towards the development of the livelihood of the people and did not necessarily include other aspects mentioned in the framework. BPRMO rationalized this in two ways.

## REFLECTION ON THE INITIATIVES

First, while primarily livelihood programs were implemented, these were grounded on sustainable-development principles and concern for the environment. Population, health and education concerns were occasionally dealt with. Second, the framework for poverty reduction concerns all other offices outside BPRMO, which have regular and ongoing activities in other aspects of the framework. Poverty reduction was argued to be not just BPRMO's concern because every national and local agency has a poverty-reduction mandate and program.

For example, the Department of Public Works and Highways[16] takes care of farm-to-market roads while the Department of Health alleviates malnutrition, mortality and morbidity concerns. The Provincial Tourism Office has programs that increase tourism activities to reduce poverty because the province is one of the country's primary tourist destinations. The Bohol Environmental Management Office manages sustainable resource use while the Bohol Investment Promotion Centre promotes the province's capacity to absorb financial capital. In close coordination with the Department of Tourism, the Bohol Tourism Office coordinates tourism activities in the province while the Bohol Employment and Placement Office helps deploy overseas workers and employs students in summer jobs. The Philippine National Police and the Armed Forces of the Philippines reduce crime incidence and insurgency, respectively. All these efforts are directed towards reducing poverty and building peace.

Other programs try to reduce poverty and encourage peace. The provincial government instituted the Kauban sa Reporma (Companions in Reform) program, which sought to rehabilitate former armed rebels (members of CPP-NPA) by providing training and livelihood programs. It conducted regular monthly civic action in barangays affected by insurgency in order to bring the government closer to the people by the extension of medical, agricultural, nutrition and other social services.

The Bohol Local Peace Forum was conducted regularly to talk about local concerns, more often those of the leftist groups seeking redress from the government.[17]

An important feature of the program was establishing the Local Poverty-Reduction Action Program (LPRAP) software, which is a computer-based data system to identify and locate the poor people in the province using a set of criteria. The 42 municipalities have installed the software that maps poverty in their respective municipalities using a set of 20 criteria.[18]

PROGRAM OUTCOMES

Almost seven years after the provincial government launched its poverty-reduction and peace program, the province reported impressive results. First, Bohol is no longer one of the 20 poorest provinces in the country but occupies the 52nd poorest slot out of a total of 81 provinces and is ranked as the second most improved province in terms of poverty reduction in 2003.[19] Poverty incidence, even using the self-rated poverty measure, has decreased since 1999.[20]

Second, barangays affected by local insurgency dropped from 305 in 2001 to 46 in 2005 while the number of armed rebels decreased from 283 in 2001 to 39 in 2008.[21] The Armed Forces reported that the CPP-NPA now holds only a single armed front, compared to the four they had in 2000, and have moved the regional headquarters from Bohol to the nearby province of Leyte. Public opinion poll results showed the dramatic decrease in the "felt presence of armed men" in Bohol by 50% since 2001.[22]

Third, the towns reported increased resettlement in areas previously threatened by occasional armed encounters between the Philippine military and the armed guerrilla movement. Over the years, this has led to an increased number of rebel members returning to the fold of the law and even participating in provincial campaigns against insurgency. This result, however, is couched in the scepticism that the decrease in insurgency in the province is caused by the weakening of the communist movement in the country and elsewhere in the world.

Consequently, Bohol and its provincial government became the recipients of numerous awards in local governance practice, the most prestigious of which is the Award for Continuing Excellence (ACE) in local governance conferred by the Galing Pook Foundation, an independent award-giving body that recognizes excellence in local governance practices in the country since decentralization reform was initiated in 2001. It is hoped that Bohol's Poverty Reduction Program for Peace and Development will be implemented in other parts of the country.

## WHAT IS THE ROLE OF GOVERNANCE AND SECURITY IN PEACE AND DEVELOPMENT?

Two questions can be interposed. First, is there a cause for celebration? Is it really the provincial government program that made the impressive achievements in well-being and peace? Second, if it is true, does this achievement lend credence to the argument that waging a war against poverty means building the foundation of peace?

### THE DEVIL IS IN THE DETAILS

Table 1 below presents the profile of the poorest municipalities in terms of poverty and insurgency by comparing results between two periods where data is available. Several generalizations can be derived from the table. First, the poorest municipalities are located in the second and third districts, which are farthest from Tagbilaran, the provincial capital and the political, economic and cultural centre of the province. Second, not all municipalities that were ranked as poorest are rebel-infested, infiltrated or influenced as the case of CPG, Bien Unido, and Trinidad would suggest. Third, most of the poorest municipalities have improved their insurgency classification while improving poverty. On the other hand, the remaining CPP-NPA fronts are not the poorest municipalities in the province and are located in the mountainous areas with relatively dense forest cover.

As these details would suggest, there may be other explanations for the decrease in poverty in the province and other causes of the declining insurgency in certain areas. In a paper that seeks explanations for the decline in poverty, one major factor was the notion of "place" and "access."[23]

Table 1. Profile of Poorest Municipalities in Terms of Poverty and Insurgency Classification (PPDO, 2002, 2005; PPOC 2008)

| Municipality | District | Distance from Tagbilaran | Area Classification Predominant characteristic | Poverty Rank (2001) | Poverty Rank (2004) | Insurgency Classification (2001) | Insurgency Classification (2008) |
|---|---|---|---|---|---|---|---|
| | | (in KM) | | 1 as poorest | | | |
| CPG | 2nd | 130 | Island | 1 | 1 | - | - |
| Ubay | 2nd | 124 | Coastal | 2 | No data | Infiltrated | - |
| Bien Unido | 2nd | 108 | Coastal | 3 | 2 | - | - |
| Inabanga | 2nd | 71 | Coastal | 4 | 10 | Infiltrated | - |
| San Miguel | 2nd | 86 | Upland | 5 | 12 | - | - |
| Alicia | 3rd | 103 | Upland | 6 | 3 | Infiltrated | - |
| Buenavista | 2nd | 83 | Coastal | 7 | 8 | Influenced | - |
| Pilar | 3rd | 76 | Upland | 8 | 15 | Infiltrated | - |
| Danao | 2nd | 92 | Upland | 9 | 13 | Infiltrated | - |
| Trinidad | 2nd | 98 | Coastal | 10 | 29 | - | - |

Rebecca Blank suggests that the place (the natural environment) has a strong bearing on the incidence of poverty. In her paper, she argues that isolation, one of the components of the natural environment and defined as "limited accessibility from location to specific markets or nearby population centres" creates distance, limits market exchange, affects labour markets, and hampers an area's ability to benefit from comparative advantage, thus leading to meagre achievements in poverty reduction.[24]

Bohol's case exemplifies this theoretical ground. When it conducted the poverty-mapping exercise in the province, PPDO noted that poverty is more pronounced in small islands–coastal zones and in upland communities where access to basic services such as health and education were limited due to poor road conditions, inadequate transport services, and the inherent resource limitation of local governments to deliver basic services.[25] This argument is exemplified by the poorest municipality in the province, the island of CPG, indicated in Table 1 above. It also acknowledged that the distance of these areas from economic centres results in limited access to livelihood and productive work opportunities for people who are traditionally dependent on farming and fishing.[26]

On a related note, a study conducted on poverty and development programs revealed that while poverty is generally found in the northeastern municipalities (District 2), development programs, more particularly by non-governmental organizations (NGOs), are concentrated in the southern half of the province, which has greater access to Tagbilaran.[27] This is confirmed by another study that reports greater and more concentrated spending of NGOs in Districts 1 and 3 compared to the poorer District 2.[28]

As pointed out above, the poorest municipalities are farther away from Tagbilaran City, the provincial capital, while the better-off ones surround it. This situation mirrors Lipton's "urban-bias" argument on development, where resources are transferred or used to benefit urban areas to the detriment of rural places.[29] In the early days of Bohol's development as a province, governmental projects and social assistance as well as NGO development programs are clustered in areas surrounding Tagbilaran.[30] This finding is based on provincial data but analysis of municipal data also reveals that the farther the barangay is from the town centre, the more likely it is to experience poverty.

There are several reasons for this. First, the offices of service providers, both governmental and non-governmental, are normally stationed in provincial and town centres. Second, the accessibility of municipalities and barangays, in terms of roads and transport, is necessary for providers to deliver services in certain areas. Given limited funds, the less accessible the area, the higher are the delivery costs. Third, people are unable to access the services of providers because of the high transport costs. Fourth, and a more serious contention, is that representation of people on the periphery is low in governments and organizations and their interests are underrepresented in the local development discourse. In this respect, it is argued that "place" is an important characteristic in poverty reduction[31] especially when the poor's access to the benefits of both markets and social provision is affected.[32] In this process, the marginalization of certain places is brought about by conscious decisions made by development agents such as governments and non-governmental organizations.

Correspondingly, "place" may be an explanation for the presence or rebels and insurgency activities in certain barangays. For tactical and strategic reasons, remote areas are normally rebel-infested because they are far from town centres with police stations. These are areas where government and non-government programs are minimal or non-existent. Remote areas normally have thick forest cover, difficult mountainous terrain, and lack power and other utilities, which frees up the mobility of rebel soldiers and means their operations are covert. Consequently, the areas where communities hardly experience the presence of a functional government are more vulnerable to indoctrination from left-leaning groups and places where mass-based support of the CPP-NPAs easily takes root.

The remaining armed front of the CPP-NPA in Bohol is clustered in towns in the interior. The darkly-shaded areas in Figure 2, above, remain as influenced barangays and are reported to have been the location of the last remaining armed front in the province. These areas are mountainous and have relatively dense forest cover. Access is limited because roads are sometimes impassable during the rainy season. Government and NGO programs are sporadic and minimal.

## THE RURAL AREA MORE VISIBLE, THE GOVERNMENT MORE PRESENT

The poverty-reduction program initiated by the provincial government indicated a shift in the way development would be pursued in the province. First, the poverty research did not identify only where the critical interventions should be implemented, but encouraged accountability on the part of local government officials and civil society actors. It made both public and private agents rethink their development strategies and priorities. They began to attend to areas that have been marginalized by previous programs and projects. The imperative, then, was to go where interventions were needed, beyond the areas of comfort. These shifts in development thinking and practice made the rural areas more visible.

- Road projects were pursued by the provincial government;
- Community health projects were undertaken by non-governmental organizations in partnership with local and national governmental agencies;
- Several projects in enterprise and livelihood development were initiated by various organizations; and
- Participatory governance was made a conscious process and goal by both public and private actors.

All these processes were undertaken alongside an increased military presence in areas identified as critical in terms of insurgency activities.

In several evaluations of projects undertaken by non-government organizations and by local government units,[33,34] a comment regularly made by community leaders and local citizens (more particularly in deprived communities) is how they have felt the increasing concern of government and other local actors, as shown by programs and projects implemented in their area. As the province is predominantly agricultural, the various support mechanisms implemented to boost farmers' income from the land were greatly appreciated. The mechanisms included investment in rural infrastructure (e.g., roads, bridges, post-harvest facilities), agricultural research (e.g., trial farms of different varieties), financial assistance (e.g., micro-credit, micro-enterprise financing), and capability building (e.g., training in livelihood skills and management). Road and transportation improvements decreased the price of agricultural inputs, increased the leverage of farmers in terms of agricultural output, and even decreased the price of basic commodities. The people felt that they had been excluded from the development process but they are now gaining a place in the collective effort towards poverty eradication.

## POVERTY AND INSURGENCY: LOOSE CONNECTIONS?

It was argued that poverty is one of the causes of communal conflict. Oxford economist Paul Collier, for example, challenged the conventional argument that ethnic hatred and power mechanics caused modern-day conflicts. He declared that the main predictors of violence were not these arguments but weak economic growth, low income, and natural-resource dependence.[35] Edward Miguel and his colleagues at Berkeley (using an analysis of 41 countries) argued that increases in poverty, on their own, increase the likelihood of conflict. They made the point that violent conflict is driven by poor economic outcomes, and not the other way around.[36] Other works have indicated that economic recession increases the likelihood of conflict.[37]

As a pragmatist, Susan Rice posited that poverty and inequality breed resentment, hostility and insecurity as the poor become open to accepting help even from violent groups that have an extremist agenda.[38] In a related context, David Keen suggests that poverty and poor social services can be reasons for people to embrace violence (or insurgent activities) as a probable solution to problems of their own.[39] Poverty, coupled with discontent about the way governments perform, can fuel the poor's grievance against institutional structures. This situation is fertile ground for violent opposition groups to expand their influence and support as well as legitimize violent actions.[40]

The links between poverty and insurgency have taken root in recent literature. In Nepal, for example, it was argued that there was some evidence for correspondence between insurgency and the poverty level; the poorer the area was, the higher the degree of insurgency. So it is in the interests of Maoist groups to capitalize on the issues of socially excluded groups to gain mass-based support.[41] In Central and Eastern Europe, as well as the Commonwealth of Independent States, there is "an unfortunate correlation between the low level of human development (and a corresponding high level of human insecurity) and the armed conflicts that have occurred in most of the countries."[42]

The links between poverty, conflict, and insurgency are admittedly far from robust. It is argued to have reverse causality problems because conflict and insurgency are important causes of poverty and destitution.[43] Places where conflict is prevalent were reported to have staggering effects on social welfare.[44] Poverty, consequently, is seen to have weakened governing institutions, depleted resources and crushed hope, leading to a cycle of desperation and instability.[45] Inequality, too, is seen to have played a crucial role in the occurrence of conflict.[46]

Using the Bohol experience I would argue, nevertheless, that poverty and the relative exclusion of the poor in the development process have caused people to support, if not participate, in the rebel movement. The stark reality of government's failure to address social problems anchored on lack of choice for upward mobility has prompted the poor to find comfort elsewhere. The persistence of victimizing processes embedded in unjust political, social and economic structures has reinforced the grievances of the rebel group. Thus it has gained the support of people, more particularly in areas where the government presence is least felt.

When more options have been made available through different programs implemented by both government and non-governmental organizations, people have gained renewed optimism and trust in institutions that they expected to offer help. This situation is complemented by the increased presence of military forces in the areas that have shown the government's ability to maintain the rule of law. The excesses of the military and their ability to suppress as well as oppress has increased the grievances of civilians and their sympathy toward the rebel cause. This circumstance was checked on by civil society groups that monitor human rights abuses and by fact-finding teams commissioned by the government and the local church.

## INSTITUTIONS OF ACCESS AND ACCOUNTABILITY

As the links between poverty and insurgency are not conclusive, the argument for poverty reduction programs to attain "peace" is far from being empirically proven. A direct causal relationship cannot be established since there are several mechanisms and processes that occur alongside efforts to reduce poverty leading to certain peace achievements. As the nature of poverty is a complex problem,[47] so are its possible solutions.

The Bohol case suggests that, given a particular peace context, certain institutions, when present, may make poverty-reduction programs effective pathways for the attainment of peace.

Institutions have been defined as the "humanly devised constraints that structure political, economic, and social interaction."[48] In economic theory, the term "institutions" refers to a set of formal and informal socio-political arrangements that would either promote or deter the development of an economic behaviour appropriate and conducive to growth.[49] A few examples would be property rights, regulatory institutions, the rule of law and independence of the judiciary, among others.

In the case of Bohol, several institutions have achieved both well-being and peace. First, a competent bureaucracy has implemented several programs for the benefit of the poor, which consequently garnered the latter's trust and confidence. Participatory governance mechanisms made governmental programs more responsive as people were consulted about their needs and aspirations. The novel initiative of profiling households and municipalities in all barangays in the province made local government officials more accountable because the poverty ranking of their respective area indicates their ability to solve the problems of their constituents.

Second, the local government, with the aid of the national army, was able to maintain the rule of law, which would assure people that their lives and property are protected from the threat of violent activities. In the past, people left home when their community was ravaged by violent encounters between the military and the Philippine Armed Forces. In these communities, investment in people involved in livelihood activities was scarce and poverty more pronounced. The relative "peace" that the communities were able to experience caused them to invest again in rural livelihoods that were assisted technically and financially by both public and private actors.

The maintenance of peace in the province has worked to the benefit of local tourism. Eco-tourism is one of Bohol's primary development strategies.[50] Its competitive advantage is the presence of the famous Chocolate Hills, white pristine beaches on its islands, diving sites, and world-class cultural attractions.[51] Investment and promotional activities in the tourism sector were increased along with the conscious effort to maintain peace in the province. These collective efforts have caused a dramatic rise in tourist arrivals in the province since 2001.

The increase in tourist arrivals has fuelled economic activity in the capital city of Tagbilaran primarily because of the demand for services to cater to the tourist inflow.[52] The tourist numbers correlated to increases in manufacturing, services, trading and agricultural establishments as well as employment – the backward and forward linkages contributing to an increase in prosperity.[53]

Third, civil society engagement in the development process has made actors more accountable to the public and more responsive to pressing community needs. The Bohol Poll, an annual public opinion survey (conducted by the independent HNU Centre for Research and Local Governance) monitored satisfaction ratings and opinions of people regarding government service delivery. The poll takes the pulse of the public on major development processes. The participation of the Catholic Church, people's organizations, and associations in the various local councils (e.g., Provincial Development Council, Provincial Peace and Order Council) has allowed consideration of people's opinion of government plans and made the discussions on development issues public.

## CONCLUSION

The case in Bohol presents achievements in human development and peace goals as well as goals of good governance and security. The challenge lies in how these initial gains are to be sustained. If the provincial government envisions "development" as not just embracing the satisfaction of material want, and "peace" as not just the absence of insurgency, then it is necessary to widen the focus on destitution and government intervention. Governance, Girouard argues, is the human interface between the nation's laws and its citizens and it should be applied to protect the citizenry. If governance does not deliver, by default, a freedom, then it fails the litmus test. Governance should pay attention to processes that would realize the removal of conditions that perpetuate the cycle of poverty. These processes should foster conditions that would help the poor lift themselves out of destitution.

Poverty is one of the manifestations of what Galtung referred to as structural violence.[54] If poverty denotes the absence of positive peace, eradicating poverty does not just mean providing poor people with access to basic needs. It is necessary to eliminate structures that perpetuate the cycle of structural violence. If poverty is multi-dimensional[55] and involves "a deprivation of essential assets and opportunities to which every human being is entitled,"[56] then eradicating economic and social poverty is insufficient. In this regard, Girouard identifies the need to examine the general malaise of the disenfranchised and vulnerable. He concludes that good governance for peace and development is about the will, power and vision delivering on the hopes of those in need.

When people who are no longer economically poor are denied their human rights to peace and when the courts are corrupt, they may still raise their fist or take up arms to fight a government, in which case peace is disrupted. For as long as violence is built into the power structures of society where benefit unjustly accrues to one at the expense of another, there will always be an opportunity for grievance to take root.[57]

## REVIEW QUESTIONS

1. Is peace a necessary pre-condition of development? Or is it its consequence?
2. Are *conflict* and *underdevelopment* symptoms of the same problem? If so, what do you think is the cause for both? If not, why not?
3. What should be the role of governments in promoting peace? What strategies should governments use in order to achieve safety, security and peace for its communities and citizens?
4. What is the role of "place" in the context of peace and conflict? What is the role of "place" in economic development? How shall governments ensure that spatial strategies address both peace and development concerns?

5. Can an enabling environment for peace and development be created by governments? What sets of institutions do you think are needed to create this enabling environment?
6. When poverty is reduced are there attendant effects on conflict?
7. Whose responsibility is the maintenance of peace and order in a given community? Why do you think so?
8. Do you agree with the following statements? Why or why not?

   • Poverty and inequality intuitively breed resentment, hostility and insecurity, as the poor become vulnerable to accepting help even from violent groups that have an extremist agenda (see Susan Rice, 2007).

   • Violence, for some sectors in society, serves an economic function. It is not always that all people lose as a consequence of violence; some may profit in the process (see David Keen, 2000).

   • Poverty is also violence. There is no long-term solution to violence that does not take into account the removal of barriers that prevent people from achieving their realisations (see Galtung, 1969).

## REFERENCES

Abucejo, I., J. Arawiran, A. R. Caballo, M. Cadiz, J. Cemine, F. Dote, D. Jayectin, B. Mijares, V. Millanar, J. Tagaro, and C. A. Villares. *Assessment of Municipal Local Poverty Reduction Action Plan (LPRAP)-Poverty Data Monitoring System (PDMS) Implementation.* Tagbilaran: HNU Centre for Research and Local Governance, 2007.

Acejo, I., F. Del Prado, and D. Remolino. *Tourism Fuels an Emerging City: The Case of Tagbilaran City, Bohol.* Discussion Paper Series 2004-53. Philippine Institute of Development Studies: Manila, 2004.

Asian Development Bank. *Fighting Poverty in Asia and the Pacific: The Poverty Reduction Strategy.* Manila: Asian Development Bank, 2001.

Bautista, M.C. R. *Ideologically-motivated conflicts in the Philippines: Exploring the Possibility of an Early Warning System.* Background Paper for the Human Development Report, 2005.

Blank, R. M. "Poverty, Policy, and Place: How Poverty and Policies to Alleviate Poverty are Shaped by Local Characteristics." *International Regional Science Review* 28, no. 4 (2005): 441-464.

Blomberg, S. B., and G. Hess. *The Temporal Links Between Conflict and Economic Activity.* Wellesley College Working Paper Series 2000-11.

Bohol Poverty Reduction and Management Office. *Accomplishment Report for CY,* 2006.

Brainard, L., D. Chollet, and V. LaFleur. *Ending Poverty, Promoting Peace: The Quest for Global Security.* Brookings Global Economy and Development, 2006.

Canares, M. *PO Evaluation: Assessing Organizational Sustainability.* An Evaluation Report Submitted to Bohol Alliance on Non-Governmental Organizations, 2004.

Canares, M. *Are We Talking of the Same Poverty?* Discussion Paper. Step Up Consulting Services, 2006.

Canares, M. *Beyond Targeting Poverty: Scrutinizing the Decline in Poverty in Bohol, Philippines.* Dissertation submitted to the London School of Economics, 2007.

Chambers, R. "What is Poverty? Who Asks? Who Answers?" In *Poverty in Focus,* edited by D. Erenphreis. Brazil: International Poverty Centre, 2006.

Collier, P. "The Market for Civil War." *Foreign Policy* (May/June 2003): 38.

Corbridge, S., and G. Jones. *The Continuing Debate About Urban Bias: Its Thesis, Its Critics, Its Influence, and Implications for Poverty Reduction.* Research Papers in Environmental and Spatial Analysis No. 99. LSE: UK, 2005

Dutta, I., and A. Mishra. *Does Inequality Lead to Conflict?* WIDER Research Paper 2005/34. United Nations University, 2005.

Galing Pook Foundation. *Kaban Galing: A Case Bank of Innovative and Exemplary Practices in Local Governance.* Manila: Galing Pook Foundation, 2006.

Galtung, J. "Violence, Peace, and Peace Research." *Journal of Peace Research* 6, no. 3 (1969): 167-191.

Goodhand, J. "Enduring Disorder and Persistent Poverty: A Review of the Linkages Between War and Chronic Poverty." *World Development* 31, no. 3 (2003): 629-646.

Gurong, H. *Social Exclusion and Maoist Insurgency.* Paper presented at National Dialogue Conference on ILO Convention 169 on Indigenous and Tribal Peoples, Kathmandu, 19-20 January 2005.

Holy Name University Centre for Research and Local Governance. *Bohol Poll 2006.* Tagbilaran: HNU, 2006.

Justino, P., and P. Verwimp. *Poverty Dynamics, Conflict and Convergence in Rwanda.* Working Paper no. 16, Households in Conflict Network, Institute of Development Studies at the University of Sussex, Brighton, 2006.

Keen, David. "Incentives and Disincentives for Violence." In *Greed and Grievance: Economic Agendas in Civil Wars*. Edited by M. Berdal and D. M. Malone. London, UK: Lynne Rienner, 2000, 19-42.

Lipton, M. *Why Poor People Stay Poor: Urban Bias in World Development*. London, UK: Temple Smith, 1977.

Mascarinas, R. *The Bohol Response to the Insurgency Challenge*. A Report to the Department of Interior and Local Government, 2007.

Miclat, S., R. Soriaga, and P. Walpole. *Communities and Watershed Governance: Visayas, Philippines*. Bohol: Asia Forest Network, 2004.

Miguel M., S. Satyanath, and E. Sergenti. "Economic Shocks and Civil Conflict: An Instrumental Variables Approach." *Journal of Political Economy* 112, no. 4 (2004): 725.

National Statistical Coordination Board. *Estimation of Local Poverty in the Philippines*. Manila: NSCB, 2005.

National Statistical Coordination Board. *Provincial Poverty Incidence Profile*, 2007.

North, D. *Institutions, Institutional Change and Economic Performance*. New York, NY: Cambridge University Press, 1991.

National Economic and Development Authority, 2010.

Paredes, R. *Private and Public Sector Engagement in Bohol*. Presentation on the Philippines Development Forum on Enhancing Coordination and Management of ODAs by LGUs. November 23, 2006 in Bohol, Philippines.

Polestico, R. *Towards a Culture of Peace: The Role of Civil Society in the Philippines*. A Conference Paper read during the 17th Annual Assembly of the Okumenische Philippinenconferenz in Wurzburg, Germany, October 27-28, 2001.

Provincial Planning and Development Office. *Bohol Agenda for Poverty Reduction, Peace, and Development*. PowerPoint Presentation to the Peace and Order Council, 2001.

Provincial Planning and Development Office. *Bohol Program Framework on Poverty Reduction: The Current Poverty Situation in the Province and the Need for a Cohesive Response*. Policy Document, 2003.

Provincial Planning and Development Office. *Annual Development Plan*. PPDO Reports, 2006.

Rasul-Bernardo, A. *Ethnic Conflict, Peace, and Development: A Philippine Case Study*. Paper presented at the 6th CSID Annual Conference, Washington, DC. April 23-25, 2005.

Relampagos, R. "Eco-tourism in the Bohol Province: The Philippines." In *Linking Green Productivity to Eco-Tourism: Experiences in the Asia Pacific Region*. Edited by T. Hundloe. Tokyo: Asian Productivity Organization, 2002.

Rice, S. "Poverty Breeds Insecurity." In *Too Poor for Peace? Global Poverty, Conflict, and Security in the 21st Century.* Edited by L. Brainard and D. Chollet. Washington, DC: Brookings Institution Press, 2007.

Rodrik, D., A. Subramanian, and F. Trebbi. "Institutions Rule: The Primacy of Institutions Over Geography and Integration in Economic Development." *Journal of Economic Growth* 9 (2004): 131-165.

Rummel, R. J. *Understanding Conflict and War.* Beverly Hills, CA: Sage, 1981.

Schelzig, K. *Poverty in the Philippines: Income, Assets, and Access.* Manila: Asian Development Bank, 2005.

Spoor, M. "Inequality, Poverty and Conflict in Transition Economies." In *Globalisation, Poverty, and Conflict.* Edited by Max Spoor. The Netherlands: Kluwer Academic Publishers, 2004.

Stewart, F., and V. Fitzgerald. *War and Underdevelopment. The Economic and Social Consequences of Conflict* (vol. 1). Oxford, UK: Oxford University Press, 2000.

Streeten, P. "Beyond Six Veils: Conceptualizing and Measuring Poverty." *Journal of International Affairs* 52, no. 1 (1998): 1-31.

World Health Organization. *World Report on Violence and Health.* Geneva, Switzerland, 2002.

802nd Infantry Brigade. *Provincial Peace and Order Briefing.* PowerPoint presentation during the Provincial Peace and Order Council Meeting on 3 March 2008.

## ENDNOTES

[1] R. J. Rummel, *Understanding Conflict and War* (Beverly Hills, CA: Sage, 1981).

[2] J. Galtung, "Violence, Peace, and Peace Research." *Journal of Peace Research* 6 no. 3 (1969): 167-191.

[3] M. C. R. Bautista, *Ideologically motivated conflicts in the Philippines: Exploring the Possibility of an Early Warning System.* Background Paper for the Human Development Report, 2005.

[4] A, Rasul-Bernardo, *Ethnic Conflict, Peace, and Development: A Philippine Case Study.* Paper presented at the 6th CSID Annual Conference, Washington, DC. April 23-25, 2005.

[5] R. Polestico, *Towards a Culture of Peace: The Role of Civil Society in the Philippines.* A Conference paper read during the 17th Annual Assembly of the Okumenische Philippinenconferenz in Wurzburg, Germany, October 27-28, 2001.

[6] (NEDA 2010).

7   Provincial Planning and Development Office. *Annual Development Plan.* PPDO Reports, 2006.

8   National Statistical Coordination Board. *Estimation of Local Poverty in the Philippines.* (Manila: NSCB, 2005).

9   Provincial Planning and Development Office. *Bohol Agenda for Poverty Reduction, Peace, and Development.* PowerPoint Presentation to the Peace and Order Council, 2001.

10  National Statistical Coordination Board. *Estimation of Local Poverty in the Philippines.* (Manila: NSCB, 2005).

11  Galing Pook Foundation. *Kaban Galing: A Case Bank of Innovative and Exemplary Practices in Local Governance* (Manila: Galing Pook Foundation, 2006).

12  For more details on the CPP-NPA, visit http://www.philippinerevolution.net/cpp/index.shtml

13  The barangays is the basic political unit in the country. The nation is administratively subdivided into regions, provinces, districts, municipalities, and finally, barangays.

14  Provincial Planning and Development Office. *Bohol Program Framework on Poverty Reduction: The Current Poverty Situation in the Province and the Need for a Cohesive Response.* Policy Document, 2003.

15  Current rate of a Philippine peso to the Euro used by the Belgian Embassy is Php69: 1 Euro.

16  A "Department" is a national agency in contrast to local agencies which are usually labeled as "Provincial" or the name of the province, as in the this case, "Bohol."

17  R. Mascarinas, *The Bohol Response to the Insurgency Challenge.* A Report to the Department of Interior and Local Government, 2007.

18  The software was hailed by some and criticized by others as an effective anti-insurgency software because it creates a profile of families and members of their households, including their location and current affiliations.

19  National Statistical Coordination Board. *Provincial Poverty Incidence Profile,* 2007.

20  Holy Name University Centre for Research and Local Governance. *Bohol Poll 2006.* (Tagbilaran: HNU, 2006).

21  (8021B 2008).

22  Holy Name University Centre for Research and Local Governance. *Bohol Poll 2006.* (Tagbilaran: HNU, 2006).

23  M. Canares, *Beyond Targeting Poverty: Scrutinizing the Decline in Poverty in Bohol, Philippines*. Dissertation submitted to the London School of Economics, 2007.

24  R. Blank, Poverty, Policy, and Place: How Poverty and Policies to Alleviate Poverty are Shaped by Local Characteristics. *International Regional Science Review* 28 no. 4 (2005): 441-464.

25  Provincial Planning and Development Office. *Bohol Program Framework on Poverty Reduction: The Current Poverty Situation in the Province and the Need for a Cohesive Response*. Policy Document, 2003.

26  Provincial Planning and Development Office. *Bohol Program Framework on Poverty Reduction: The Current Poverty Situation in the Province and the Need for a Cohesive Response*. Policy Document, 2003.

27  S. Miclat, R. Soriaga and P. Walpole. *Communities and Watershed Governance: Visayas, Philippines*. (Bohol: Asia Forest Network, 2004).

28  I. Abucejo, J. Arawiran, A. R. Caballo, M. Cadiz, J. Cemine, F. Dote, D. Jayectin, B. Mijares, V. Millanar, J. Tagaro and C. A. Villares. *Assessment of Municipal Local Poverty Reduction Action Plan (LPRAP)-Poverty Data Monitoring System (PDMS) Implementation*. (Tagbilaran: HNU Centre for Research and Local Governance, 2007).

29  M. Lipton, *Why Poor People Stay Poor: Urban Bias in World Development*. (London, UK: Temple Smith, 1977).

30  Presentation on the Philippines Development Forum on Enhancing Coordination and Management of ODAs by LGUs. November 23, 2006 in Bohol, Philippines.

31  K. Schelzig, *Poverty in the Philippines: Income, Assets, and Access* (Manila: Asian Development Bank, 2005).

32  S. Corbridge and G. Jones. *The Continuing Debate About Urban Bias: Its Thesis, Its Critics, Its Influence, and Implications for Poverty Reduction*. Research Papers in Environmental and Spatial Analysis No. 99. London, UK: London School of Economics, 2005.

33  M. Canares, *PO Evaluation: Assessing Organizational Sustainability*. An Evaluation Report Submitted to Bohol Alliance on Non-Governmental Organizations, 2004.

34  M. Canares, *Are We Talking of the Same Poverty?* Discussion Paper. Step Up Consulting Services, 2006.

35  P. Collier, The Market for Civil War. *Foreign Policy*, May/June 2003, 38.

36  (Miguel et al 2006). M. Miguel, S. Satyanath and E. Sergenti. Economic Shocks and Civil Conflict: An Instrumental Variables Approach. *Journal of Political Economy* 112 no. 4 (2004): 725.

37  S. B. Blomberg and G. Hess. *The Temporal Links Between Conflict and Economic Activity*. Wellesley College Working Paper Series 2000-11.

38  S. Rice, "Poverty Breeds Insecurity," in *Too Poor for Peace? Global Poverty, Conflict, and Security in the 21st Century*, eds. L. Brainard and D. Chollet (Washington, DC: Brookings Institution Press, 2007).

39  David Keen, Incentives and Disincentives for Violence. In *Greed and Grievance: Economic Agendas in Civil Wars*, eds. M. Berdal and D. M. Malone (London, UK: Lynne Rienner, 2000), 19-42.

40  F. Stewart and V. Fitzgerald. *War and Underdevelopment. The Economic and Social Consequences of Conflict* (vol. 1). (Oxford, UK: Oxford University Press, 2000).

41  H. Gurong, *Social Exclusion and Maoist Insurgency*. Paper presented at National Dialogue Conference on ILO Convention 169 on Indigenous and Tribal Peoples, Kathmandu, 19-20 January 2005.

42  M. Spoor, Inequality, Poverty and Conflict in Transition Economies. In *Globalisation, Poverty, and Conflict*, ed. Max Spoor (The Netherlands: Kluwer Academic Publishers, 2004), 47-65.

43  P. Justino and P. Verwimp, *Poverty Dynamics, Conflict and Convergence in Rwanda*. Working Paper no. 16, Households in Conflict Network, Institute of Development Studies at the University of Sussex, Brighton, 2006.

44  World Health Organization. *World Report on Violence and Health*. Geneva, Switzerland, 2002.

45  L. Brainard, D. Chollet and V. LaFleur. *Ending Poverty, Promoting Peace: The Quest for Global Security*. Brookings Global Economy and Development, 2006.

46  I. Dutta and A. Mishra. *Does Inequality Lead to Conflict?* WIDER Research Paper 2005/34. United Nations University, 2005.

47  P. Streeten, Beyond Six Veils: Conceptualizing and Measuring Poverty. *Journal of International Affairs* 52 no. 1 (1998): 1-31.

48  (North 1991). D. North, *Institutions, Institutional Change and Economic Performance*. (New York, NY: Cambridge University Press, 1991).

49  D. Rodrik, A. Subramanian and F. Trebbi. Institutions Rule: The Primacy of Institutions Over Geography and Integration in Economic Development. *Journal of Economic Growth* 9 (2004): 131-165.

50  Provincial Planning and Development Office. *Bohol Program Framework on Poverty Reduction: The Current Poverty Situation in the Province and the Need for a Cohesive Response*. Policy Document, 2003.

51  R. Relampagos, Eco-tourism in the Bohol Province: The Philippines. In T. Hundloe Ed. *Linking Green Productivity to Eco-Tourism: Experiences in the Asia Pacific Region*. (Tokyo: Asian Productivity Organization, 2002).

[52] I. Acejo, F. Del Prado and D. Remolino. *Tourism Fuels an Emerging City: The Case of Tagbilaran City, Bohol.* Discussion Paper Series 2004-53. Manila: Philippine Institute of Development Studies, 2004.

[53] I. Acejo, F. Del Prado and D. Remolino. *Tourism Fuels an Emerging City: The Case of Tagbilaran City, Bohol.* Discussion Paper Series 2004-53. Manila: Philippine Institute of Development Studies, 2004.

[54] J. Galtung, "Violence, Peace, and Peace Research." *Journal of Peace Research* 6 no. 3 (1969): 167-191.

[55] R. Chambers, What is Poverty? Who Asks? Who Answers? In D. Erenphreis (Ed.), *Poverty in Focus.* Brazil: International Poverty Center, 2006.

[56] Asian Development Bank. *Fighting Poverty in Asia and the Pacific: The Poverty Reduction Strategy.* (Manila: Asian Development Bank, 2001).

[57] J. Goodhand, Enduring Disorder and Persistent Poverty: A Review of the Linkages Between War and Chronic Poverty. *World Development* 31 no. 3 (2003): 629-646.

**SECTION VII**

---

# NON-EUROPEAN GOVERNANCE

---

# HARMONY AND ORDER: GOVERNANCE AND SECURITY THE AZTEC WAY

GRAHAM KEMP, PhD

Modern studies of governance and security may become trapped in a Eurocentric view that is based on Hellenistic and Roman cultural concepts of government. These concepts matured through two thousand years in Europe and were exported worldwide via colonization to dominate the modern view of governance. Today, most academic institutions are established in countries dominated by such Eurocentric concepts. Other traditions have developed independently from Hellenistic European ideas, however, and may provide a mirror by which to examine the Euro-world of governance. These other traditions offer different answers to some of its weaknesses but also reveal its strengths. They may indicate where we have choices in terms of workable human governance and security by showing alternative cultural solutions. Humans learn from others so we need to cast our net out to other cultures to find paths to good governance that ensure human security.

This chapter examines one such alternative, the Mesoamerican political development (pre-Columbian), which developed independently from the Eurocentric world: the Aztecs. We know little of earlier cultures such as the Olmecs and Toltecs but Aztec culture developed from them and was well documented by their Spanish conquerors. At the heart of the Aztec Empire were the Mexica and their great city of Tenochtitlan, a city of an estimated 700,000 souls in AD 1500.

In terms of Mexica governance, the polity created a secure, well-ordered city, which would be the envy of many modern city governments. Girouard proposes: "Governance, as a theme, is familiar to all cultures and regimes." Where concomitant security exists, good governance remains sustainable; where security is absent, good governance is replaced. The former was the socio-political environment in Mexica in 1500. On one hand, the Mexica's belief in their city and governance processes united them and motivated them to defend it. On the other hand, Mexica's rule of the Aztec Empire was less inclusive, which resulted in many Aztecs rising up against them, allying themselves with Cortes and the Spanish. This chapter examines the Mexica's governance and security processes, including its strengths, weaknesses and the lessons it may hold for today's Eurocentric view of governance.

## THE MEXICA (AZTECS)

In approximately 1170, the Toltec civilization in central Mexico collapsed and their great city, Tula, was abandoned. However, the city-states it had ruled in the Valley of Mexico lived on as independent states. Shortly after the Toltec collapse, a nomadic group of people known as the Mexica arrived. The Mexica came from the barbaric wastes to the north, an uncouth and uncivilized tribe searching for land. They were initially rejected by the residents of the powerful city-state of Culhuacan and its ruler Cocoxtli, who later allowed them to settle in the marshes and wasteland on the shores of Lake Texcoco. The Mexica started to build their community on the marshes in the southwest corner of the lake. They were a people with a mission, led by their god, Huitzilopochtli, to a chosen land.[1] They did not see marshes but a small island with an eagle holding a snake on a cactus. They declared that this image was the sign that the island was their chosen place. In 300 years, that small island in the marshes would become the site of a great temple complex at the heart of one of the world's biggest 16th century cities. At its head was the largest empire Mesoamerica would boast, the Aztec Empire ruled by the Mexica.

In achieving this dominance, the Mexica proved to be accomplished engineers. They turned the marsh into productive farmland and dug canals through the marshes and swamps. Then they piled up the mud they had excavated, alternating it with layers of weeds, creating rectangular cane frames between the canals. Trees were planted on the corners, which thus secured a field on the lake, known as a chinampa. The field was just a few feet above water level and proved highly productive because of the richness of the soil and easy access to water.

The growing wealth in agriculture, complemented by good governance and a powerful security force (the Mexica often acted as mercenaries for local warring states) meant that they emerged as a powerful regime. In 1328, under their leader, Itzcoatl, they formed a triple alliance with the city-states of Texcoco and Tlacopan to overthrow the dominant power in the valley, the Tepanec state of Azcapotzalco. In the following two centuries, the Mexica and their two city allies pushed their power beyond the valley as far as the Caribbean to east, the Pacific to the west, the wastelands to the north, and the lands of the Maya to the south in what is now Guatemala and the Yucatan peninsula.

The territory was known as the Aztec Empire but by the 16th century, the people who ruled it were the Mexica.[2] The empire would consist of 50 to 60 city-states, only surpassed in size by the Inca Empire of South America. At its heart lay the Mexica city of Tenochtitlan (the place near rock-cactus), founded in 1325 on the island where the Mexica claim they saw the eagle with the snake on the prickly cactus. By 1519, when the Spanish arrived in the region, Tenochtitlan had a population of over 600,000, larger than any European metropolis with the possible exception of Constantinople. What amazed the Spanish even more than its size was the harmony and order that existed in this massive metropolis, a manifestation of good governance and security.

## GOVERNANCE AND SECURITY AMONG THE MEXICA: THE CITY-STATE OF TENOCHTITLAN

At the heart of Aztec governance was the calpulli, which was the central unit of governance originally based on the family. As the population increased, it became a unit of several families usually of common ancestry. In cities characterized by a flow of people, the calpulli became a geographical unit centred on trades such as feather work or goldsmithing.

The most powerful unit was the Cueopan calpulli, the district of the long-distance merchants (pochteen/pocteca).

In Aztec society, individuals did not own land; it was owned by the calpulli, which was responsible for its distribution and use within the group. One of the main advantages of the calpulli was its relatively small size, allowing everyone to know those in the community. The result was greater control over order, security and the collection of taxes. Education was universal for all Mexica members (male and female) of the calpulli and it ensured that social mores remained deeply rooted in the society.

The small, tightly knit structure of the calpulli allowed its own culture and subculture to develop, each with its own gods, priests and traditions.[3] Each calpulli had a governing council and its most capable leaders formed the tribal council or city government. Thus, the government represented the breadth of the population and was composed of members well versed in public service. An executive of four chiefs was elected from the city council, the leader of which would be the Tlatoani (literally meaning the Speaker) who was responsible for the religious and external affairs of the city. One of the other four chiefs conducted the internal affairs. This strength of the bond among the Mexica under the calpulli system was later reflected in their determination as they fought street by street for their city against the Spanish and their allies, despite knowing that there was little hope.

A second aspect of Mexica society observed by the Spanish was the contentment of those at the bottom of the social scale, despite their low status. There were a number of reasons. The first reason was the social mobility between classes. The Aztec world was class ridden and this was echoed in what you could do, eat, wear or even which stones you were allowed in your jewellery. Yet, classes were not exclusive. With the exception of the merchant class, class position was not hereditary. Your position in society was determined on merit, particularly military merit. Anyone could rise to the rank of the nobility if he were able to capture four prisoners of war. Equally, the position of a noble's adult sons was determined by the same rule. If a noble failed to capture four prisoners of war, the sons lost their position in the nobility. It is noteworthy that the sons of nobles had the benefit of better military education and opportunities provided by their father's position; thus, these advantages tended to mitigate the potential for loss of status. Even so, the perception was prevalent that nobility was based on merit rather than birthright. This circumstance meant that lower classes had an invested interest in preserving the privileges, wealth and status of their betters so that when they joined the elite, they would share them. Hence, the threat to security by the have-nots rising up to destroy the haves was considerably lessened. Governance and security of societies elsewhere in the world often collapsed when such means of social mobility were unavailable. In modern European societies, wealth (legally or illegally obtained) is the main means of social mobility, so the opportunity for wealth creation remains a sacred institution. For the Mexica, social mobility was based on the military meritocracy system. Unfortunately, it condemned the Mexica to a state of perpetual war.

The second reason for the contentment of the lower classes may have been a product of the justice system in the Aztec world. Mexica and Aztec justice was harsh and swift, yet weighted against the social elite. For the Mexica, the status of nobility came with responsibility. The nobles were expected to set an example; therefore, punishment for the elite was far more severe than for those who came from the lower social orders. For example, it was a capital offence to be found drunk in public. If you were from the lower classes you were given a second chance but the nobility had to pay the penalty immediately.

The use of alcohol was interesting and, unlike modern societies, hallucinogenic drugs were not banned or criminalized. Drugs were used for religious or recreational purposes. The exception was alcohol; drunkenness was a capital offence. In their edited book on *Peaceful Societies*, Kemp and Fry (2004) noted that in nonviolent societies, the common theme was the intolerance of alcohol. Such societies believed that alcohol changed the nature of people, leading them to lose control of their behaviour and break social norms, causing disorder and violence. It is possible that Aztecs singled out alcohol as the drug that damages the health and good order of society, rather than just the individual.[4] Certainly, Aztecs suffered, as all Native Americans did, from a greater intolerance to alcohol, which made them more susceptible to its effects. After the

Spanish conquered the Aztecs and lifted the ban on alcohol, alcohol remained a major disruptive, problematic factor in Mexican society.

Aztec society was divided into several classes. The nobles included priests, warriors and administrators. The common people (macehual) were the artisans, soldiers, farmers, and labourers, indeed, the bulk of Aztec society. Merchants were common people but were regarded in many societies in Europe and the Far East as almost a separate class. All commoners had to undertake military service and public service such as canal and dyke building. For the Mexica, as in early Rome, it was a citizen army but had an elite professional class, the Jaguar and the Eagle warriors, based on military merit and those with noble status.

Below the macehual, a landless class of people lived on the fringes of society. They were descendents of conquered people brought to the city or those who lost their position in the Mexica world. They acted as serfs to the Mexica and were obliged to fight and do public service, but had no rights in communal affairs.

The Mexica also had slaves but slavery was a form punishment for crime or failure to pay tribute or taxes. Unlike the European system of slavery in the 17th to 19th centuries, slaves had many more rights. Their families were not regarded a slaves, they could marry whom they pleased, their children were regarded as freeborn, and they could work to buy back their freedom. Slavery, therefore, was a form of severe communal service and a Mexica alternative to our prison system.

One of the factors that amazed the Spanish when they came to Tenochtitlan was the main market. The market was in the fifth district of the city, once the separate city of Tlatelolco. The Spanish were impressed by the secure, orderly and peaceful conduct of the approximately 60,000 merchants and patrons who attended each day. This behaviour reflected the acceptance of certain social mores by the Mexica who acknowledged the swift consequences of any misdemeanour or disorder. Magistrates dealt with the misdemeanour, setting up their courts around the market to enact prompt and harsh punishment. The law was visibly present and its judgements were rapid.

By 1519, the gap between poor and rich had widened considerably in Mexican society yet the Spanish found no discontent, as one would expect. The calpulli system of local accountable government, visible security, fairness of the judiciary system, opportunity to advance through merit, and social mores of responsibility may have accounted for this relative socio-economic stability. As mentioned above, education was freely available for all in Mexican society with the possible exception of landless serfs. In addition, Mexica had one of the world's most beautiful languages, Nahualt. It was expressive and poetic in its communication of ideas, enjoyment and clear thought. This factor may have contributed to the harmony and order of the Mexica world.

## TO RULE AN EMPIRE: THE MEXICAN RULE OF THE AZTEC EMPIRE

On the surface, the Mexica Empire, with its subservient partners of the triple alliance, appeared secure and in good order. As the Mexica extended their rule across Mesoamerica, they brought roads, communications and trade, which enhanced the lives of the Mexica but not their subject peoples. The Mexica Empire was based on trade and tribute. The Mexica did not want to rule these conquered cities, only to impose tribute (taxation) and provide advantageous trading rights for Mexican merchants. It was a much looser empire than any Europeans had experienced. This apparently mercantile empire lasted as long as tribute was paid and trade continued; the subject peoples could rule themselves. The system appears to be an example of good governance and secure empire, yet when the Spanish arrived, the empire rapidly collapsed. Its members rose up in rebellion and allied to the Spanish to crush the hated Mexica. The reason might have been because their emperor was a despot but in fact Montezuma was not.

The Aztec Empire was ruled by a council of 30 lords, including the rulers of the partners in the empire, the Texcocans and Tlacopans. The council formed an electoral college to elect an executive of four. The leader of these four, the Huey Tlatani (Great Speaker) was what the Spanish called the emperor. However, Montezuma was president of a cabinet government rather than an emperor as perceived by the Spanish. This was not despotic rule. The Mexica Huey Tlatani was selected from the ruling family but strict heredity was not practised; instead, merit within the family was the greater consideration. Montezuma was the eighth son of a previous emperor, but succeeded his uncle. His role as the Speaker of the new empire included being responsible for religious and external affairs. He was divine in the sense that he was the high priest, closer to the gods, but not divine because he was anointed by a god and thus chosen supernaturally, as in Europe. Nor was he a god. Internal Mexican affairs were not his remit, but that of the Cihuscoatl, one of the other four. Among the four was the heir apparent, another family member. These four were chosen for life but could be deposed if they lost their legitimate right to govern, with the consent of the Mexican people. The Spanish made the error of seeing Montezuma as the supreme ruler, so they took him hostage in order to rule the empire through him. In the process of the kidnapping, they took the whole council as well, which was where the real power existed. Feeling they were safe with the "Emperor," the Spanish allowed one member of the four, Montezuma's brother, Cuitlahauc, to negotiate with the rebellious Mexica. The Mexica accepted Cuitlahauc as the Huey Tlatani, unceremoniously deposing Montezuma as a failed leader. The Spanish thus lost their hold on any power they had over the Mexica.

Despite the benefits the Mexica may have brought to their subject people, they controlled the empire through governance and security by fear. Fear of the Mexica's power formed the basis of the empire's security so it was not the rule of a despotic ruler but of a despotic people that caused the defection.

One of the religious aspects of Aztec life was human sacrifice, which was not universally supported. Many in the Aztec world were disquieted by it. It has been argued that the Toltec civilization fell due to religious strife over the issue. Like most peoples of the empire, the Mexica carried out human sacrifice but they did so on a greater and more dramatic scale than most, sacrificing sometimes as many as 20,000 people at a time before the assembled members of the empire's city-states. For the Mexica, the ceremony was not just about religion but about terror and instilling fear into those who might defy them.

The manner in which the Mexica conquered city-states also reflected

the use of fear to achieve dominance. If the Mexica wanted to incorporate a city-state in their empire they would send representatives of the
Tlacopans (the most junior partner in the triple alliance). The representatives would invite the city-state to join the empire, asking for trade
preferences and not tribute, but at the same time discussing the horrors
of war. They gave city-states 20 days to join. If no acknowledgement was
received within 20 days, representatives of the Texcocans would arrive,
again inviting the city-state to join the empire, but now tribute as well
as trade preferences were demanded. They would discuss what would
be done to the rulers of the city-state if force had to be used. Then they
would leave, giving 20 more days for compliance. If the city-state had still
not responded, the representatives of the Mexica would arrive, giving
another 20 days' grace. This time if the state did not comply, it would see
its rulers sacrificed, its people enslaved and its temples destroyed, with
no mercy shown. Once a city-state joined the empire, the Mexica would
maintain a presence by sending its tax collectors to ensure that tribute
and trade priorities were enforced. In addition, they would monitor the
economic and social activities of the city-state to ensure that it kept the
interests of the Mexica as its highest priority. Behind this "negotiation"
lay the might of a large dedicated army of citizens and professional
nobles keen to seek military merit. The army would dare the state to
take them on, knowing, as the Mexica were keen to demonstrate, what
happened to all prisoners.

Governance through a policy of fear means that threats need to be
followed up with action, should circumstance dictate. When the Mexica
reached the limits of their conquest, their need for war to earn merit
led them to conduct "flowery" (in Nahuatl) or institutionalized battles,
rather than conquests. They allowed the city-state of Tlaxcala, for example, to be independent of the empire, simply by conducting regular
wars and battles for the purpose of acquiring prisoners. Allowing Tlaxcala to be independent gave it a sense of its importance, which added
to the humiliation of being defeated each year by the Mexica in their
flowery war. Tlaxcala was a real enemy and knew it had the might to defeat the Mexica in a real war. In fact in 1517 and 1518, Tlaxcala inflicted

defeat on the mighty Mexica in the flowery wars, destroying the apparent invincibility of the Mexica.

When Cortes arrived on the coast of the empire, he chained up two of the Mexica's taxpayers, which impressed the local people of the city-state of Totonecs. As a direct result, they immediately offered to be his first allies against the Mexica. The Tlaxcala saw him as an invader, however, and attacked the small force. When they realized the might of the Spanish army, they called off their attacks and sought alliance with the Spanish because they saw a chance to defeat the hated Mexica. When Cortes was driven from Technotitlan, losing two-thirds of his army, and struggled back to Tlaxcala, the Mexican leader, Cuitlahauc, demanded that the Tlaxcala destroy Cortes. As the Spanish army struggled back, the Mexican army fell on them at Otumba but was soundly defeated. Seeing the defeat of the Mexica, the Tlaxcala remained loyal to the Spanish, supplying most of the forces (as many as 200,000 men) in the subsequent attack on Technotitlan. In the final days of Technotitlan when the Spanish suffered a major reverse and took to their tents, the Tlaxcalans spurred them on by continuing the fight.

Cortes took on the Mexica at their own game by taking the small state of Tepeca, putting all the men to the sword and selling the women and children into slavery. He proved to be a greater terror than the Mexica, and city-states that had been reluctant to abandon the Mexica began to do so. The cities of Huexotzinco and Cuetlaxtlan immediately capitulated to Cortes as a result. Once you are not afraid, fear quickly fails as a form of governance and security. The Mexica experienced this reversal and failed alone, abandoned by the triple alliance allies.

If you rule by fear, the temptation is to be arrogant toward your subjects. The Mexica were no exception. They sent representatives to all city-states to oversee tribute collections, taxes, and trade relations. The representatives expected to be treated royally and deferred to but the arrogance of the Mexica to what were semi-independent city-states offended them greatly. The influence of economic advisors may be resented as strongly as any political dominance. Indeed, many of the empire's city-states resented the Mexican tribute collectors and traders.

It is useful to compare economic empires of today. In 1916, Lenin wrote that the true British Empire was South America, consisting of independent nations ruled economically by British merchants and bankers. The US rules this empire now and it can be said that the true crime of Cuba was not so much that it was communist but that it defied the economic interests of the US in order to be independent.

## CONCLUSION

"Harmony and order" were the words used by the Spanish on seeing Technochtitlan, a great city of 600,000. The security of that metropolis was maintained by a combination of:

1. Closely knit forms of local governance, which elected the city government from its members;
2. Order, peace, education, tax collecting, and land distribution conducted at the local level and not from above;
3. Universal education, which enforced social mores of conduct;
4. A class system that allowed social movement based on merit;
5. A swift and harsh justice system that did not discriminate against the poor or powerless; in fact, one that required higher standards from the social elite, who were expected to set an example; and
6. Recognition of the influence of alcohol in causing social disorder.

At the heart of this apparent harmony and order was governance from the bottom up, rather than the top down. All Mexican citizens, rich or poor, fought as a community against the Spanish and their allies to defend this structure. European concepts of governance were imposed on democratic institutions. Top-down rule is not centred on the grassroots; justice still discriminates against the powerless. We may have a long way to go to learn that with power comes real, not token, responsibility.

In some nation-states today we have social mobility that is not based on military merit but on the merit of wealth, although some European-type societies in the developed world use the military as a means of social mobility. Wealth creation is essential for those at the bottom to join the ruling elite, whether legally, illegally or by the lottery. Thus, just as the right to go to war and capture prisoners was sacred to Mexica society, wealth creation may well be as sacred to the modern world. For the Mexica, the need for perpetual war required a permanent enemy in the empire (Tlaxcala), which aided their downfall. It can be said that the sacredness of wealth creation may threaten our civilization, undermining initiatives to counter global warming.

Harmony and order were not prevalent in the Aztec Empire. Under the Mexica, harmony and order were achieved through a loose empire of quasi-independent states. It was a mercantile rather than political empire and had a governance structure led not by a single leader but by ruling families and an appointed leader. The Mexica brought wealth to their empire but incurred deep resentment because of their economic dominance. More importantly, security for the empire was achieved through fear.

The Mexica had an effective form of governance while fear remained but as security through fear dissipated and governance collapsed, security vanished. The collapse of the Aztec Empire was swift but did not result from the military superiority of the Spanish. Instead, it resulted from the subject peoples no longer fearing the Mexica and turning against them. Cortes' skill was his diplomatic realization of the weakness in the empire and harnessing the hatred and resentment against the Mexica. Thus, the Mexica were alone, their subject peoples either fighting as allies of Cortes or remaining neutral. Even their allies, the Tlacopans and Texcocans, turned against the Mexica. European cultures have yet to learn this lesson: you cannot rule for long through fear and terror. Without good governance and security, nation-states fail, as in Romania in 1989 and the Middle East in 2011.

By examining political traditions of governance other than the dominant Eurocentric view of the world today, we may learn better ways of conducting internal and external affairs to increase good governance and security. The Aztec world has gone but their history is a mirror for us to learn from. We need to look for answers not only from the Aztecs but across the broad spectrum of human experience of governance and security. Girouard correctly concludes that the view of governance must focus on "those who have the will and the power and the vision delivering on the hope of those around us in need." We also need security to achieve this in the contemporary global city-state.

## REVIEW QUESTIONS

1. What are main differences in style and content of the Aztec (Mexica) governance of themselves and their empire? How secure did this make them?
2. What would you assess as the strengths and weaknesses of Aztec governance and security?
3. How could present-day societies learn from Aztec governance and security?

### REFERENCES

Joseph, A. M. *500 Nations*. New York, NY: Knopf 1994.

Katz, F. *The Ancient American Civilizations*. London, UK: Phoenix, 1997.

Kemp, G., and D. P. Fry, eds., *Keeping the Peace*. London, UK: Routledge, 2004.

Pagden A., and H. Cortes, eds., *Letters from Mexico*. New Haven, CT: Yale University Press, 1986.

Soustelle, J. *Daily Life of the Aztecs*. Translated by Patrick O'Brien. New York, NY: Macmillan, 1962.

Thomas, H. *The Conquest of Mexico*. London, UK: Hutchinson, 1993.

Wright, R. *Stolen Continents, The Indian Story*. London, UK: Murray, 1992.

Vaillant, G. C. *Origin, Rise and Fall of the Aztec Nation*. New York, NY: Doubleday, 1962.

### ENDNOTES

[1] This is likely to be a Mexican fable: the Mexica burnt all books to destroy inconvenient history. They wanted to be seen as a chosen people, true inheritors of the great Toltecs.

[2] The Aztec empire was an empire of a triple alliance of three cities – the Tlacopans, Texcocans and the Mexicans. As time passed, the former became increasingly subservient to the Mexica so when the Spanish arrived, it seemed that the Mexica were the Aztec empire. One can make a distinction between the Mexica and their Aztec empire, like the English and their British Empire.

3    The closest example of this is the canton system in the Italian city of Sienna, which has been argued to encourage a low crime rate in the city.

4    There was exception to law regarding alcohol consumption; it did not apply to anyone over 50. But then groups of drunken 50-year-olds have not been seen causing disorder compared to the youth in societies where alcohol is open to all.

# GOVERNANCE, TURTLE-ISLAND STYLE

## BARBARA ALICE MANN, PhD

---

## INTRODUCTION

I have a few Pueblo friends who would take great exception to Roger Girouard's reference to the *"Anastazi"* ("Anastazi," a Diné term meaning, "Our Ancient Enemies"). The Pueblos, who claim a direct descent from the Cliff Dwellers (not "Anastazi"), would like to hear Mr. Girouard explain how exoticizing their ancestors fits with his theory of anthropological correctitude.[1]

For the record, Native North Americans did not romantically disappear in *pre*-history. We are still here. Moreover, Native American history did not begin with contact, nor were we (in the pre-contact era) so primitive as to lack time to develop sophisticated writing systems. Besides the playful, multiple-choice phonetic script of the Central American Mayas, there is also North America's two-colour, character writing system of bead *wampum* and the seventeen-coloured, knotted-string *khipu* of South America. These may not resemble Europeans' understanding of writing, yet they extend into deep antiquity as recording media.[2]

## AN ETIOLOGY OF DEMOCRACY

On Turtle Island (North America), the Woodlands peoples, or those living east of the Mississippi River, thought long and hard about governance, trying a totalitarian method or two, under the Mound-Builder priesthoods before hitting upon participatory democracy.[3] Western scholarship likes to confine discussion of our democratic forms exclusively to the Iroquois League. Although the Haudenosaunee League was more frequently pestered by scribbling anthropologists than, say, the Guales (whom the Spaniards set about destroying in earnest after their effective revolt of 1597–1601), all Woodlands cultures used some version of the constitutional democracy expressed most famously by the Iroquois League.

Our democracies are ancient, too. The League of the Haudenosaunee was founded in the year 1142 C.E., after a long civil war to end the priest-controlled system that preceded it.[4] It was a joint effort by the women (blood), under the head mother, *Jigonsaseh*, and the men (breath), under the stuttering Peacemaker, whose sacred name is not to be uttered, except in a ceremonial telling of this tradition.[5] Despite Western anthropology's damaging attempt to impose a Lone Male Hero script on this history (including promoting "Hiawatha" to the Peacemaker's role) the structure of the democracy was co-founded and put together in a *joint* female-male effort. Furthermore, it was based on an extant model of the Attiwendaronks, operating in Ontario. Finally, the traditional Haudenosaunee story includes a recalcitrant priest, Adodaroh (or Tadadaho) and a priest-allied clan mother. This doubled double (F–M / M–F) entirely matches Woodlands' "common sense," which operates by endlessly replicating the binary, blood-breath balance of the cosmos, evident in the commonplace Native North American symbology of the circle-square and the nested half- and full-circle schematics of the mounds (see Figure 1).

Native North American binaries require repetition because any binary, say the East-West axis, consists of halves (½, ½) that combine to become one. The E–W "one" thus conceived, needs a mirror-image repetition to be balanced, in this instance the North-South (N | S) axis, another halved whole. The resultant + looks like four points to Western eyes but is really just the crossed, halved wholes (—, |) in an arrangement that, to Native North Americans, feels "complete." This explains why four parties are necessary to a proper reading of wampum messages: the two speakers ($_{\backslash blood}/^{breath}$) for each clan half addressing cross-wise ($^{breath\backslash}_{blood}$) the clan-halved audience, in an X ( / , \ ) motif. Often, the + motif is doubled into a ╬ to emphasize the continued doubling.

Figure 1. Native North American Symbology in the Mounds

Shows two different mound schematics from the Ohio Valley, showing variant motifs of the cosmic halves.

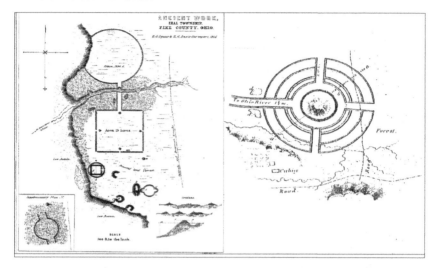

(SOURCE: Ephraim George Squier and E. H. Davis, *Ancient Monuments of the Mississippi Valley: Comprising the Results of Extensive Original Surveys and Explorations*, Smithsonian Contributions to Knowledge, vol. 1 (1848; reprint, New York: Johnson Reprint Corporation, t1965). Seal Township Earthworks, facing page 66; and Portsmouth Group, facing page 78)

In Figure 1, all the designs delineate the same concept of breath/sky–blood/earth to achieve the cosmic balance. On the left, the Seal Township Earthworks include not only the ○–■ circle-square (○ breath/sky – ■ blood/earth) motif, so common to the Ohio Valley mounds, but also the double-circle and semi-circle symbols found more often in the Mississippi Valley mounds. There is a very interesting square within a circle in the Seal Township group. On the right, the Portsmouth Group in Kentucky shows an intricate nested circle motif, replicating the Lenapé notion of dimensions as something peeled away in layers, like an onion.[6] The outermost ○ circle of breath/sky leads to the innermost · circle of blood/earth, which is literally a burial mound.

When Europeans try to discuss such concepts, the result usually comes out as "dialogic," in the sense that Mikhail Mikhailovich Bakhtin proposed dialogism, but Native North Americans are talking about a necessary unit that just *looks* like "two" or "four" to Europeans.[7] For

Native North Americans, the human community is one unit, composed of clan halves (blood), mirrored by national halves (breath) that together, equal one. In wampum writing, the community is symbolized by a ♦ diamond, for the common council fire, composed of the $_{\text{Turtle/blood}}$/Wolf/breath clans and the Elders/breath\$_{\text{Youngers/blood}}$ nations. (Turtle and Wolf are the designations of the Iroquoian clan halves. Other groups use different terms for their clan halves.)

## GOVERNANCE

The community includes everybody in sight. Exclusion is an act of suicidal cruelty and not to be countenanced. Instead, inclusiveness of all comers becomes a primary object and traditionally Native North Americans went out of their way to ensure that everyone "ate from the same bowl," a living metaphor, acted out to make two or more groups one.[8] As shown in Figure 2, people are seen as scattered within the circle of community. If anyone happens to fall outside that circle, the circle is simply widened to encompass that person. Inclusiveness is the key to solid governance, which is why so many missionaries were adopted. The religious dogma they were peddling was entirely beside the Native point of inclusion.

Figure 2. Native North American Inclusive Communities

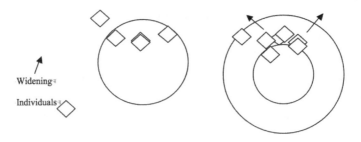

As shown in Figure 2, the Native North American community strives for inclusiveness, not exclusiveness.

It easily widens to include newcomers.

Although Native North American forms are sometimes brought up in Western discussions of governance, it is either in the whimsical mode or as a nod of courtesy, for the structures of our inclusive binaries are certainly never canvassed. To Western readers, the lip service aimed generally in our direction may give the impression of considerateness but if it were real, the published models of governance would not all look so suspiciously Western in their fundamental assumptions of:

- Capitalist markets
- A military-industrial complex
- Nation-statehood
- Hierarchical structures
- Militarism as security

## NATIVE NORTH AMERICAN STRUCTURE

What I do not see on the list are any quintessentially Native North American structures of governance, including:

- The gift economy
- Identity as geo-lineal
- Parallel governance structures mirroring the binary cosmos
- The Native North American method of security
- Sacred clowning

There seems to be a lack of any real discussion about an economic system other than the capitalist market system. In fact, all mainstream Western media confidently assure us that, since the "fall of communism," no competition for capitalism exists. This is just not true. Well into the colonial period, Turtle Island in its entirety operated on the gift economy. This did not mean that we were scrounging about in some "savage" subsistence mode[9] because poverty did not hit us until the Europeans arrived.

The plenty produced under the gift economies of the Woodlands regularly staggered European observers and conquerors. In 1687, for instance, French troops under the Marquis de Denonville spent twenty-four days destroying 1.2 million bushels of corn, the harvest of just four towns.[10] In 1779, during the genocidal attack on Iroquoia ordered by George Washington, the US Revolutionary Army destroyed "great Quantities" of "the best corn" that the soldiers, most of them farmers, had ever seen, in "quantity immense, and goodness unequalled," so as to stagger the "civilized" mind.[11] The gift economies of the Woodlands produced such plenty that the people had never had any homeless or hungry citizens. Even as late in the colonial game as 1890, a true nadir of our existence with traditional cultures in tatters under forced assimilation, the Iroquois still had but one indigent citizen and his clan provided for him under the gift economy.[12] Although beset on all sides particularly on the government-controlled reservations, among our own communal groups, modern Native North Americans still practise gifting as a sort of parallel albeit underground economy. How strong and inevitable can capitalism really be, if it cannot wipe out the gift economy after five hundred years of dedicated trying?

Neither are Native North Americans the only cultures to practise gift economics, for gift economies are the identifying feature of all matriarchies. Although battered by the concerted, modern onslaught of first colonial capitalism and second Moaism, the gift economy of the Lahu, or mountain people of southern China, continues in operation.[13] The Berber women in Kabylia as well as the Minangkabau of Sumatra use the gift economy.[14] The Sami ("Laplanders") of Finland, despite Scandinavian invasion and Soviet oppression, continue with their gift economies.[15] Other gift economies exist and considerable theoretical work has been done on the operation of the gift economy in matriarchies.[16]

Thus, when governance is the topic, we need to quiz the reflexive insistence on capitalism and, worse, the military-industrial complex it has spawned, as necessary features. *Are* they necessary? Are they just *Western*? If they are just Western, then why are they allowed to dominate the discussion? Before any discussion of governance can bear fruit, there must be a critique of capitalism, not starting with its current excrescences but starting where all good inquiry begins, at the beginning.

## CAPITALISM EXAMINED

Capitalism is rooted in the culture of the raid. In its simplest form, it consists of young ruffians bopping people on the head to expropriate the fruits of creative labour that said ruffians either cannot equal or do not wish to perform. As such, raiding is a criminal enterprise. No matter how complex the system becomes, the raiding continues. The complexity lies mainly in methods of deflecting responsibility for the harm done to anyone who is handy. Part of being handy is being too socially weak to make an objection. Whole conventions and institutions exist simply to define and contain capitalism's designated "weak," keeping them available for exploitation.

To prevent the peasants from noticing that the books are being cooked, deflection rhetoric has it that "no one" understands economics and that scams such as derivatives are too complex for anyone lacking a seat on the Federal Securities and Exchange Commission to grasp. The penalty for pointing at the power elites behind the curtain is to be declared a conspiracy theorist.

Instead, people are supposed to play along with the fiction that market forces are impersonal. Intentional, traceable greed, causing the goods and services necessary to life to be overpriced and/or withheld from the designated weak, are portrayed as "unintended consequences." Since most people would rather not fight, the extortion continues, with the capitalists as latter-day warlords in Armani suits.

The capitalist sleight-of-hand only worsens when the military-industrial complex obtrudes because governmental secrecy prevents critics from inquiring into the whereabouts of the public money that is run through its private coffers. Should "black" or unaccounted-for budgets be quizzed, the expedient is simply to declare the money missing without trace. On 10th September 2001, then US Secretary of Defence Donald Rumsfeld openly admitted that 2.3 trillion dollars had gone from the US public coffers this way.[17] This was the day before the Department of Defence began squandering money in Iraq and Afghanistan, lavishing unaccountable, billion-dollar contracts on the industrial (private) side of its military-industrial complex.

Just because amounts that are literally unimaginable are distributed through the Byzantine misdirection of the military-industrial complex does not mean that capitalism is working. In fact, it means that capitalism is in crisis. Continued capital raiding of the environment as well as of the peoples in the system ultimately sustains neither Mother Earth nor the life dependent on Her.

## THE ESSENCE OF THE GIFT ECONOMY

Instead of going down with the capital ship, let us modernize the gift economy, which has a track record of managing plenty in totally transparent ways for the benefit of all. The magic in this system is in the size of the community. Historically, Woodlanders knew that, when a community is so large that its functionaries no longer personally know its constituents, the group is asking for trouble. If one ceases to witness, up close and personally, the suffering caused by one's decisions, then it becomes possible to make impersonal decisions of the massively destructive sort. Woodlanders came by this insight the hard way, through their experience of large populations living under the Mound-Builder priesthoods, which grew extremely brutal, avaricious, and corrupt, even as the population centres boomed. Warfare became its chief activity and the class lines hardened into a stratospheric elite (the priesthood), a subaltern military, and large masses of peasant farmers struggling to support the groaning superstructure.[18]

After the overthrow of the Mound-Builder culture, Woodlanders kept towns no larger than 12,000 to 15,000 people, and any of that size were capital cities.[19] The more common town populations ranged between 500 and 2,000 people. We knew that human beings could not effectively interact with numbers larger than that while retaining human sentiment. Thus, whenever a community became so large that people did not know one another any more, we broke them up into smaller, sister communities. This strategy kept leaders knowing the people and known to their constituents. The only people who could nominate anyone to office were the grandmothers – the same grandmothers who could and did impeach wrongdoers, publicly delineating their misdeeds in removing them from office.

## WE GREW FROM THE GROUND ON WHICH WE STAND

Nation-statehood is a crumbling concept that I for one am not sorry to see go because the larger the polity and the more removed the leaders from the "grass roots" (a Native North American term for "the people"), the more likely said leaders will morph into criminal elites, who consider only what is good for people like themselves rather than what is good for all the people. Dissolving nation-states do not necessarily cue slugfest chaos or corporate, multi-national police states. Instead, with the Internet as a factor, global sub-communities are an exciting and productive possibility. (Native North Americans just *love* the Internet.) The community may be virtual but the results work well for all. In this context, it is worth realizing that the big reason that Barak Obama was elected president of the US in 2008, prevailing against hugely moneyed if backward interests, was the insightful use his campaign made of the Internet to reach American virtual communities.

Although our umbrella polities are called nations, Native Americans do not have nation-states, a Western ideological structure that has always puzzled us. The homeland is a deep component of our psyches but in a mystical rather than a political sense. In a metaphor that is understood by farmers, it is commonplace for Native North Americans to say that we grew from the ground on which we stand. Other metaphors of belonging include the poignant assertion that our homeland, for the first five feet down, is made of our ancestors. Yet-to-be-conceived children are often depicted as smiling little faces looking up hopefully from beneath the ground. This kind of imagery bespeaks a close confederacy with Our Mother, the Earth that includes "indigeneity and sovereignty." It is not ownership but "a particular way of seeing and being in the land," as my Abenaki sister, Lisa Brooks, puts it.[20] Westerners lack this spiritual umbilicus to Mother Earth, the common pot (here, womb) nurturing All Our Relatives.

Instead, Westerners view the "nation" as a politically engendered entity of accidental co-citizens living within expedient, re-drawable boundaries. Operating with this understanding of the term, Westerners always ask Native North Americans what our nation is, ignoring our primary political identification through the clan, the matrilineal club we belong to, either through birth or naturalization. In our concept of space, female-identified clans of blood interpenetrate the male geographical units of air, now miscalled nations. The blood and breath halves comingle in one polity. The correct questions to ask Native North Americans are: "What is your clan? Who are your elders? Where are your sacred places? What ground did you grow from?"

A member of the Heron Clan is a Heron everywhere. Despite the geographical area she visits in the League, she has unquestioned admittance into Heron clan houses. Thus, our Heron Clan Mother might live in Mohawk, roughly eastern upstate New York, but travel to Erie, the lands south of Lake Erie, and still "belong" there. Malleability of citizenship is not completely unfamiliar to Westerners. In a similar vein, modern Americans are citizens of their respective states as well as of the federal United States and may travel anywhere in any of the states without question. The European Union is creating the same flexibility for its member states. I do not know that the binary identity of "South Hamptonite" and "Englishman" are quite as strongly felt, but they are still similar in their simultaneity. Thus, Westerners do have some idea of how to deal with multiple identities through simultaneous, internal and external structures, such as those that Internet groups establish. The groups co-habit reality; they do not cancel out one another. The existence of one does not require the annihilation of the other.

## WOODLAND GOVERNANCE

Politically, our customary binaries pop up everywhere in Woodlands governance as a means of ensuring that everyone has a hand and a stake in the polity. Although Western colonialism played havoc with our councils, damagingly androgynizing them while making them subject to the settler government, traditionally governance councils were foursquare. The overall binary consisted of the youngers (—, the blood half) and the elders (|, the breath half). The youth councils were then split into the blood half (—) of the young matrons, including the children, and the breath half ( | ) of the young men (always mistranslated as "warrior"). The elder councils were likewise halved again, into the grandmothers' (— blood) and grandfathers' (| breath) councils. This yielded the familiar ǂ doubled doubles, a sturdy structure that resists hierarchy.

Organizationally, the grandmothers meet to consider all matters first, handing off matters to the grandfathers after they reach some sort of consensus. Meanwhile, the young matrons and children bring matters to the grandmothers, even as the young men bring them to the grandfathers so that democracy bubbles up rather than trickling down. Thus, the sets of binary units, the = and ||, sit in a binary foursquare structure ǂ, gathering intelligence from the "grass roots" in both halves.[21]

Between the halves, the elders have the edge and in the elders' councils, the grandmothers have the edge but this does not mean that any of the four entities is in a position to bully the rest into line. In each subgroup, consensus must be reached before a matter moves forward and then the whole group must reach consensus before anything is put into place. This process obviously takes time. Native American cultures view speed as an expression of callow, thoughtless youth rather than something to be valued, let alone stand as an organizing principle. Instead, ideas ripen in their own time and produce the best and most mature ideas. If that means it takes fifty years to agree on an approach to a policy, then so be it. Because the economy operates on continual gifts, no economic repercussions result from the slow process of consensus. The people are fed, housed and cared for, regardless of the political issues.

Historically, the Woodlands law stated that only the grandmothers could appoint soldiers and call wars and second, that only one engagement at a time could be authorized, which quelled militarism.[22] Furthermore, it was against the law for any member of the Iroquois Confederacy to make war on another member. At the same time all members were called upon to stand by any threatened member. Since there were eventually over sixty nations living under the shade of the Tree of Peace, this made war fairly impractical until, of course, the Europeans showed up with their weapons of mass destruction and their forever wars, using

Native proxies. My point here is not that the League method of govern-ance cannot be destroyed but that it can and did work for centuries. This is not unknown to Westerners. In fact, the League of Nations is thought to have been modelled on the Iroquois League.[23]

## SECURITY AND
## THE WOODLANDS LAW OF INNOCENCE

This brings me to the Native American definition of "security." It does not consist of an ever-heightening militarization of the culture but quite the opposite. In matriarchies, there is a widening gift circle that works to disarm hostilities. Violence is simply an unacceptable response to gifting. The basic premise of Native North America is that everyone on Earth is related. We take our cue from Our Mother, the Earth, who continually gives to us all. Our proper stance, then, is continually to give to others. Once gifting is established, there is no need to take anything, as every-thing is available to whoever needs it. Let me emphasize once more that this is not some fantastic, socialist utopia but the demonstrable operation of Woodlands gifting for hundreds of years *before* the Europeans arrived and the dominant native economy for at least three hundred years *after* Europeans arrived.

Under such a system, the definition of security falls under the Wood-lands Law of Innocence. It is the absolute duty of all young men to use their physical prowess in acts of protection and support of the women, the children, the elderly, and the physically or mentally challenged.[24] Be-cause it was the absolute right of the Innocents to enjoy physical safety and security, it became the main duty of the young men to ensure as much. It was not unusual for the grandfathers to hush young men, eager for a fight, by telling them bluntly to stay home to "take care of the women and children, and not to trouble themselves" about war.[25]

The first Law of Innocence accounts for what Europeans have long seen as a puzzling fact of the 1779 US invasion of Iroquoia under cover of Revolutionary warfare with England: that the young men but once, and then reluctantly, stood to fight the US invasion force. This was not cowardice but attention to duty. The rest of the time they were hurrying women, children, and elders, physically carrying many of them to safe havens before the US army marched into their towns. The 400 young men, our entire army, accomplished this task so brilliantly that the US Army, 5,000-strong, took only four Iroquoian captives during the summer-long campaign.

## GOVERNANCE AND SACRED CLOWNING

There is another element of governance that Native North America finds fairly important but to which Europeans seem oblivious: sacred clowning. This is not the same as simple satire. Sacred clowning is a *duty* of the body politic, an *institutionalized* form. Sacred clowning involves backwards medicine, like saying the opposite of what one means or doing things in a riotously backwards way, say, climbing up sacred poles upside-down, as some Plains peoples do at ceremonial times.[26] This keeps people from thinking that sacred means grimly tyrannical, for the binary twin of awe is laughter, not fear. By and large, sacred clowning keeps anyone from taking her or himself too seriously. Long ago, the elders noticed that the people were in for hardship once the leaders decided, as my grandmother used to put it, "that theirs didn't stink."

Entire groups of self-important people are publicly targeted, as were the Moravian missionaries in Ohio in 1781. An Ottawa clown commandeered a horse and missionary garb and rode back and forth in front of the missionaries, wearing not only their day clothes but also a ridiculous "white night cap on his head." At each pass, he nodded at them in a patronizing way, causing guffaws among all the spectators, including the missionaries.[27] Similarly, in 1971, after Native Americans mounted an "invasion" of the abandoned prison island of Alcatraz in the San Francisco Bay, they issued a proclamation claiming the land for Native America, citing the fact of vacant land, *terra nullius*, a Western legal notion under Discovery Doctrine.[28] Clowns began distributing bumper stickers, "US out of North America." Although many mainstream histories of the Alcatraz invasion now treat it as deadly serious, it was an act of sacred clowning.

Western settlers unconsciously supplied another hilarious instance.

To commemorate the 1794 Battle of Fallen Timbers (in which the US defeated the Ohio Union in the struggle for the control of Ohio) and as an emblem of their victory, Ohio settlers showcased what they thought was "Turkey Foot Rock" in Side Cut Park in Maumee, Ohio. In fact, the gargantuan piece on the pedestal was never Turkey Foot Rock, as all Ohio Natives had long known. The real rock, a much smaller spirit rock, had long since been squirreled away for safekeeping by the faith-keepers. As sacred clowning, we had had quite a long-standing chuckle over letting the settlers go on thinking that their gaudy monument was the Real Deal. The joke only improved in February 2008, when archae-ologists realized that, after landscaping in 1941, park workers had reset the impostor rock upside down![29] As an act of backwards medicine, we could not have thought of anything better ourselves, so we asked that the monument not be "righted."

## GOVERNANCE AND NATURAL PROPORTIONS

The egalitarianism behind sacred clowning is not incidental but essential to good governance. It is a dangerous cult that bans good-natured laugh-ter from its precincts. It is a totalitarian dictator who wants genuinely funny yet gentle critics like Victor Borge dead. The beauty of sacred clowning is that natural proportions of governance are re-established without anyone being materially injured. Skewered pomp deflates pom-posity to natural proportions that no longer impinge on anyone else's space. Moreover, even the targets can laugh heartily at the joke as they did in 1781, 1971, and 2008. Targeted people may feel a little sheepish for a while but they are not so injured as to seek revenge. In fact, they are not even driven from office. They are just reminded that theirs stinks, too. The usual effect is that they carry on but more humbly and more mindfully than before.

## SUMMARY OBSERVATIONS

Toward a vibrant discussion of governance, I will close by noting that peoples besides the Native North Americans have long histories of successful, constitutional governance, for instance, the Icelanders, whose Althing (literally all things; general assembly) dates from about 930 C.E. Therefore, I strongly urge more voices to be invited to this conversation on what is good governance. We simply cannot do without the intellectual contributions of *all* our relatives. Here, I return to my critique of Girouard's discussion. His is just one voice; mine is another.

## REVIEW QUESTIONS

1. Western culture fundamentally exists on precepts of exclusivity, whereas Native North America accepts everyone else as a necessary relative of a common Mother Earth. Obviously, distinct warrants will evolve from these premises. How are these systems to co-exist without injury?

2. Given the interfaces of democratic matriarchy and the gift economy, on the one hand, and patriarchal hierarchy and capitalism, on the other hand, could any sort of mutually respectful economic system result?

3. Standing armies and wars are taken for granted and heavily funded among Western cultures, whereas both are actively undercut in Native North American cultures, with wealth used instead to ensure that all people are provided for. If Westerners are to be included in governance pacts, how is this fundamental mismatch to be resolved?

## REFERENCES

Armand, Louis, and Baron de Lahontan. *New Voyages to North America*, ed. Rueben Gold Thwaites, 2 vols. 1703; Chicago: A. C. McClure & Co., 1905.

Bakhtin, M. M. *The Dialogic Imagination: Four Essays*, ed. Michael Holquist, trans. Caryl Emerson and Michael Holquist. Austin, TX: University of Texas Press, 1981.

Brinton, Daniel, G. *The Myths of the New World: A Treatise on the Symbolism and Mythology of the Red Race of America* (2nd ed. rev.). New York, NY: Henry Holt, 1876.

Brooks, Lisa. *The Common Pot: The Recovery of Native Space in the Northeast.* Minneapolis, MN: University of Minnesota Press, 2008.

Calloway, Colin G. *Crown and Calumet: British-Indian Relations, 1783-1815.* Norman, OK: University of Oklahoma Press, 1987.

Carr, Lucien. "On the Social and Political Position of Woman among the Huron-Iroquois Tribes." Peabody Museum of American Archaeology and Ethnology, *Reports* 16 & 17, 3.3–4 (1884): 223-24.

Converse, Harriet Maxwell. *Myths and Legends of the New York State Iroquois,* ed. Arthur C. Parker. New York State Museum Bulletin No. 125, Education Department Bulletin No. 437. Albany: University of the State of New York, 1908.

Cook, Frederick. *Journals of the Military Expedition of Major General John Sullivan against the Six Nations of Indians in 1779.* (1887, reprint). Freeport, NY: Books for Libraries, 1972.

Du, ShanShan. *"Chopsticks Only Work in Paris:" Gender Unity and Gender Equality among the Lahu of Southwest China.* New York, NY: Columbia University, 2002.

Heckewelder, J. *History, Manners, and Customs of the Indian Nations Who Once Inhabited Pennsylvania and Neighboring States.* 1820/1876. New York, NY: Arno Press and *New York Times,* 1971.

Heckewelder, J. *History, Manners, and Customs,* 136, and (n 1) 136. [Alexander McKee], "Minutes of Debates in Council on the Banks of the Ottawa River (Commonly Called the Miami of the Lake), November, 1791" (Philadelphia: William Young, 1792), 21.

Heckewelder, J. *Narrative of the Mission of the United Brethren among the Delaware and Mohegan Indians from Its Commencement, in the Year 1740, to the Close of the Year 1808.* 1818; New York, NY: Arno Press, 1971.

Hewitt, J. N. B. "Wampum." In *Handbook of American Indians North of Mexico.* Edited by Frederick Webb Hodge. New York, NY: Rowman & Littlefield, 1911/1965.

Hewitt, J. N. B. "Some Esoteric Aspects of the League of the Iroquois." *Proceedings of the International Congress of Americanists* 19 (1915): 325.

Hewitt, J. N. B. "Ethnological Studies among the Iroquois Indians." *Smithsonian Miscellaneous Collections* 78 (1927): 240-41.

*Hitakonanu'laxk* ["Tree Beard"]. *The Grandfathers Speak: Native American Folk Tales of the Lenapé People.* New York: Interlink Books, 1994.

Johansen, Bruce E., and Barbara Alice Mann, eds. "Wampum." *Encyclopedia of the Haudenosaunee.* Westport, CT: Greenwood, 2000.

Johansen, Bruce E., and Barbara A. Mann. "The Second Epoch of Time; The Great Law Keeping." *Encyclopedia of the Haudenosaunee.* Westport, CT: Greenwood, 2000.

Kuokkanen, Rauna. "The Logic of the Gift: Reclaiming Indigenous Peoples' Philosophies." *The Australian Journal of Indigenous Education* 34 (2005): 251-71.

Lahontan, *New Voyages to North America*, 1: 58;

Lockwood, Rod. "History on the Rocks: Researcher Says Turkey Foot Rock Is Upside Down." *The Toledo Blade* <http://www.toledoblade.com/article/20080227/ART16/802270316> (27 February 2008).

MacGowan, D. J. "Secret Indian Societies." *The Historical Magazine* 10, no. 5 (May 1866): 139-41.

Makilam. *The Magical Life of Berber Women in Kabylia.* New York, NY: Lang, 2007.

Mann, Barbara A., and Jerry L. Fields. "A Sign in the Sky: Dating the League of the Haudenosaunee." *American Indian Culture and Research Journal* 21, no. 2 (1997): 105-63.

Mann, Barbara A. *Iroquoian Women: The Gantowisas.* New York, NY: Lang, 2000.

Mann, Barbara A. *Native Americans, Archaeologists, and the Mounds.* New York, NY: Peter Lang 2003.

Mann, Barbara A. *George Washington's War on Native America.* Lincoln, NB: University of Nebraska Press, 2008.

Mann, Barbara A. *The Tainted Gift: The Disease Method of Frontier Advance.* Santa Barbara, CA: Praeger, 2009.

Mann, Charles C. "Appendix B: Talking Knots." In *1491: New Revelations of the Americas before Columbus.* New York, NY: Alfred Knopf, 2005.

McLellan, Howard. "Indian Magna Carta Writ in Wampum Belts." *New York Times* (7 June 1925): n.p.

Native American Graves Protection and Repatriation Act (NAGPRA) 25 U.S.C. 3001, also included in US Department of the Interior, National Park Service, and Cultural Resources Programs, *Federal Historical Preservation Laws* (Washington, D.C.: Government Printing Office, 1993) whole law, 63–74; cultural unidentifiability, 65, Sec. 3, (a) (1) (C), 1990.

Nordenskiöld, G. *The Cliff Dwellers of Mesa Verde of Southwestern Colorado*, trans. D. Lloyd Morgan. Chicago, IL: P. H. Norstedt & Söner, 1893.

O'Callaghan, E. B., ed., "Letter from M. de Dennville to the Minister [of France]." *Documentary History of the State of New York*, 4 vols. Albany, NY: Weed, Parsons, 1850.

Parker, Arthur C. *The Constitution of the Five Nations, or the Iroquois Book of the Great Law.* Albany, NY: The University of the State of New York, 1916.

Peet, Stephen D. *Cliff Dwellers and Pueblos.* Chicago, IL: Office of the American Antiquarian, 1899.

Sanday, Peggy Reeves. *Women at the Center: Life in a Modern Matriarchy.* Ithaca, NY: Cornell University Press, 2002.

Sundstrom, Linea. *Storied Stone: Indian Rock Art of the Black Hills Country.* Norman, OK: University of Oklahoma Press, 2004.

"The War on Waste." *CBS Evening News.* <www.cbsnews.com/stories/2002/01/29/eveningnews/main325985.shtml> (29 January 2002).

Trowbridge, Charles C. *Meearmeear Traditions,* ed. Vernon Kinietz. Ann Arbor, MI: University of Michigan Press, 1938.

Winton, Ben. "Alcatraz, Indian Land." *Native Peoples Magazine* (Fall, 1999): 2.

Vaughan, Genevieve, ed. *Women and the Gift Economy: A Radically Different Worldview Is Possible.* Toronto, ON: Inanna Publications and Education, 2007.

## ENDNOTES

[1]  That the modern Pueblos are the descendants of the Cliff Dwellers has been known and accepted since before the turn of the twentieth century. See Stephen Denison Peet, *Cliff Dwellers and Pueblos* (Chicago: Office of the American Antiquarian, 1899), 245; G. Nordenskiöld, *The Cliff Dwellers of Mesa Verde of Southwestern Colorado,* trans. D. Lloyd Morgan (Chicago: P. H. Norstedt & Söner, 1893), 168. Any question about this today reflects attempts to get around the Native American Graves Protection and Repatriation Act (NAGPRA) of 1990, which requires the return of all human remains and grave goods to the peoples from whom they were stolen. The loophole in this law is that any items from "culturally unidentifiable" groups may be retained by archaeologists, spurring a sudden spike in claims that this or that group is "culturally unidentifiable." For the Act, see 25 U.S.C. 3001, also included in US Department of the Interior, National Park Service, and Cultural Resources Programs, *Federal Historical Preservation Laws* (Washington, D.C.: Government Printing Office, 1993) whole law, 63–74; cultural unidentifiability, 65, Sec. 3, (a) (1) (C). For an extended discussion of the vagaries of NAGPRA law, see Barbara Alice Mann, *Native Americans, Archaeologists, and the Mounds* (New York: Peter Lang Publishing, 2003), 255–58.

[2]  Wampum was a binary writing system, using white and "black" (dark purple) *wampum,* knotted into characters, which were read and understood throughout the woodlands. John Heckewelder, *History, Manners, and Customs of the Indian Nations Who Once Inhabited Pennsylvania and Neighboring States* (1820; 1876; New York: Arno Press and *New York Times,* 1971), 108; Daniel G. Brinton, *The Myths of the New World: A Treatise on the Symbolism and Mythology of the Red Race of America,* 2nd ed. rev. (New York: Henry Holt and Company, 1876), 16; J. N. B. Hewitt, "Wampum" in Frederick Webb Hodge, ed., *Handbook of American Indians North of Mexico* (1911;

New York: Rowman and Littlefield, 1965), 904–909. For more on wampum, see Bruce Elliott Johansen and Barbara Alice Mann, eds., "Wampum," *Encyclopedia of the Haudenosaunee.*(Westport, CT: Greenwood Publishing Group, 2000), 325–29. For khipu, see Charles C. Mann, "Appendix B: Talking Knots," in *1491: New Revelations of the Americas before Columbus* (New York: Alfred Knopf, 2005), 345–49. Charles Mann is no relation to the author of this article.

For the Mound-Builder priesthood system and its overthrow, see Mann, *Native Americans, Archaeologists, and the Mounds*, 161–68.

3    For the Mound-Builder priesthood system and its overthrow, see Mann, *Native Americans, Archaeologists, and the Mounds*, 161–68.

4    Barbara A. Mann and Jerry L. Fields, "A Sign in the Sky: Dating the League of the Haudenosaunee" *American Indian Culture and Research Journal* 21.2 (1997): 105–63.

5    Johansen and Mann, "The Second Epoch of Time; The Great Law Keeping," in *Encyclopedia of the Haudenosaunee*, 265–84.

6    *Hitakonanu'laxk* ["Tree Beard], *The Grandfathers Speak: Native American Folk Tales of the Lenapé People* (New York: Interlink Books, 1994), 32.

7    M. M. Bakhtin, *The Dialogic Imagination: Four Essays*, ed. Michael Holquist, trans. Caryl Emerson and Michael Holquist (Austin: University of Texas Press, 1981).

8    Arthur Caswell Parker, *The Constitution of the Five Nations, or the Iroquois Book of the Great Law* (Albany: The University of the State of New York, 1916), 45, 103.

9    Barbara Alice Mann, *Iroquoian Women: The Gantowisas* (New York: Lang, 2000), 204–37; Barbara Alice Mann, The Tainted Gift: The Disease Method of Frontier Advance (Santa Barbara, CA: Praeger, 2009), 2–5.

10   Louis Armand, Baron de Lahontan, *New Voyages to North America*, ed. Rueben Gold Thwaites, 2 vols. (1703; Chicago: A. C. McClure & Co., 1905), 1: 130; E.B. O'Callaghan, ed., "Letter from M. de Dennville to the Minister [of France]," *Documentary History of the State of New-York*, 4 vols. (Albany: Weed, Parsons & Co., Public Printers, 1850), 1: 147.

11   Frederick Cook, *Journals of the Military Expedition of Major General John Sullivan against the Six Nations of Indians in 1779* (1887, reprint; Freeport, NY: Books for Libraries, 1972) "best corn," 27' "quantities immense," 163. For an overview of the 1779 attack and the crop types and quantities destroyed, see Barbara Alice Mann, *George Washington's War on Native America* (Lincoln, NB: University of Nebraska Press, 2008), 71–76.

12   Harriet Maxwell Converse, *Myths and Legends of the New York State Iroquois*, ed. Arthur C. Parker, New York State Museum Bulletin No. 125, Education Department Bulletin No. 437 (Albany: University of the State of New York, 1908), 134.

13   ShanShan Du, *"Chopsticks Only Work in Pairs:" Gender Unity and Gender Equality among the Lahu of Southwest China* (New York: Columbia University, 2002), especially 97-106.

14   Makilam, *The Magical Life of Berber Women in Kabylia* (New York: Lang, 2007), especially 47-76; Peggy Reeves Sanday, *Women at the Center: Life in a Modern Matriarchy* (Ithaca: Cornell University Press, 2002), especially 79–86

15   Rauna Kuokkanen, "The Logic of the Gift: Reclaiming Indigenous Peoples' Philosophies," *The Australian Journal of Indigenous Education* 34 (2005): 251–71.

16   See, for instance, the anthology, ed. Genevieve Vaughan, *Women and the Gift Economy: A Radically Different Worldview Is Possible* (Toronto: Inanna Publications and Education, 2007).

17   "The War on Waste," *CBS Evening News*, 29 January 2002. <www.cbsnews.com/stories/2002/01/29/eveningnews/main325985.shtml>

18   D. J. MacGowan, "Secret Indian Societies," *The Historical Magazine* 10.5 (May 1866): 139–41. Mann, *Native Americans, Archaeologists, and the Mounds*, 166–67.

19   Lahontan, *New Voyages to North America*, 1: 58; O'Callaghan, "M. de Denonville to the Minister," 1: 147.

20   Lisa Brooks, *The Common Pot: The Recovery of Native Space in the Northeast* (Minneapolis: University of Minnesota Press, 2008), 251.

21   J. N. B. Hewitt called these mirroring binaries of blood and breath, respectively, the "Mother" and "Father" sides of the Iroquois League. J. N. B. Hewitt, "Some Esoteric Aspects of the League of the Iroquois," *Proceedings of the International Congress of Americanists* 19 (1915): 325; J. N. B. Hewitt, "Ethnological Studies among the Iroquois Indians," *Smithsonian Miscellaneous Collections* 78 (1927): 240–41. Although his discussions focused on the Iroquois, it described traditional woodland structures, generally.

22   Lucien Carr, "On the Social and Political Position of Woman among the Huron-Iroquois Tribes," Peabody Museum of American Archaeology and Ethnology, *Reports* 16 & 17, 3.3–4 (1884): 223–24; Colin G. Calloway, *Crown and Calumet: British-Indian Relations, 1783–1815* (Norman: University of Oklahoma Press, 1987). 197.

23   Howard McLellan, "Indian Magna Carta Writ in Wampum Belts," *New York Times*, 7 June 1925, n.p.

24   Heckewelder, *History, Manners, and Customs*, 136, and (n 1) 136. [Alexander McKee], "Minutes of Debates in Council on the Banks of the Ottawa River (Commonly Called the Miami of the Lake), November, 1791" (Philadelphia: William Young, 1792), 21.

25   Charles Christopher Trowbridge, *Meearmeear Traditions*, ed. Vernon Kinietz (Ann Arbor: University of Michigan Press, 1938), 14.

26   Linea Sundstrom, *Storied Stone: Indian Rock Art of the Black Hills* Country (Norman, OK: University of Oklahoma Press, 2004), 145.

27   John Heckewelder, Narrative of the Mission of the United Brethren among the Delaware and Mohegan Indians from Its Commencement, in the Year 1740, to the Close of the Year 1808 (1818; New York: Arno Press, 1971), 272.

28   Ben Winton, "Alcatraz, Indian Land," Native Peoples Magazine (Fall, 1999): 2.

29   Rod Lockwood, "History on the Rocks: Researcher Says Turkey Foot Rock Is Upside Down," *The Toledo Blade* (27 February 2008) <http://www.toledoblade.com/article/20080227/ART16/802270316>

# SECTION VIII

---

# A COMPREHENSIVE APPROACH

---

# THE COMPREHENSIVE APPROACH: AN IDEA WHOSE TIME HAS ARRIVED

PETER GIZEWSKI, PhD

## INTRODUCTION

Recent years have witnessed a growing chorus of claims that sustainable responses to insecurity and the challenge of providing good governance, both at home and abroad, are unlikely to be achieved through any single agency or organization. Instability, crisis and conflict involve an increasingly complex mixture of ethnic, religious, ideological and material drivers. It is essential to achieve coordination and bring to bear all instruments of national and coalition power and influence (e.g., diplomatic, economic, military, informational) on a problem in a timely fashion to achieve lasting results. It is also essential to consult and, if possible, constructively engage the views and reactions of the public, both domestic and international, as operations unfold.

The need to practise a more coherent, holistic approach to the challenges of governance and security has become evident among academics and policymakers in Canada and elsewhere. Perhaps most notable is the fact that officials in Canada and other states (e.g., the United States, the United Kingdom and other NATO allies) are calling for the adoption of a more "Comprehensive Approach" (CA) to security challenges. Such an approach would involve a more integrated orientation to both policy and campaign planning. This orientation would draw upon a range of diplomatic, defence, development and commercial resources as well as a range of players (both official and private) to discuss the key security issues of the day. The result, advocates claim, would be a more effective response to any challenge.

The concepts underlying such an approach are hardly unique. In fact, elements of the CA have existed for decades, if not centuries. That said, formal articulation and concerted efforts to develop and implement the concept *is* a relatively recent phenomenon. So too is the growing interest in its institutionalization. What accounts for this rise in interest? What issues bear on the CA's acceptance, implementation and practice? Moreover, what are the implications of an established, effective CA for its practitioners and the manner in which security challenges are met? Answers to such questions are important.

The following chapter examines these questions in an effort to illuminate the character of the CA, its current status and future prospects. To this end, the chapter describes the essential elements of the CA and some of its historical antecedents. It then examines the factors leading to the growing currency of such thinking as a means of meeting security challenges and their underlying forces. In particular, the chapter notes that growing interest in a CA is largely a function of the evolving security environment. This environment has created conditions that increase the need for such an approach and the capacity to practise it. In surveying current initiatives aimed at developing the approach, the chapter concludes by noting that the CA represents a marked evolution in the development of organizational interaction and collaboration which, given time, may well yield revolutionary results in future approaches to governance and security challenges.

## THE COMPREHENSIVE APPROACH: KEY ELEMENTS

Definitions of the CA vary.[1] While some see the approach as a means of interacting with a myriad of national and international entities to resolve security challenges, others have used the term to refer primarily to government and/or interagency coordination. Still others have loosely employed the term to refer to simple coordination mechanisms at the tactical level of operations.

In general, however, such thinking calls for increasing the capacity and willingness of separate agencies to collaborate in achieving policy objectives. It entails developing an improved capacity, where needed, to interact with such players in a more cooperative, constructive manner. It generally involves creating a capacity for interaction and collaboration that cuts across departments and dispenses with "stovepipes" (tunnel vision). In fact, the idea has roots in the private sector management theory of re-engineering and aims at streamlining processes from input to output in order to maximize efficiency and remove overlap and duplication. In a theoretical sense, re-engineering seeks to create an end-to-end process that cuts across traditional "stovepipes" leading to an organization that runs more smoothly and efficiently.[2] Such an approach would involve:

- The adoption of a more team-oriented approach to developing integrated plans in order to realize objectives in operations;
- The willingness to consider second- and third-order effects in planning processes;
- The ability to plug into joint organizational operating systems to interoperate effectively;
- The ability to facilitate the building of interagency and multinational interoperability through collaborative planning mechanisms and protocols;
- An ability to connect non-governmental agencies and provide liaison to support these agencies in the execution of the mission;
- The ability to implement effective communication with joint and other multinational agencies;
- The capacity to access key information in an efficient and timely manner so as to identify targets for influence as well as determine resources required in operations; and
- The ability to communicate mission goals, objectives and actions to the public and members of the media *as required*.

Advocates of the CA contend that the practical results flowing from the implementation of such capabilities might yield a number of benefits. With all actions based upon agreed principles and collaborative, cooperative processes, greater organizational efficiencies would be obtained. In addition, traditional organizational "stovepipes" would be overcome where necessary through enhanced synergies. Information sharing between organizations would be improved (e.g., through the establishment of greater inter- and intra-organizational trust and hence more effective interaction between players). The strategic framing of issues and campaign planning would be improved (e.g., through greater organizational interaction and cooperation in assessment and planning). A degree of organizational awareness, interaction, integration, coherence and consistency would emerge when confronting security threats rarely if ever seen before. Beyond this, the CA could work to ensure a greater level of legitimacy both domestically and internationally for those security operations undertaken.[3]

## PRECURSORS: THEORY AND PRACTICE

Much of the logic underlying the CA has existed for decades, if not centuries. The concept of grand strategy offers a case in point. Much like the CA, grand strategy calls for the marshalling of a range of resources (e.g., economic, diplomatic, military) to accomplish a national end. Indeed, as Colin Gray notes, it involves the "purposeful employment of all instruments of power available to a security community."[4] Stephan Metz is more precise still, defining grand strategy as "the integrated use of power resources in pursuit of national objectives."[5]

Counterinsurgency doctrine (COIN) does much the same with its strong emphasis on prevailing in irregular conflicts less by the use of military might than by winning the allegiance of an indigenous population through the use of political, economic, civic and psychological actions. This fact is reflected in its characterization by some as a "grand strategy in miniature."[6] Doctrines of civil-military cooperation (CIMIC) are also notable, particularly given their endorsement of the importance of developing constructive military–civilian linkages (e.g., liaison, coordination, joint planning) as an essential means of enhancing mission effectiveness.[7]

Beyond this, history reveals a variety of instances in which precursors to a modern CA were pursued by states as a means of addressing domestic and international challenges (although with varying degrees of success). The planning and implementation of the post-World War II reconstruction of Japan (1945-46) and the development and implementation of the Marshall Plan in Europe (1947-51) stand out as particularly prominent cases of success.

In the former case, successful integration of the U.S. Government's military and civilian assets led to the creation of a practical strategy for reform and the reconstruction of occupied territory. Under the State-War-Navy Coordinating Committee (SWNCC), civilian and military officials generated an interagency strategic and tactical approach, which established a coherent set of objectives and a flexible action script for occupation when U.S. forces arrived in August 1945. In fact, prompt adoption of the Committee's key recommendations was central to the transformation of Japan from a pre-modern, semi-feudal nation to a modern democratic capitalist state.[8] The latter not only involved the sustained cooperation of military, diplomatic and trade personnel but also an active campaign aimed at explaining key aspects of the initiative to the U.S. public and allies. The practical result was the creation of a foreign aid plan that provided the crucial step toward European reconstruction after World War II.

The Commonwealth campaign against Communist insurgents during the Malayan Emergency (1948-60) similarly reflected aspects of CA logic. Especially noteworthy was the use of layered coordination committees. A committee of military, police and civilian administration officials assumed authority at all levels of government (national, state, and district levels). This allowed intelligence from all sources to be rapidly evaluated and disseminated, and anti-guerrilla measures to be coordinated. The result was an integrated political–military campaign that contributed to victory over the Malayan National Liberation Army (MNLA) (i.e., the military arm of the Malayan Communist Party).[9]

Examples of inter-agency integration and collaboration have been evident on the domestic front as well. In 1964, for instance, state and local bureaucracies collaborated to maintain Alaska's viability as a state in the aftermath of the most severe earthquake ever registered in North America. Here, success derived in no small measure from U.S. President

Lyndon Johnson's creation of the Federal Reconstruction and Development Planning Commission for Alaska. The Commission was a Cabinet-level agency that developed a Rehabilitation Strategy and managed implementation through a division of labour among those agencies most engaged in recovery efforts.[10]

Until recently, most efforts to achieve greater organizational coordination and cooperation in security affairs were relatively sporadic and ad hoc in character. Generally prompted by a sense of urgency, most were cobbled together quickly in response to immediate crises and therefore featured makeshift institutional mechanisms, structures and processes. Many required the full and active support of top political leaders and bureaucrats. While collaboration was occasionally achieved under these conditions, it was primarily inter-departmental and interagency in character. Most efforts were of relatively limited duration with collaboration and cooperation dwindling once crises subsided and key tasks and objectives were achieved. Concerted efforts to devise an approach aimed at sustained inter-agency cooperation through the development of enduring practices, procedures and principles rarely materialized.

## COLD WAR ENVIRONMENT: LIMITED INCENTIVES AND LIMITED CAPABILITIES

Past limits on organizational and inter-agency interaction, cooperation and collaboration were due to a variety of factors. Yet a central obstacle was an international security context, which for the most part provided neither the incentives (i.e., the need) nor the means (i.e., capabilities or wherewithal) to practise and institutionalize a strong culture devoted to such an approach.

For much of the past century, international politics were driven by the primacy of the state and realist thinking. Security equated heavily and almost exclusively with state interests, their preservation and pursuit, as defined by governmental decision-makers. It was also strongly shaped by the "high politics" of inter-state armed conflict. This tended to elevate certain issues and organizations over others. It also limited the degree to which organizational collaboration was valued and sought.

During the Cold War, for instance, military and ideological competition became the overriding preoccupation of Western nations. Accordingly, the requirements of superpower deterrence and containment eclipsed all other issues as major security concerns. Competition ensured the growth of large military, intelligence and diplomatic bureaucracies all with deeply entrenched mandates, interests and agendas. Such interests were not only actively pursued but judiciously guarded, creating a strong organizational aversion to collaboration with others.[11] Hence, while individual departments carried out those parts of policies directed by leaders in their primary areas of responsibility, collaboration on tasks involving shared responsibilities was rare.[12] Regularized interaction with non-governmental organizations was rarer still. Not only were such actors relatively few in number but, given the chief security preoccupations of the state, were generally limited in terms of their perceived policy relevance and hence, their influence.

A lack of interconnectedness could only heighten obstacles to interaction and collaboration. Without today's information and communication technologies, the capacity to network quickly, regularly and economically was less available.[13] Accordingly, awareness of organizations beyond government was constrained and the ability to interact regularly with others was limited. Beyond this, restricted global interconnectedness tended to ensure that events in other parts of the world were viewed as more contained both in terms of their salience and impact. The effects of instability in one region were less apparent and less of a concern. Once again, the perceived need to identify and tap new organizational resources to act in such cases could only suffer.

Achieving an approximate stability in the superpower relationship nevertheless served to ensure that, for the most part, such realities remained unchanged for decades. While occasional cases of organizational cooperation were evident, the need for a drastic revision of existing, still largely "stove-piped" organizational practices and procedures was neither desired by governments nor viewed as particularly pressing.

## POST-COLD WAR ENVIRONMENT: NEW DEMANDS AND NEW CAPABILITIES

The end of the Cold War altered this reality, dramatically changing the calculus connected with both the need and the capacity to engage in greater organizational cooperation in security affairs. Increasingly, a range of new security challenges eclipsed concerns over bipolar, state-on-state confrontation and superpower deterrence. These challenges included: (a) the danger of attack from transnational terror groups, (b) political instability and civil wars arising from fragile and failed states, (c) ethnic and sectarian violence, and (d) the destabilizing societal effects of organized crime and such forces as resource depletion and global climate change.

Such challenges emanated less from strong state entities than from a lack of effective governance. They involved a wider range of issues and actors than ever before. Their importance was magnified by globalization, particularly in the form of cascading information and communication technology. Indeed, such forces generated greater interconnectedness globally. They allowed previously disparate and marginalized groups and movements to organize and influence events. They heightened prospects that even local turmoil and instability (along with the character of responses to it) could generate not only regional but global consequences. Increasingly, distant crises could affect global economies, disrupt international trade and commerce, trigger inter-state rivalries, and influence the political standing and legitimacy of distant governments.[14]

At the same time, notions of human security began to compete with national security as an important consideration in global affairs. The security and well-being of individuals in society were being accorded a status equal if not greater than the well-being of the state.[15] The number of domestic and international actors, seen as the key to meeting the security challenges, proliferated.[16]

Incentives for approaches that were less focused on the use of military power alone, less on state than human security, and less on deterring states and overrunning governments than stabilizing and reconstructing them, correspondingly increased. So too did a growing realization of the need for more integrated, coordinated responses that would engage a wider range of issues, actors or participants in developing effective approaches to the challenges.[17]

Meanwhile, exponential advances in information and communication technologies offered an increasing capacity to fashion such responses. These innovations made it possible to network quickly, regularly and efficiently with a wide variety of organizations. Beyond this, the advances heightened the need to do so. In a world in which globalized communications offered near-instantaneous information about distant events, public demands for government action increased and so did the wider scrutiny of the actions taken. Given a wired world, the response to security challenges affected perceptions of government legitimacy.[18]

## INSTITUTIONALIZING INTERACTION: TOWARD THE COMPREHENSIVE APPROACH

Such an environment bred demands for greater organizational collaboration in meeting security challenges and strongly suggested a need to extend it. Indeed it has produced both a growing need as well as an increasing ability to practise a more comprehensive approach to security operations. In this regard, a complex range of challenges and threats has stimulated an approach capable of drawing upon all available resources in an efficient manner. At the same time, the proliferation of new players and actors, along with the growing connectivity of modern information and communication technologies, offer the capacity to realize it.

Initial reflections of the changing mindset have been evident in concepts such as Defence, Diplomacy, Development and Commerce (3D+C), as well as Whole of Government (WOG), Comprehensive Crisis Management and Interagency Approaches. Growing recognition that a *truly* inclusive and effective response to contemporary security challenges has generated support for a CA and could well involve entities beyond official government departments and agencies.

In essence, articulation of the CA marks a direct response to the realities of the changed security environment. Indeed, the concept seeks to meet the challenges it poses by offering a less "stove-piped," more inclusive means by which interaction and, if necessary, collaboration between organizations can be achieved in the support of enhanced governance and security.[19] In fact, its very articulation and pursuit signals a marked progression in thinking about how governments must approach these tasks in the contemporary international system. The concept has received endorsement both nationally and internationally and a rising level of activity is devoted to its development.

Indeed, the level of activity is increasingly devoted to its development on the part of national governments and international organizations. Such activity is both varied and intense. It includes efforts aimed at the CA's conceptual elaboration and at developing programs aimed at educating and training both military and civilian personnel to apply the ideas it advances. Initiatives are afoot to identify and develop the enabling technologies, organizational structures and processes most suitable to its practice. Researchers are engaged in projects to ensure the proper organizational mindset upon which the approach depends. This initiative requires identifying the psychological requirements essential to building nurturing and extending trust and more effective interaction, coordination and cooperation within and between organizations.[20]

More notable still is the fact that efforts to apply more integrated and "CA-like" approaches to security operations are increasingly apparent. For instance, over the course of Western involvement in Afghanistan, coalition allies have combined counterinsurgency operations involving Special Forces and regular infantry with broader efforts aimed at stabilization and reconstruction of the country. Such principles and practices have been increasingly evident in operations in Iraq and Haiti.

Military, diplomatic, development and law enforcement personnel are in fact working together in a relatively collaborative framework to help realize the Afghanistan National Strategy (ANS) and thus bring stability, prosperity and good governance to the country. Despite the range of problems and obstacles, reports indicate that Provincial Reconstruction Teams (PRTs) operating in the country "have played important roles in everything from election support to school-building to disarmament and mediating factional conflicts."[21] Beyond this, the concept is somewhat mirrored in the integrated operational planning process of the

United Nations (UN). It has gained official standing and growing currency in NATO and has begun to influence thinking in the development and practices of a number of operational military commands. In this regard, the civilian command, interagency modalities and "soft power" mandate of U.S. Africa Command (USAFRICOM) is exemplary. So too is the "collaborative approach" of U.S. Southern Command (e.g., USSOUTHCOM).

To be sure, the concept continues to confront a number of obstacles. Lack of clarity in mission definition and goals can pose one such obstacle. Indeed, lack of clarity may impede the degree to which the CA approach is organized and applied so that component players rationally interact and work together to achieve desired outcomes. Beyond this, devising practices and procedures allowing work between organizations (each with its own culture, mindset, agendas and goals) is no easy task. Such efforts often confront issues of cultural and professional bias, problems of information sharing, constraints stemming from resource asymmetries between organizations, and concerns related to the protection of organizational credibility and essence. Nor is it entirely clear how the benefits of such an approach, if and when implemented, should be reliably measured and assessed.[22]

Not surprisingly, full acceptance and institutionalization of the CA has yet to be achieved, despite growing endorsement of the concept in principle. Bureaucratic incentives to promote and engage in the approach remain on the whole underdeveloped, and resources devoted to the broad implementation of a CA continue to be limited.

Nevertheless, given that the approach remains at a relatively early stage in its development, progress thus far has been noteworthy. Not only has the CA generated intense discussion and debate, but also widespread interest both nationally and internationally from a variety of institutions. It has prompted a varied and growing agenda of scientific investigation and experimentation. Most importantly, it has resulted in a growing shift in attitudes, in both official and unofficial circles, regarding the manner in which security operations should be conducted. In particular, it has resulted in a clear acknowledgement that today's security challenges require a more institutionalized, less "stove-piped" and more inclusive approach in order to be effective.

## FUTURE PROSPECTS: A NEW NORM FOR GOVERNANCE AND SECURITY OPERATIONS

The degree to which the obstacles facing adoption of the CA can be overcome remains unclear. In the event that present challenges are surmounted, however, continued pursuit of the CA agenda holds the possibility of more substantial and far-reaching change in the years ahead. In fact, full development and implementation of such thinking could, over time, usher in a fundamental change in the way in which organizations view one another and how they interact to meet problems and challenges.

In this regard, evidence suggests that the CA is already generating a subtle but nonetheless significant shift in organizational mindsets regarding the way operations are conducted. In the case of allied militaries, for instance, growing familiarity with the concept has been accompanied by a move away from viewing other organizations as simply resources to be used in support of the demands of the military mission. They tend to appreciate the need of the military to integrate in support of the broader objectives of the mission as a whole – objectives that often include integration of the goals and viewpoints of a range of other players.[23]

Should the CA become more widely accepted and institutionalized, the prospect of other organizations becoming socialized to engage in similar shifts in perspective cannot be ruled out. Indeed, such regularized interaction and the "give and take" that it entails may stretch organizational perspectives, sensitizing organizations to new ways of looking at security and its conduct. This shift could affect not only thought and planning but also action. It may even work to broaden organizational identities and mandates. The result may well be the creation of a new norm governing how future security operations are conducted.[24]

## CONCLUSION

Interest in the development of the CA is widespread and growing. Yet many of the concepts underlying the approach are not entirely new. Not only have elements long existed but efforts to practise a more "CA-like" approach to operations are evident throughout history. Such practice was primarily ad hoc and sporadic in character, limited in the scope of organizational interaction both sought and achieved, and heavily dependent on the initiative of key leaders for their success. In fact, such efforts took place in a security context that provided neither the incentive nor the capacity to support a more institutionalized, regularized form of organizational interaction.

Changes in the security environment following the end of the Cold War have, nonetheless, increased both the need for such an approach as well as the opportunity to implement and practise it. By and large, such forces account for the articulation of the CA and efforts aimed at its development and implementation.

At present, movement towards the CA remains a gradual, evolutionary process. Much more remains to be done. In this regard, endorsement of the concept itself and the championing of its development and implementation by leadership are important. So too is the development of effective training and education programs.

Beyond this, the creation of a comprehensive approach is likely to require a genuine willingness on the part of those organizations and agencies involved to undertake fundamental alterations in their respective policy cultures and practices. Such alterations may involve more conceptual and practical collaboration with others as well as greater emphasis on collaborative mission planning. It may require the creation of new incentive structures and arrangements aimed at encouraging collaborative efforts. It will surely demand clarity in mission definition and goals on the part of the government so that such an approach can be organized and applied in a manner in which component players rationally interact to achieve desired outcomes.

Nevertheless, the need for more multidisciplinary approaches to governance and security has gained considerable traction both in government and the private sector. The concept of the CA is drawing ever more interest. To the extent that such an approach is adopted, the upshot may well be a new norm for addressing challenges and one that reflects the dynamics of current and future security environments.

**NB**: A previous version of this paper appears in Michael Rostek and Peter Gizewski (Eds.), *Canadian Perspectives on a Comprehensive Approach* (Kingston, ON: McGill-Queens University Press, 2011).

## REVIEW QUESTIONS

1. Comment on the argument that there is a need to practise a more comprehensive approach (CA) to the challenges of governance and security.
2. Do you agree or disagree that full acceptance and institutionalization of the CA has yet to be achieved?

### REFERENCES

Boutros-Ghali, Boutros. *An Agenda for Peace: Preventative Diplomacy, Peacemaking and Peace Building,* Report of the Secretary General United Nations, A/47/277-S/24111, 1992. <www.un.org/docs/SG/agpeace.html> (accessed 3 January 2011) and United Nations Development Program, Human Development Report (New York: Oxford University Press, 1994).

Department of National Defence and the Canadian Forces. The Management Command and Control Re-engineering Project. (1990s)

Djik, Gert. "Comprehensive Approach ... and Why It's a Big NATO Issue." Paper presented to CIOR Symposium on "NATO's Comprehensive Approach and the Role of Reservists." Stavanger, NO. <http://www.cior.net/News/2010/COMPREHENSIVE-APPROACH...and-why-it-is-a-big-NATO.aspx>

(11 August 2010).

Friis, Karsten, and Pia Jarmyr (eds.), *Comprehensive Approach: Challenges and Opportunities in Complex Crisis Management.* NUPI Report No. 11 (Oslo: Norwegian Institute of International Affairs, 2009), 3.

Gallant, Bruce, Dale Reding, and Peter Gizewski. "Assessment of the TTCP Ad Hoc Study Group: Science and Technology for the Comprehensive Approach, Final Report." *Briefing Note,* January 2010.

Gizewski, Peter, and Lt. Col. Michael Rostek. "The Canada First Defence Strategy: The Need for a Comprehensive Approach," in *Canada and the Changing Strategic Environment: The Canada First Strategy and Beyond.* Edited by Phil Orchard. Proceedings of the Annual Conference of the Security and Defence Forum Centres 2008. Vancouver, BC: Centre for International Relations, University of British Columbia (2009): 36-8.

Gizewski, Peter, and Lt. Col. Michael Rostek, *Toward a Comprehensive Approach to Military Operations: The Land Force JIMP Concept.* DRDC CORA TM 2007-60, 2007.

Government of Canada. Comprehensive Approach Inter-departmental Working Group (Core Team). *Concept Paper, Strategic Level: The Comprehensive Approach (Expeditionary), Draft 1.0,* December 2009.

Gray, Colin. *War, Peace and International Relations – An Introduction to Strategic History.* Oxford, UK: Routledge, 2007.

Gray, Colin. *Designing Government Strategies and Drawing Them Together.* Remarks presented to the Conference Sustaining the Force-Soldier First RUSI/DEM Future Land Warfare 08, Banqueting House, Royal Palace at Whitehall & Royal United Services Institute, United Kingdom 12-13 June 2008.

Ink, Dwight A. *The 1964 Alaskan Earthquake, Case Study for the Project on National Security Reform* Washington DC: Project on National Security Reform and the Centre for the Study of the Presidency, 2008. <http://www.pnsr.org/web/page/653/sectionid/579/pagelevel/3/parentid/590/interior.asp>(15 November 2010).

Locher III, James R. "National Security Reform: A Prerequisite for Successful Complex Operations." *Prism* 1, no. 1 ( 2009): 79. < http://www.ndu.edu/press/prism1-1.html> (1 December 2011).

McNerney, Michael J. "Stabilization and Reconstruction in Afghanistan: Are PRTs a Model or a Muddle?" *Parameters* (Winter 2005-06).

Metz, Stephen. "American Grand Strategy: Concepts, Theory, History and Futures." Presentation at the US Army War College Strategic Studies Institute, August 2008, <http://www.scribd.com/doc/2419351/Grand-Strategy>.

North Atlantic Treaty Organization, *NATO Civil-Military Cooperation*, Allied Joint Publication 9. (Brussels: North Atlantic Treaty Organization; 2003). <http://www.nato.int/ims/docu/AJP-9.pdf> (accessed 13 December 2010).

Nagl, John. *Counterinsurgency Lessons from Malaya and Vietnam: Learning to Eat Soup with a Knife.* Westport, CT: Praeger, 2002.

NATO's definition of CIMIC: The co-ordination and co-operation, *in support of the mission*, between the NATO Commander and civil actors, including national population and local authorities, as well as international, national and non-governmental organizations and agencies. Allied Joint Publication 9, page 1-1, Art 102.

Ramo, Joshua C. *The Age of the Unthinkable.* New York, NY: Little and Brown, 2009.

Schaefer, Peter. F., and P. Clayton Schaefer, *"Japan after WWII,"* Case Study for *the Project on National Security Reform.* Washington DC: Project on National Security Reform and the Centre for the Study of the Presidency, 2008) <http://www.pnsr.org/web/page/659/sectionid/579/pagelevel/3/parentid/590/ interior.asp> (15 November 2010).

Thompson, Robert. *Defeating Communist Insurgency: The Lessons from Malaya and Vietnam.* New York, NY: Praeger, 1966.

## ENDNOTES

[1]   A draft study conducted by the Canadian Government's Comprehensive Approach Inter-departmental Working Group (Core Team) defines the approach as the interaction of a diverse range of actors in a cooperative, collaborative and constructive manner in order to bring coherence to the planning, implementation and evaluation of efforts to resolve complex problems. See Concept Paper, Strategic Level: The Comprehensive Approach (Expeditionary), Draft 1.0, December 2009.

[2]   The mid 1990s saw a plethora of "re-engineering" projects in response to the dramatic budget cuts of the time. In Canada's case, the Department of National Defence and the Canadian Forces undertook a re-engineering project - The Management Command and Control Re-engineering project, which resulted in scattered "tactical" successes. However, the cause is different today and the experience and knowledge gained from the successes and failures of past re-engineering projects may provide the CF pivotal experience and information in creating a comprehensive approach.

[3]   The extent to which the CA will in fact yield such benefits remains unclear and subject to an assessment of evidence. That said, the discussion above captures many of the key motivations and claims advanced by those pursuing it. For additional detail, see Karsten Friis and Pia Jarmyr (eds.), *Comprehensive Approach: Challenges and Opportunities in Complex Crisis Management,* NUPI Report No. 11 (Oslo: Norwegian Institute of International Affairs, 2009), 3.

[4]   Colin Gray, *War, Peace and International Relations – An Introduction to Strategic History,* (Oxford, UK: Routledge, 2007), 283.

[5]   Stephen Metz, "American Grand Strategy: Concepts, Theory, History and Futures," presentation at the U.S. Army War College Strategic Studies Institute, August 2008, <http://www.scribd.com/doc/2419351/ Grand-Strategy>.

6    Colin Gray, "Designing Government Strategies and Drawing Them Together," remarks presented to the Conference Sustaining the Force-Soldier First RUSI/ DEM Future Land Warfare 08, Banqueting House, Royal Palace at Whitehall & Royal United Services Institute, United Kingdom 12-13 June 2008.

7    See for instance, North Atlantic Treaty Organization, *NATO Civil-Military Cooperation*, Allied Joint Publication 9. (Brussels: North Atlantic Treaty Organization; 2003). <http://www.nato.int/ims/docu/AJP-9.pdf> (accessed 13 December 2010).

8    See Peter F Schaefer and P. Clayton Schaefer, *"Japan after WWII,"* Case *Study for the Project on National Security Reform* (Washington DC: Project on National Security Reform and the Centre for the Study of the Presidency; 2008) <http://www.pnsr.org/web/page/659/sectionid/579/pagelevel/3/ parentid/590/interior.asp> (accessed November 15, 2010).

9    Solid analyses of the Malayan Insurgency can be found in Robert Thompson, *Defeating Communist Insurgency: The Lessons from Malaya and Vietnam.* (New York: Praeger Publishers, 1966) and John Nagl, *Counterinsurgency Lessons from Malaya and Vietnam: Learning to Eat Soup with a Knife* (Westport, CT: Praeger Publishers, 2002).

10    See Dwight A. Ink. *The 1964 Alaskan Earthquake, Case Study for the Project on National Security Reform* (Washington DC: Project on National Security Reform and the Centre for the Study of the Presidency, 2008), available at http://www.pnsr.org/web/page/653/sectionid/579/pagelevel/3/parentid/590/ interior.asp (15 November 2010).

11    Concerted efforts to institutionalize effective inter-organizational coordination and collaboration are not only time consuming, but can also have profound resource implications both in financial and human terms. Often organizations have vastly unequal capabilities for supporting such approaches. Beyond this is the fact that such collaboration can threaten organizational identities, interests and agendas. Indeed not only does such practice by its very nature require considerable inter-agency dialogue, but at times a willingness to compromise and thus dilute key aspects of one's own agenda. As such, it can pose a challenge to organizational visibility and status. Accordingly, in the absence of forces compelling inter-agency interaction and collaboration such practice tended to be the exception rather than the rule.

12    See James R. Locher III, "National Security Reform: A Prerequisite for Successful Complex Operations." *Prism*, Vol. 1 No. 1, 2009, p. 79. < http:// www.ndu.edu/press/prism1-1.html> (1 December 2011).

13    Joshua Cooper Ramo, *The Age of the Unthinkable* (New York: Little and Brown, 2009), 35.

14    Ramo, 2009, 35-6.

15    The initial references to the Human Security concept can be found in Boutros-
      Ghali, Boutros, *An Agenda for Peace: Preventative Diplomacy, Peacemaking
      and Peace Building,* Report of the Secretary General United Nations,
      A/47/277-S/24111, 1992. <www.un.org/docs/SG/agpeace.html> (accessed
      3 January 2011) and United Nations Development Program, Human
      Development Report (New York: Oxford University Press, 1994).

16    According to Joshua Cooper Ramo "more than 90 percent of all non-
      governmental organizations" in the world have been created in the past ten
      years. Ramo, 2009, 35.

17    The fact that existing mechanisms failed to meet the challenges of security,
      governance and development in war-torn regions such as the Balkans
      and Africa only served to emphasize the need for the development and
      institutionalization of a broader, more holistic approach.

18    Indeed, one need only consider the widespread international fallout
      concerning the U.S. response to Hurricane Katrina (2005) and President
      George W. Bush's declaration proclaiming "the end of major combat
      operations in Iraq" (2003) to appreciate the degree to which global
      communications magnify issues of government legitimacy (or lack thereof).

19    See Peter Gizewski and Lt. Col. Michael Rostek, *Toward a Comprehensive
      Approach to Military Operations: The Land Force JIMP Concept.* DRDC
      CORA TM 2007-60, 2007.

20    For a summary of research being conducted in a Canadian context, see Bruce
      Gallant, Dale Reding and Peter Gizewski. "Assessment of the TTCP "Ad
      Hoc Study Group: Science and Technology for the Comprehensive Approach,
      Final Report," Briefing Note, January 2010.

21    For a useful discussion, see Michael J. McNerney, "Stabilization and Recon-
      struction in Afghanistan: Are PRTs a Model or a Muddle?" *Parameters*, Win-
      ter 2005-06.

22    See Peter Gizewski, and Lt. Col. Michael Rostek, *Toward a Comprehensive
      Approach to Military Operations: The Land Force JIMP Concept.* DRDC
      CORA TM 2007-60, 2007, 42-3.

23    The change is clear when one compares how a CA would differ from CIMIC.
      As one observer notes in the case of CIMIC, "[M]ilitary members are
      used to being "in the lead" and calling the shots, playing the military card
      whereby all activity is directed towards the military objective. Under [the]
      old philosophy, when planned activities were executed, all means, military
      and civilian, were used to reach the militarily defined objective, as clearly
      defined in NATO's definition of CIMIC: The co-ordination and co-operation,
      *in support of the mission,* between the NATO Commander and civil actors,
      including national population and local authorities, as well as international,
      national and non-governmental organizations and agencies. (Allied Joint
      Publication 9, page1-1, Art 102). With this definition, the commander's
      intent always prevailed in planning and executing the mission. The most

significant change in adopting CA <u>is the understanding that the mission is not only a military objective but can be an objective used to integrate a broader approach, leading to an end state that is not simply military in character</u>. By the incorporation of CA, the planning of operations would mean that we would not look to the use of civilian organizations as a means of supporting a military mission, <u>but recognizing that we have to share the planning table with other actors; actors who want to achieve their own objectives</u>!" See Gert Djik, "Comprehensive Approach … and Why It's a Big NATO Issue," paper presented to CIOR Symposium on "NATO's Comprehensive Approach and the Role of Reservists," 11 August 2010, Stavanger (NO). <http://www.cior. net/News/2010/COMPREHENSIVE-APPROACH-…--and-why-it-is-a-big-NATO.aspx>

[24]    For an elaboration of this point in a military context, see Peter Gizewski and Lt. Col. Michael Rostek. "The Canada First Defence Strategy: The Need for a Comprehensive Approach," in Phil Orchard (ed.), *Canada and the Changing Strategic Environment: The Canada First Strategy and Beyond. Proceedings of the Annual Conference of the Security and Defence Forum Centres 2008.* (Vancouver: Centre for International Relations, University of British Columbia, 2009), 36-8.

# SUMMARY OF OUR ASPIRATIONS

# CONCLUSION:
# GOVERNANCE AND SECURITY –
# A UNITARY CONCEPT

## GRAHAM KEMP, PhD

## INTRODUCTION

This book is a response to Roger Girouard's call for a better understanding of governance and security. It is particularly necessary at a time when humankind is facing major global insecurity, particularly with climate change induced by global warming. The book throws open the subject, covering many aspects of this topic. It includes a wide range of studies not just from the academic world but also from those with more direct experience of the failings and successes of human governance and security in the field from the failures of Somalia (Cairns) and Kenya (Neal and Muthoki) to success stories such as in Bohol in the Philippines (Canares). The book seeks to inspire a fuller study of human governance and security. With major global problems anticipated, it is necessary to establish a proper science of governance and security to ensure a better future for all.

"Our experience is not the only experience" (Cairns).

To understand this topic, one needs to be aware of the narrow constructs and political subjectivities that influence perceptions on the topic and that may undermine its full and proper examination. For example, Girouard defines governance in the following terms: "Governance is the human interface between a nation's laws and its citizens."

As this book demonstrates, nations are not the only form of human society. It is said that the world is divided into over 180 nations but ten thousand human societies; however, that statement refers only to the cultural divisions of humanity. Many other human societies exist in nation-states with their own forms of governance and security. For example, Tom Rippon refers to motorcycle gangs and Les Chipperfield indicates that police forces are societies in their own right, with their own governance and security. He talks of a "policing universe." Thus, macro societies such as nation-states include micro societies, each with their own governance and security issues. There is a corresponding need to understand the interaction between them.

Theissen's chapter on the interaction between the First Nations of Canada and the Canadian macro society is a good example. In reference to the police, Les Chipperfield states, "It takes a strong, knowledgeable person to lead any police organisation." This statement echoes Theissen's opinions on First Nation leadership in its interaction with Canadian macro society. The real value of Theissen's chapter is not merely a comment on First Nations problems; it is a good analysis of micro-macro society interaction and problems of their own governance and security engendered by that interaction. However, if we regard a nation-state as a macro society, such states are coming together in super-macro societies; for example, the European community (Fry). European governments have to negotiate joint governance and security while ensuring that of their own country.

Some human society interaction is global but not between nations; for example, NGOs and multinational corporations which know no borders (see Christenson on project management). Barbara Mann suggests that, from the eastern Native American perspective, the nation-state is purely a European construct; there are no Native American nations. Native individuals belong to clans that cross borders.

We must be careful not to fall into the trap of assuming that the Western way is the best and that the panacea for good governance and security is democracy and capitalism just because they dominate the most stable parts of the planet. President George W. Bush suggested that the insecurity of the Middle East would be solved if Arab states were allowed to adopt the Western model. Although an apparently successful system for stable governance and security, the Western model has weaknesses; hence, it may *not* be the best, as is often assumed.

Winston Churchill commented:

> Many forms of government have been tried, and will be tried in this world of sin and woe. No one pretends democracy is perfect or all wise. Indeed, it has been said that democracy is the worst form of government except for all those other forms that have been tried from time to time.[1]

For example, the Western democratic model has not translated well into other parts of the world, as Neal and Muthoki indicate with the failing governance of Kenya. They quote the Kenyan Elspeth Huxley: "It is not possible to have Western style democracy in a country divided deeply on racial, linguistic and religious lines." Cairns argues in the same vein in her chapter on the failed state of Somalia.

One of the problems with the Western democratic model is that it is not as democratic as it declares – governance for the people by the people. Historically, it is a compromise between a ruling oligarchy and its ruled masses. In exchange for preserving the privileges of wealth, power and social position, the ruling oligarchy has allowed its ruled masses to participate and share in some of that wealth and power. First, through elections, it allows the masses a political voice in the governance of the country; second, through social mobility whereby some of the masses may join the ruling elite.[2] The Western democratic model maintains, by its nature, an unequal share of wealth and power. Social mobility offers an escape from poverty rather than an attempt to abolish poverty.[3]

The Western democratic model has not shown itself to be sufficiently robust against political manipulation, as revealed by the examples of Hitler and Mugabe, among others. This does not mean one should dismiss the model. One needs to be sceptical of even the apparently best models and be wary of their self-perception and propaganda. In fact, one of the strengths of the Western democratic model, as argued in a recent article, is that it has greater ability than most other forms of governance to adapt to change when circumstances demand. It addition, democracy tends to be more responsive to the needs of its members, a reflection of the "compromising spirit" that lies at heart of its evolution.[4]

Equally, one must be wary of the triumphal tide of capitalism over the past two centuries and particularly since the Cold War. Marx argued that capitalism was inherently unstable. Not only was it a great source of wealth creation but also of unrest and insecurity. It is a profit-driven system that seeks to maximize profits by reducing costs. The largest cost, Marx argued, was labour. Thus, by its nature, capitalism will attack labour costs, pushing down wages, seeking cheaper labour, using machines in preference to humans and, in the process, creating deep political unrest. This is hardly a secure basis for good governance and security.[5]

Barbara Mann declares that, to Native Americans, capitalism is just a form of piracy. The adherents of capitalism may regard this statement as farfetched but one need only look at Africa, the wealthiest continent in resources and ask, "Where is its wealth?" In the 18th and 19th centuries, Latin America was the gold producer of the world but this industry did not benefit its people. The gold went to European banks, which funded the industrial capitalist systems of the West.[6]

Capitalism may have succeeded as an economic system without causing great unrest for three reasons:

1.  It developed in democratic states, whose ability to adapt allowed adjustments between political unrest and profit demands, to keep the system stable;
2.  Governments used public money to establish welfare to offset the unrest that capitalism caused by pushing down labour costs, as well as enforcing greater wealth distribution through taxation strategies; and
3.  It exported the problem elsewhere – from Disraeli's two nations of 19th century England, to the two worlds of the 21st century. For example, the political unrest and lack of security in the Congo does not undermine the security or the governance of the countries that use its resources and cheap labour.

Capitalism may not be the only successful economic system. Again, Barbara Mann talks of the Native Americans' "Gift Sharing" economy which, she argues, has proved more successful in wealth generation and fairer in its distribution of the wealth; thus, it has created fewer security problems than capitalism. Interestingly, the success of the European Union may rest on economic structure not unlike "gift sharing." The EU redistributes its wealth from its richer to its poorer members, stimulating greater growth in all parts of the Union and avoiding the severe deprivation that would cause political unrest and instability.[7]

In order to explore human governance and security, we should avoid making assumptions about what is right (from our own experience) and be prepared to challenge our own cultural viewpoints. We need to think out of the box and we are delighted to have two such chapters in this book: Kemp on Aztecs, and Mann on Native Americans.[8] They challenge dominant Western perspectives of good governance and security. I was fascinated by the "sacred clowning" of Native American governance, which is echoed in Western societies as satire, without enjoying the same importance as in Native American society.

## SECURITY AND GOVERNANCE AS A UNITARY CONCEPT

What are the coherent themes to be drawn from this diverse sweep of chapters: the beginnings of a framework for greater understanding or an unravelling of what Girouard described as a complex and murky subject? Ironically, it is the diversity of the material in the book that allows a clearer framework to develop. Two themes emerge: first, what is meant by governance and security as a unitary concept and their interaction, and second, the key characteristics of human governance and security.

Let us begin with security. Traditionally, security has been perceived as the maintenance of internal order and prevention of external physical threat. This perception reflects the traditions of Western history, when ruling elites saw their security based on preventing rival elites from stealing their resources (external security), and keeping the masses from stealing their wealth.[9] This book shows that human security is a much broader concept. Tom Rippon sums it up in his introduction:

By security, one does not mean just physical security, but

also human, environmental, economic, resource and cultural security.

Contributors talk of security in terms of education (Adjapawn), water (Abitbol), environment (Neal and Muthoki), gender (Balbuena González), children (Villarreal, Adjapawn), exploitation (Villarreal), poverty (Canares), and culture (Theissen) as well as physical well-being; this is by no means an exhaustive list. Reading through the chapters, one realizes that it is necessary to turn over the metaphorical card. Human security includes human rights: the rights to water, food, peace, physical well-being, cultural identity, language, happiness, and, in some cases, accumulated or inherited wealth and prestige (birthright). Human rights and human security are one and the same, possibly differing only from the perspective of the writer.[10] Several contributors use the terms interchangeably, thus reinforcing the assertion that governance and security are a unitary concept.

Turning to governance, one must be aware of presumptive norms. In establishing governance, it may be noted that the contributors refer to agreements (Rippon, Cairns, Mann), co-operation (Arbitol, Fry), and interfacing (Girouard, Theissen) underlying the process of governance and security. In 17th century political thought, this was termed the Social Contract (Rousseau, Hobbes). From a social contract between members of a society, governance guides how best to secure rights.

It does not need to be a fair contract. The Mafia protection racket of "obey and we will protect you from any harm that we might inflict on you" is found among many human governance systems (e.g., Norman feudal system, Aztec Empire) and is a contract of fear. The need for security led humans to form social contracts and establish governance systems to protect their rights. The contract need not be formal or in writing; most are established through oral traditions and customs. It is not governance that creates security but security that creates a need for governance, which feeds back into establishing (or failing to establish) those security needs. This system makes biological and evolutionary sense.

Present-day humans, Homo sapiens, are the only hominids believed to have organized themselves beyond mere family groups. Humans form communities. The importance of decoration in body, dress or in flags and symbols is peculiar to Homo sapiens. It reflects the way humans moved from biological communities of family to larger cultural groupings. This change, however, created greater insecurity for the individuals in these larger groups; thus, they negotiated a form of governance to create security. The governance may not be designed to meet everyone's needs but it reflects power relationships in the group.

From this point, humans evolved into ever larger communities and the larger the group, the less the human contact. With less contact, a greater need arose for more formal governance systems to meet their security needs and rights. The complexity of that governance increased the need for societies to grow within even larger societies, and societies to interlink and cross each other's boundaries. This is where the murkiness and complexity of human governance and security lies, as Girouard suggests. Examination of the chapters of this book reveals three common elements that form a framework to unravel the murkiness and complexity.

## NATURE OF GOVERNANCE AND SECURITY

The first factor is the cycle in which security creates governance. The resultant success or failure of that governance in respect to security (or human rights), feeds back into governance and develops the cycle of interchange. This results in a dynamic rather than a static concept. Human governance and security is an evolving process.[11] Fry talks of the evolution of governance and security; Gizeweski proposes gradual evolution; Cairns argues that you cannot impose governance and security on a failing community. It needs to evolve within the community. In terms of the success of Bohol's development of better governance and security, Canares identifies this feedback loop as an evolutionary process. Others identify this interaction by including the dynamic interplay between the community of the police and the wider community (Chipperfield, Vidalis), and between the police and motorcycle gangs (Rippon). The interaction takes the form of negative or regressive evolution, as Neal and Muthoki argue in the case of Kenya. For good or ill, governance and security are experiencing dynamic evolution.[12]

Second, stemming from this dynamic process is the need to establish pathways of communication. Breakspear writes on intelligence-gathering as an essential component of good governance. Gizeweski emphasizes that a "lack of interconnectedness only heightens obstacles to interaction and collaboration." This pathway of communication is not impersonal but human. With larger and more complex societies, it develops into agencies, the agents of security. We naturally think of the police or the military but that is a norm we need to look beyond. There are, in fact, many other agents or agencies; for example, factory and health and safety inspectorates, a free press with investigative journalism, and trade unions, to name a few. Cullen emphasizes security agents of the ruling executives. These agencies, as indicated above, become informal communities developing their own governance and security rights. It is necessary to examine this interaction between the agencies and the macro society.

The third element is not readily apparent, yet it is in almost every chapter. It is suggested that there is a moral dimension to human governance and security. It is not just a dimension but a human need to succeed (Gizeweski). Girouard talks about those who have the will and power *and the vision* to deliver on the hopes of those around us [my italics]. Rippon talks of a moral contract as "good governance with a moral reflection." Barbara Mann discusses the "spiritual vision behind Native American governance."

Gizeweski discusses the "moral dimension," Canares the "moral sphere," and Cairns talks of a "need to build trust" in restoring governance and security to a community. When Confucius taught the warring Chinese states a new concept of governance to create a more secure realm, he emphasized the moral dimension. Mohammed did the same for warring tribes in Arabia; he did not supply just a new political system but one with a theological basis.

Although God is not evoked in the US constitution itself, it is evoked in its maintenance.

"From this nation, under God, shall have a new birth of freedom, and that government of the people, by the people, for the people, shall not perish from the earth" (Lincoln, *Gettysburg Address*). If we ever forget we are One Nation under God then we will be a nation gone under (President Ronald Reagan). The first US president, George Washington, noted:

> Now I make it my earnest prayer that God ... would incline the hearts of the citizens to cultivate a spirit of subordination and obedience to the government to entertain brotherly affection and love for one another.... And finally, that God would most graciously be pleased to dispose us all to do justice, to love mercy, and demean ourselves with that charity, humility and pacific temper of mind, which were the characteristics of the Divine Author of our blessed religion, and without an humble imitation of Whose example in these things, we can never hope to be a happy nation. (George Washington, 1783)

Cullen's chapter on corruption reveals the calamity in governance and security when faith, trust and morality are eroded through corruption. In researching governance and security, it is necessary to appreciate the need for morality, religion and vision in human governance and security.

## CONCLUSION

Humanity stands at a turning point in its cultural evolution. At no point in human history has the world joined as one. Globalization is a new development. Governments are beginning to talk of co-operation on a global scale with a world governance and world security. As this book demonstrates, world governance need not require a formal agreement. Examples of agents of this global security would be NGOs and the United Nations.

The Internet has created global human connections, increasing the call for human security and rights, and creating concepts not unlike the clan system that Barbara Mann writes about; she comments that Native Americans love the Internet. A moral dimension of the global vision is developing. Theo Lentz identified this development over thirty years ago and called it Humatriotism – the human interest in peace and survival.[13] He likened it to patriotism, the moral component underlying nation-states' governance and security. Humatriotism does not mean loyalty to one's country but to humanity as a whole, irrespective of race, creed or religion. If we are to advance towards this loyalty, we need to:

1. Break with conventional viewpoints on governance and security and think out of the box;

2. Understand the breadth of human governance and security across the planet and across time;

3. Understand the social contracts or agreements made to establish a society's governance and security;

4. Comprehend the complexity of interactions between human societies and the impact on their governance and security;

5. Study the dynamics, the cyclic evolutionary process of governance and security;

6. Examine the communication pathways, the means of intelligence gathering and its effectiveness, and study the human agents and agencies of security; and

7. Comprehend and look for the moral needs in human governance, in trust and belief in the system, and note how it can be undermined through corruption (Cullen).

This book is the beginning of what we hope will be a better science of human governance and security.

## REFERENCES

Galeano, Eduardo. "Open Veins of Latin America, Five Centuries of the Pillage of a Continent." *Monthly Review Press* (1997).

Churchill, Winston. *Summary Information for Mr Winston Churchill, 1947*. <http://hansard.millbanksystems.com/people/mr-winston-churchill/1947>

Jones, Owen. *The Demonization of the Working Class.* London/NY: Verso Books, 2011.

Lentz, Theo. *Humatriotism – Human Interest in Peace and Survival*. St Louis, MO: The Future Press, 1976.

Oldfied, S. *Women Against the Fist – Alternatives to Militarism 1900-1989.*
Oxford, UK: Blackwell, 1989.

Penn, W. *An Essay Towards the Present and Future of Peace in Europe (1693).*
Hildesheim, Germany: Olms Verlag, 1983.

"Pro Constitution" quotations. <http://www.proconstitution.com/under_god/>
(n.d.)

Roberts, D. *Europe – First Continent of Lasting Peace.* London, UK: Harney and
Jones, 1983.

Runciman, D. "Will it be Alright in the End?" *London Review of Books* (January
2012): 3-5.

## ENDNOTES

[1] Hansard, November 11th, 1947. <http://hansard.millbanksystems.com/people/
mr-winston-churchill/1947>

[2] As in the American dream.

[3] Owen Jones. *The Demonization of the Working Class.* (London/NY: Verso
Books, 2010).

[4] D. Runciman. "Will it be Alright in the End?" *London Review of Books*
(January 2012).

[5] In its pursuit of cheap labour globally, capitalism has left its once beneficiaries
of capitalism bereft of rights and security e.g., the fate of the Motown cities
of Ohio. Also, in the pursuit of ever-cheaper labour, many have argued it can
seriously undermine security and rights, e.g., Coca Cola has been criticised for
undermining water security in India.

[6] Eduardo Galeano. "Open Veins of Latin America, Five Centuries of the
Pillage of a Continent." *Monthly Review Press* (1997).

[7] The EC economic system is about the whole union, not a Euro zone in the
union.

[8] To be more precise, the woodland dwellers of the eastern United States, the
Iroquois, Shawnee, etc.

[9] Until the 20th century, crimes against property were regarded as much worse
than crime against the person in Western law, and some would argue that it
still carries undue representation in present criminal codes.

[10] "Good governance and security is about freedom from abuse" (Balbuena
González).

11    Events in Cairo's Tahrir Square to the development of new governance in
      Egypt can be seen as an example of this cycle.

12    See Fry on his examination of the evolution of the development of
      governance.

13    Theo Lentz. *Humatriotism – Human Interest in Peace and Survival*. (St. Louis,
      MO: The Future Press, 1976) (see Canares' chapter in this light).

CPSIA information can be obtained at www.ICGtesting.com
Printed in the USA
LVOW011141040113

314264LV00005B/18/P